ADVANCE HEALTH CARE DIRECTIVES

A HANDBOOK FOR PROFESSIONALS

CAROL KROHM, M.D.
SCOTT SUMMERS

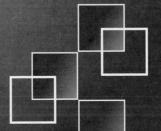

**Defending Liberty
Pursuing Justice**

Cover design by Vicki Freyman.

The materials contained herein represent the opinions of the authors and editors and should not be construed to be the action of either the American Bar Association or the Senior Lawyers Division unless adopted pursuant to the bylaws of the Association.

Nothing contained in this book is to be considered as the rendering of legal advice for specific cases, and readers are responsible for obtaining such advice from their own legal counsel. This book and any forms and agreements herein are intended for educational and informational purposes only.

Library of Congress Cataloging-in-Publication Data
Summers, Scott K., 1949–
   Advance health care directives / Scott K. Summers, Carol Krohm.
      p. cm.
   Contains legislation.
   Includes bibliographical references.
   ISBN 1-59031-008-X
   1. Advance directives (Medical care)—United States. 2. Medical care—Law and legislation—United States. 3. Informed Consent (Medical law)—United States. I. Krohm, Carol, 1953– II. Title.
[DNLM: 1. Advance Directives—United States. 2. Patient Advocacy. 3. Ethics, Medical.]
   R726.2 .S85 2001
   362.1—dc21   2001053388

Discounts are available for books ordered in bulk. Special consideration is given to state bars, CLE programs, and other bar-related organizations. Inquire at Book Publishing, ABA Publishing, American Bar Association, 750 North Lake Shore Drive, Chicago, Illinois 60611.

www.ababooks.org

Contents

Foreword xiii

Preface xv

Acknowledgments xvii

Frequently Asked Questions xix

CHAPTER 1
Five Counterintuitive Precepts 1
§ 1.01 Introduction 1
§ 1.02 Directives? Who Cares? 2
§ 1.03 Directives Breed Conflict 2
§ 1.04 Directives Are Vulnerable to Failure 3
    § 1.05—Conflicting Philosophies and Value Judgments 3
    § 1.06—Physicians and Agents May Be Disinclined to Honor Directives 5
    § 1.07—Directives Lack Permanence 5
    § 1.08—Poorly Drawn or Ambiguous Directives 6
    § 1.09—Absence of Good Footprints 6
§ 1.10 Directives Are Rights without Remedies 6
§ 1.11 Directives Won't Work in Most Emergency Situations 7
§ 1.12 Conclusion 7

CHAPTER 2
What Are Advance Health Care Directives? 9
§ 2.01 Introduction 9
§ 2.02 Durable Power of Attorney (or Proxy) for Health Care 9
§ 2.03 Ancillary or Limited Use Directives 10
    § 2.04—Living Wills 10
    § 2.05—Declarations of Preferences for Mental Health Treatments 12
    § 2.06—Durable Power of Attorney for Property; Trusts 12
    § 2.07—Organ Donation 13

§ 2.08—Oral Expressions   15
§ 2.09—Nomination of Guardian   16
§ 2.10   Some Comments—and Cautions—about Durable Powers
of Attorney   16
§ 2.11—Controlling Implementation   16
§ 2.12—Selecting an Agent   17
§ 2.13—Keeping Direct Control   17
§ 2.14—Indicating the Existence of Directives   18
§ 2.15—Updating Directives Regularly   18
§ 2.16   Diversions   19
§ 2.17   Conclusion   20

CHAPTER 3
The Ethics of Advance Health Care Directives   23
§ 3.01   Introduction   23
§ 3.02   Negotiating the Straits   24
§ 3.03—Advance Directives   24
§ 3.04—Substituted Judgement   24
§ 3.05—Best Interests   25
§ 3.06   The Lighthouses   26
§ 3.07—Respect for Autonomy   26
§ 3.08—Nonmaleficence   27
§ 3.09—Beneficence   27
§ 3.10—Justice   28
§ 3.11   Professional Ethics   28
§ 3.12—Lawyers   28
§ 3.13—Health Care Professionals   29
§ 3.14—Allied Professionals   29
§ 3.15   Institutional Ethics Committees   29
§ 3.16   Conclusion   30

CHAPTER 4
Competence and Incompetence   33
§ 4.01   Introduction   33
§ 4.02   Check Applicable Statute   34
§ 4.03   The American Bar Association Position   34
§ 4.04   When in Doubt, Include a Medical Assessment   35
§ 4.05—The Medical Examination   35
§ 4.06   The Lawyer–Client Interview   36
§ 4.07   Some Comments—and Cautions—about Lay
Observations of Competence   36

§ 4.08—Avoid Snap Judgments 36

§ 4.09—Competence Is Essentially a Threshold
            Concept 37

§ 4.10—Capacity on Occasion (Episodic Lucidity) 38

§ 4.11—Be "Decision-Neutral" 39

§ 4.12—Strange? So What? 39

§ 4.13—Refusal to be Evaluated 39

§ 4.14—Temporary Incapacity 39

§ 4.15—Dementia 39

§ 4.16—Psychiatric Disorders 40

§ 4.17—A Special Note about Depression 41

§ 4.18   Legal Standards of Capacity 41

§ 4.19   Incapacity as the Effectuating Event 42

§ 4.20   Conclusion 42

CHAPTER 5
Client Issues 45

§ 5.01   Introduction 45

§ 5.02   Summary of Literature 46

§ 5.03—Individuals Most Likely to Complete
            Directives 46

§ 5.04—Why People Don't Have Advance
            Directives 47

§ 5.05—A Need for Discussion 48

§ 5.06—Ethnic Trends 48

§ 5.07—Increasing Interest in Directives 49

§ 5.08   Common Misconceptions 49

§ 5.09—"I'm in Good Health, I Don't Need
            a Directive." 49

§ 5.10—"They're All 'Pull-the-Plug' Documents.
            I Don't Want That." 50

§ 5.11—"I Want Everything Possible Done for Me.
            Directives Won't Permit That." 50

§ 5.12—"Directives Are Permanent. I Won't Be Able to
            Change My Mind." 51

§ 5.13—"With Directives, I Lose the Right to Decide for
            Myself." 51

§ 5.14—"Directives Are Just Arbitrary Checklists.
            They're Not at All Responsive to What
            I Want." 51

§ 5.15—"I Don't Need Directives. My Family Knows
            What I Want." 52

§ 5.16   Barriers to Acceptance   52
    § 5.17—Society's Conflicted Views on Life
        and Death   52
    § 5.18—Cultural or Religious Beliefs   53
    § 5.19—Reluctance to Rely on "Elastic Clauses"   54
    § 5.20—Ceding Autonomy   55
    § 5.21—Opinions and Feelings of Others   55
    § 5.22—Foreclosure of Medical Advances
        by Directives   55
    § 5.23—Procrastination and Fear   55
§ 5.24   Barriers to Implementation   56
    § 5.25—Failure of PSDA Protocols   56
    § 5.26—Cost   57
    § 5.27—Meeting with Professional Advisors   57
    § 5.28—Obtaining Forms   58
    § 5.29—Complexity of Documents/Readability   58
    § 5.30—Lag Times in Drafting   58
    § 5.31—Delays in Meeting with Family   59
    § 5.32—Formalities of Execution   59
    § 5.33—Failures in Communication   59
§ 5.34   Critique of Case Study   59
§ 5.35   Conclusion   62

CHAPTER 6
The Perspective of Family and Friends   67
§ 6.01   Introduction   67
§ 6.02   The Role of Immediate Family   68
    § 6.03—The Role of Extended Family and Friends   70
§ 6.04   Literature Review   70
    § 6.05—Family Members as Decision-Makers   70
    § 6.06—Validity of Decisions   71
§ 6.07   Common Misconceptions   72
§ 6.08   Barriers to Acceptance   73
§ 6.09   Barriers to Implementation   74
§ 6.10   Critique of Case Study   77
§ 6.11   Conclusion   77

CHAPTER 7
The Attorney Perspective   79
§ 7.01   Introduction   79
§ 7.02   The Genesis of Advance Health Care Directives   80
§ 7.03   The Lawyer's Role   81

§ 7.04—Initiating Discussion   82
§ 7.05—Drafting a Checklist   83
§ 7.06—Moving it Forward   84
§ 7.07—Issues of Capacity   85
§ 7.08—Comments—and Cautions—About Durable
           Powers of Attorney   85
§ 7.09—Causes of Action if Directives Are not
           Honored   85
§ 7.10   Critique of Case Study   86
§ 7.11   Conclusion   87

CHAPTER 8
The Health Care Provider Perspective   93
§ 8.01   Introduction   93
§ 8.02   The Patient–Physician Relationship   94
§ 8.03   Review of Literature   94
§ 8.04—Finding the Facts   95
§ 8.05—Discussing the Issues   95
§ 8.06—Executing the Directives   95
§ 8.07—Improving Provider Participation   96
§ 8.08   Common Professional Misconceptions   98
§ 8.09   Barriers to Acceptance among Medical Professionals   98
§ 8.10   Barriers to Implementation within the Medical
           Profession   99
§ 8.11—Professional Education   99
§ 8.12—Available Time   99
§ 8.13—Opportunities for Patient Education   101
§ 8.14—Questions about Capacity   103
§ 8.15—Cultural/Ethnic/Spiritual Barriers   104
§ 8.16—Conflicts   104
§ 8.17—Weaknesses of the Patient Self-Determination
           Act   106
§ 8.18—Difficulty Determining Prognosis   107
§ 8.19—Limited Use of Protocols for Providers   107
§ 8.20—Poor Footprints   107
§ 8.21   Legal Issues   108
§ 8.22   Countermanding or Overriding Patient Directives
           or Instructions of Agents   109
§ 8.23   Tailoring Clinical Situations to Directives   109
§ 8.24   The Ever–Changing Continuum of Health Care
           Directives   111

§ 8.25   Critique of Case Study   112
§ 8.26   Conclusion   113

CHAPTER 9
Involvement of Clergy and Spiritual Advisors   117
§ 9.01   Introduction   117
§ 9.02   The Benefits of a Multidisciplinary Approach   119
    § 9.03—Religious/Spiritual Leaders and End-of-Life
       Issues   120
§ 9.04   Religious and Spiritual Precepts about Advance
    Directives   120
    § 9.05—Buddhism   121
    § 9.06—American Baptist   122
    § 9.07—The Church of Christ, Scientist (Christian
       Science)   122
    § 9.08—Jehovah's Witnesses   122
    § 9.09—Evangelical Lutheran   123
    § 9.10—The Lutheran Church—Missouri Synod   123
    § 9.11—Roman Catholic   123
    § 9.12—United Church of Christ   124
    § 9.13—Hinduism   124
    § 9.14—Islam   124
    § 9.15—Church of the Brethren   125
    § 9.16—United Methodist Church   125
    § 9.17—Presbyterian Church (U.S.A.)   126
    § 9.18—Mennonites   126
    § 9.19—Navajo   126
    § 9.20—Judaism   127
    § 9.21—Unitarian Universalist Association   127
    § 9.22—Eastern Orthodox   128
    § 9.23—Latter–Day Saints   128
    § 9.24—Anglican Church   128
    § 9.25—Seventh-day Adventists   129
§ 9.26   Barriers to Acceptance   129
§ 9.27   Barriers to Implementation   130
§ 9.28   Accomodation of Faith   131
§ 9.29   Critique of Case Study   131
§ 9.30   Conclusion   131

CHAPTER 10
Alternatives in the Absence of Directives   135
§ 10.01   Introduction   135
§ 10.02   Diversions   135

§ 10.03—Informal Practice   135
§ 10.04—Surrogacy Statutes   136
§ 10.05—"Do Not Resuscitate" (DNR) Protocols   136
§ 10.06—Guardianship   137
§ 10.07—Proceedings   137
§ 10.08—Limitations   138
§ 10.09—Avoiding Guardianship   138
§ 10.10—Health Care Ethics Committees   139
§ 10.11—A Word about Euthanasia or "Mercy Killing"
        or "Assisted Suicide"   140
§ 10.12 Conclusion   141

CHAPTER 11
Special Circumstances   143
§ 11.01 Introduction   143
§ 11.02—Anencephalic Infants   143
§ 11.03—Anatomical Donation   143
§ 11.04—Autopsy   144
§ 11.05—Cord Blood   144
§ 11.06—Cryonics   144
§ 11.07—Defective, Inoperative, or Stale
        Directives   144
§ 11.08—Divorce or Dissolution or Annulment of
        Marriage; Termination of Domestic
        Partnership   145
§ 11.09—Domestic Partners/Companions   145
§ 11.10—Embryos, Ova, and Sperm   146
§ 11.11—Expressions by Decisionally
        Incapacitated   146
§ 11.12—Guardianship and Conservatorship
        and Directives   146
§ 11.13—Foreign Nationals   146
§ 11.14—Health Care Providers Serving as Agents
        or Proxies   147
§ 11.15—International Travel   147
§ 11.16—Military Personnel on Active Duty   147
§ 11.17—Minors   147
§ 11.18—No Agent or Proxy or Surrogate   148
§ 11.19—Organ Donation   149
§ 11.20—Out of State Travel or Relocation   149
§ 11.21—Pregnancy   150
§ 11.22—Prisoners   150

§ 11.23—Revocation of Directives   151
§ 11.24—Spiritual or Religious or Philosophical
        Imperatives   151
§ 11.25 Conclusion   151

CHAPTER 12
The Future of Advance Health Care Directives   153
§ 12.01 Introduction   153
        § 12.02—Questions to Ask   153
        § 12.03—Ethical Issues   154
        § 12.04—The Future of Directives   154
§ 12.05 Better Methods of Implementation   155
        § 12.06—Details, Details   155
        § 12.07—Palliative Care and Hospices   155
        § 12.08—Quality Improvement   155
        § 12.09—Ethics Consultants   156
        § 12.10—Legislation, Regulation, and Other
                Oversight   157
        § 12.11—Saturation Marketing   157
        § 12.12—Technology   158
§ 12.13 Better Education   158
        § 12.14—Educating the Public   158
        § 12.15—Educating Professionals   159
§ 12.16 Shifting Attitudes   159
§ 12.17 Dilemmas   159
        § 12.18—Forum Shopping   159
        § 12.19—Utilization   160
§ 12.20 One Last Look   161
§ 12.21 Conclusion   161

Afterword   163

Appendices   167
(Available on CD-ROM also)

Appendix A: Federal Statutes: 169
              (i) The Patient Self-Determination Act   169
              (ii) Military Advance Medical Directive   173
Appendix B: Glossary   175
Appendix C: Uniform Health-Care Decisions Act   183
Appendix D: Values History Form Packets   213
              (i) English   213
              (ii) Español   219

Appendix E: Spanish Language Directives   224
              (i) Poder médico   224
              (ii) Directiva   228
Appendix F: Religious Directives   233
              (i) Jewish Law Halachic Forms   233
              (ii) Catholic Directives   240
                  (a) Health Care Proxy   240
                  (b) Advance Medical Directive   241
Appendix G: Mental Health Directives: 243
              (i) Oklahoma   243
              (ii) Advance Directives for Mental Health Care
                  (Not on CD-ROM)   246
Appendix H: Uniform Anatomical Gift Act (As Enacted by
              North Dakota)   268
Appendix I: The Oregon Death With Dignity Act   276
Appendix J: Statutory Citations (by State, with Analysis)   288
              (i) Health Care Power of Attorney and Combined
                  Advance Directive Legislation   288
              (ii) Surrogate Consent in the Absence of an
                  Advance Directive   302
              (iii) Health Care Surrogate Decision-Making
                  Legislation   317
              (iv) Health-Care Decisions Statutes Citations   318
Appendix K: Consumer Education (How to Make a Community
              Presentation on Advance Directives)   325
Appendix L: Internet Resources   328
Appendix M: Selected Bibliography   332
Appendix N: Sample Wallet Cards   334
Appendix O: Sample Letter from Lawyer to Client Upon
              Execution of Advance Health Care
              Directives   336
Appendix P: Sample Instructions to My Agent About My
              Advance Health Care Directives   338

Advance Health Care Directives: State Statutes
(CD-ROM Only):

Alabama	Connecticut
Alaska	Delaware
Arizona	District of Columbia
Arkansas	Florida
California	Georgia
Colorado	Guam

Hawaii
Idaho
Illinois
Indiana
Iowa
Kansas
Kentucky
Louisiana
Maine
Maryland
Massachusetts
Michigan
Minnesota
Mississippi
Missouri
Montana
Nebraska
Nevada
New Hampshire
New Jersey
New Mexico

New York
North Carolina
North Dakota
Ohio
Oklahoma
Oregon
Pennsylvania
Rhode Island
South Carolina
South Dakota
Tennessee
Texas
Utah
Vermont
Virginia
Virgin Islands
Washington
West Virginia
Wisconsin
Wyoming

About the Authors   339

Index   341

Foreword

In February 1990, Terri Schiavo suffered a massive heart attack. She was 26 years old. The flow of oxygen to her brain was cut off for at least six minutes, and she has been in a persistent vegetative state ever since.

Today, Terri is 37. Her parents have not given up hope that she can get better. They argue that while she is severely disabled, Terri should continue to receive tube feedings until doctors discover an effective treatment or cure. Her husband, however, says that Terri never wanted to live as she does, a prisoner in an almost lifeless body. For three years, he has been seeking permission from the courts to end his wife's tube feedings, and thus her life.

Terri Schiavo did not have a living will, so it is debatable how she wanted to live or die. These days, there are many such stories, with families struggling with gut-wrenching emotional dilemmas that pit loved one against loved one to do what they think their incapacitated family member would want. Many of these family tragedies can be avoided by filling out advance health care directives.

As lawyers, we play an integral role in advising our clients about advance health care directives, because they are legal documents. We are uniquely qualified to counsel our clients on the best way make certain their wishes about health care and end-of-life decisions are enforced. Indeed, we have an obligation to help our clients work through these difficult decisions so they avoid situations such as Terri Schiavo's.

The ABA is an ardent supporter of advance health care directives, and has been a leader in the movement by providing the most current information about them to lawyers and the public.

That's why "*Advance Health Care Directives: A Handbook for Professionals*" is such a valuable resource. This book will help lawyers deal with complex, emotional issues such as: knowing when to approach the topic of a living will with your client; developments and changes in the laws; and bioethical questions surrounding the laws.

I congratulate the ABA on continuing its long tradition of helping provide important information about advance health care directives to the public. This information can spare families the heartache experienced by Terri Schiavo's family.

Martha Barnett
ABA President 2000-2001

Preface

Looking for an easy "how-to" on advance health care directives? This isn't the book for you. A panacea? Sorry. A missionary–style guide on spreading the word about the importance of directives? Can't help. A rehash of opinion? No. Categorical conclusions about right ways and wrong ways to approach advance directives? If only it were so easy!

Advance health care directives aren't necessarily imbued with high reason and lofty principle. Rather, they often reflect and refract the marvelously irrational things that make us human: fear, loathing, ignorance, disgust, disdain, revulsion, misunderstanding, trepidation, anger, and sloth, to list but a few. Unfortunately, emotions may be at their most volatile when the subject is advance directives; confronting mortality can be excruciatingly difficult. There is no simplistic or "right" way to broach the subject with patients and clients: each encounter necessitates—provokes, actually—a tailor-made approach.

By dint of being an ABA publication, this book is, of course, metered largely in the lexicon of lawyers. But because the subject is multidisciplinary in nature, we have striven to provide a straightforward, even handed, and (above all) practical guide and point of departure on the subject of advance health care directives for use by *all* professionals—lawyers, physicians, clerics, ethicists, social workers, psychologists, nurses, palliative caregivers, administrators, and every allied walk—endeavoring to assist a patient or client in the completion of an advance directive. Although this volume is not designed as a self-help resource, we expect that thoughtful lay readers too will find these materials informative.

Recognizing the severe time constraints under which most professionals labor, the book is organized to provide cogent briefings from four principal perspectives: lawyer, physician, cleric, and patient/client. Those preferring a condensed read might best refer to Chapters 1, 2, 5, 6, and 10, plus selective review of pertinent chapters of professional interest. Those availing themselves of a complete reading will, we think, glean valuable detail and perspective; indeed, we hope most will go cover-to-cover with us. However, this four-way design necessarily entails some repetition of thoughts and ideas. We trust that the "marathoners" (as opposed to the "sprinters") in our audience will indulge us this bit of awkwardness.

Those eager for more information will, we hope, avail themselves of the meticulous and immensely useful resources that are available. We merely attempt to synthesize and supplement—not supplant—the outstanding scholarship in the field. Our companion website, http://www.AdvanceHealth CareDirectives.com, points the way to but a sampling.

All the statutes and case law and research and scholarship in the world will never, ever, be able to substitute for the wisdom and compassion essential to the approach of advance directives. It is not nearly enough for we professionals to merely bring our knowledge and skills to bear upon what arguably is the most essential set of decisions a person is ever to make. We must also strain the sinews of goodness and grace. The kind and stout hearts among us will not shirk from so high a calling.

Carol Krohm and Scott Summers

Dedication and Acknowledgments

In memory of Luis Kutner (1908–1993): poet, author, human rights lawyer, and originator of the living will.

The authors are grateful for the insights of those from many perspectives—medical, legal, ethical, religious, and lay—who reviewed early drafts of the manuscript. Thanks to Dianne Arakawa, Kevin Cullinane, Debra Kelsey, Mary Mahowald, Pat Mikos, Lois Summers, Andrew Teton, Burton Vander-Laan, Stephen Washburn, and Holly Wehmeyer for their fastidious readings and superb suggestions.

Special thanks to the webmeisters at www.AdvanceHealthCareDirectives. com—our sons, Benjamin Summers and Geoffrey Summers.

CK and SKS

Frequently Asked Questions

What is an advance health care directive?

Simply put, it's a personal contingency plan (usually written) on how medical decisions are to be made in the event of decisional or communicative incapacity. With a directive, you can prospectively state wishes and instructions about treatments you want and don't want—just in case you're unable at some future time to understand or communicate with health care providers.

You're speaking about living wills and health care powers of attorney, aren't you?

Generally, yes—although there are related issues and documents to consider, such as organ donation and declarations of preferences for mental health treatments. Note well, though, that these all are exclusively health and personal care matters. A "big picture" contingency plan also should touch on trusts and powers of attorney for property, so that your finances can be managed for you just in case you can't do it yourself.

How does an advance health care directive work?

There are two principal mechanisms: naming an agent (a "deputy") to decide for you if you can't, or leaving a set of instructions. Health care powers of attorney (or proxies) are predicated on appointing an agent to "step into your shoes" and take over decision making for you if you can't do it. Living wills, on the other hand, generally are direct instructions to doctors about end-of-life care and do not require appointment of a third party agent or "deputy."

So which is better—a living will or a health care power (or proxy)?

Most people will find that a health care power of attorney (also called a proxy in some jurisdictions) is the preferred vehicle, for two reasons. First, state laws are expansive about how it may be used: it does not necessarily run solely to end-of-life treatments. Almost any health care contingency may be addressed. Second, it is a more flexible approach, thereby permitting you to write out a personalized set of instructions for your "deputy." Living wills (or declarations), on the other hand, are far more limited in scope. They typically are pointed instructions for doctors to discontinue heroic medical treatments in terminal situations and to allow a "natural" death. (Note well that living wills are most emphatically *not* directions to "pull-the-plug" and *not* instructions to completely cease all care: many also pointedly provide that death is not to be hastened, and that various levels of comfort care are to continue.)

Should I have both a living will and a health care proxy (or power)?

This may—or may not—be a good idea, depending largely on state law. Most jurisdictions have provisions for both documents, but a few have only one or the other. In instances where both are permitted, a living will can be employed as a "backup" if the proxy or power fails for some reason (for example, the agent is unavailable or has predeceased). However, this can cause problems if state law is silent on which document is controlling. In short—carefully check both statute and case law in your jurisdiction if both documents are contemplated.

When do directives take effect?

Usually upon the onset of decisional or communicative incapacity. Directives typically are not invoked if a patient has sufficient ability to (1) weigh treatment alternatives and (2) render informed consents.

Are my directives good anywhere I go?

Not necessarily. The good news is that for travel within the U.S., most states specifically recognize directives executed in other states (see Chapter 11, "Special Circumstances"). The bad news is that they may not be recognized in foreign countries. For individuals who permanently change residence from one state to another, it probably is a good idea to destroy or revoke "old" directives are re-execute them with the formalities of the "new" jurisdiction.

Okay, I'm mostly sold—I think. But please go over the advantages and disadvantages of advance health care directives.

Make no mistake: there are drawbacks to directives. Due to cultural, philosophical, religious, and ethical reasons, they're not for everyone. If inartfully drawn and executed, or if inarticulate or conflicting, they can cause problems and misunderstandings. They're utterly worthless if no one—agents, doctors, family, friends, advisors—knows about them. They may not work at all in emergency situations.

On the other hand, directives are smart personal planning for many people. You can use them to help guide your health care if, for whatever reason, you cannot understand or communicate. Advance health care directives can help you preserve your privacy and autonomy, too. Employing them can preclude (or at least minimize) the chance of "living probate"—that is, judicial involvement in your health care choices through the appointment of a guardian or similar functionary. And they're *not* permanent: they can be revoked and changed and re-executed at any time, as your thinking or personal preferences or needs change.

In short, directives are tricky. They require lots of thinking, hard work, and patience to draft and implement. Even with the best of intentions, they don't always work as intended. The following pages will help point the way to effective use.

CHAPTER I

Five Counterintuitive Precepts

§ 1.01 Introduction

Here is a leading question: What are the most important legal documents our clients (or we) will ever sign?

A home mortgage? A will? Surely these have ranked—and will continue to rank—at the forefront for many.

But advance health care directives surely join the short list. Arguably, they now go to the very top: through them, it is possible to direct the circumstances—and, indeed, the timing—of our deaths. This is an extraordinary development.

There is more. Properly executed and applied, advance directives can guide the scope of medical care from palliative (comfort) care to aggressive. Privacy and autonomy for our most intensely personal decision-making are, seemingly, assured. Agents or proxies can direct health care, finances, and living arrangements in the event of incapacity, thereby obviating the need for "living probate": guardianship and conservatorship.

Advance directives might even be considered mandatory. The federal Patient Self Determination Act (PSDA)[1] requires Medicare/Medicaid funded hospitals, long term care facilities, hospices, and home health care agencies, to provide written information about state-specific health care (but not property) directives to patients upon contact. Execution remains voluntary.

The conclusion is compelling: advance directives—powers of attorney for health care (or health care proxies) in particular—have become integral parts of both personal and estate planning.

The authors freely admit an abiding belief—more plainly, a bias—in favor of advance health care directives. However, the case for directives is not easily made.

1

Consider five counterintuitive precepts:

- Directives? Who cares?
- Directives breed conflict.
- Directives are vulnerable to failure.
- Directives are rights without remedies.
- Directives won't work in many emergency situations.

§ 1.02 Directives? Who Cares?

Remember the introduction of "new Coke" a few years back–and the reaction it engendered? How about the once-ballyhooed IRA–style Medical Savings Accounts that have never really caught on? Or the Susan B. Anthony dollar coin?

At the risk of sounding flippant, advance health care directives seem to be another "product launch" that has, well, flopped. At best, public reaction seems to range generally from no knowledge about the subject to lukewarm to indifferent to reluctant. Impacts of the Patient Self Determination Act (PSDA) on public behavior appear mixed.[2]

A 1991 Gallup poll indicated that 20 percent of Americans had advance directives.[3] Therein lies a sobering and cautionary tale: for all that directives may seem to be a good idea, they aren't catching on. Why? Aversion? Fatalism? Fear? Ignorance? Intimidation? Disgust? Sloth? Procrastination? Lousy marketing? Cultural issues? All of the above?

And do directives save health care resources at the end of life? Be they aggressive or palliative or somewhere in between, medical services at the end of life can be both copious and costly. Scholars have mixed opinions on whether advance directives actually lead to monetary savings.[4] Some bristle altogether at the notion that advance directives might possibly be used as tools to ration care at the end of life; they would prefer to keep discussion of directives entirely apart from issues of medical economics.

§ 1.03 Directives Breed Conflict

The acts of executing and subsequently carrying out the terms of an advance health care directive may provoke sharp controversy.

For example, an attending physician may disagree with either a directive or an agent (or both). The doctor may decide to treat an uncomprehending patient against that patient's seemingly misguided written wishes, yet be completely in conformity with community medical standards. Who is right? Who is wrong? For that matter, *is* there any right or wrong here?

Family members and agents may argue about treatments, with deleterious effects on the interests of the patient. Agents may be badly misinformed about a patient's/principal's desires, or quail in crisis; as a result, care entirely inconsistent with the patient's wishes might be rendered. What then?

What if a designated agent or proxy has an interest—real or imagined—in a dying principal's estate? Or what if an agent is financially responsible for the medical care being rendered to a principal at the end of life? Might the agent be disinclined to direct heroic life support measures in these instances, even if the patient wanted them and even if they are consistent with commonly accepted standards of medical care?

Perhaps a nursing home or other care facility requests consent to a Do Not Resuscitate (DNR) order as a condition of admission. What then is an agent to do in the face of a principal's care directives to the contrary? Sign the principal in and hope for the best?

A patient with, say, terminal emphysema may wittingly or unwittingly impose crushing financial and caregiving burdens upon family members by directing, via an agent or proxy, that patently futile care be rendered. What then?

Perhaps a patient (either knowingly or unknowingly) signs a consent agreeing to defibrillation or emergency open-heart surgery in the event that a contemplated cardiac catherization or angioplasty goes badly. If the advance health care directive pointedly excludes the contingent procedures described in the consent—or, more ambiguously, specifies "no heroic measures"—which document is controlling? Is it even possible that carefully and thoughtfully drawn directives may be rendered moot by hastily signed written consents to medical procedures?

These scenarios illustrate that advance health care directives do not necessarily solve problems. The counterintuitive implication is that they can foment conflict and *cause* problems.

§ 1.04 Directives Are Vulnerable to Failure

Advance health care directives are not panaceas. They obviously can fail (either fully or in part) on the basis of any of the situations previously described. They also can fail for myriad other reasons. A few of them are:

- Conflicting philosophies and value judgments.
- Physicians and agents may be disinclined to honor directives.
- Directives lack permanence.
- Poorly drawn or ambiguously worded directives.
- Absence of good "footprints."

§ 1.05—Conflicting Philosophies and Value Judgments

The most obvious cases of conflict are when the agent/proxy (hereafter, "agent") or attending physicians disagree with one other or with the patient/principal (hereafter, "patient"). It is incumbent upon patients to locate doctors and agents sympathetic to their wishes; absent this effort, the perceived benefits of tailor-made advance directives may be entirely for naught.

The idea of advance directives stems from the premise of substituted judgment—that is, acting strictly on the basis of what the patient would have wanted. These wishes may be deduced in several ways: through the directive itself, through completion of a value judgments inventory (see Appendix D) by the principal, other memorializations or writings, and from first hand knowledge of the patient's philosophical, moral, and spiritual beliefs. With substituted judgment, the agent and doctors are to put their own opinions and beliefs entirely aside and, in effect, "stand in the patient's shoes." (The premise of substituted judgment will be discussed in more detail in Chapter 3).

The authors believe that substituted judgment is most manifestly expressed not so much through the instructions contained in a directive but rather through the choice of an agent or proxy. Consider the broad range of authority often conferred on an agent. In attempting to extrapolate the values of an uncomprehending principal, the agent may start jumbling the patient's values with his or her own beliefs. Physicians, family, and others may exert influence upon an agent that steers care away from the types that the patient would have desired. In effect, substituted judgment may in practice morph into the premise of "best interests"—a much more conservative standard that may have the unintended effect of rendering medical decisions the principal may not have wanted. (See Chapter 3.)

Consider, too, the diverse perspectives and training of the professionals who may come to have considerable impact and influence upon an advance directive: physicians, lawyers, nurses, clergy, and social workers, among others. The training of physicians is grounded in the Hippocratic Oath and the premise of "first do no harm." Simplistically put, death is an end-game: it is to be outflanked, outwitted, and held off for as long as possible. Perhaps the western medical view of death is finally starting to change: given the increased life expectancies and "high tech" medical interventions of the past half century, dying now has become merely the consequence of a long life. In any event, it can be extremely difficult for some physicians to let go of a patient and, hence, "fail" by not exhausting all possible death-delaying interventions, irrespective of what the patient or agent purports to want. This is but one small dimension of the very human calculus of advance directives that may lead the application of directives entirely awry.

The law brings its own perspective to bear—a perspective that can be at variance not only with other points of view but one that conflicts within itself. In the interests of personal autonomy and privacy, a zealous advocate surely would champion the "substituted judgment" standard. But such advocacy sets down upon a false horizon. Substituted judgment is not a doctrine unto itself, existing in a vaccuum apart from all others. Asserting the wishes of an uncomprehending patient has impacts on other people—family and friends in particular—which cannot be denied. So at what point might substituted judgment change over to best interests? No one can really say.

More poignant for lawyers is that substituted judgment and best interests sometimes are competing doctrines. In the absence of advance directives, a guardianship may be required. This highly conservative proceeding compels our judiciary to employ the best interests tests, rather than substituted judgment. State interests in preserving human life also can be diametrically opposed to the precepts of substituted judgment: in effect, a state, acting by and through a guardianship judge, may, inadvertently or otherwise, superimpose its values rather than defer to what a patient might have wanted.

The religious beliefs of a patient may be among the most compelling reasons to have a directive. However, clergy also may become ensnared in conundrums. Most denominations seem amenable to advance directives, to the extent that they mirror both a reverence for life and the premise of death with dignity. But it is not so simple, of course. One denomination prohibits the transfusion of blood and blood products. Another eschews the medical healing arts. Who is to say when—or if—religious precepts are to be countermanded by agents, physicians, or by the state? And to what extent do advance health care directives add to, or detract from, bereavement and spiritual healing?

Intimately involved with daily patient care needs and instrumental as consensus builders, social workers and nurses can be indispensable to a dying patient and his family. But they, too, are compelled to handle conflict and contradiction. Some conflicts may be irreconcilable. How does one facilitate acceptance and moving on?

§ 1.06—Physicians and Agents May Be Disinclined to Honor Directives

One study by the Robert Wood Johnson Foundation determined that attending physicians countermand preferences to forego cardiopulmonary resuscitation (CPR) with surprising frequency and, instead, perform heroic death-delaying interventions.[5] This may be attributable to the "do no harm" rubric, mixed messages from family or other professionals, or to a lack of understanding about (or even suspicion or disdain for) advance directives. Agents and family members, in their very real grief over the imminent death of a loved one, may themselves suddenly run roughshod over directives.

§ 1.07—Directives Lack Permanence

Advance directives are *not* forever! As a principal's interests and needs change over a lifetime, it is entirely permissible—indeed, perfectly proper—to revoke and re-execute directives from time to time. This built-in flexibility can have a disconcerting side effect, however; directives can be rendered moot in an instant.

Note well that in some jurisdictions (Arizona, Arkansas, District of Columbia, Wisconsin, Indiana for example), statute provides that the faintest and most disjointed oral statement of an enfeebled principal on the cusp of death can serve to revoke or countermand the most carefully crafted directives, irrespective of patient capacity or what a physician or agent may think or want. Physical destruction (e.g., tearing, obliterating, burning, as in the method of revoking a last will and testament) is not necessary. For example, say that a patient executed documents directing "no heroic life-sustaining measures" and requesting "comfort care only." If, near death and struggling to breathe, the patient suddenly was to gasp, "Save me! Save me! Don't let me go!" the directive would have to be disregarded and heroic life-sustaining measures (e.g., a ventilator) started.

§ 1.08—Poorly Drawn or Ambiguous Directives

A directive can be overly broad, or poorly drawn, or ambiguous. Perhaps a patient categorically specifies "no ventilator." What, then, is a surgeon to do if a "vent" is required for a brief period of time after, say, a complicated emergency appendectomy? Let the patient suffocate and die, in slavish obedience to an inartfully drawn instruction? "Of course not!" most of us would say. But the patient's expressly stated wishes will have been overridden. Just where do we draw the line?

§ 1.09—Absence of Good Footprints

It is the quintessence of futility to execute directives and not tell others that they exist. If the maker of a directive does not tell family, or friends, or doctors, that she or he has directives—or does not carry some kind of indication alerting emergency personnel that directives are to be had—then the exercise is pointless.

People are not mind readers. Individuals who execute directives need to make it easy for those persons (both known and unknown) who may be called upon to help in a medical emergency. Those who go to the trouble of executing directives *must* leave good footprints. (See the sidebar in Chapter 5 "Client Issues").

§ 1.10 Directives Are Rights without Remedies

Advance health care directives exist in some form in all fifty states, plus the District of Columbia, Guam, and the U.S. Virgin Islands. (At present, there are no statutory provisions for directives in the Commonwealth of Puerto Rico.) In other words, directives are almost universally ours as a matter of statutory right. And many of the jurisdictions so providing carry civil and/or criminal penalties for noncompliance.

Yet pragmatically speaking, directives don't really have much in the way of remedies or enforcement. Recourses are largely fumbling or impractical;

unheeding or impulsive pursuit of them inadvertently may lead to greater problems. (See Chapter 7 "The Attorney Perspective" for a discussion).

§ 1.11 Directives Won't Work in Most Emergency Situations

What about emergency response teams such as paramedics, firefighters, police, and hospital emergency room staffs? (For that matter, what about Good Samaritans?) Can we realistically expect them to spend precious seconds of response time—with life and death seemingly hanging in the balance—first having to locate and then having to read copious treatment instructions before deciding what to do? Face it: if in doubt, they're going to (and they're supposed to) treat first and ask questions later.

In other words, highly dedicated and motivated people working in emergency situations and with the very best of intentions are largely duty bound to treat *irrespective* of the existence of directives. In fact, statutes governing advance health care directives in New Jersey, North Dakota, Pennsylvania, and Tennessee (for example) pointedly provide exemptions for treatments rendered by emergency health care providers.

The only way to have a chance of effectively eschewing emergency medical care is to carefully conform to laws, regulations, or protocols governing out-of-hospital DNR orders. Forty-four states and the District of Columbia have such provisions (exceptions: Iowa, Mississippi, Nebraska, North Dakota, Pennsylvania, and Vermont).[6] Protocols run from government-issued DNR bracelets to prescribed forms on colored paper. Precise compliance is essential.

§ 1.12 Conclusion

Directives are not panaceas. Still largely uncommon, they may on occasion foment (rather than ameliorate) problems. They don't always work as intended. Although now largely universal in U.S. jurisdictions, they are statutory rights without much in the way of remedies. And they may not work well (if at all) in emergency situations.

Still, as the following chapters will illustrate, advance health care directives can be invaluable personal planning documents. By adjusting our expectations, and by adapting for their flaws and failings, directives can be made to serve—and serve well.

Notes

1. Patient Self-Determination Act, 42 U.S.C.A. § 1395cc(f) (1992). *See* Appendix A.
2. S. Wolf, et al., *Special Report Sources of Concern About Patient Self-Determination Act* 325 NEW ENG. J. MED. 1666 (1991); E. Emanuel et al., *How Well is the Patient Self-Determination Act Working? An Early Assessment,* 95 AM. J. MED. 619 (1993).

3. G. Gallup, & F. Newpurt, "Mirror of America: Fear of Dying." The Gallup Poll News Service, Vol. 55, No. 33, January 6, 1991. p. 3.
4. E. Emanuel, *Cost Savings at the End of Life: What Do the Data Show?* 275 JAMA 1907 (1996); R. Kellogg et al., *Code Status Decision-Making in a Nursing Home Population: Processes and Outcomes,* 43 J. AM. GERIATRICS SOC'Y 113 (1995), W. Weeks et al., *Advance Directives and the Cost of Terminal Hospitalization,* 154 ARCHIVES OF INTERNAL MED. 2077 (1994); C. Chambers et al., *Relationship Advance Directives to Hospital Charges in a Medicare Population,* 154 ARCHIVES OF INTERNAL MED. 541 (1994); E. Emanuel et al., *Special Articles: Economics of Dying: The Illusion of Cost Savings at the End of Life,* 330 NEW ENG. J. MED. 540 (1994).
5. N. Wenger et al., *Physician Understanding of Patient Resuscitation Preferences: Insights and Clinical Implications* 48 J. AM. GERIATRICS SOC'Y 544 (2000).
6. *End-of-Life Law Digest.* "State Laws and Protocols Governing Nonhospital Do-Not-Resuscitate Orders," Partnership for Caring, Inc., Washington, D.C. (September, 2001).

CHAPTER 2

What Are Advance Health Care Directives?

§ 2.01 Introduction

So just what are advance health care directives?

Directives are personal contingency plans: they are guidance (usually written) on how medical choices are to be made in the event of decisional or communicative incapacity.

Depending on statutory expression, directives are cast in one of two ways—as treatment instructions, or as delegations of authority to consent to treatments. With one particular exception, they are completely revocable—at least up to the point where a patient becomes incapable of communicating revocation.

The principal style of directive now is the durable health care power of attorney (or proxy). Ancillary or limited purpose health care directives are best used—if used at all—to augment such a proxy or power.

§ 2.02 Durable Power of Attorney (or Proxy) for Health Care

Given its far ranging and flexible nature, this has become the directive of choice for most. A relatively new statutory creation, the power of attorney for health care (or, in some jurisdictions, the health care proxy) may permit a patient to delegate **any or all** decisions (including both routine and end-of-life treatments) regarding her or his own health care—and in some states (Illinois and North Carolina, for example), health care for minor children—to a proxy or agent or surrogate. The individual so designated is authorized (in effect, "deputized") to confer with attending physicians and to render informed treatment consents in the patient's stead. The agent is called upon to act on the uncomprehending patient's behalf and to make decisions consistent with what the patient would have wanted.

9

At common law, power of attorney lapses if a principal (i.e., the maker of a power) becomes unable, for whatever reasons, to make decisions or give directions. By pointedly casting a power as *durable* (in accordance with statute), then its purported effect and authority can, if desired, outlast incapacity: the agent can continue to make health care decisions on the uncomprehending principal's behalf. Note well, then, that health care powers or proxies may be rendered utterly useless unless expressly written as a durable (or similarly styled) power. Colorado, Idaho, and Vermont are among the jurisdictions that impose such a requirement. Consult applicable statute.

Depending on the patient's direction, a durable health care power may be very narrow (for example, granting authority to consult about hernia surgery for only the period of time the patient is under anesthesia on a given day—much like the highly limited delegation of presidential authority Lyndon Johnson once conferred upon vice president Hubert Humphrey while the president underwent surgery in the mid-1960s). Or it may be very broad and powerful (for example, allowing withdrawal of nutrition and hydration in the event of a terminal condition). The patient also may specify types of treatments to be provided or withheld. To give the agent guidance in the event of unforeseen medical situations, the patient often may express a generalized preference for level of care (e.g., instructions to aggressively attempt all possible death-delaying interventions; or directions to withhold heroic life support and provide comfort care only in the event of a terminal condition.)

A broad grant of authority—one that completely delegates all decisions for health care and living arrangements with few (if any) exceptions or limitations—generally has the ancillary benefit of obviating the need for appointment of a guardian of the person. As a contingency, the proxy or power may serve to nominate the agent as guardian if one becomes required for some reason (for example, if the grant of authority in the health care power is limited or silent or ambiguous about particular treatments that may later be required. States so providing include Illinois, Hawaii, and Minnesota. See applicable statutes.)

Be aware that powers and proxies are predicated on the most gossamer and fleeting of consents. In addition to traditional means of physical destruction, some jurisdictions (Delaware, Iowa, and Nevada, for example) pointedly provide for oral revocation, irrespective of mental state. If revoked, it is over—no matter how incongruous or implausible or inopportune or irrational the revocation may seem to be.

§ 2.03 *Ancillary or Limited Use Directives*

§ 2.04—*Living Wills*

A statutory forerunner of the durable health care power or proxy, living wills—which are on the books in forty-seven states—now are largely in eclipse.[1] This is due to their single-scenario nature of non-curative illness. Because they are cast as explicit instructions (rather than as delegations of authority, like powers or proxies), living wills may, however, still serve in a useful backup role.

Euphemistically, the living will (also known as a "declaration" in some jurisdictions) is widely perceived by lay persons as a "pull the plug" document. This is not necessarily so. It is, more correctly, a "death with dignity" directive.

Through a living will, an individual instructs attending physicians to withhold death-delaying procedures and to provide only comfort care in the event of a terminal condition. Note well that some jurisdictions (Illinois and Missouri, for example) do not permit the withdrawal of artificial hydration and nutrition under the terms of a living will if such withdrawal (rather than the terminal condition itself) would be the cause of death. On the other hand, enabling legislation for powers or proxies in forty-one states specifically authorize the agent to withhold sustenance. This issue is not addressed in Arkansas, California, the District of Columbia, Kansas, Massachusetts, Michigan, Montana, North Dakota, Rhode Island, and Wyoming.[2] Refer to applicable statute.

Because they seem to have more "name recognition" than powers or proxies, living wills may provide a useful starting point for a client discussion on advance directives. Be mindful that persons unfamiliar with directives commonly consider health care powers and living wills to be two different names for the same style of document. Some also continue to confuse the living will with a last will and testament. Take pains to point out the distinctions.

A crucial difference about the living will is that it is a succinct written instruction to physicians about end-of-life treatments: no third party is necessary to make it operative (as is the case with health care powers or proxies). Accordingly, it may become the document of choice for individuals who do not, for whatever reason, have a designated agent or proxy. The document also may have some use as a "fallback" in the event an agent named in a contemporaneously executed health care power has predeceased, declines to serve, or is unavailable.

Be especially alert to possible overlaps and conflicts between living wills and durable health care powers or health care proxies. Some jurisdictions (for example, Alabama and Georgia) provide that both may be executed, with the power taking precedence if there is an agent available and ready to act. Some jurisdictions lack specifics in this area. Therefore, lawyers must review applicable statutes and case law with great care if contemplating execution of both the health care power and the living will. Because the majority of jurisdictions (among them: Alaska, California, Florida, Maine, Nebraska, Ohio, South Carolina, Vermont, and West Virginia) provide for some form of reciprocity in recognition of living wills, clients—especially those who travel widely—may be wise to prepare this directive regardless of its limits in scope.

§ 2.05—Declarations of Preferences for Mental Health Treatments

A handful of states (for example: Alaska, Illinois, Minnesota, and Oklahoma) now provide for this ancillary directive. For the most part, it roughly parallels the generalized health care power or proxy: the principal or patient designates an individual to render consent to treatments in the event of mental illness. Specific treatments (psychotropic medications, electroconvulsive therapy) may be pointedly authorized or excluded, as the patient directs.

Similarly, these documents also may be revoked during periods of lucidity or remission. One difference is that some states (South Dakota and Texas, for example) specifically provide for sunset dates (e.g., three years from the date of execution) or some other form of automatic expiration.

These expressions are particularly useful for those who suffer from episodic mental illness. However, note well and be exceedingly cautious about *the utterly irrevocable nature* of these so-called Ulysses directives.[3] Upon onset, the agent may continue to act, and the doctors may continue to treat, for the duration of the illness or episode no matter how strident the attempted revocation, and no matter how bitterly the patient may protest. This is a radical difference from other types of health care powers or proxies.

§ 2.06—Durable Power of Attorney for Property; Trusts

Strictly speaking, of course, these are not advance health care directives at all. However, carefully drawn instructions for the management of property and finances in the event of decisional or communicative incapacity are integral to a holistic contingency plan. Accordingly, they are referenced here as ancillary documents. Note that some clients may believe that property powers encompass health care needs, when in fact two distinct documents may be required to cover all functions. Examine state statute and counsel clients carefully.[4]

In some jurisdictions (California, Hawaii, and Michigan, for example), property powers are designed to operate in parallel or in tandem with health care powers—that is, the former purport to run to all financial decision-making in the event of incapacity. Designated agents may be the same person (e.g., a spouse) under each power.

Clients with simple needs or modest means may find that a property power executed simultaneously or contemporaneously with a health care proxy or power will address their needs very satisfactorily. In order to minimize the potential for guardianship or conservatorship, it is important to execute both health care **and** property powers. Review the following section on cautions to consider when employing powers of attorney.

Those with extensive or complex financial matters are, of course, more likely to opt for intervivos trusts and related arrangements. A review of estate planning concerns is beyond the scope of this book. Refer to one of the many fine reference texts available.

§ 2.07—*Organ Donation*

How many of our clients—and how many of us—have considered organ donation?

Given recent improvements in transplant techniques and immunosuppressive therapies, the need for organs and tissue has grown enormously. The supply is woefully small: some transplant candidates wait in suspense and agony (both physical and mental) for weeks and months, hoping against hope to win a figurative footrace between donation and death. Sadly, many die for lack of a donor.

Organ donation is, of course, a highly charged emotional issue. To some family members, consenting to donation may be tantamount to a death sentence: it can represent "giving up" on a loved one, no matter how compromised the life of that loved one has become. Unfortunate nomenclature compounds the difficulty. (Who wants their organs "harvested"?)

Donation also has become an economic and political issue. Allocation of organs and tissue long has been done on a regional basis. Proposed U.S. Department of Health and Human Services regulations establishing a national allocation system based on "greatest need" have met withering criticism, thus delaying implementation.

Although the authors consider anatomical gifts to be a corollary to the subject of advance health care directives, their importance cannot possibly be overstated. Of course, organ donation is not for everyone. Emotional, economic, and political (as well as semantic) issues aside, we as professionals have a profound societal—indeed, humanitarian—responsibility to facilitate it through education of patients and clients who are receptive to the concept.

Intent to donate organs or tissue often may be expressed in accordance with an applicable organ or anatomical gift act (now enacted in all states), a health care proxy, or a durable power of attorney for health care. One may specify certain organs or tissues, or direct donation without restriction. Note, however, that in some states the immediate family of a prospective donor may need to give consent before organs or tissue can be removed, irrespective of prior written intent or direction. In some jurisdictions, "required request" legislation compels hospital staff to ask a family to consider organ donation. (The Omnibus Reconciliation Act of 1986, implements "required request" at all hospitals certified for Medicare reimbursement.).[5]

Practically speaking, signing the back of a driver's license or carrying a properly executed donor card is most effective. Providing instruction solely within a difficult-to-locate health care power may, from a medical standpoint, frustrate the donor's intent. State the donation instructions consistently in both a health care power and donor card or driver's license. Also, consider listing with a regional or state donor registry (where available) or online service: this may provide helpful guidance to grieving family members when they are asked by hospital staff to donate.

Help dispel some of the following myths and misconceptions:

- "The doctor won't try hard to save me if I donate." False. Every effort is made to save a patient's life before anatomical gifts are even considered. Death now is determined through brain function: when it ceases, heart and lung activity also stops unless the patient is temporarily connected to a respirator. As a safeguard, death is always pronounced first by a doctor who has absolutely no connection to the organ procurement or transplant team.
- "We don't want to pay for giving organs or tissue." Not true. There is no charge—nor is there payment—for donating. (The National Organ Transplant Act of 1984 prohibits sale.)[6]
- "Organ donation will mutilate the body. We won't be able to have an open casket funeral." Incorrect. There is no disfigurement. The surgical team removes the organs and tissue in the hospital and leaves the body intact.
- "It's against my religion." If this is so, then it is imperative that applicable religious tenets be respected. Most major religions are generally supportive of the concept of brain death; moreover, they largely view organ and tissue donation as the final act of giving. Be alert, however. Organ transplantation may raise theological issues among Muslims. Most Christian Scientists reject the practice. (See Chapter 9.)
- "The patient never signed a donor card, so we can't do it." Not true. So long as the family has knowledge of what the patient wanted, then consent may be given.
- "I'm too old (or too sick). My organs won't be useful to anybody." Wrong. Women and men of any age, and of any race, may donate: determinations of suitability are made on a case-by-case basis, after death.
- "The wealthy and famous can buy their way to the top of the list." Incorrect. Committees and teams employ strict and exhaustive criteria to screen potential recipients (both medically and psychologically) and rank them on the basis of suitability, availability, urgency of need, and elapsed waiting time—never on ability to pay.
- "Caucasians are helped by transplants more than African Americans or other minorities." False. The majority of transplants received by African Americans come from Caucasian donors.
- "I can donate organs and tissue, and then donate my body to a medical school for study and research." Generally, it is not possible to donate a body from which any part (except eyes) has been removed. Those wishing to donate their bodies for research (to the exclusion of organ donation) usually must register in advance. Contact a local medical school, or the office of the local coroner or medical examiner, for information.
- "There's not really all that much that can be transplanted." It is widely known that hearts, kidneys, livers, and corneas are used. It is also

possible to transplant lungs, the pancreas, small bowel, bone and bone marrow, skin, and tendons. A single donor can give health—and life—to several individuals.

The "Tissue Trade": A Cautionary Tale—An investigative series by the *Chicago Tribune* in May, 2000 revealed possible abuses in procurement and distribution of human tissues (not organs), including questionable representations to next of kin and startling financial markups by some intermediaries for "processing" and "handling." It appears that the U.S. Department of Health and Human Services is developing new regulations. In short: for the present, do not be sanguine about tissue donations. Make pointed inquires before consenting.

Can You Feel It in Your Bones?—One needn't wait until the end of life to give a life saving gift. Consider registering with the National Marrow Donor Program. For information, call 1-(800) MARROW-2 or visit http://www.marrow.org.

Cord Blood—Umbilical cords—which until recently have been routinely discarded at birth—contain stem cells that are proving to be immensely useful for treating leukemia and other diseases. Please see the discussion in Chapter 11.

A Pint-Sized Favor—By the way—you can be a hero. You can save a life. Today. Just by rolling up your sleeve.

How? You can give blood or blood components. Donation takes only a bit of time, and the discomfort is minimal. Generally, donors must be at least eighteen years old (or 16 or 17 with parental permission), over 110 pounds, and in good health. Temperature, pulse, blood pressure, and hemoglobin must be within acceptable ranges. Blood may be donated every eight weeks. Platelets may be given even more frequently. Be aware: in order to protect the supply from blood-borne pathogens, very personal questions now are asked about sexual practices, non-prescription needle use, and the like.

Give organs. Give tissue. Give marrow. Give blood. Give life!

§ 2.08—Oral Expressions

Occasionally, a hospitalized or institutionalized patient may decline to fill out a directive but make known to the treating physician her or his wishes for treatment. Although plainly not as desirable as a written directive (might oral statements be pointedly excluded under state law?), these expressions may prove to be of some use. Physicians might consider noting such statements in the chart. Perhaps the patient might be encouraged to countersign such notes. As an alternative, consider having another person sign as a "witness" to the oral expression of treatment preferences. In some states, this is addressed by statute. In Texas, "A competent, qualified patient who is an adult may issue a directive (i.e., a living will) by a nonwritten means of communication."[7] Maryland allows oral expression; Florida permits oral or written statements.

§ 2.09—Nomination of Guardian

In contexts apart from property and health care powers, some states specifically provide for nomination of guardians. Writings of this nature commonly assume many of the formalities of a last will and testament (e.g., one or more witnesses). Similarly, parents may nominate guardians and successor guardians for their minor or decisionally incapacitated children within the context of a last will and testament.

Such designations, perhaps, are best thought of as "once removed" from advance directives: they represent contemplative expressions as to preferences for a contingent health care decision maker, and do not run at all to treatment preferences or scope. Still, the mere act of identifying a potential health care decision-maker may be of some use.

Help clients overcome a common misconception. With but few exceptions, we cannot appoint our own guardians; appointment is strictly a judicial function. However, we may *nominate* a guardian for a judge's future consideration. A judge is likely—but is not obligated—to appoint an individual so nominated.

§ 2.10 Some Comments—and Cautions—about Durable Powers of Attorney

Given their simplicity and low cost, durable powers of attorney for health care (and property) can be exceedingly effective. And let's be candid about it: a number of people simply do not require professional assistance to draft and execute them.

However, if there are complex health or financial situations to be governed by powers, or if they are inartfully drafted or imprudently applied, or if they fall into the hands of the unscrupulous, property and health care powers may become tools of abuse. Be certain to advise clients on both the benefits and drawbacks of these powerful documents.

Clients need to know that the statutorily suggested language associated with each type of power usually grants the broadest authority. It is incumbent on the principal to "chip away" at the language to limit or modify it to suit his or her wishes. This may be done in two ways: by controlling the implementation, and by specifying or otherwise limiting the duties of the agent.

§ 2.11—Controlling Implementation

Controlling the timing of implementation is probably the better method. Unless otherwise stated, the effectiveness of the powers might begin at the moment of signing and run until death. (In some jurisdictions—Georgia,

Indiana, and Kansas for example—health care powers may be extended for the limited purposes of consenting to autopsies, organ donations, and disposition of remains.) If desired, one may insert a future date for it to become effective, as well as a "sunset" date for expiration.

A "springing" power may be appropriate. Consider this language: "This document shall become effective upon the independent determinations, in writing, of two medical doctors that I am totally incapable of making personal decisions." (With respect to the property power, substitute "financial" for "personal" decisions.) Note that absent a contrary statement, a document executed under the Model Uniform Health-Care Decisions Act format (see Appendix C) becomes operative only when the primary physician determines that the patient is no longer able to make health care decisions.

§ 2.12—Selecting an Agent

Advise clients that the careful selection of an agent (and successor agents) is absolutely essential to the effectiveness of these documents. Obviously, a highly trustworthy agent well known to the patient is necessary for effective discharge of property duties in the event of the patient's decisional or communicative incapacity. Similarly, a concerned, loving, and courageous individual is to be chosen as agent under the durable health care power, as the agent may be called upon to make life-and-death health care decisions.

The growing awareness of these powers might result in increasing numbers of unscrupulous individuals who press those of marginal decision-making capacity to grant far-ranging authority. Agents working under durable property powers have the opportunity to wreak havoc: bank accounts can be cleaned out, beneficiaries on insurance policies changed, titles transferred, and so forth. Conceivably, health care decisions may be colored by an expectancy in an estate, or by the pecuniary interests of an agent who is financially responsible for the medical care of the patient.

Accordingly, be alert to undue influence (inadvertent or otherwise) on a marginally capable person. Be as concerned about bedside powers as one may be about bedside wills. Preparing durable powers well in advance of any crisis is, of course, desired. If any professional ever is in doubt about a patient's or client's ability to grant durable powers, always err on the side of caution. Ask a medical doctor to examine the individual and provide a written opinion about capacity. If there is insufficient capacity, one may have to proceed with a guardianship.

§ 2.13—Keeping Direct Control

In addition to controlling the timing of implementation, clients should consider holding the powers under their direct control. Some may prefer a safe-deposit box, for example. (This is not, however, recommended by the authors.) As another approach, some may wish to leave powers with counsel or another third party, to be delivered to the agent only upon the indicated date or circumstance.

With the permission of clients, keep photocopies on file, along with notations as to where the originals may be found. Physicians and health care facilities should be informed of health care powers, and photocopies provided for their charts and other records. The principal may choose whether agents and/or successor agents should have copies.

Note well that differentiating between originals and copies may be of no consequence in a number of jurisdictions: some statutes pointedly provide that a photocopy of a proxy or power shall be as valid as an original.

§ 2.14—Indicating the Existence of Directives

Individuals should carry a pocket card in a wallet or purse (or wear a bracelet or medallion or necklace) indicating the existence of directives and where they may be found. (See Appendix N for a sample of a wallet card). Copies (which note where the originals are located) should be left at work and home in places such as a top desk or dresser drawer where others are likely to look in case of an emergency. Louisiana has a statewide registry; North Carolina will operate a registry beginning in 2002. In Wisconsin, documents may be filed with the register in probate in the county of residence. New online services also serve as clearinghouses for directives.[8]

Although many state-suggested forms now provide for addresses and telephone numbers of designated agents, be expansive. Include both work and residence numbers for all agents and successor agents. Also incorporate, as appropriate, wireless phone, fax, pager, and e-mail information. Precious time may be lost in an emergency situation if health care personnel are compelled to contact directory assistance or similar resources in a distant city.

An aside about property powers: it may be astute to prospectively advise banks, stockbrokers, and other financial advisors and intermediaries of their existence. In fact, it may be prudent to preemptively provide duplicate originals, as some entities may (rightly or wrongly) refuse to honor photocopies of a power. Similarly, it is important to carefully anticipate contemplated functions: financial entities may be reticent to abide by "elastic clauses" and may decline to honor attempts by an agent to undertake activities such as gifting unless expressly provided for in a property power. Incidentally, gifts made by an agent (as opposed to a principal) may have unintended—and unfavorable—tax consequences. Consult appropriate estate planning resources.

§ 2.15—Updating Directives Regularly

Advise clients that durable powers are revocable documents—at least, up to the point of decisional or communicative incapacity. Given that wishes and needs may change, they should consider reviewing and changing these documents from time to time. Lawyers should also be alert to statutory change

Important Caveats for Changing Directives

- It's easier said than done! Note well this risk: revoked directives may someday (and somehow) surface as rogue directives. Innocent parties may be unaware of subsequent revocations and in good faith construe them as definitive and current. Pointedly gather up and destroy all copies—including photocopies—of revoked directives. And who has copies? Agent/proxy and successors? Doctors? Residential facility? Family/friends? Lawyer? Clergy? Registry services? Be aware, however, that some jurisdictions (California, Delaware, Minnesota, and Mississippi, for example), as well as the Model Uniform Health-Care Decisions Act format expressly provide that copies have the same effect as originals. By the way—might directives have found their way into electronic or computer-stored records systems? More and more hospitals and doctors are abandoning paper charts for computerized records.
- State in the new directives that the "old" ones are revoked. In jurisdictions where suggested forms lack a revocation clause, suggest language to this effect: "I hereby revoke all health care proxies/powers/living wills previously made."
- Consider methods of closely holding documents to minimize the potential for "rogue directives." Some possible approaches: stipulate in the directive that photocopies are for informational purposes only and lack the force and effect of originals (applicable only in jurisdictions that are silent on the use of photocopies—see above); rely on duplicate originals rather than photocopies; refrain from wide distribution of copies; disseminate *data* about directives (e.g. unsigned documents) to need-to-know individuals, rather than copies of the directives themselves; have a third party hold the originals (or duplicate originals) for delivery to the agent or proxy only upon the indicated date or circumstance.
- Declarations of preferences for mental health treatments (provided for in states such as Alaska, South Dakota, and Texas)–the so-called "Ulysses" directives—typically may **not** be revoked if the patient is under active treatment.

and new case law in this area, and mark pertinent files for occasional review. Clients who move out of state should re-execute both health and property powers in conformance with the laws of the new jurisdiction.

§ 2.16 Diversions

See Chapter 10 (Alternatives in the Absence of Directives) regarding diversions or fallbacks in the event there are no advance health care directives.

§ 2.17 Conclusion

Advance health care directives are exceedingly important personal planning documents. The health care power of attorney or proxy is, for most, the preferred vehicle: it is the most far-reaching, flexible, and adaptable style of document. Ancillary or special purpose directives (living wills, mental health declarations, organ donation) can augment and enhance a power or proxy.

Patients and clients should work with statutorily suggested forms and "tailor make" powers that, on a broadbrush basis, pointedly state their preferences and needs. The most essential choice by far is the selection of agent or proxy. No matter how carefully thought out, the power will be useless (or, worse, counterproductive) if the designated "deputy" is unwilling to act or is disinclined to honor treatment instructions.

Avoid being exhaustive in crafting directives; inordinate detail may only complicate implementation. Opt for figurative signposts over reams of prose. Append a values history to a directive if desired (see Appendix D). At some point, each of us must let go with our directives and trust our agents to faithfully interpret our wishes.

Family and friends and care providers and emergency personnel are not mind readers. We must each leave good "footprints" as to where directives (and agents or proxies) are to be found. (See the sidebar in Chapter 5.)

Directives demand courage. Help give clients and patients the courage they need to complete them—and put them into action.

Notes

1. Alaska is the only state providing solely for living wills. Massachusetts, Michigan, and New York authorize the appointment of health care agents only and do not provide for living wills. Forty-six states and the District of Columbia provide for both living wills and powers of attorney (or proxies) for health care.
2. *End-of-Life Law Digest*, "Artificial Nutrition and Hydration in Statutes Authorizing Health Care Agents." Partnership for Caring, Inc., Washington, D.C., March, 2001.
3. Recall that portion of Homer's *Odyssey* where Ulysses (Odysseus) encounters the Sirens. Wishing to hear for himself their unspeakably beautiful singing, and mindful that mere mortals would be driven mad and leap off their ships (and subsequently drawn) upon hearing it, Ulysses ordered his crew to lash him to the mast and to plug their own ears. As they sailed past, Ulysses begged to be freed. The crew, however, resolutely ignored their captain's pleas until they were safely away.
4. It should be noted that it may not be necessary to have an attorney or other professional prepare a property power of attorney or a trust. However, lay-prepared documents may be the falsest of all economies. Individuals with large estates or complex financial issues are particularly well advised to obtain requisite assistance.

5. Pub. L. No. 99-509, 100 Stat. 1874, 2009 (1986).
6. National Organ Transplant Act, 42 U.S.C. 273.
7. V.T.C.A., Vol. 5, Health and Safety, Natural Death Act, § 672.005(a).
8. The U.S. Living Will Registry electronically stores advance directives and makes them available directly to health care providers across the country by telephone through an automated computer-facsimile system. For more information, see http://www.uslivingwillregistry.com.

CHAPTER 3

The Ethics of Advance Health Care Directives

§ 3.01 Introduction

You're navigating an unknown archipelago in the dead of night, and you and your crew must pick the best way to ferry your passengers and ship to safety.

You are compelled to choose from three straits: Advance Directives, Substituted Judgment, and Best Interests. All are fraught with tricky currents and unseen reefs and rocks. Out on the horizon, ominous storms gather.

Charts tell you the strait of Advance Directives probably is, on balance, the best: despite the currents and shoals, it is the shortest route, and the water is fairly deep. If it cannot be negotiated, the strait of Substituted Judgment is the next choice. If both are unnavigable, then you will get to port through the strait of Best Interests, even though it may be the slowest and shallowest and most indirect of the three.

Fortunately, you have four lighthouses to guide you: Autonomy, Non-maleficence, Beneficence, and Justice. You may return to these beacons at any time and check bearings. Once there and reoriented, change course for another strait, or simply drop anchor and wait for better conditions. Never forget—all hands are counting on you.

The ethics of advance health care directives should be considered in two parts: drafting and implementation.

This volume emphasizes the drafting of directives. The exquisitely excruciating ethics of application and implementation are largely beyond our scope. The authors defer, with admiration, to the ethicists and scholars in the field[1] for authoritative discussion and review.

That said, all professionals still must have commanding knowledge of the essences of ethics. The following discussion should be construed as but the briefest of introductions.

§ 3.02 Negotiating the Straits

§ 3.03—Advance Directives

The personal contingency plans collectively called *advance directives* are contemplative and affirmative instructions for health care in the event of incapacity. When they exist—and recall that directives presently appear only in a minority of cases—they generally are to be favored, because they are most likely to either approximate, replicate or actually be an authentic set of patient choices. Directives also do the most to further the precepts of privacy and autonomy in medical decision-making.

However, a predisposition or predilection for directives should not—indeed, cannot—be automatic or slavish. A number of figurative reefs and shoals may force us as professionals to discount or even disregard directives and turn back: questions about competency upon execution, undue influence, insufficient information, ambiguity, silence, contradiction, instructions inadvertently at variance with clinical situations the patient did not anticipate, conflicts of interest, and directions to treat irrespective of medical futility, to name but a few.

§ 3.04—Substituted Judgement

In the event directives either do not exist or cannot be negotiated or implemented, the next figurative strait to be attempted usually is that of *substituted judgment*. Beauchamp and Childress provide the definition:

> The standard of substituted judgment appears initially to be autonomy-based, and several influential judicial opinions have so viewed it. However, it is at best a weak autonomy standard. Substituted judgment begins with the premise that decisions about treatment properly belong to the incompetent or nonautonomous patient by virtue of rights of autonomy and privacy. The patient has the right to decide but is incompetent to exercise it. It would be unfair to deprive an incompetent patient of decisionmaking rights merely because he or she is no longer (or has never been) autonomous. Nonetheless, another decisionmaker should be substituted if the patient is currently unable to make autonomous decisions.[2]

Under this approach, a surrogate who purports to have personal knowledge of the values and mores of a once competent patient volunteers (or at times is even conscripted) as a substitute decision-maker. A surrogate typically relies on recollections about the values of a patient and attempts to interpolate, extrapolate and impute medical decisions that are thought to comport with what the patient, if competent, might have wanted.

In short, substituted judgment is the equivalent of celestial navigation by dead reckoning. Unable to fix a position because of darkness, or because clouds, fog or mist shroud the sun or stars, we must estimate our figurative position based only on estimates of course and speed. We attempt to respect and preserve autonomy and privacy while simultaneously trying to approximate the position of a formerly competent patient. We hope to be close; we may be way off. The possibility that we may be way off should forever give us pause.

Unheeding deference to the precepts of substituted judgment also carries a figurative risk of running aground. Recalled patient expressions may be fragmentary or misconstrued. Candidates for surrogate may have conflicting or even opposite recollections. Even the most well meaning of surrogates may inadvertently superimpose or jumble her or his values with those of the formerly competent patient. On occasion, underlying motives of a surrogate may lie at cross-purposes to a patient's supposed wishes. Any one of these "hazards to navigation" may compel the most seasoned crews to abandon transit of these figuratively treacherous waters.

§ 3.05—Best Interests

The *best interests* approach effectively is the antithesis of patient privacy and respect for autonomy—and, accordingly, can be diametrically opposed to the precepts of advance directives and substituted judgment. It is, for all practical purposes, the default or fallback standard. According to Beauchamp and Childress,

> Under the best interests standard a surrogate decisionmaker must determine the highest benefit among the available options, assigning different weights to interests the patient has in each option and discounting or subtracting inherent risks or costs. The term *best* (emphasis is original) is used because the obligation is to maximize benefit through a comparative assessment that locates the highest net benefit. The best interests standard protects another's well-being by assessing risks and benefits of various treatments and alternatives to treatment, by considering pain and suffering, and by evaluating restoration or loss of functioning. It is therefore inescapably a quality-of-life criterion.[3]

Best interests may also run the risk of third parties imposing their will on uncomprehending patients. Treatment decisions may be completely at variance with what an individual might have wished. As with the other routes, we must navigate this figurative strait with skill and care.

Unfortunately, the best interests standard of surrogate medical decision making for the previously competent may at times seem—to no one's fault—overbearing, oppressive, arbitrary, autocratic, cumbersome, expensive (as in the instance of having to seek judicial appointment of a guardian), and entirely without regard to what a given patient might really have wanted. Unfortunately there is usually no other way: perhaps the previously competent patient was reticent to write or speak on the subject of possible decisional incapacity, or no one seems to have knowledge of relevant prior patient expressions. Or perhaps the other straits to medical decision-making—advance directives and substituted judgment—cannot for whatever reason be navigated.

§ 3.06 The Lighthouses

§ 3.07—Respect for Autonomy

For better or worse, we as a society are plunging headlong into an era of patient privacy and autonomy in medical decision making. Federal and state statutes are trending decidedly in favor of the "lighthouse of autonomy"—to the point of partially subjugating (or even almost trumping) the other three ethical precepts to be discussed in this section. How is this so?

All the states, the District of Columbia, Guam, and the U.S. Virgin Islands now provide in some form for the quintessential expression of individualized health care decisionmaking: advance directives. (The Commonwealth of Puerto Rico does not so provide.) Consider, too, the federal Patient Self-Determination Act (codified as 42 USC Sec. 1395cc(f)—see Appendix A), which buttresses the concept of directives by mandating the distribution of information about them (but *not* execution) upon contact with federally funded (i.e., Medicare and Medicaid) hospitals, hospices, home health agencies, and nursing homes. In an effort to afford even higher degrees of respect for patient autonomy and privacy (and, some might believe, medical expediency), 28 states and the District of Columbia now have prescribed substitute medical decision-making hierarchies through passage of health care surrogacy (or similarly styled) laws.[4]

Case law also is coming to bear. As signaled in *Cruzan* and *Vacco* (see Chapter 7, "The Attorney Perspective," for a discussion), the U.S. Supreme Court now is pointing to the Fourteenth Amendment's liberty interest as a harbinger of patient autonomy. Although expressly declining to rule on whether or not a state must give effect to the decision of a surrogate decision-maker for health care, Justice O'Connor's separate concurrence in *Cruzan* plainly is receptive to the concept of advance health care directives:

> Few individuals provide explicit oral or written instructions regarding their intent to refuse medical treatment should they become incompetent. States which decline to consider any evidence other than such instruction may frequently fail to honor a patient's intent. Such failures might be avoided if the State considered an equally probative source of evidence: the patient's appointment of a proxy to make health care decisions on her behalf. Delegating the authority to make medical decisions to a family member or friend is becoming a common method of planning for the future.... These procedures for surrogate decisionmaking, which appear to be rapidly gaining in acceptance, may be a valuable additional safeguard to the patient's interest in directing his medical care ... (Please also refer to additional excerpts from Justice O'Connor's opinion on page 81.)[5]

Once again, note well that the only absolute in the field of ethics of advance health care directives is that there are absolutely no absolutes. Unheeding deference to the precepts of patient autonomy carries its own set of perils—for patients and professionals alike. If compromised, patient autonomy must be discounted or even abandoned in favor of the substituted judgment or best interests means of surrogate health care decision-making.

§ 3.08—Nonmaleficence

At its core, the ethical concept of nonmaleficence "... asserts an obligation not to inflict harm intentionally."[6] It is a premise readily recognizable to health care professionals in the Hippocratic maxim "first do no harm."

The distinction between nonmaleficence and beneficence is, to some, a fine one: the former connotes a degree of passivity (i.e., "One ought not to inflict evil or harm"[7]), and the latter is couched as affirmative duties to act.

These differences actually straddle a fault line of medical ethics, because some of the biggest temblors emanate from here:

- Withholding and withdrawing life-sustaining treatment
- Extraordinary (or heroic) and ordinary treatment
- Artificial feeding and other life-sustaining medical technologies
- Intended effects and merely foreseen effects[8]

§ 3.09—Beneficence

The "lighthouse" of beneficence represents affirmative efforts to prospectively act for a patient in a positive fashion. Beauchamp and Childress define the term:

> Morality requires not only that we treat persons autonomously and refrain from harming them, but also that we contribute to their welfare. ... (P)rinciples of beneficence potentially demand more than the principle of nonmaleficence because agents must take positive steps to help others, not merely refrain from harmful acts. ... In ordinary English the term *beneficence* (emphasis is original) connotes acts of mercy, kindness, and charity. Altruism, love, and humanity are also sometimes considered forms of beneficence. *Beneficence* refers to an action done for the benefit of others...[9]

Beauchamp and Childress also cast the concept in another way:

- One ought to prevent evil or harm.
- One ought to remove evil and harm.
- One ought to do or promote good.[10]

In the best sense, then, the ethical concept of beneficence can augment and enhance patient autonomy rather than detract from or supplant it. If the precepts of patient autonomy cannot be invoked—or, for some reason, must be abridged—health care surrogates and their professional advisors then may employ beneficence as an ethical tether.

Beneficence has shortcomings. Those who take on the solemn responsibility of surrogate decision-making and act within the construct of beneficence must not inadvertently perform in patently patronizing or paternalistic ways. Despite this risk, the precept of beneficence in its noblest form draws upon "the better angels of our nature."[11] We do well to rely upon it for bearings even when autonomy or nonmaleficence or justice are largely controlling.

§ 3.10—Justice

Access to health care. Rationing of care. The plight of the uninsured and underinsured. Cost shifting. Cost containment. Scarcity. Efficiency. Efficacy. Equity. Utility.

Justice in health care delivery? That's a Gordian knot if ever there was. And advance health care directives are but the merest few wisps of fiber in that patently impossible knot.

So where stands the "lighthouse" of justice, and how do advance health care directives take bearings on it? Agents and professionals may begin with the following rhetorical questions:

- Will the contemplated course of medical decision-making abridge (or, worse, subvert) either an advance directive or an uncomprehending patient's inherent right to just care?
- Will the course of medical decisions contemplated by a surrogate or stipulated in an advance directive result in a level of care at variance with that afforded similarly situated patients?
- If enacted, will the prior expressions of an uncomprehending patient (or the instructions of a surrogate) result in a level of care either so remarkably extraordinary or so patently futile as to compromise scarce societal resources, thereby diminishing the just level of care that might be afforded to others?

§ 3.11 Professional Ethics

Pertinent codes of ethics and rules of conduct apply to all professionals engaged in the field of advance health care directives.

§ 3.12—Lawyers

Lawyers practicing in this field may frequently find themselves beset by contradictions and conundrums. On one hand, the duty of zealous advocacy may compel fervent articulation of patient/client rights to autonomy and privacy in medical decision-making, unfettered by third party intervention. On the other hand, lawyers have duties of fealty to clients of questionable capacity and may at times be compelled to hew to the best interests standard of substituted decision making, particularly if cause arises to petition for guardianship or conservatorship. In such instances, the responsibility for zealous advocacy of privacy and autonomy interests may come to be completely at loggerheads with an obligation to passively allow—or even actively assist in—the stripping away of liberty interests and civil rights (e.g., through a guardianship or conservatorship or other protective proceeding) if a client is at peril of exploitation or physical harm.

Many state codes of professional responsibility and conduct address the contingency of clients under disability. Refer to the relevant rules. (Also refer to Chapter 7, *infra*, "The Attorney Perspective.")

§ 3.13—Health Care Professionals

Ethical precepts and codes of conduct exhort physicians, nurses, psychologists, ethicists, social workers, and associated administrative and support personnel to some of the most selfless service society can inspire. The Hippocratic Oath and associated principles come immediately to the minds of most. Physicians might also refer to the American Medical Association's Code of Medical Ethics.[12]

Of all the professions interfacing with advance health care directives, those involved in direct patient care are the ones with the preponderance of day-to-day (and even hour-to-hour and moment-to-moment) ethical issues. Reflect again on just a few:

- Withholding treatment (e.g., Do Not Resuscitate)
- Withdrawing treatment
- Medical futility
- Cost of care

Please refer to Chapter 8, *infra*, "The Health Care Provider Perspective," for related discussion.

§ 3.14—Allied Professionals

Social workers, clergy, mental health professionals, palliative caregivers, and spiritual advisors are of course governed by their own respective sets of ethical and moral tenets. Please refer to Chapter 9, "Involvement of Clergy and Spiritual Advisors."

§ 3.15 Institutional Ethics Committees

Another venue for weighing the ethics of advance health care directives are the institutional ethics or biomedical ethics committees now often constituted in larger hospitals and medical centers. These deliberative groups can provide immeasurable help with issues running from poignant to excruciating to seemingly intractable. Buchanan and Brock provide a cogent description:

Ten Rules for Professionals
Aiding in the Execution of Directives

1. Abide by professional tenets (e.g., codes of responsibility, rules of conduct, Hippocratic Oath). "The only absolute in the ethics of advance health care directives is that there are absolutely no absolutes."
2. Be clear on who you are helping—almost always the client/patient/ principal, to the exclusion of family, friends, and concerned others, well-meaning as they all may be.
3. Guard against undue influence. Even if multiple parties (e.g., family members) are involved at the express wish of the patient/client, conduct at least a portion of an interview privately and one-on-one.
4. Verify. Check and recheck client wishes and understanding. When prudent and possible, conduct more than one interview.
5. If you doubt client capacity to execute a directive, be very conservative. Include a formal medical assessment.
6. Insufficient capacity? Then the patient/client cannot execute directives. However, do not categorically rule out or dismiss expressions by a decisionally incapacitated individual. Aided by a surrogate decision-maker or court appointed guardian, she or he may be able to articulate some treatment preferences. Strive very hard to accommodate these.
7. Perpetually burnish your good moral compass. Use it heavily.
8. When in doubt, get third party perspective.
9. Common sense hardly ever fails.
10. Always ask, "Is this how *I* would want to be treated?"

Institutional ethics committees can perform several valuable functions: They can serve as a focus for bioethics education in the institution and community; they can provide ethics consultation services for staff, patients, and family; and they can serve as a forum for complaints about the decisions of any of the parties involved in treatment decision making, sometimes achieving a satisfactory resolution of conflicts without recourse to the courts or other government agencies. . . .(Even the) most enthusiastic supporters must acknowledge that (committees) are no panacea, but at best only one element of a complex set of social arrangements needed to assure responsible decision making for incompetent people.[13]

In addition to a committee or similar deliberative structure, staff ethicists also may be "in house" as a service, making rounds in larger institutions and promptly available for case-by-case consultations upon request.

§ 3.16 Conclusion

As with advance health care directives themselves, there is no single or simplistic "right way" governing the ethics of their drafting and implementation. When in doubt, be cautious. Collaborate—and corroborate—with others.

Remember, the goal is to get your passengers and crew to port safely, maddeningly slow and shallow as the straits may be.

This chapter's nautical analogies now conclude with a bit of naval history. Remember Admiral Farragut's Civil War battle at Mobile Bay? His memorable "damn the torpedoes, full speed ahead" approach surely stirs romantic images of seafaring courage and verve and derring-do. But we all know deep down how very risky this approach can be if applied to the construct of the ethics of advance health care directives. Those feckless and reckless enough to espouse and embrace this approach are destined to plunge ignominiously to the figurative bottom—in very short order.

One final thought: Healthy humility produces marvelous leavening. Resolve to be a "perpetual student" of the ethics of advance health care directives. Hardly any of us are good enough to be figurative (or literal) professors.

Notes

1. *See infra* appendices and bibliography for reference to some of these sources.
2. T. BEAUCHAMP & J. CHILDRESS, PRINCIPLES OF BIOMEDICAL ETHICS 171 (1994).
3. *Id.* at 178-79.
4. Twenty-two states do not have health care surrogacy statutes: Alaska, California, Georgia, Idaho, Kansas, Massachusetts, Michigan, Minnesota, Missouri, Nebraska, New Hampshire, New Jersey, New York, North Dakota, Oklahoma, Pennsylvania, Rhode Island, South Dakota, Tennessee, Vermont, Washington, and Wisconsin. Twenty-nine jurisdictions that authorize surrogate decisions in the absence of health care directives are: Alabama, Arizona, Arkansas, Colorado, Connecticut, District of Columbia, Delaware, Florida, Hawaii, Illinois, Indiana, Iowa, Kentucky, Louisiana, Maryland, Maine, Mississippi, Montana, Nevada, New Mexico, North Carolina, Ohio, Oregon, South Carolina, Texas, Utah, Virginia, West Virginia, and Wyoming. *End-of-Life Law Digest*, "State Statutes Governing Surrogate Decisionmaking", Partnership for Caring, Inc., Washington, DC (March, 2001).
5. Cruzan V. Director, Mo. Dep't of Health, 497 U.S. 261, 289 (O'Connor, J., Concurring).
6. T. BEAUCHAMP & J. CHILDRESS, *supra* note 2, at 189.
7. *Id.* at 192.
8. *Id.* at 196.
9. *Id.* at 259-60.
10. *Id.* at 192.
11. President Abraham Lincoln, First Inaugural Address (Mar. 4, 1861).
12. AMERICAN MED. ASS'N, CODE OF MEDICAL ETHICS (1997).
13. A. BUCHANAN & D. BROCK, DECIDING FOR OTHERS: THE ETHICS OF SURROGATE DECISION MAKING 148-49 (1995).

CHAPTER 4

Competence and Incompetence

§ 4.01 Introduction

Competence—or lack of it—is the most poignant and nettlesome issue associated with advance health care directives.

As a matter of law, we all are presumed competent upon attaining majority. The burden of proof typically is on those who would assert otherwise—petitioners in guardianship cases, for example. Were it only so stark and simple in everyday practice!

The question of competence comes to bear on advance health care directives at two junctures: execution and effectuation. In other words, one must be competent to execute a directive and usually must be incompetent to effectuate it. This is a startling dichotomy.

Each of us makes subjective evaluations about the competence of others every single day. Whenever clients come to a lawyer's office to execute wills, witnesses affix signatures attesting to the "sound mind and memory" of testators, based perhaps only on a few furtive moments of observation. For the most part, advance directives are witnessed with even less formality and absolutely no pomp.

At the risk of sounding glib, we all know competence (and incompetence) when we see it. Untold numbers of business transactions occur daily predicated only on subtle and highly subjective lay evaluations of competence. Our society could hardly be expected to function if disinterested third parties had to pass on the competence of every single person entering into a contract.

So it is with advance directives. The vast majority of them surely are composed and signed and witnessed without medical or legal involvement and without formal evaluations of competence.

The rub comes, of course, at the margins. What is to be done when a client or patient fails some or all of the intuitive and subtle lay screenings each of us routinely use on one another?

§ 4.02 Check Applicable Statute

The first step is to check applicable statute. A number of jurisdictions define capacity to (a) make health care decisions or (b) execute directives, or (c) both, within the context of relevant legislation. Here are some examples:

- District of Columbia. "Presumption of capacity. An individual shall be presumed capable of making health-care decisions unless certified otherwise (by two physicians, one of whom shall be a psychiatrist) . . . " Inferences about capacity based on mental health status are pointedly curbed.[1]
- Indiana. "An individual . . . may consent to health care unless, in the good faith opinion of the attending physician, the individual is incapable of making a decision regarding the proposed health care."[2]
- Minnesota. "The principal is presumed to have the capacity to execute a health care directive and to revoke a health care directive, absent clear and convincing evidence to the contrary."[3]
- Mississippi. "Unless otherwise specified in a written advance health-care directive, a determination that an individual lacks or has recovered capacity . . . must be made by the primary physician."[4]
- New York. "(E)very adult shall be presumed competent to appoint a health care agent unless such person has been adjudged incompetent or otherwise adjudged not competent to appoint a health care agent, or unless a committee or guardian of the person has been appointed . . ."[5]

What, then, is to be done about evaluating capacity in furtherance of state statute—or in the absence of statutory construction?

§ 4.03 The American Bar Association Position

The American Bar Association's Commission on Legal Problems of the Elderly has promulgated a three part test to evaluate decision-making capacity. It is a highly useful touchstone for professionals:

- Is the patient aware of his or her needs and alternatives for meeting them?
- Is the patient able to express a preference regarding the alternatives?
- Does the patient demonstrate a factual understanding of the risks, benefits, and alternatives of treatment or no treatment?

§ 4.04 When in Doubt, Include a Medical Assessment

Here is the rule of thumb: no capacity, no directives. Professionals must be very conservative when they take either drafting or advisory roles with respect to living wills, health care proxies, durable powers of attorney for both health care and property, and related documents. If questions exist about one's capacity to provide informed consent, request an examination and written evaluation of the individual by a medical doctor before drafting any documents. This helps eliminate any possible appearance that a professional or other party is, inadvertently or otherwise, exerting undue influence.

There are, of course, downsides to seeking medical evaluation of a marginally capable client. First of all, a *medical* determination of competence is not necessarily a *legal* determination of competence. (See the following discussion of legal thresholds of competence.) Furthermore, the very fact that a professional seeks third party medical evaluation of an individual is, to some, a tacit indication that the professional thinks (if only subjectively) that there *is* a question about competency; on this basis, any subsequent document may carry at least a tinge (or even stigma) of doubt. The authors believe that on balance, however, the interests of all concerned are collectively best served by a third party medical evaluation whenever capacity is an issue.

§ 4.05—The Medical Examination

If only as a point of departure, a medical examiner may employ any one of several brief mental status examinations. Most widely known is the Folstein Mini-Mental State Examination (MMSE),[6] which can be administered to most patients in less than ten minutes. Note well that it (or any other brief scale) should not be relied upon exclusively for diagnosis: depending on variables such as underlying intelligence and extent of formal education, false positives and false negatives may result.

A complete neurologic and psychiatric examination and evaluation typically begins with a thorough history and physical. A clinical interview will assess orientation to person, time and place, memory, recall, language skills, degrees of consciousness, behaviors, attention, learning ability, cognition, and the like. The examiner likely will administer two or more neuropsychologic test batteries. Ancillary laboratory and radiological studies may be considered to exclude medical conditions that may lead to transient or potentially reversible mental status changes. Although not necessarily required, a board-certified psychiatrist is mildly preferred for these purposes, especially if judicial review is anticipated.

Clinical determinations of competence should include several areas of patient function: extent (if any) of decisional impairment; ability by degrees to make personal and/or financial decisions; problem-solving ability;

sufficiency with activities of daily living (ADLs); extent of supervision (if indicated); appropriate living arrangements; and (if applicable) potential for rehabilitation or restoration.

If the scrivener suspects that client deficits are so pronounced as to possibly implicate guardianship or conservatorship or both, provide the medical examiner with any indicated evaluation form or written criteria. In the event the doctor states that the individual has insufficient capacity, directives are, simply speaking, out. The lawyer then has immediately at hand the requisite written evaluation to petition for guardianship.

In case questions are subsequently raised, the lawyer should retain medical evaluations and reports indicating sufficient capacity along with copies of directives and ancillary documents that are subsequently prepared. The exceedingly cautious may wish an audio or video recording of the MMSE, plus any other contemporaneous statements the client may choose to make (but only, of course, with consent of the patient/client). New Jersey provides for this possibility (see below.)

§ 4.06 The Lawyer–Client Interview

Lawyers should keep careful notes about all client interviews for their files. As appropriate, and with prior client consent, consider using disinterested third parties as witnesses to lawyer interviews. Record names and addresses of witnesses in contemporaneous lawyer notes. If witnesses are to be privy to an interview, it is probably best to seek some sort of affirmative assent to a limited waiver of the lawyer–client privilege. (Note, however, the wry—if not untenable—irony of asking a client to sign a waiver if client capacity is the issue!)

A more suitable method for lawyers to prospectively involve extra witnesses is to simultaneously employ jurisdictionally prescribed methods for testamentary attestation whenever directives are executed, even if this is "overkill" not called for by advance directives statutes or provided for in forms. In this fashion, the awkwardness of witnesses attending lawyer–client interviews is avoided. If for whatever reason patient/client capacity at the time of signing becomes an issue at a future time, all concerned will know preemptively from the faces of the directives that multiple witnesses observed execution. By extension, the witnesses presumably may be called to testify in the highly unlikely event of a court contest.

§ 4.07 Some Comments—and Cautions—about Lay Observations of Competence

§ 4.08—Avoid Snap Judgments

A single encounter or observation hardly ever is sufficient. Illnesses, medications, meals (or lack thereof), sleep deprivation, stressors, distractions and even time of day cause occasional stumbles and bumbles among us all. In other words, let's cut one another some slack. We *all* have times when we don't present well.

§ 4.09—*Competence Is Essentially a Threshold Concept*

In only a minority of circumstances—coma or profound mental retardation, for example—does the question of capacity or competence even remotely approach becoming a simple yes-or-no issue. *Always* be very reticent to make global or categorical or absolute observations about the capacity of another person.

Buchanan and Brock provide a useful summary on competence:

- Competence is competence *for some task*, competence *to do something.* More specifically, the concern is with competence *to make a decision* (e.g., regarding health care, living arrangements, financial affairs, and so on).
- The necessary decision-making capacities include:
  Understanding and communication
  Relatively stable values and views of life
  Reasoning and deliberation
- Appropriate standards for competence will focus primarily on the *process* of reasoning, not on the content of the decision itself.
- The function of a competence determination is to sort people into two classes: those whose decision must be respected, and those whose decision will be set aside and for whom others will be designated as surrogate decision-makers. Competence, then, is not a matter of degree—a person either is, or is not competent to make a particular decision. Thus competence is a *threshold* concept, not a comparative one.
- Setting the proper level of decision-making competence involves balancing two important values: protecting and promoting the individual's well being, and respecting the individual's self-determination. . . .
- No single standard of competence is adequate for all decisions. . . . The more serious the expected harm to the patient from acting on a choice, the higher should be the standard of decision-making capacity, and the greater should be the certainty that the standard is satisfied. . . .
- Some treatment refusals may reasonably trigger competence investigations, but refusal of treatment itself is not ever proof or even evidence that a patient is incompetent. . . .
- In cases of questionable competence to decide medical treatment, general mental status exams are not sufficient, and must be supplemented by an evaluation of the patient's understanding and reasoning in the specific decision at hand.

- Because of the potential for conflicts of interest, judicial determinations of competence for decisions about financial matters and living arrangements are generally necessary. . . . Determinations in medical settings may remain . . . informal, except when ineliminable conflicts about competence require referral to the courts for formal adjudication of competence.[7]

An individual may be entirely capable of making some types of decisions but not others. For example, a compulsive gambler may be utterly unable to manage money and require a conservator or guardian of the estate—but be entirely capable of making personal decisions (including choices about advance health care directives). Another person's decision-making capability may amount to what color sweater to wear or what cereal to eat for breakfast—insufficient capacity, most would say, for making personal and financial decisions. Others may have partial or diminished capacity and remain capable of some decision-making—shopping for a few items if given a small "walking around" stipend, and expressing some generalized preferences for health care treatments and living arrangements. Don't forget the special case of maturing minors. Although universally presumed incompetent as a matter of law, many will articulate highly astute health care treatment preferences.

Accommodate these individuals! To the extent that someone desires advance health care directives, or wishes to make some limited or partial expression about health care treatment preferences, help her/him achieve that goal. Tempting—and easy—as it surely may be to make global determinations or judgments about capacity ("Yes—or no?"), assist those whose circumstances are either challenged or compromised, and help tailor-make written health care expressions that comport with their abilities and understanding.

§ 4.10—Capacity on Occasion (Episodic Lucidity)

Some enfeebled clients and patients may be a bit like weak radio stations: by turns faint but clear, or full of cross talk and static, or unintelligible, or "off the air" altogether.

These instances can be the trickiest of all. To determine capacity for advance health care directives, we as professionals are collectively looking for the "faint but clear" events. (This is all the more reason *not* to rely on one-time encounters for lay evaluations.)

Coming upon episodes of lucidity may be a matter of plain luck. However, do what you can to take luck out of the mix. Ask caregivers about possible patterns of patient alertness and try to time interviews accordingly. Sometimes it is helpful to visit in the morning: "signal strength" may be strongest then. Interviews an hour or so after a meal are another possibility. When circumstances permit, attempt multiple interviews. To minimize the possible appearance of undue influence, have disinterested witnesses observe a lucid interview. Consider making a video or audio record. (Of all the jurisdictions, only New Jersey so provides: "An advance directive may be supplemented by a video or audio recording."[8])

If you have reason to suspect episodic lucidity but are unable to discern it yourself, be absolutely certain to have a medical doctor evaluate the individual. Even if you get an interview at a "good" time, it is very wise to obtain medical corroboration about capacity.

§ 4.11—Be "Decision-Neutral"

Consider an end-stage emphysema patient who, upon consultation with his physician, chooses to forego ventilator treatment. The family may be vehemently opposed and demand that the patient's decision be overridden and the ventilator employed, asserting that the patient has somehow "lost it" by dint of this decision.

Just because someone makes a disagreeable or repugnant or even seemingly appalling decision does not for a moment mean that she or he has lost capacity. Help concerned others understand this crucial premise. Be "decision-neutral". Capacity turns on the ability to understand and reason, not on subsequent choices.

§ 4.12—Strange? So What?

Do not make lay judgments about capacity solely on the basis of another person's appearance or habits, peculiar (or even offensive) as they may be. Eccentricity and poor grooming of themselves are *never* dispositive of capacity.

§ 4.13—Refusal to be Evaluated

Exasperating and disconcerting as it may be for those attempting to divine capacity of another, declining an evaluation never of itself is grounds for a summary finding of decisional incapacity.

§ 4.14—Temporary Incapacity

Perhaps it is unlikely, but don't rule out the possibility that a temporary or transitory medical issue may cloud capacity. Here are some possible conditions: head trauma, dehydration or nutritional deficiency, drug or alcohol intoxication or withdrawal, electrolyte imbalance, side effects from medication or treatments, delirium (see below), sensory loss (e.g., deafness), metabolic disorders (e.g., hypothyroidism, hypoglycemia), neoplastic disease (cancer), cerebrovascular accident (CVA, or stroke), transient ischemic attack (TIA, a precursor of stroke), hypoxia (lack of sufficient oxygen), and shock.

§ 4.15—Dementia

If dementia is a seeming obstacle to capacity, some special issues must be considered, especially as they relate to the elderly. Common types of dementia, such as Alzheimer's Disease, are characterized by gradual deterioration over a number of years. Another common form, vascular dementia, may be triggered by apparent or occult strokes that lead to decline in function. Uncommon forms of dementia (which may vary in speed of onset) include Huntington's disease, Pick's disease, Creutzfeld-Jakob disease, and Lewy body dementia.

If the onset of dementia is abrupt, all concerned should be alert for "reversible" types. Vitamin B-12 deficiency and low thyroid level may be uncommon causations. Depression (which sometimes is mistaken for dementia, especially among the elderly) may improve with appropriate recognition and treatment, including courses of medications, counseling, or both.

A syndrome like delirium, which can present itself in a form much like dementia, may be entirely reversible with appropriate treatment. In the elderly, common causes of delirium may be medication toxicity, infections, fluid or electrolyte imbalances, or uncontrolled chronic medical conditions. The deterioration in mental capacity is abrupt and severe. Treatment of underlying conditions frequently will reverse completely the deterioration in mental status.

Other causes of dementia, such as neurosyphilis, normal pressure hydrocephalus, brain tumors, HIV, and Parkinson's, also may be affected or mitigated by appropriate therapies.

The diagnosis of many of these conditions may be had from simple blood tests and in some cases by diagnostic radiology such as computerized tomography (CT) scans. These causes of "reversible" dementia may not be completely resolved with therapy, but may improve a patient's condition enough to render sufficient capacity to contemplate and execute advance health care directives.

§ 4.16—Psychiatric Disorders

Psychiatric disorders do *not* connote categorical lack of capacity. An individual suffering from depression or anxiety is perfectly capable of rendering treatment consents and executing directives so long as the psychological condition itself does not affect her or his understanding about advance directives and their implications. And please—a little compassion goes a long way. Individuals so afflicted are highly vulnerable and may be in utter agony: the very fact that they seek your assistance with directives sometimes takes remarkable courage. Ask to build a "team" with therapists and treating physicians, and tailor-make the mental health treatment portion of directives in a manner consistent with the underlying condition(s). As appropriate, employ (in jurisdictions that have them, such as Alaska, Illinois, and Texas) the special purpose "Statement of Preferences for Mental Health Treatments" (or similarly styled document). As warranted, and with permission, obtain a written opinion about capacity to execute directives from a treating psychologist and/or psychiatrist before drafting documents.

§ 4.17—A Special Note about Depression

A profoundly crippling injury (an accident, say, resulting in paraplegia), or a terminal illness, may "incubate" a depressive illness that can become florid and itself life threatening. Clinically depressed individuals may harbor suicidal ideas ranging from fleeting to end-stage plans for killing themselves.

In short, depression and directives may be a bad mix. Some argue that advance health care directives stop just short of euthanasia and assisted suicide—or that directives even cross these thresholds. (Interestingly, the Oregon Death with Dignity Act [Appendix I] pointedly anticipates this exigency and forecloses application by a patient "suffering from a psychiatric or psychological disorder or depression causing impaired judgment."[9] Thus a fearsome rhetorical question: might directives somehow abet depressed patients intent on killing themselves? For that matter, might a severely depressed person with suicidal intent lack capacity (if only temporarily) to complete directives?[10]

Be vigilant about clients you think may be profoundly depressed. Be reticent to draft directives and estate planning documents if you have cause to believe that a depressive episode or illness is affecting or dictating choices that are at cross-purposes with prior client expressions. *Always* take very seriously any open talk of suicide, even if it's couched "in the abstract" or camouflaged as "a joke." It is never that: it is a horribly painful shriek from a debilitated and desperate person. "Help get help." This is far too tricky for lay intervention.

Also help throw off depression's shroud of stigma. This shockingly common (and widely untreated) condition now is highly responsive to a wide range of new therapies and medications. Be supportive and sympathetic. With clinical depression at bay or in remission or even seemingly "burnt out" or cured, clients so afflicted are in far better positions to make clear and cogent choices about advance health care directives (and, for that matter, wills and trusts and property powers). *Mental* illnesses (such as depression) should engender the same sorts of caring and compassion among us that *physical* illnesses do.

§ 4.18 Legal Standards of Capacity

The various states treat general issues of capacity differently. Be certain to carefully review both statute and case law. As a point of departure, refer to Clark, Boardman and Callaghan, *Mental Capacity: Legal and Medical Aspects of Assessment and Treatment, Second Edition* (1994), with updates, which contains state-by-state synopses on burdens of proof for mental capacity, testamentary capacity, donative capacity, contractual capacity, and undue influence.

Generally, legal thresholds of capacity or competence are matters of degree. More exacting standards apply to, say, entering into a contract than for execution of a will or for assenting to marriage. In other words, it is possible that a person may lack sufficient acumen to enter into a contract to purchase a house or car, yet be able to comprehend the nature and extent of personal bounty and the objects of his or her affection and execute a will.

§ 4.19 Incapacity as the Effectuating Event

The authority conferred by directives commences either upon execution or at some future time or circumstance. The Model Uniform Health-Care Decisions Act (Appendix C) becomes effective "when my primary physician determines that I am unable to make my own health-care decisions," unless a box is marked that confers decision-making authority upon execution.

A directive that comports with the uniform act, or which contains a similar "springing" style provision, typically requires a *medical* judgment that the principal has lost capacity to make her or his own health care decisions. This determination should be in writing and appended to the patient's medical records or entered into the chart.

Note again that some states (Arizona, Colorado, Connecticut and Nebraska, for example) provide for revocation of a directive (in writing or orally) *irrespective* of capacity. If the patient regains decision-making ability, then the authority of agents or proxies presumably becomes suspended or mooted or revoked. Similarly, the attending physicians should insert a written evaluation of regained capacity into the patient's records; such an evaluation should pointedly rescind the prior determination by date and other relevant particulars.

§ 4.20 Conclusion

Treat issues of competence and incompetence with the utmost care. Your judgments—clinical or subjective—may literally alter the course of another person's life.

When in doubt, take your time. Involve others. Always concede the benefit of the doubt and resolve all close calls in favor of the patient.

None of us wants to be victimized by some distant and autocratic individual unilaterally making crass, simplistic and cavalier judgments about our own decision-making abilities. Don't dare do that to a fellow human being. Pledge to make conscience and compassion your guides.

This above all: check yourself. Now and forever, ask one simple question: "Is this how *I* would want to be treated?"

Notes

1. D.C. CODE ANN. §§ 21-2203 and 21-2204.
2. IND. CODE ANN. § 16-36-1-4.

3. MINN. STAT. ANN. § 145C.10(a).
4. MISS. CODE ANN. § 41-41-205(6).
5. N.Y. PUB. HEALTH LAW § 29-C § 2981(1)(b).
6. Marshal Folstein, Mini Mental State Examinations (available in multiple languages). For copies contact Marshal Folstein, M.D., Chairman, Department of Psychiatry, New England Medical Center, NEMC# 1007750 Washington St., Boston, MA 02111, or email him at *Marshal.Folstein@es.nemc.org.* "The 7-Minute Screen" is a recently developed neurocognitive tool designed to be more sensitive to detecting patients with Alzheimer's Disease. Validation Studies are ongoing. For information, contact Paul Solomon, Ph.D., Williams College, Williamstown, MA.
7. A. BUCHANAN & D. BROCK, DECIDING FOR OTHERS: THE ETHICS OF SURROGATE DECISION MAKING (1995).
8. N.J. STAT. ANN. § 26:2H-56.
9. OR. REV. STAT. § 127.820.
10. L. Ganzini et al., *The Effect of Depression Treatment on Elderly Patients' Preferences for Life-Sustaining Medical Therapy*, 151-11 AM. J. PSYCHIATRY 1631 (1994); L. Ganzini et al., *Is the Patient Self-Determination Act Appropriate for Elderly Persons Hospitalized for Depression?* 4 J. CLINICAL ETHICS 46 (1993); L. Ganzini and M. Lee, *Authenticity, Autonomy, and Mental Disorders*, 4 J. CLINICAL ETHICS 58 (1993).

CHAPTER 5

Client Issues

§ 5.01 Introduction

Charlie Krumplewski is a 74-year-old widowed male who three years ago first demonstrated problems with memory and judgment. Worried that he was exhibiting symptoms of Alzheimer's Disease, his adult children brought him to their family physician. Although no abnormalities were found upon physical exam or through laboratory or x-ray testing, Charlie continued to show gradual decline in his ability to care for himself. Concerned for his safety, the family encouraged him to move to an assisted care retirement home.

Six months after the move to assisted living, Charlie was hospitalized for pneumonia. During that time, he became increasingly disoriented. On the first night following return to his apartment, he was found wandering outdoors in freezing temperatures. Over the next several weeks, this pattern reoccurred frequently enough to prompt anxiety on the part of both family and retirement home staff. After a family conference, Charlie agreed to move to a nursing home.

Upon admission, Charlie was presented with information on advance health care directives. He and his family watched a video describing the use of directives and he signed a living will.

Charlie experienced progressive deterioration characteristic of Alzheimer's dementia. It became pronounced: on the second anniversary of Charlie's admission, he became wheelchair bound, and by the third year he was nonverbal and confined to bed. Staff observed some choking difficulties during meals. Charlie's weight declined; the dietitian recommended a swallowing evaluation. Unbeknownst to the family, and while the primary care physician was out of town one weekend, the nursing home's medical director intervened and signed an order to begin tube feedings.

Shortly thereafter, Charlie's daughter visited her father. Surprised by the tube, she pointed out the living will to the staff and argued that her father would never wish to live this way. The facility director and the medical director both were indifferent.

National studies show that most adults have not completed an advance health care directive.[1] Although surveys indicate that many acknowledge in concept the importance of stating preferences about end-of-life situations, acceptance of directives in the adult population is far from universal. Patients who are receptive to the idea of directives often have gaps in knowledge about them, or experience logistical issues that interfere with implementation. It is, accordingly, incumbent on professionals to view advance health care directives from a patient or client perspective.

Professionals wishing to inform their clients or patients about the availability and viability of advance health care directives must be sensitive to tremendous variations in knowledge, attitudes, and behaviors about them. Discussion should begin with an assessment of the patient's understanding and values. Only then will professionals be in a position to provide better understanding of what the documents can and cannot do.

The following examination will help professionals identify common misconceptions, personal attitudes and obstacles to implementation from the patient perspective. By understanding this perspective more fully, sensitive practitioners may be better able to anticipate concerns and questions and subsequently facilitate completion of these exceedingly important documents.

§ 5.02 Summary of Literature

Pertinent literature from the past decade includes surveys, educational interventions, and responses to scenarios. Through these interventions, investigators have contributed to our knowledge of patient attitudes, understanding, and behaviors relating to the use of directives.

A cautionary note: many of these examinations focus on the elderly and chronically ill, to the partial or complete exclusion of other populations. Some may be skewed by their reliance on self-identifying volunteers and subjects who are either interested in or experienced with directives. Despite these limitations, many provide valuable information that may help professionals anticipate both patient concerns and behaviors about directives.

§ 5.03—Individuals Most Likely to Complete Directives

A 1991 Gallup poll indicated that 20 percent of American adults had advance directives.[2] It does not appear that extensive studies about the incidence of directives have occurred since that time.

An intriguing dichotomy exists: although few individuals seem to have executed advance health care directives, surveys show that high numbers of people are philosophically predisposed to concepts fostered by these documents.[3] Gamble's 1991 study[4] of elderly in North Carolina shows that 52 percent were familiar with living wills. Eighty-six percent stated a preference for comfort care only in the event of terminal illness, while none had completed the document. Recent work by Joos shows that 72 percent were knowledgeable.[5]

Other surveys have attempted to identify characteristics of individuals most likely to complete a directive. They suggest that older[6] and white[7] individuals, as well as those with higher cognitive abilities[8] and individuals with formal estate plans[9] are among the persons most likely to accept the concept of advance health care planning. Additionally, Sugarman has demonstrated a higher incidence of directives among those who know someone with one.[10]

The inclination to complete a directive also may be dependent on a combination of personal values with specific medical conditions such as Acquired Immunodeficiency Syndrome (AIDS),[11] Amyotrophic Lateral Sclerosis (ALS, or "Lou Gehrig's Disease"),[12] kidney dialysis,[13] and terminal cancer.[14] Several authors reviewing the preferences of community residents and nursing home patients have determined that care settings may influence patient interest in directives.[15]

§ 5.04—Why People Don't Have Advance Directives

Reasons why patients choose not to complete advance directives are categorized by a number of investigators. Frequently cited rationales are lack of knowledge and procrastination.[16]

Despite seeming interest in directives and concurrence in the concept, multiple studies have shown that few individuals discuss them with physicians[17] or family.[18] Investigators also have identified difficulties (and resultant minimal impacts on subsequently provided health care) when directives are not available to care providers at the time of admission to facilities.[19]

Other examinations include the amount of education people receive about directives. These studies show that the manner in which data is presented[20] and descriptions of possible treatments[21] all can influence an individual's medical decision-making.

Educational interventions and scenario studies have isolated other factors that may influence completion of directives. Frequency of clinic visits and patient continuity with a care provider[22] have been found to influence the completion of a directive. Mental and physical functioning,[23] patient understanding of prognosis,[24] and likelihood for success of interventions such as cardiopulmonary resuscitation (CPR)[25] also may influence the decision to choose less aggressive treatment.

§ 5.05—A Need for Discussion

Lo's work[26] shows that the vast majority of patients have good responses to discussion of advance directives. A very small percentage felt nervous, sad, or hopeless. The majority felt in control, cared for, or relieved to discuss these topics. Others have shown that even decisionally incapacitated elderly are not distressed by the topic of directives.[27] Henderson discerns lower anxiety measures in those who complete directives.[28]

Many clients wish to discuss this topic with physicians.[29] Lo's examination shows that 53 percent of those interviewed felt relieved discussing life-sustaining treatments and most *wanted* their physicians to raise the issue.[30]

Timing may be relevant to the initiation of discussion. Although most agree that ambulatory discussion with individuals not in crisis may be the most appropriate, investigators have found that clients still are receptive to discussion while hospitalized.[31] Studies of patients newly diagnosed with AIDS confirm that discussion of directives is important to the patient, but should be initiated only after the patient has had time to adjust to the diagnosis.[32]

Family involvement is pivotal to most patients. Investigations show that when close family ties exist, individuals often informally discuss medical treatment preferences even if those preferences are not subsequently formalized or memorialized through completion of a directive. Gamble's 1991 study[33] shows that 93 percent want a spouse or family to make decisions about terminal care. This is in contrast to individuals without family, who are more likely to formalize their wishes in a document.[34]

§ 5.06—Ethnic Trends

Studies to date have found a higher use of directives in white populations and a preference for more aggressive medical interventions in the African American and Hispanic populations.[35] Eleazer's work shows that Hispanics studied were the least likely to make use of directives. Subjects of Asian ancestry seem similarly reluctant to use directives but also appear reluctant to agree to aggressive medical treatments.[36]

The study by Murphy and colleagues confirms earlier observations showing that knowledgeable European Americans are the most likely to have directives.[37] Their investigation showed that Mexican Americans and Korean Americans had negative reactions toward the concept of advance health care planning. These ethnicities seem to have preferences for decision-making by family members, not patients. Similarly, family members had negative feelings about extending bad clinical news to ill relations. Differences in outlook were discerned among Mexican Americans based on acculturation (i.e., either in Mexico or in the United States). African Americans were found to be positive about advance care planning generally but negative about formally executing advance health care directives. The Murphy team concluded that among the ethnicities studied, advance directives are most likely to meld with the outlooks of European Americans.

Possible variations in the use of directives may be attributable to socioeconomic status, education, and predisposition to estate planning techniques. Undoubtedly, other ethnic-oriented factors affect use (and nonuse) of directives. New studies apparently are beginning to examine the decision-making processes of some ethnic groups based on cultural values and traditions.

Definitive studies examining differences in attitudes, knowledge, and behaviors by race and ethnicity have not yet been completed. There are preliminary indications that culturally sensitive educational interventions comport with increased receptivity to and completion of directives among African Americans and Hispanics.[38]

§ 5.07—*Increasing Interest in Directives*

For the population as a whole, interventions to increase interest in completing directives or defining treatment preferences have shown some promising results. Most of these studies have been designed to include counseling by a health professional and distribution of educational materials. Most of these have shown favorable completion rates.[39] In other cases, no change in completion rates has been discerned through intervention.[40]

Some have expressed concern that the treatment preferences outlined within a directive may not remain constant or stable over time. Preliminary investigations of this possible "moving horizon" of patient philosophy and desires seem, rather, to support the likelihood of stability in patient preferences over time.[41] Although preferences indeed may prove to be stable, one should remain cautious about inferring or imputing preferences based on specific scenarios.[42]

§ 5.08 *Common Misconceptions*

For many, misunderstandings and even fears about what directives are designed to do—and why they are important—become the basis for reticence or reluctance to accept or complete a living will or durable health care power or proxy. Some are disinclined because they view these documents as unduly complex or highly technical. Because advance directives are not widely used, much misinformation may exist.

§ 5.09—*"I'm in Good Health, I Don't Need a Directive."*

Many individuals readily recognize the utility of directives for the chronically ill or elderly. Counterintuitively, however, they may be far more important for younger (and usually more healthy) persons who experience sudden illness or debilitating injury. Recall that the two most widely known subjects—Karen

Ann Quinlan and Nancy Cruzan—fall precisely into this category. As the Quinlan and Cruzan cases so sorrowfully showed us, health care decision-making by third parties can be especially difficult in these situations. For that matter, the need for family members and health care providers to discern or divine or recollect what a Cruzan or a Quinlan might have wanted becomes especially excruciating and poignant. The implication? Extra effort should go into reaching young adults.

§ 5.10—"They're All 'Pull-the-Plug' Documents. I Don't Want That."

Many are concerned that an advance care directive is essentially a "no care" directive. In other words, directives are construed as "pull-the-plug" documents—something to employ when there is no hope for recovery from illness or injury and a passive (or "natural") demise is contemplated.

Typically, neither a living will nor a durable health care proxy or power stipulate or even imply "pull-the-plug" or cessation of all care—rather, only the withholding of heroic measures which would needlessly prolong a terminal situation. Comfort care and relief of suffering are very much consistent with the philosophical intent (indeed, literal reading) of many advance directives.

§ 5.11—"I Want Everything Possible Done for Me. Directives Won't Permit That."

It is important to re-emphasize that advance directives are *not* necessarily "pull-the-plug" documents. They may in fact be structured as "don't you *dare* touch that plug!" Directives actually may be instrumental—indeed, essential—in advocating zealous and unfettered preservation and maintenance of life. Although not commonly used to specify preservation of life "no matter what," durable health care powers most assuredly may be used to express precisely that: a preference for aggressive medical interventions that most individuals—lay and clinical—might deem hopeless.

Indiana, for example, expressly provides for this possibility through its statutory "Life Prolonging Procedures Declaration", which is reproduced in the accompanying CD-ROM. (See Indiana Code Ann. Sec. 16-36-4-11.) However, patients so inclined must be aware of the cons: the physically punishing and painful nature of some treatments, the emotional or psychological trauma possibly visited upon the patient and loved ones, the potentially crushing financial burdens (might insurers or other third parties decline to pay?), and the possibly untoward misdirection of societal medical resources. (Might ever there come a point when hundreds of thousands of dollars spent on life support for one person in an irreversible coma should be redirected to, say, immunizations or prenatal care for scores of others?)

§ 5.12—"Directives Are Permanent. I Won't Be Able to Change My Mind."

Another misconception is that once executed, advance directives are irrevocable. The opposite is true: directives may (perhaps *should*) be reviewed, revoked, and re-executed from time to time. Principals need to do more than just restate treatment instructions, however. They should use the opportunity to include modifications in health status, personal relationships, and life experiences. Similarly, those re-executing directives should reappoint or change agents (or proxies) and their successors, and update addresses, telephone numbers (including residential, work, wireless, pager, and fax), and e-mail. Those with chronic or terminal conditions should consult with their doctors to structure directives that are medically comporting.

§ 5.13—"With Directives, I Lose the Right to Decide for Myself."

Directives are personal contingency plans—not abdications or waivers. They usually "kick in" only when patients cannot direct their own care due to unconsciousness or mental incapacity. (An exception is Minnesota, where a principal pointedly *may* authorize an agent to make decisions even though the principal retains capacity.[43]) So long as an individual is alert and able to measure the advantages and disadvantages of treatment choices, only he or she will be asked to direct health care providers. In the event of anesthesia or administration of medications that may cloud judgment, or in instances of high stress, painful, or complex medical treatment programs, an otherwise competent person may wish to delegate either limited or complete authority under a health care proxy or power. This too is allowed if specified in the document.

Ease patient concern about implementation of directives by employing springing powers. With these, triggering events (rather than dates or other time-specific circumstances) establish when an agent or proxy is to assume authority. If not provided for in suggested forms, consider language to this effect: "This proxy (or power) becomes effective only upon the written determinations of two (or one) medical doctors that I am totally incapable of making personal decisions." (For property powers, substitute "financial" for "personal".)

§ 5.14—"Directives Are Just Arbitrary Checklists. They're Not at All Responsive to What I Want."

Although the states may impose limitations on use and interpretation of living wills, health care proxies, and durable health care powers, document designs generally are flexible enough to allow incorporation of a range of client preferences and concerns. Competent individuals who execute directives are not necessarily "signing a blank check" (although they *may* end up doing so, due either to nonchalance or inattentiveness about filling in blanks and checking off boxes): rather, they may customize or personalize their documents in fashions consistent with their values, medical situation, and life experiences. Most forms provide room for narrative statements and may allow detailed descriptions (such as values histories—see Appendix D) as attachments. These types of inventories should be suggested to those individuals who (understandably) find directives too simplistic or too confining or too limited for their needs.

It is important to observe that even in states with suggested forms, they are usually just that: suggested. A principal often may write out a directive on her or his own terms and be confident that it will be honored. Generally, it is a good idea to use state-suggested forms, at least as a point of departure: physicians and other caregivers tend to recognize them and, for the most part, now are comfortable with them.

§ 5.15—"I Don't Need Directives. My Family Knows What I Want."

Many feel that close family or friends in whom they have confided will honor informally expressed wishes. This highly common practice probably works just fine for many people.

It's not foolproof, however. Informality produces only strong recommendations to direct medical treatment choices. And like it or not, these may be cast aside.

In states with health care surrogacy or similarly styled laws (Arkansas, Iowa, Louisiana, Maine, Mississippi, Montana, North Carolina, and Wyoming, for example), caregivers are compelled to turn to a prescribed hierarchy of decision-makers in the event there are no directives. Even in informal practice, doctors are likely to turn to similarly described kindred: first spouse, then adult children, then parents, then adult siblings, and so forth. These may not at all be the individuals in whom the patient confided. In effect, it boils down to this: No directive? Then no (or, at best, remote or diminished) standing for non-kindred.

Patients and clients should not blithely rely on informality. Those who do tempt fate. Worse yet, they risk placing some of their most personal decision-making in the hands of people they may dislike or distrust. For peace of mind, it is best to formalize and memorialize health care contingency plans through use of advance directives.

§ 5.16 Barriers to Acceptance

§ 5.17—Society's Conflicted Views on Life and Death

American culture has been characterized by some as death-denying if not altogether death-defying. The most casual and infrequent observer of movies, magazines, and other media can hardly help but be bemused (if not astonished or swept away) by riptides of youth adulation and siren songs of sexuality and longevity and perpetual good health. "It just ain't so," of course.

Additionally, rituals of death and dying were largely "sanitized" during the twentieth century: the sad reality of an individual's passing was often stripped from community (and familial) consciousness. In other words—death has become distasteful. Discussions of death are taboo. For some, death is a foe to be openly mocked and taunted and challenged through open denial or even personal risk taking. Perhaps this overly simplistic and mockingly rhetorical statement makes the point: "Huh? Advance health care directives? You mean "no care" directives! If I had one, it'd mean I was gonna die. Forget it!"

In aggregate, this makes directives a hard sell. Professionals dealing with the notion of advance health care directives may, therefore, expect at times to encounter formidable resistance—even contempt—for the entire subject.

Many feel that directives are useful for those individuals with serious or chronic illness and may defer their consideration until a time when they feel more personally or medically vulnerable. Some patients with more serious illness may not be fully aware of their prognosis or may be in denial of the prognosis. Frank discussions helping clients prepare for unexpected catastrophic illnesses may be appropriate.

§ 5.18—Cultural or Religious Beliefs

Cultural or religious affiliations may espouse values relevant to medical decision-making in the face of serious illness (see Chapter 9). Prohibitions may be well-defined and published (e.g., rejection of blood products by Jehovah's Witnesses; refusal of medical treatment by Christian Scientists). Similarly, some cultural and ethnic groups may be reluctant to discuss these issues openly, thereby making the introduction of the topic by professionals awkward and potentially unwelcome. Strive to be sensitive to these issues.

Some clients may hold personal or spiritual convictions that maintain life is precious and must be preserved and maintained irrespective of physical or financial cost. Others construe advance directives as either a ruse or charade for euthanasia or as a form of subterfuge to ease out or even deny care for the enfeebled, the elderly, and the physically disabled or mentally incapacitated. Accordingly, some may think the entire concept of directives repugnant and may reject them categorically. These *are* plausible and legitimate points of view and must be respected.

Some scholars have provided commentary on the effects of culture and ethnicity in patient expressions of preferences for medical care.[44] Disillusionment with and disfranchisement from the medical system may adversely influence acceptance of the concept of directives. Although personal autonomy may be prized in mainstream American culture, it is minimized and even suppressed in other parts of the world: individual action for the greater good is held in much higher societal regard. On this basis, the very concept of advance health care directives may seem disproportionately or even inappropriately self-centered.

Additionally, intricate family relationships in other cultures give rise to different approaches and responsibilities for care of the sick and dying. For example, end-of-life decision-making may be assumed (according to tradition or custom) by family members; a terminally ill individual may be effectively insulated from health care choices. This is because speaking of death in front of an ill patient may be seen as disrespectful.

Similarly, multigenerational families may be fundamentally predicated on close relationships and oral communication. The idea of writing down health care preferences on paper might seem unnecessary and impersonal.

Upon reflection, the implications are sobering: the entire concept of advance health care directives may be disconcerting, distasteful, alien, and perhaps even offensive to some cultures and traditions. Simplistic, shrill, and strident advocacy of the concept of directives may, then, be deleterious to all concerned.

§ 5.19—Reluctance to Rely on "Elastic Clauses"

Try as we might, it is of course utterly impossible to anticipate all medical contingencies. It is for this reason that directives in several states (e.g., Illinois, Nevada, Vermont) contain generalized (and often optional) statements of treatment preferences—"elastic clauses," for short. For example, the principal/patient might choose one of the following gradations as an augmentation or enhancement of specific medical treatment choices:[45]

- I do not want my life to be prolonged nor do I want life-sustaining treatment to be provided or continued if my agent believes the burdens of the treatment outweigh the expected benefits. I want my agent to consider the relief of suffering, the expense involved and the quality as well as the possible extension of my life in making decisions concerning life-sustaining treatment.
- I want my life to be prolonged and I want life-sustaining treatment to be provided or continued unless I am in a coma that my attending physician believes to be irreversible, in accordance with reasonable medical standards at the time of reference. If and when I have suffered irreversible coma, I want life-sustaining treatment to be withheld or discontinued.
- I want my life to be prolonged to the greatest extent possible without regard to my condition, the chances I have for recovery or the cost of the procedures.

Some clients may have difficulty choosing among generalized statements to guide unanticipated health crises. To some, the imprecise and inartful nature of this exercise is, understandably, both intellectually and emotionally challenging (if not outright distasteful or reprehensible). Although potential medical scenarios and detailed responses to certain treatments may be inserted (or referenced in an accompanying medical or values history), some would argue that an unanticipated or unforeseen health care emergency cannot at all be honestly or realistically be addressed by "elastic clauses."

On the other hand, choice of a generalized treatment preference may be immeasurably valuable guidance to an agent/proxy and family. Do not press one way or the other. Instead, help clients/patients objectively review the pros and cons of this sensitive issue.

§ 5.20—Ceding Autonomy

Autonomy may be a serious issue for some clients. This concern about self-determination may lead some to reject out-of-hand the idea of selecting a "back up" decision-maker. Some might choose the open-ended alternative of no directive rather than leaving ultimate control in the hands of one individual. Particularly in those jurisdictions where health care surrogate acts exist (e.g., District of Columbia Kentucky, North Carolina, Rhode Island, South Dakota, Tennessee, Washington), some may prefer to have decisions deferred to the designated hierarchy, especially if that hierarchy actually represents their preferred decision-makers.

§ 5.21—Opinions and Feelings of Others

Some clients will be strongly influenced by the opinions of family and professional contacts. Negative feedback from these sources may soften the client's interest in completing a directive. Also, clients may assume that family or friends will be distressed by a discussion of sensitive end-of-life concerns and may avoid discussion of advance health care directives to spare their feelings.

§ 5.22—Foreclosure of Medical Advances by Directives

In our culture, some individuals stand in awe of and have come to depend on the possibilities offered through advances in medical technology. These clients may see advance directives as documents that may inadvertently frustrate (or altogether deny) applications of as-yet-unknown medical technologies. Similarly, they may not at all wish to delineate between useful applications of technology and potentially harmful or futile ones. Once again, there is no right way: these points of view must be respected.

§ 5.23—Procrastination and Fear

Human nature being what it is, these barriers will forever be a part of what impedes execution of advance health care directives. However, isolate these issues before working to address them: be certain that ethnic, cultural, and spiritual issues first are out of the mix. (None of us wants to have our efforts in this respect inadvertently misconstrued as proselytizing.)

As appropriate, resort to all professional (and practical) wiles: reason, logic, repeated explanations, alternative explanations, time for reflection, encouragement, patience, cultivated insight, possible scenarios in the absence of directives, and so forth. Be philosophical—and back off—when efforts to overcome procrastination and fear don't work. As one wag observes, "You can't reason a person out of a position he didn't reason himself into in the first place."

§ 5.24 Barriers to Implementation

§ 5.25—Failure of PSDA Protocols

As noted elsewhere, the federal Patient Self-Determination Act (PSDA) (42 USCA 1395 cc (f) - see Appendix A) compels dissemination of state-specific advance health care directives upon contact with federally funded hospitals, long term care facilities (e.g., nursing homes), hospices, and home health care agencies. There may be many pitfalls at this crucial time.

- Because of illness or injury, the admittee's judgment may be clouded or impaired. She or he may not at all be in a position to think or speak.
- Facility personnel may have superficial (or no) instruction in the PSDA or in advance directives. Accordingly, some may provide mistaken or even patently incorrect information. Some may assert that the PSDA *requires* execution of directives. (This is false; execution is optional.)
- Inadvertently or otherwise, others may use the requirements of the PSDA as a vehicle to effect grievously wrong results—for example, compelling perfectly healthy patients to unnecessarily sign DNR consents.
- Some patients may be asked to sign acknowledgments that they have been told about advance directives in accordance with the PSDA and then mistakenly think that the acknowledgment is actually a directive. Similarly, other patients may be asked to sign a statement that they already have an advance directive (when in actuality they do not) and misconstrue this as execution of a directive.
- Some patients may receive an unexplained directive in admissions documentation and either not sign it or execute it without regard to or knowledge of the contents or the implications.
- Some patients may lack knowledge about the severity of their illness and the prognosis. Even if philosophically predisposed to directives, some individuals may defer execution until such time as they perceive their illnesses have become critical or irreversible. Those with serious chronic illness such as cancer may not always inquire as to their prognoses and may, in the mistaken belief that they are not profoundly ill, inadvertently defer completion of directives until they are too sick

to do so. On occasion, patient ignorance about a serious condition may be compounded by the reticence of some practitioners to initiate discussion due to difficulty in scientifically predicting prognosis.

Many clients and patients are intellectually and philosophically comfortable with the concept of directives. However, they may encounter obstacles that may indefinitely delay execution. Complex and emotionally challenging documents that they are, one would not expect the completion of advance health care directives without counsel from trusted family and professionals and without careful reflection. Multiple steps may lie between the initiation of the idea and completion. The passage of time between each step may weaken the client's resolve to complete the project. All good intentions aside, little benefit is gained from discussions and reflection if the client does not formalize intentions by completing the directive and informing affected parties.

§ 5.26—Cost

Some clients may defer completion of directives because of anxiety about the cost of preparation. Allay fears about this essentially insignificant issue. First of all, directives generally are simple and straightforward documents; lawyers do not charge (nor are they likely to get) high fees for consultation and preparation. Second, let's be realistic: a considerable number of individuals simply don't require professional assistance with this, any more than they need a lawyer to defend a parking ticket or a doctor to treat a sniffle.

On the other hand, directives are at their core legal documents. As stated at the outset of this book, they arguably may be the most important legal documents any of us will ever sign. Patients/clients with uncertainties about legal implications, or those with complex issues and needs, are well advised to seek out and retain the most comprehensive and thorough and thoughtful legal assistance available.

The issue reduces quite starkly to personal choices about living and dying. Those with legal questions who remain reticent to retain a lawyer for assistance with directives merely because of cost may end up doing themselves an extraordinary disservice—perhaps even grievous harm. Allied professionals (physicians, nurses, hospital/nursing home staffs, social workers, palliative caregivers, psychologists, and clergy) with clients who are in doubt about directives should *always* "counsel retaining counsel." The modest lawyer fees involved surely will be a downright bargain for peace of mind.

§ 5.27—Meeting with Professional Advisors

Although not required, some may wish to seek medical practitioner assistance in outlining treatment preferences, particularly if they are specific or detailed. Those with chronic conditions may find it particularly beneficial to obtain physician guidance in crafting a directive that is consistent with treatment scenarios for underlying illnesses. Others will seek the assistance of clergy or other spiritual leaders or advisors. Clients/patients may find it difficult to find the right time, place, and circumstance to discuss this topic with medical and spiritual advisors.

Even after consulting with their advisors of choice, clients may be confronted with disinterest or conflicting advice. Lack of support from professional advisors may effectively delay the implementation of directives indefinitely. Be vigilant about these exigencies.

§ 5.28—Obtaining Forms

Although virtually all jurisdictions make materials on advance health care directives available to the public, some individuals may experience difficulty locating them. Professionals can facilitate this process by referring clients to low-cost and no-cost documents and forms that contain suggested or statutory language. Here are some possible sources:[46]

- State and local bar associations
- State and local medical societies
- Doctor and lawyer offices
- Hospitals and nursing homes
- Health maintenance organizations (HMOs) and health insurance carriers[47]
- Agencies on aging and senior citizen centers
- Libraries, stationary stores, legal forms publishers, and websites
- The CD-ROM packaged with this volume
- Links through the website maintained by authors Krohm and Summers: http://www.AdvanceHealthCareDirectives.com

§ 5.29—Complexity of Documents/Readability

Regrettably, some preprinted documents may be downright intimidating. They may be in unduly small print,[48] verbose, inordinately technical, long on jargon and short on step-by-step instructions. Poorly designed information and document preparation packets may have the inadvertent effect of completely frustrating client/patient intent: individuals may give up in exasperation or feel unnecessarily compelled to seek professional assistance to obtain basic instruction.

§ 5.30—Lag Times in Drafting

Some directives allow value selections or customized statements. It is also possible to append values inventories or histories (Appendix D). While these exercises may provide extremely useful detail, clients may unduly delay completion of the principal documents (the proxy or power or living will) while they compose accompanying text or develop a values inventory or research technical or treatment options.

Suggest to such individuals that they execute "provisional" directives un-til their values inventory or research is complete. (Remember that directives—including "provisional" ones—may be revoked at any time.) For those desiring customized directives, consultation with health care professionals may greatly facilitate progress toward completion—especially where a treatment for a given disease or condition essentially dictates the parameters of directives.

§ 5.31—Delays in Meeting with Family
Most individuals prefer to discuss their preferences and agent/proxy selection with family before committing them to paper. Finding the right time to gather and speak with family may be a challenge for many clients. This may be particularly so if family members are geographically dispersed or disinterested in the topic.

§ 5.32—Formalities of Execution
In most jurisdictions (for example, Arizona, California, Hawaii, Iowa, Kansas and Kentucky) directives must be witnessed or notarized or both. These for-malities may be yet another barrier to implementation: clients may find it inconvenient or inopportune to assemble the requisite witnesses or go before a notary. An aside: strongly suggest to clients/patients that witnesses/notaries be disinterested parties. Avoid even the remotest appearance of undue influ-ence. Refrain from calling upon a close family member, or a prospective agent or proxy, or a health care provider, or a person responsible for paying medical bills, to witness an advance health care directive. Be certain to check applicable statute: certain classes of individuals (e.g., attending physicians, nursing home personnel) may be curbed, curtailed, or pointedly excluded as witnesses.

§ 5.33—Failures in Communication
Clients may complete the entire process and then forget to communicate completion of a directive to important parties. At a minimum, provision of copies to the proxy or agent and treating health care provider should be considered. Absent dissemination, the existence of this document may not be known by key decision-makers, thereby utterly frustrating intent. (See the accompanying sidebar, "Leaving Good Footprints".)

§ 5.34 Critique of Case Study

It was inappropriate (to mince words) for the medical director to unilaterally order tube feedings in the absence of the attending physician. It was also unfortunate (to put it mildly) that this was done without notice to the family and in contravention of the living will that was in the chart. But note too the issue of competence: Mr. Krumplewski arguably may have lacked capacity to sign the living will in the first place. Might the document thereby have been rendered voidable or void had the adult children pressed the issue?

Directives are not fail-safe. No one—patients, family, agents, care providers—should blithely assume that once invoked, advance directives operate on some kind of "automatic pilot," assuring that health care decisions are perpetually and unerringly made precisely on their terms. They require constant vigilance and zealous advocacy if they are to stand a chance of being carried out as intended. Even that may not be good enough.

From a practical standpoint, Mr. Krumplewski and his family seemingly have next to no options. They could seek an institution and physician receptive

---

Leaving Good Footprints

Remember how the fairytale children Hansel and Gretel thought to drop crumbs to mark their way?

When it comes to advance health care directives, each of us must begin with the same realization—plus a bit more sophistication as to the types of markers we leave. For our purposes, let's call them "footprints."

First of all, tell the need-to-know people who will implement your directives that you have them. Included will be the agent or proxy you designate (plus any successors), your primary care physician (plus specialists, as medical conditions may indicate), a hospital or nursing home or other care facility, family members, friends, neighbors, clergy, and lawyer. As warranted, provide photocopies. (See the discussion on pages 18 and 19 about photocopies of directives.)

Secondly, *talk about what you want. Verbally validate and reiterate your directives.* Those who may be thrust into making decisions for you must be comfortable with both what you want, and your charge to them to act on your behalf. Know that many people are *not* comfortable with this subject. Note cues and compensate accordingly. Ask them to synthesize and feed back their understandings of what you have said. Additionally, try to have "refresher" talks from time to time (e.g., once a year).

Carry in a wallet or purse a pocket card that indicates directives exist and where they may be found. (See Appendix N for a sample.)

Wear a medallion or bracelet with information similar to that contained in a pocket card. Medi-cAlert (among other organizations) provides such devices. (These may also provide indicia of medical conditions, allergies, etc.) Visit   http://www.MedicAlert.org for more information. For those seeking to conform to state DNR protocols, be *certain* to follow the prescribed procedures (e.g., *government-issued* bracelet) precisely.

(continued)

to Charlie's plight and ask to have the tube removed in accordance with his living will. But with the tube already inserted, a facility and doctor so inclined might be difficult to find. All concerned (Mr. Krumplewski's children in particular) surely would be greatly troubled by the unintended appearance of euthanasia.

The family might seek court appointment of a guardian and subsequent authorization to remove the tube. But this is not a good prospect, either: judges in some jurisdictions may be highly reticent to permit removal of life support. Counsel for a guardian likely would have to carry a daunting burden of proof in any event.

Place your directive with a registry. In some communities, local hospitals provide such services. Louisiana has a state registry. Private online services (not necessarily endorsed by the authors or the American Bar Association) such as http://www.uslivingwillregistry.com also are available.

Think critically about where emergency personnel might look, and place footprints there. How about a top desk or dresser drawer? A bulletin board? A copy among your important papers? Be as critical as you can: ask yourself, "If I had to be searching, where would I look?" (Also, place a footprint at your workplace or other regular daytime location.) Two interesting programs keyed for emergency medical personnel are Vial of Life (www.stormnet.com/~Kerry/Kpage/vial.html and File of Life (http://www.folife.org), which provide for placement of important papers and medical information on or in home refrigerators.

Directives in a safe deposit box? This can be one location, especially if duplicate originals are employed. But because of the limited hours of access (i.e., bank business hours), and possible procedural encumbrances (e.g., might a court order be required for a non-owner to drill the box?) this is not the recommended repository for sole copies of originals. Note that retrieval of originals may not be an issue in your state: many jurisdictions provide that a photocopy is just as valid.

You needn't confine your footprints solely to your advance directives. Seize the opportunity to consolidate emergency medical information in one place: names and phone numbers of doctors and other caregivers, emergency treatment instructions, chronic medical conditions, allergies, lists of prescription medicines, health insurance carriers and policy numbers, and so forth.

Other people will *want* to help you in your time of need. Make it as easy for them as you can. Take Hansel and Gretel one step beyond. Leave enduring footprints about your advance health care directives—and leave them in multiple places.

The Right Client for Directives:

- Is of legal or statutory age (usually age 18. Alabama and Nebraska specify age 19 for execution of directives.)
- Is competent
- Is fully informed about medical choices and their implications
- Upon reflection and review of pros and cons wants directives

The Wrong Client for Directives:

- Is not of legal or statutory age
- Is psychologically unstable
- Is ambivalent about having directives
- Is mentally incapacitated with no insight into discussion
- Is being subjected to undue influence
- Is medically unstable with judgment or insight clouded as a result

---

The family could file complaints with state agencies against the physician and the facility, but that would do absolutely nothing to alleviate Charlie's immediate physical distress and the contravention of his wishes. The family could even sue—but once again, a protracted lawsuit might be of possible "benefit" only to Charlie's family and estate and provide absolutely no physical or spiritual relief to the uncomprehending and slowly dying patient. Filing suit also might engender unwanted public attention.

And talk about the quintessential Pyrrhic victory. Would Charlie—or, for that matter, any of us in Charlie's condition—really get excited about the possibility that his Fourteenth Amendment liberty interest *might* someday be vindicated?

Perhaps a glimmer of hope remains for Mr. Krumplewski, his family, and those similarly situated. In a recently decided case, *Estate of Taylor ex rel. Taylor v. Muncie Medical Investors, L.P.,* 727 N.E. 2d 466 (Ind. App. 2000), a facility intubated an uncomprehending patient over the objections of her adult children. It was held that the children, believing that their mother did not want her life artificially prolonged, had recourse to enforce their wishes pursuant to Indiana's Health Care Consent Act.[49]

§ 5.35 Conclusion

The subject of advance health care directives is exceedingly difficult for many people. Consideration of the subject may be clouded by misunderstanding, misinformation, loathing, fear, procrastination, peer pressure, trepidation, and distaste and disgust, to name but a few possible impediments. Additionally, cultural and spiritual issues abound.

Try very hard to view directives from a patient or client perspective. Do not proselytize. Do not cajole or force. Make information passively available in neutral settings, and go about assisting only those who self-identify as interested. Advance health care directives are not for everyone.

Notes

1. G. Gallup & F. Newport, "Mirror of America: Fear of Dying". The Gallup Poll News Service, Vol. 55, No. 33, January 6, 1991, p. 3.
2. Id.
3. L. Emanuel et al., *Advance Directives for Medical Care–A Case for Greater Use,* 324 NEW ENG. J. MED. 889 (1991); K. Stelter et al., *Living Will Completion in Older Adults,* 152 ARCHIVES INTERNAL MED. 954 (1992).
4. E. Gamble, P. McDonald, & P. Lichstein, *Knowledge, Attitudes, and Behavior of Elderly Persons Regarding Living Will,* 151 ARCHIVES INTERNAL MED. 277 (1991).
5. S. Joos et al., *Outpatients' Attitudes and Understanding Regarding Living Wills,* 8 J. GEN. INTERNAL MED. 259 (1993).
6. B. Reilly et al., *Promoting Completion of Health Care Proxies Following Hospitalization,* 155 ARCHIVES INTERNAL MED. 2202 (1995); P. Duffield & J. Podzamsky, *The Completion of Advance Directives in Primary Care,* 42 J. FAMILY PRAC. 378 (1996).
7. J. Sugarman, M. Weinberger, & G. Samsa, *Factors Associated with Veterans' Decisions About Living Wills,* 152 ARCHIVES INTERNAL MED. 343 (1992); H. Silverman et al., *Implementation of the Patient Self-Determination Act in a Hospital Setting,* 155 ARCHIVES INTERNAL MED. 502 (1995).
8. J. Cohen-Mansfield et al., *The Decision to Execute a Durable Power of Attorney for Health Care and Preferences Regarding the Utilization of Life Sustaining Treatments in Nursing Home Residents,* 151 ARCHIVES INTERNAL MED. 289 (1991); K. Stelter, B. Elliott, & C. Bruno, *Living Will Completion in Older Adults,* 152 ARCHIVES INTERNAL MED. 954 (1992), H. Silverman et al., *supra* note 7.
9. E. Emanuel et al., *How Well Is the Patient Self Determination Act Working? An Early Assessment,* 95 AM. J. MED. 619 (1993).
10. J. Sugarman, M. Weinberger, & G. Samsa, *supra* note 7.
11. J. Teno et al., *The Use of Formal Prior Directives Among Patients with HIV-related Disease,* 5 J. GEN INTERNAL MED. 490 (1990); R. Steinbrook et al., *Preferences of Homosexual Men with Aids for Life Sustaining Treatment,* 314 NEW ENG. J. MED. 457 (1986).
12. M. Silverstein et al., *Amyotrophic Lateral Sclerosis and Life-Sustaining Therapy: Patients' Desires for Information, Participation in Decision Making, and Life Sustaining Therapy,* 66 MAYO CLINIC PROC. 906 (1991).
13. A. Sehgal et al., *How Strictly Do Dialysis Patients Want Their Advance Directives Followed?* 267 JAMA 59 (1992).
14. J. Garrett et al., *Life-Sustaining Treatment During Terminal Illness,* 8 J. GEN. INTERNAL MED. 361 (1993).
15. S. Joos et al., *supra* note 5; J. Cohen-Mansfield et al., *supra* note 8.
16. J. Roe et al., *Durable Power of Attorney for Health Care: A Survey of Senior Center Participants,* 152 ARCHIVES OF INTERNAL MED. 292 (1992).
17. S. Joos et al., *supra* note 5; J. Roe et al., *supra* note 16; J. Virmani, L. Schneiderman, & R. Kaplan, *Relationship of Advance Health Care*

Directives to Physician-Patient Communication, 154 ARCHIVES OF INTERNAL MED. 909 (1994); J. Cohen-Mansfield, J. Droge, & N. Billig, *The Utilization of the Durable Power of Attorney for Health Care Among Hospitalized Elderly Patients*, 39 J. AM. GERIATRICS SOC'Y 1174 (1991).

18. S. Joos et al., *supra* note 5; J. Roe et al., *supra* note 16; J. Cohen-Mansfield et al., *supra* note 17.

19. R. Johnson, T. Baranowski-Birkmeier, & J. O'Donnell, *Advance Directives in the Medical Intensive Care Unit of a Community Teaching Hospital*, 107 CHEST 752 (1995).

20. D. Mazur & J. Merz, *How the Manner of Presentation of Data Influences Older Patients in Determining Their Treatment Preferences*, 41 J. AM. GERIATRICS SOC'Y 223 (1993); D. Mazur & D. Hickam, *The Effect of Physicians' Explanations on Patients' Treatment Preferences*, 14 MED. DECISION MAKING 255 (1994); B. McNeil et al., *On the Elicitation of Preferences for Alternative Therapies*, 306 NEW ENG. J. MED. 1259 (1982).

21. T. Malloy et al., *The Influence of Treatment Descriptions on Advance Medical Directive Decisions*, 40 J. AM. GERIATRICS SOC'Y 1255 (1992).

22. P. Duffield & J. Podzamsky, *supra* note 5; D. Meier et al., *Marked Improvement in Recognition and Completion of Health Care Proxies*, 156 ARCHIVES INTERNAL MED. 1227 (1996).

23. P. Raymark et al., *Advance Directives: A Policy-capturing Approach*, 15 MED. DECISION MAKING 217 (1995).

24. R. Phillips et al., *Choices of Seriously Ill Patients about Cardiopulmonary Resuscitation: Correlates and Outcomes*, 100 AM. J. MED. 128 (1996).

25. D. Murphy et al., *The Influence of Probability of Survival on Patients' Preferences Regarding Cardiopulmonary Resuscitation*, 330 NEW ENG. J. MED. 545 (1994); D. Miller et al., *Cardiopulmonary Resuscitation: How Useful?* 152 ARCHIVES OF INTERNAL MED. 578 (1992).

26. B. Lo, G. McLeod, & G. Saika, *Patient Attitudes to Discussing Life-Sustaining Treatment*, 146 ARCHIVES OF INTERNAL MED. 1613 (1986).

27. T. Finucane et al., *Establishing Advance Medical Directives with Demented Patients: A Pilot Study*, 4 J. CLINICAL ETHICS 51 (1993).

28. M. Henderson, *Beyond the Living Will*, 30 GERONTOLOGIST 480 (1990).

29. E. Gamble, P. McDonald, & P. Lichstein, *supra* note 4.

30. B. Lo, G. McLeod, & G. Saika, *supra* note 26.

31. B. Reilly et al., *supra* note 6; SUPPORT Principal Investigators, *A Controlled Trial to Improve Care for Seriously Ill Hospitalized Patients*, 274 JAMA 1591 (1995).

32. J. Littrell et al., *Negotiating Advance Directives for Persons with AIDS*, 23(2) SOCIAL WORK IN HEALTH 42 (1996).

33. E. Gamble, P. McDonald, & P. Lichstein, *supra* note 4.

34. D. High, *Who Will Make Health Care Decisions for Me When I Can't?* 2 J. AGING & HEALTH 291 (1990).

35. G. Eleazer et al., *The Relationship Between Ethnicity and Advance Directives in a Frail Older Population*, 44 J. AM. GERIATRICS SOC'Y 938 (1996); P.V. Caralis et al., *The Influence of Race on Attitudes Toward Advance Directives, Life-prolonging Treatments, and Euthanasia*, 4 J. CLINICAL ETHICS 155 (1993).

36. G. Eleazer et al., *supra* note 35.

37. S. Murphy et al., *Ethnicity and Advance Care Directives,* 24 J. LAW, MED. & ETHICS 108 (1996).

38. D. Meier et al., *Enhancement of Proxy Appointment for Older Persons: Physician Counselling in the Ambulatory Setting,* 44 J. AM. GERIATRIC SOC'Y 37 (1996); Dupree, Claretta, The Attitudes of Black Americans Toward Advance Directives, Journal of Transcultural Nursing, Vol. 11, No. 1, Jan 2000, 12–18.

39. D. High, *Advance Directives and the Elderly: A Study of Intervention Strategies to Increase Use,* 33 GERONTOLOGIST 342 (1993); R. Schonwetter et al., *Educating the Elderly Cardiopulmonary Resuscitation Decisions Before and After Intervention,* 39 J. AM. GERIATRICS SOC'Y 372 (1991); D. Meier, *supra* note 38; D. Meier et al., *Marked Improvement in Recognition and Completion of Health Care Proxies,* 156 ARCHIVES INTERNAL MED. 1227 (1996); D. Bailly & E. DePoy, *Older People's Responses to Education About Advance Directives,* 20 HEALTH & SOCIAL WORK 223 (1995); P. Duffield & J. Podzamsky, *supra* note 6; J. Hare & C. Nelson, *Will Outpatients Complete Living Wills? A Comparison of Two Interventions,* 6 J. GEN. INTERNAL MED. 41 (1991); S. Rubin et al., *Increasing the Completion of Durable Power of Attorney for Health Care,* 271 JAMA 209 (1994); K. Richter et al., *Promoting the Use of Advance Directives,* 4 ARCHIVES OF FAMILY MED. 609 (1995).

40. G. Sachs, C. Stocking, & S. Miles, *Empowerment of the Older Patient? A Randomized, Controlled Trial to Increase Discussion and Use of Advance Directives,* 40 J. AM. GERIATRICS SOC'Y 269 (1992); E. Siegert et al., *Impact of Advance Directive Videotape on Patient Comprehension and Treatment Preferences,* 154 ARCHIVES INTERNAL MED. 207 (1996).

41. L. Emanuel, *Advance Directives: What Have We Learned So Far?,* 4 J. CLINICAL ETHICS 9 (1993); L. Schneiderman et al., *Relationship of General Advance Directive Instructions to Specific Life-Sustaining Treatment Preferences in Patients with Serious Illness,* 152 ARCHIVES INTERNAL MED. 2114 (1992); M. Everhart & R. Pearlman, *Stability of Patient Preferences Regarding Life-Sustaining Treatments,* 97 CHEST 159 (1990).

42. R. Walker et al., *Living Wills and Resuscitation Preferences in and Elderly Population,* 155 ARCHIVES INTERNAL MED. 171 (1995).

43. MINN. STAT. ANN. §145C.05(2)(1).

44. G. Yeo, *Ethical Considerations in Asian and Pacific Island Elders,* 11 CLINICS IN GERIATRIC MED. 139 (1995); J. Berger, *Culture and Ethnicity in Clinical Care,* 158 ARCHIVES INTERNAL MED. 2085 (1998); J. Lipson, S. Dibble, & P. Minarik, Culture and Nursing Care UCSF Nursing Press, San Francisco, CA, 1996.

45. Illinois Statutory Short Form Power of Attorney for Health Care, 755 ILL. COMP. STAT. 45/4-10.

46. *See* Appendix for listings of helpful websites and telephone numbers.

47. A number of jurisdictions forbid health insurers from requiring directives as a condition of coverage.

48. This is of course a decided impediment for both blind and visually impaired individuals. The authors are unaware of any resource that provides directives in either Braille or audio formats. Help visually impaired persons by scanning documents into word processing programs and then maximizing font sizes.

49. Indiana's Health Care Consent Act, Ind. Code § 16-36-1-8.

CHAPTER 6

The Perspective of Family and Friends

§ 6.01 Introduction

Corazon ("Cory") Hernandez, a 40-year-old female, presents to her family physician with sleeplessness and lack of energy. Upon detailed questioning, her physician discovers that the symptoms developed after the three month anniversary of her sister's death. The patient and her sister had been very close to the point where her sister had named her as the agent under her durable health care power. Several years after the power was executed, Cory's sister suffered a severe brain injury in a boating and diving accident that left her in a persistent vegetative state.

After twelve months in this condition and numerous hospitalizations for complications resulting from her sister's immobility and severe debilitation, Cory was invited to a care conference at the nursing home. The assembled multidisciplinary team of health care professionals presented the facts relating to her sister's poor state of health and continued deterioration. The primary care physician asked Cory, as the agent under the power, to consider whether continued hospitalizations for complications would be what her sister would have wanted.

Absent specific language in the directive to guide her, Cory was forced to make these decisions based on memories of her sister. She knew her to value her intellectual ability and accomplishments and recalled how her sister had prized her independence. With these thoughts in mind, Ms. Hernandez reluctantly directed the treating physician to provide comfort care and "low tech" nursing home interventions only. Hospitalizations were to be foregone.

Two months later, Cory's sister developed aspiration pneumonia. She received hydration and antibiotics orally. However, infection overtook her and she died within three days.

Within weeks of her sister's death, Hernandez felt overwhelmed with feelings of anguish and loss. She confided in friends a profound sense of guilt for "not doing enough" for her sister and "betraying" her. Increasingly listless and eating and sleeping poorly, Ms. Hernandez found suicidal thoughts welling up occasionally, then daily, then almost hourly. Her friends feigned comfort and consolation at first, and then finally told Hernandez in exasperation that she had to "get a grip."

§ 6.02 The Role of Immediate Family

Family members (by both blood and marriage), domestic partners, companions, and close and enduring personal friends—"family", for short—play pivotal roles in making health care decisions for loved ones. Those designated as proxies or agents in advance directives typically come from this group of concerned individuals. In the absence of directives, health care providers regularly seek surrogates (both formal and informal) from this same pool.

The impact of family goes well beyond substituted judgment or best interests decision-making for the decisionally incapacitated: they also may

---

DILEMMAS FOR SURROGATE DECISION MAKERS
Weighing the Efficacy of Treatments

Think of the advice you as a professional may be called on to render to a family. Here are some ideas you may want to convey.

Revisit for a moment an old conundrum: does the end justify the means or do the means justify the end?

Now add a medical twist. Do the treatments justify the cure, or does the cure justify the treatments? Advance health care directives and both formal and informal decision-making mechanisms may put proxies, agents, and surrogates on the spot. Here are some treatment scenarios:

1. Cardiopulmonary resuscitation. CPR is hardly benign. In fact, it can be a series of highly aggressive last ditch physical insults: cardiac compressions, endotracheal intubation, artificial ventilation, defibrillation (electric shocks to the chest), and cardiac medications (among other procedures). Whether or not successful (and "success" may be relative—if not altogether dubious—in this context), CPR may result in rib fractures, neurological damage (due not to the procedure itself but rather because of prior oxygen deprivation), internal bleeding, stroke, pneumonia, and renal failure—and, of course, pain. The type and course of any underlying disease is a factor as well. Consider this: the success rate of CPR performed on patients with pervasive metastatic cancer, end-stage AIDS, and advanced dementia is essentially zero. Why resort to heroics when there is no hope?
2. Artificial hydration and nutrition. Recent research has found that tube feedings of demented patients do not contribute to survival rates.[17]

(continued)

heavily influence patient acceptance of directives in the first place. In addition, studies show patients to believe that family members acting as proxies effectively will extend their own self-determination and autonomy.[1]

Patients do not make decisions about advance health care directives without advice from many sources. Acceptance (and completion) of directives often is influenced by family reaction and moral and logistical support. In limited circumstances, it is possible for family to override directives altogether: some states provide that organ donation and autopsy instructions, for example, are subject to family review and consent.

In a society as culturally rich and diverse and resilient as ours, the expansive definition of "family" given above surely may be given credence in health care matters. Any "family" member may be consulted in the execution of a directive; one of them frequently is designated as a health care proxy or agent.

However, in states with formal hierarchies for health care decision-making in the absence of directives, this expansive definition of "family" is largely or even entirely inapplicable: statute may direct that surrogate decision-makers are to be drawn almost exclusively from traditional blood and marriage relationships and in fashions typical of laws for descent and

---

Some assert anecdotally that reduced oral intake is a natural part of dying, and that artificial nutrition is not necessarily justified unless the patient expresses hunger or thirst. Accordingly, choices about artificial hydration and nutrition may be truly momentous ones for an uncomprehending patient: she or he may either slip away or linger for weeks or months. Carefully consider both patient prognosis and patient wishes when grappling with this issue.

3. In short, do not summarily or reflexively consent to *any* medical procedure. Weigh the implications carefully. Get all of the good and reasoned advice possible. Consider what the patient might have wanted (an agent's or proxy's substituted judgment pursuant to an advance health care directive) or what is best (a surrogate's or guardian's conservative determination of best interests). Weigh the short and long term medical prognoses, the prospects for cure or recovery (are they good, risky, or futile?), the potential for mitigating or alleviating pain and suffering, the prospective quality of life, the emotional toll, and (distasteful as it surely is) the financial implications. And remember this: *it is much more difficult to discontinue treatments than to start them.* Be realistic about high tech procedures. Some interventions are particularly aggressive—so much so as to be physically punishing while having only marginal success in maintaining or reviving the patient. How many of us *really* are willing to endure a lot of pain—especially if our chances are slim? Actually, what we personally think does not really even matter. Would the *patient* have been willing to undergo an ordeal in the face of long odds and poor quality of life?

distribution. Even when expansive relationships are provided for (e.g., Illinois includes "close friend" toward the end of its statutory hierarchy), such categorizations usually are last or nearly last in preference or priority.

§ 6.03—The Role of Extended Family and Friends

Accordingly, it is essential for a patient/client favoring an enduring friend or a life or domestic partner or a principal companion—"extended family"—to formally designate her or him as agent or proxy in an advance health care directive. Otherwise, kindred of the closest degree may effectively "trump" a patient's informally or inartfully expressed preference for surrogate. This may be utterly distasteful (if not disastrous) for the patient if the statutorily (or even informally) indicated surrogate—spouse, adult child, or parent, for example—is estranged.

Clearly, the patient's stated preferences for medical interventions and surrogate decision-makers are preferred.[2] A health care proxy or durable health care power is likely to be the vehicle of choice for most in accomplishing this purpose. Absent a health care directive, doctors have little choice but to first turn, formally or informally, to surrogates. The patient will not have preferred some of these surrogates. Further, if consensus cannot be obtained from an entitled class (e.g., a group of adult children) or is otherwise conflicted or challenged, legal proceedings such as guardianship may be the only way to obtain health care decision-making authority for a decisionally or communicatively incapacitated person.

In addition to prospective service as decision-makers, family and close friends have other influences on the patient contemplating completion of a directive. This may range from support and encouragement to neutrality or nonchalance, to philosophical, logistical or even physical barriers. Professionals advising a client on the use of directives should be alert to possible undue influence on either the acceptance or implementation of directives. Case studies describing potential abuses by surrogate decision-makers have already been described in the medical literature (detailed below under "Literature Review").

Despite occasional difficulties or conflicts with individual surrogate decision-makers, some specialty medical societies specifically endorse and categorize as useful the involvement of proxies and agents.[3]

§ 6.04 Literature Review

§ 6.05—Family Members as Decision-Makers

Studies have shown that patients typically prefer family to make health care decisions for them in the event of incapacity[4]; further, they generally expect that family will be involved in medical decisions if they become unable to render their own medical consents. This informal recognition of family involvement in health care decisions leads some individuals to neglect formalizing such recognition in the form of a proxy or agent.[5] Although many of these studies were done with elderly populations, results probably may be generalized and extended to younger and more diverse groups.

The importance of family in health care decision-making also may be illustrated (somewhat indirectly, perhaps) by the choices made by those without family. Absent a prospective agent or proxy, the only plausible written document to be employed is, generally, the living will. Absence of a viable choice for proxy or agent may add to the procrastination or inertia most of us experience in prospectively delegating health care decisions, or prompt avoidance altogether.[6]

§ 6.06—Validity of Decisions

Although most clients assume their proxies or agents will be involved in decisions, few devote much energy to informing their surrogate decision-makers about their treatment preferences.[7] Interestingly, clients seem to accept the concept that proxy decision-makers may not comply with their wishes as stated in a directive.[8]

A separate body of investigation has explored the validity of the authority of proxy decision-makers. Many studies have confirmed a troubling result: proxy decision-making often does not comport with decisions the patient may have made if able. Some of these studies have compared patient preferences after survival from a cardiac arrest and have shown that physicians as proxy decision-makers do not conform to what the patient would have wanted.[9]

Another approach for validating the accuracy of proxy decision-making is through scenarios with decisions made by patients and their selected proxies. These too show significant differences in patient and proxy choices and decisions. One study examined physician and spouse accuracy as proxies. It determined that physicians consistently underestimate the resuscitation preferences of patients and that spouses tend to overestimate.[10]

A second scenario study examined middle generation proxies and found that they use the same criteria for decision-making (e.g., mental incapacitation, burden on family) but tend to underestimate resuscitation choices of the patient. Diamond[11] has demonstrated that proxies—even those with a limited knowledge of patient preferences—disapprove of "high tech" interventions. Others have discerned disagreement between patient and proxy.[12]

The dilemma for the proxy decision-maker is that she or he may be compelled to make decisions based on little (or limited) information from the patient. Patients infrequently discuss their preferences with their "deputies", even if they have executed directives.[13] In instances of limited information from patients, agents or proxies may be unable to extrapolate from written wishes expressed for one type of medical situation to unanticipated scenarios.[14] Even if patient preferences about quality of life are known, this information may not accurately predict the treatment choices exercised by family proxies in scenario studies.[15]

In such scenario studies, Tomlinson has shown that when proxy decision-makers are specifically asked to make substituted judgments or act as the patient might, the results come closer to replicating patient preferences than do best interests determinations.[16]

§ 6.07 Common Misconceptions

Family members may bring numerous misconceptions to discussions concerning the advance health care directives of loved ones. Awkward and disconcerting as such discussions may be, gently try to facilitate them. If possible, deftly encourage patients to "open up" and share their wishes about medical decisions frankly and forthrightly. Sometimes sharing copies of

---

DILEMMAS FOR SURROGATE DECISION MAKERS
Making Ethical Decisions

Help guide family members with some of the following ideas:

1. Do whatever you have to do to discern or divine or impute or extrapolate or interpolate what the uncomprehending loved one would have wanted. Try very hard not to mix up your own values and substitute what *you* might want. Work as carefully and faithfully as you can to "step into the patient's shoes" and make the choices she or he might have otherwise made. (This is the substituted judgment standard.) For the person who knows prospectively that she or he will someday act as proxy or agent, the key to serving effectively is to **listen very carefully to what the patient/principal has to say.** Take notes if that's appropriate. Feed back what was said to ascertain or verify understandings. Meet and go over the directive from time to time—yearly may be opportune—and make sure that both of you see eye to eye on key issues and scenarios. When the fateful days finally arrive, the patient will be confident—and the "deputy" ready.

   There's one more dimension, however, beyond being a knowledgeable, capable, and faithful proxy or agent who is buoyed by a modicum of certainty as to what must be done. After the death of the patient, a previously unprepared "deputy" may be faced with onsets of delayed remorse or anguish or other psychological issues attributable to lack of understanding, or to inadequate preparation, or to unease about guessing. Accordingly, principal and agent do one another loving service by communicating well. Patients, don't by your silence back your deputies into quagmires of guilt and grief by leaving them to wonder if they did the right thing.

2. If you as proxy or agent or surrogate have very little to go on, then the best interests standards apply. This is a more conservative approach than substituted judgment. Since you don't really know what the patient might have wanted, do your very best to *do* what's best. Once again, don't superimpose your personal values.

directives and (if employed) a values history—line by line, perhaps—is a good approach. The involved professional might even serve (if asked) as an informal moderator and possibly help with unanswered questions and unresolved issues. Fastidious patients may even direct that such discussions be memorialized as audio or video records; accommodate them.

In organizing and precepting such encounters, be alert: untimely or inopportune efforts may provoke unexpected confrontation and conflict.

§ 6.08 Barriers to Acceptance

Family members, like patients, may express a variety of philosophies about the use of directives. Additionally, there may be other familial attitudes or dynamics that may create barriers to acceptance of advance health care directives.

Stemming from seemingly innocuous and inconsequential exposures such as television and movies, some families may harbor idealized and even uplifting visions of death, in which a dying individual is totally conscious and in charge of his or her medical decision-making until the very last (and seemingly painless) breath. Unseen and decidedly difficult and unwanted are the agonized deaths. Although the public has been educated as to possibilities for improvements in end-of-life care through the hospice movement (making transition and death more peaceful and acceptable for both patients and family), few have had first hand experience with this type of "better death." Accordingly, some may not see any need at all for the personal contingency planning that advance directives represent.

Some family members see discussion of advance health care directives as an emotionally negative experience, and may try to "protect" the patient's feelings by avoiding discussion of this topic. Patients may interpret this as disinterest or rejection of the concept. Depending on the client's resolve, such family disinclination may at best delay implementation of a pre-existing directive.

Discussing the details of life threatening or terminal illness is left in some cultures to the family; the individual is "spared" from the details and negative implications. Likewise, cultural norms may obligate family members to do everything possible to spare the life of someone seriously or terminally ill: not doing so might be viewed as abrogation of familial responsibility.

Other possible difficulties abound. A designated and previously uninformed proxy or agent may reject service on moral or philosophical grounds. (This is, of course, perfectly acceptable.) Additionally, some family members may find it upsetting—even traumatic—to be thrust into a decision-making role for life-and-death situations, and may understandably quail. Selection of an agent or proxy may provoke crisis, conflict, and competition within some families. For these reasons, open discussion of directives may be unacceptable.

§ 6.09 Barriers to Implementation

- **Prioritizing time to discuss preferences.** Patients may be reluctant to call a family conference to discuss their health care directives, particularly if they do not perceive their medical problems as life threatening. Given geographic and time barriers, some patients may experience difficulty finding the right time and place to speak with principal family and friends. On this basis, the completion of a directive often becomes a low priority or is forgotten completely. Professionals assisting a patient may provide a useful role by inquiring from time to time on the status of directives. Although best done contemplatively and in the absence of crisis, "it's never too late" for a competent and communicative patient to express preferences. Discussion while in the throes of illness actually may be more realistic for some individuals: aware of their difficulty (indeed, peril), they suddenly may propel themselves

---

DILEMMAS FOR SURROGATE DECISION MAKERS
Get Good Advice

Again, here are some pointers to impart:

1. Making health care decisions for someone else can be very difficult. It can be emotional. There can be a lot of pressure. You may be called on to make choices that will result in the patient's death. Sometimes, people are second-guessing and even hostile. At other times, it seems like no one will help, and you feel like the loneliest person in the world. If it's too much, take heart. Get the advice you need from people you know and trust: doctors, clergy, lawyer, family, friends, and concerned others. Be as methodical as you can. And if it's *really* too much, then it's perfectly okay to step aside and let someone else take over. For all the somberness that service connotes, the role of agent or proxy or surrogate may be constructively channeled into a personal growing experience and a life experience. A "deputy" who is at once singed and seared by the experience actually may come to a greater understanding of the fullness of life—and in so doing help instill and impart measures of wisdom and compassion in others.

2. Even if you think you know the choices to be made, get good advice first. We're all aware that there are pros and cons to almost everything. Other people may have crucial information and ideas and perspective that, upon your further reflection, may just turn your decision-making inside out. Take the time if possible. Don't make hasty decisions you may later regret.

into rapid—and often highly focused and cogent—decision-making, not only about personal health care but myriad other issues such as disposition of property and care to be afforded others.

- **Lack of prior guidance.** Family discussions are important not only to get the directive-drafting process started, but also to provide guidance for the designated decision-maker. Little or no discussion on values and interests may leave the proxy or agent in the highly uncomfortable and unenviable position of having to act without direction during tense or even traumatic situations. Lack of prior guidance surely may make the substitute decision-maker's tasks emotionally excruciating. Professionals render an exceedingly important service by helping patients keep from inadvertently casting adrift the very individuals upon whom they will be relying for help.

- **Commitment of surrogate decision-maker.** The individual assigned as the agent under a health care power or proxy assumes a great deal of responsibility. The ideal agent or proxy will be in regular touch with the patient. This contact runs to much more than vigilance about current medical problems or the progression of a disease. The prospective health care decision-maker should remain ever sensitive to the patient's values and vision of quality of life: these do change over time. Despite the best of intentions, caring and concerned family members may not be astute enough (or even prepared) to make this commitment. Indeed, family members are likely to feel more comfortable if supplied with necessary information about the task at hand.

- **Family Not Familiar with Patient's Health Care Delivery System.** Family members unacquainted with a patient's personal physician may be understandably reluctant to agree with the implementation of directives, particularly if those directives are constructed to limit care.

  Wary family members first may wish to assess the quality of care provided by the patient's personal health care providers and ascertain that all reasonable options for care have been either examined or exhausted. Frank discussions between family and health care professionals and staff are essential.

- **Stale or Obsolete Directives.** Agents and proxies may be asked to make decisions based on patient instructions that predate a dramatic change in patient status; accordingly, they may have legitimate concerns about the applicability of directives. It is incumbent on professionals to assist and guide any necessary reassessment of what effectively may become stale or obsolete directives.

Be Sensitive

Your patients and clients will be eminently well served if you can help them with these points:

1. Be astute about the needs of the patient's dearest people. For example, if hope is gone and heroic interventions are to be discontinued, it may make all the difference in the world to a loved one coming from out of town to wait just a little longer so that he or she can arrive in time to say goodbye.

2. Be astute about the needs of the patient's dearest people. For example, if hope is gone and heroic interventions are to be discontinued, it may make all the difference in the world to a loved one coming from out of town to wait just a little longer so that he or she can arrive in time to say goodbye.

3. The imminent death of a loved one may provoke argument and discord. Dormant or latent hostilities may open or reopen. Some may even escalate into being venal and vicious arguments. Without really even knowing it, family members may jumble or even superimpose their own long standing quarrels and disagreements as the issues of the dying patient. Help separate out all contentions, and try to get all concerned to a figurative armistice. Subsume issues extraneous to the patient's needs, and urge unification with and behind the designated "deputy" in the best interests of the dying person. (This is, of course, exceedingly difficult.)

4. Think before you converse at the bedside. It probably always will lack evidence and proof. Perhaps it's just silly conjecture. But some believe the last sense to be lost by a dying patient is the sense of hearing. Whether or not that's true, we all can agree on the imperative for decency and respect in the presence of a seriously ill person. Think of what it is like to be in a dentist's chair and only being able to hear—and then resolve to be just as judicious as the dentist about what you say at bedside. Speak only words of comfort and love and support in the presence of an unconscious or dying patient. Conduct conversations about treatments (and funerals) somewhere else.

§ 6.10 Critique of Case Study

The immediate pressures on an agent or proxy or surrogate can be daunting and debilitating—even utterly crushing. For those of us cast—like Cory Hernandez—in the horrifically miserable and lonely position of deciding to "let go" of a loved one, there may be delayed grief, guilt and depression which, latent or undetected at first, may become at turns insidious, sinister, virulent, and profoundly dangerous.

The need for counseling does not end the instant a collective family gets through an end-of-life crisis. Survivors need help, too—sometimes lots of it, and for months and even years at a time. Read on for a much more publicized story—and the largely unknown aftermath.

Cory is at risk. Her friends probably mean well. But they haven't a clue. Spoken suicidal ideas should always be cause for alarm. Telling a profoundly depressed and suicidal person to "get a grip" or to "snap out of it" is grievously wrong advice. Ms. Hernandez (and, for that matter, those close to her) are fortunate that she still had enough mettle left to seek out her personal physician for assistance.

§ 6.11 Conclusion

Family and friends can be integral in enhancing the utility and efficacy of advance directives. As prudent and proper, help draw them in and array them in support of the patient. Help the patient validate their participation.

There is so very much we as professionals can do. We can be pathfinders. In our deft little ways, we can guide and illuminate. Some of the insights we are capable of providing can move patients and devoted families into uncommon realms of goodness and grace. May we always strive to do just this.

Notes

1. D. High, *All in The Family: Extended Autonomy and Expectations in Surrogate Health care Decision-Making,* 28 GERONTOLOGIST 46 (1988).
2. This preference is for the vast majority of cases. In the event a directive is procured by way of forgery, fraud, overreaching, undue influence, and the like, it may be necessary to resort to judicial intervention for revocation or suspension.
3. American Geriatrics Soc'y Ethics Comm., *Making Treatment Decisions for Incapacitated Older Adults without Advance Directives,* 44 J. AM. GERIATRICS SOC'Y 986 (1996).
4. D. High, *supra* note 1; D. High, *Standards for Surrogate Decision Making: What the Elderly Want,* J. OF LONG TERM CARE ADMIN., Summer 1989, at 8-13. E. Gamble et al., *Knowledge, Attitudes, and Behavior of Elderly Persons Regarding Living Wills,* 151 ARCHIVES INTERNAL MED. 277 (1991).
5. D. High, *supra* note 1; D. High, *Families' Roles in Advance Directives,* HASTINGS CENTER REP., 1994 Special Supp., at 16-18.

6. D. High, *Old and Alone: Surrogate Health Care Decision-Making for the Elderly without Families,* 4 J. AGING STUDIES 277 (1990).

7. D. High, *supra* note 4.

8. *Id.*

9. S. Bedell & T. Delbanco, *Choices About Cardiopulmonary Resuscitation in the Hospital: When Do Physicians Talk with Patients?* 310 NEW ENG. J. MED. 17 (1984).

10. R. Uhlmann, R. Pearlman, & K. Cain, *Physicians' and Spouses Predictions of the Elderly Patients' Resuscitation Preferences,* 43 J. GERONTOLOGY 115 (1988).

11. E. Diamond et al., *Decision Making Ability and Advance Directive Preferences in Nursing Home Patients and Proxies,* 29 GERONTOLOGIST 622 (1989).

12. J. Ouslander, A. Tymchuk, & B. Rahbar, *Health Care Decisions Among Elderly Long-Term Care Residents and their Potential Proxies,* 149 ARCHIVES INTERNAL MED. 1367 (1989); J. Hare, C. Pratt, & C. Nelson, *Agreement Between Patients and Their Self-Selected Surrogates on Difficult Medical Decisions,* 152 ARCHIVES INTERNAL MED. 1049 (1992); A. Seckler et al., *Substituted Judgment: How Accurate Are Proxy Predictions?* 115 ANNALS OF INTERNAL MED. 92 (1991); R. Pearlman, R. Uhlmann, & N. Jecker, *Spousal Understanding of Patient Quality of Life: Implications for Surrogate Decisions,* 3 J. CLINICAL ETHICS 114 (1992).

13. S. Joos, J. Reule, & J. Powell, et al., "Outpatients' Attitudes and Understanding Regarding Living Wills," Journal of General Internal Medicine, Vol. 8, May 1993, page 259–263.

14. R. Reilly, T. Teasdale, & L. McCullough, *Projecting Patients' Preferences from Living Wills: An Invalid Strategy for Management of Dementia with Life-Threatening Illness,* 42 J. AM. GERIATRICS SOC'Y 997 (1994); L. Emanuel et al., *Advance Directives: Can Patients' Stated Treatment Choices Be Used to Infer Unstated Choices?* 32 MEDICAL CARE 95 (1994).

15. R. Pearlman et al., *Spousal Understanding of Patient Quality of Life: Implications for Surrogate Decisions,* 3 J. CLINICAL ETHICS 114 (1992).

16. T. Tomlinson et al., *An Empirical Study of Proxy Consent for Elderly Persons,* 30 GERONTOLOGIST 54 (1990).

17. T. E. Finucane, C. Christmas, & K. Travis, *Tube feeding in patients with advanced dementia: a review of the evidence,* 282 JAMA 1365 (1999); M.R. Gillick, *Rethinking the role of tube feeding in patients with advanced dementia,* 342 NEW ENG. J. MED. 206 (2000); Z.B. Huang & J.C. Ahronheim, *Nutrition and hydration in terminally ill patients: an update,* 16(2) CLINICAL GERIATRIC MED. 313 (2000).

CHAPTER 7

The Attorney Perspective

§ 7.01 Introduction

On the night of January 11, 1983, N.C. lost control of her car as she traveled down Elm Road in Jasper County, Missouri. The vehicle overturned, and she was discovered lying face down in a ditch without detectable respiratory or cardiac function. Paramedics were able to restore her breathing and heartbeat at the accident site, and she was transported to a hospital in an unconscious state. An attending neurosurgeon diagnosed her as having sustained probable cerebral contusions compounded by significant anoxia (lack of oxygen). It was thought that N.C. had been deprived of oxygen from 12 to 14 minutes.

She remained in a coma for approximately three weeks and then progressed to an unconscious state in which she was able to orally ingest some nutrition. In order to ease feeding and further the recovery, surgeons implanted a gastrostomy feeding and hydration tube in N.C. with the consent of her then-husband. Subsequent rehabilitative efforts proved unavailing. She came to lie in what is commonly referred to as a persistent vegetative state: generally, a condition in which a person exhibits motor reflexes but evinces no indications of significant cognitive function.

After it had become apparent that N.C. had virtually no chance of regaining her mental faculties her parents asked hospital employees to terminate the artificial nutrition and hydration procedures. All agreed that such a removal would cause her death. The employees refused to honor the request without court approval.

Does this scenario sound familiar? It probably does: it is taken almost verbatim from the introduction to *Cruzan vs. Director, Missouri Department of Health.*[1] N.C. is, of course, Nancy Cruzan.

§ 7.02 The Genesis of Advance Health Care Directives

The idea of the living will was first suggested by a distinguished human rights attorney, Luis Kutner (1908–1993). Advance health care directives as we know them today stem from Kutner's vision plus a body of case law that stretches back to the nineteenth century.

A synopsis of case law begins with *Union Pacific Railway Co. v. Botsford,* 141 U.S. 250 (1891):

> No right is held more sacred, or is more carefully guarded by the common law than the right of every individual to the possession and control of his own person, free from all restraint or interference of others, unless by clear and unquestionable authority of law.

In *Schloendorff v. Society of New York Hospitals*, 102 NE 92 (N.Y., 1914), Justice Benjamin Cardozo wrote:

> Every human being of adult years and sound mind has a right to determine what shall be done with his own body; and a surgeon who performs an operation without his patient's consent commits an assault for which he is liable for damages.

A number of other cases have come to bear on this body of law. One of the leading decisions is, of course, *In re Quinlan*, 70 N.J. 10, 355 A.2d 647, cert. denied *sub nom, Garger v. New Jersey*, 429 U.S. 922 (1976), which is widely regarded as the first case dealing squarely with the termination of life support. Drawing upon the privacy rights enumerated in *Griswold v. Connecticut*[2] and *Roe v. Wade*,[3] the New Jersey Supreme Court articulated Quinlan's right to die. The Court also discerned common law and constitutional antecedents that enable an individual to refuse medical treatment.

To date, *Cruzan* is the most influential. Chief Justice Rehnquist framed the question as ". . . whether Cruzan has a right under the United States Constitution which would require the hospital to withdraw life-sustaining treatment from her under these circumstances."[4] The opinion then traced the development of the doctrine of informed consent to medical treatments, and determined ". . . (t)he logical corollary . . . is that the patient generally possesses the right not to consent, that is, to refuse treatment."[5]

The Court went on to establish a constitutional right to refuse medical treatment—a right protected as a liberty interest under the Fourteenth Amendment, subject to balance against a state's interest in preserving the lives of its citizens. Because ". . . no person (i.e., Cruzan's parents, as guardians of her person) can assume (the choice to withdraw life support) for an incompetent in the absence of the formalities required under Missouri's Living Will statutes or the clear and convincing, inherently reliable evidence absent here,"[6] the case was remanded. At rehearing, the trial court heard sufficient evidence of Cruzan's intent and authorized her parents to remove the feeding tube. She died in December, 1990.

Of particular relevance to the topic at hand is Justice O'Connor's concurring opinion:

> I also write separately to emphasize that the Court does not today decide the issue whether a State must also give effect to the decisions of a surrogate decision-maker. In my view, such a duty may well be constitutionally required to protect the patient's liberty interest in refusing medical treatment. . . . Several States have recognized the practical wisdom of such a procedure by enacting durable power of attorney statutes that specifically authorize an individual to appoint a surrogate to make medical treatment decisions. . . . Today's decision . . . does not preclude a future determination that the Constitution requires the States to implement the decisions of a patient's duly appointed surrogate. (Please also refer to additional excerpts from Justice O'Connor's opinion on page 26)[7]

In *Vacco v. Quill,* 521 U.S. 793, 117 S.Ct. 2293, 138 L.Ed.2d 834 (1997) and *Washington v. Glucksberg,* 521 U.S. 702, 117 S.Ct. 2258, 138 L.Ed.2d 772 (1997), the U.S. Supreme Court provided guidance on the degree of autonomy to be afforded a terminally ill patient. An effective distinction now has been made between dying and killing. Pursuant to the Fourteenth Amendment's liberty interest, a competent patient may refuse medical care and die. However, the equal protection clause of the Fourteenth Amendment does not bar states from outlawing the deliberate acceleration of death. The Court was particularly succinct in *Vacco: "Everyone,* regardless of physical condition, is entitled, if competent, to refuse unwanted lifesaving medical treatment; *no one* is permitted to assist a suicide." (Id. at 800. Emphasis is original.)

Accordingly, the contentious issue of hastening death in terminally ill patients is for now left to "the laboratory of the states." All U.S. jurisdictions categorically outlaw suicide, euthanasia, and physician-assisted suicide. Only Oregon, with its Death with Dignity Act[8] (see Appendix I), carves out a limited and highly controlled protocol for prescribing (but not administering) lethal doses of medication to competent, terminally ill patients who pointedly and repeatedly request it. (A related initiative was defeated in November, 2000 by voters in Maine.)

Vacco and *Washington* seem to establish outer boundaries for the applicability of advance health care directives. Interestingly, the Court differentiated the sphere of palliative (comfort) care and signaled misgivings about any state restrictions that might burden an individual with untoward pain and suffering at the end of life.

§ 7.03 The Lawyer's Role

This section contains a narrative, a checklist, and a sidebar. Although some information overlaps, each contains differing ideas and perspective. It is recommended that all three be reviewed.

Lawyers render invaluable service by acquainting clients with advance health care directives. Be proactive about it.

Tips for Lawyers

Think of advance health care directives as personal contingency plans. Introduce them to clients who seek your assistance with estate planning and wills. Look at it this way: directives have become an essential part of an estate plan. Even absent an estate planning context, wills and directives now logically should be paired.

Lawyers are especially well-suited to raise levels of awareness about directives. Place appropriate brochures in your reception area. Cover the subject in a client newsletter or on your firm's webpage. Join your bar association's speaker bureau and make community presentations. Offer guest articles on the subject to your local paper. Similarly, make yourself available to local radio and television stations (including community access cable). In your presentations, make at least passing reference to other parts of the advance directives package—organ donation in particular. Encourage people to sign up for here-and-now bone marrow and cord blood registries. Don't forget the occasional "pint-sized" favor of giving blood.

You'll need to employ several styles in your one-on-one consultations about advance health care directives. Some clients are receptive and are ready to go ahead. Others have questions—sometimes hard–to–read questions—and need (and occasionally even want) your encouragement. Be as sensitive as you can possibly be to cultural and ethnic and religious issues. Back off with clients who are obviously uncomfortable.

(continued)

Appointments to draft a will or to develop or refine an estate plan are particularly opportune times to broach the subject. Directives now should be a part of both types of client encounters.

Some empirical studies show that when it comes to advance directives, patients look to their physicians to initiate the discussion.[9] Although there are apparently no similar examinations pertaining to lawyers, some clients surely will be receptive to their lawyer bringing it up. (For all of their interdisciplinary nature, directives are, of course, legal documents.) All a client may need is your gentle encouragement.

Begin, of course, by becoming familiar with statute and case law in your jurisdiction. And once you've done that, don't put it off any longer—*execute your own directives*. You are not in much of a position to speak on the subject, counselor, unless you're personally committed to it.

§ 7.04—Initiating Discussion

Many state and local bar associations have excellent brochures on directives: place a supply in your office reception area. This is a neutral and sensitive

Need an occasional prod? Try this: "Do you think probate is bad? Then let me tell you about *living* probate. If you ever lose decisional or communicative capacity and don't have a plan, then a probate judge will have to appoint a guardian or conservator for you. And the guardian will micromanage your life. All of your finances may become public record. You can head off living hell—I mean, living probate—with advance health care directives (and trusts or property powers)."

Be careful when third parties are involved—for example, when an adult child makes an office appointment for consultation on directives for an elderly parent. More often than not, all concerned have the best of intentions. Even if the child pays your fee,

however, the *parent* is the client. Don't permit others to exert undue influence. Make a point of meeting privately with the parent for at least part of the interview (even when the parent expressly says s/he wants the child present) and carefully ascertaining his/her wishes.

Occasionally, a client presents with questionable capacity. Be very conservative in such instances. First, see if capacity to execute a directive is defined by statute. If in doubt, ask for a written assessment by a doctor before you begin drafting. Insufficient capacity? Then no formal directives. However, do everything you can to give voice to decisionally impaired individuals capable of some expression. (See Chapter 4, "Competence and Incompetence.")

By the way, counselor—have *you* executed advance directives yet?

---

introduction to an admittedly difficult and emotional subject. If your client *wants* to talk about advance health care directives, she or he will pick up the literature and walk into your office with it in hand. Take your cues accordingly. A gentle, deft, compassionate, and understanding manner is highly appropriate.

§ 7.05—Drafting a Checklist

Generally, it is best not to execute directives on a snap or on-the-spot basis. As described elsewhere, they require contemplation. Here is a partial checklist of information to be gathered. (For a more expansive discussion, please see the appendix to this chapter, Drafting Checklist, on page 89):

- Medical treatments to be included or excluded
- Levels of care desired (e.g., Aggressive? Comfort care only?)
- End-of-life care preferences
- Start and stop dates (Springing power? Escrowed directives? Immediate applicability?)

- Designation of agent/proxy and successors (including home, work, pager, wireless phone, and fax numbers, as appropriate, plus residential, work, and e-mail addresses)
- Choices regarding organ and tissue donation
- Disposition of remains/autopsy
- Religious or philosophical convictions that may affect treatments
- Known or chronic ailments (including commentary or instructions specific to them)

At the first office encounter, review the subject on a broad-brush basis and answer questions. Provide copies of the statutorily suggested language (Living will? Health care power or proxy?) or your own drafting template (or a variant), discuss pros and cons, and encourage the client to take it home and pencil in choices for a subsequent discussion. Also raise for possible consideration the various enhancements to directives (living will, organ donation, statement of preferences for mental health treatments, etc.) referred to in Chapter 2.

A values history[10] (and other tools referenced in Appendix D) also may help a client formulate choices and articulate preferences. If desired, it may be retained with subsequently drafted directives, or incorporated by reference: the proxy or agent may find the additional information particularly useful in her/his future discharge of duties.

In addition to giving the client the drafting worksheet (and, if desired, the values history form), suggest that s/he speak with friends, family members, physicians, and spiritual advisors, as appropriate, for aid in formulating choices. For that matter—do not hesitate to be involved with physicians and other advisers if the client requests it. (Offer to do so if you think it is warranted.) Facilitate and guide; lead and build consensus as circumstances may dictate. Be a steadying influence. Remember—client emotions during this phase may be surging. Those emotions may be anything from distaste to downright agony.

Unless the client is clearly disinclined to move ahead, pointedly schedule a second office appointment for follow up and execution. The two of you have gotten this far; don't run the risk of leaving the task undone.

§ 7.06—Moving it Forward

Save time, effort, and money by working in a telephone call prior to the second appointment. Clarify issues and answer questions. Suggest, perhaps, that the client work through the applicable form with pen in hand as you converse. As necessary, schedule another phone or office consultation for unresolved issues.

If comfortable with choices, perhaps the client can drop off, mail, or attach as a file to an e-mail the completed drafts in advance of the second appointment: staff then can prepare and have ready a set of documents for formal execution.

Provide the client with plenty of duplicate originals or conformed copies or photocopies, as circumstances dictate. With permission, keep copies (including the values history, if employed) for your file. Urge the "good footprints" principle suggested in the sidebar in Chapter 5—that is, s/he should keep originals in a safe place, with copies to the doctor, hospital, care facility, agent or proxy, family members, and so forth. (The copies should indicate where the original might be found unless, of course, state statute provides that photocopies are equally valid, which accordingly makes location of an original far less important.) As an extra touch, also prepare a purse or wallet card that indicates the existence of directives and where they may be located (see Appendix N). If the client favors organ donation, offer to witness on the spot the signing of the back of a driver's license or organ donor card. (Be certain that organ donation instructions are stated consistently in the directive and on the license or the card.) See Appendix O for a sample letter to the client and Appendix P for sample instructions to the proxy or agent.

A final aside: directives can be very labor and time intensive. You are not often likely to receive fees commensurate with your efforts. For good or ill, that is part of what goes with this subject. Be philosophical about it, and chalk it up to what you will: service to the profession, good deed, or cost of doing business.

§ 7.07—Issues of Capacity

Occasionally, a client presents questionable capacity to execute directives. A difficult issue also may arise if a third party—an adult child, for example— schedules and pays for consultation on advance directives for a parent. Just who is the client? See Chapter 4 for a discussion.

§ 7.08—Comments—and Cautions—About Durable Powers of Attorney

See Chapter 2 for commentary.

§ 7.09—Causes of Action if Directives Are Not Honored

As observed in Chapter 1, this can be problematic, if not enigmatic: advance health care directives are rights without much in the way of remedies. In the event a directive is not honored, it may, of course, fall to counsel to assert the rights of the principal or agent or proxy, or to intercede in some other fashion.

Begin pragmatically. Polite inquiries, informal mediation, some old style jawboning, or a pointed letter may be all that are necessary to prod an errant or misinformed or recalcitrant party to act in accordance with a directive. In fact, litigation may be entirely counterproductive and deleterious: apart from the considerable financial (and emotional) expense, the patient may be inadvertently forced to suffer physically for the duration of the proceeding, or unwelcome public and press attention may be attracted, or an unwanted protective proceeding (e.g., guardianship or conservatorship) may be imposed.

There are a handful of cases that have appeared in this new area of the law. There surely will be more. If judicial relief is to be sought, proceed very carefully. Some causes of action are somewhat new and untried; others carry daunting burdens of proof; still others are not "good fits." Here is a partial list:

- Injunctive relief or temporary/permanent restraining orders
- Petition for declaratory judgment (i.e., determination of rights of the parties)
- Construction (or rulings on validity and/or scope) of advance directives
- Violations of state laws on advance directives, or failure to honor directives
- Healing arts malpractice
- Battery (i.e., unwanted touching) or medical battery (lack of consent to treatments)
- Wrongful living or wrongfully prolonging life (i.e., forced to remain alive after request to forsake care—as differentiated from wrongful life, which runs to disabilities at birth that could have been anticipated or prevented). To date, this putative cause of action has not been well received by courts. For a related discussion, see Gregory G. Sarno, *Tortious Maintenance or Removal of Life Supports* 58 A.L.R. 4th 222.
- Breach of contract, or tortious interference with contract
- Negligence
- Apparent authority and vicarious liability (e.g., hospital responsibility for actions of a doctor)
- Severe intentional infliction of emotional distress
- Violations of civil rights (federal and state)
- Violations of constitutional rights (federal and state)
- Equitable relief
- Petition for guardianship or conservatorship
- Actions under ancillary or related federal and state statutes (e.g., hospital and nursing home protections, disability, human rights, elder abuse, financial responsibility of family members)
- Referral to local prosecutor for possible criminal action. (Note, however, that enforcement of criminal provisions regarding advance health care directives statutes are not likely to be high on a prosecutor's list of priorities—lending credence, perhaps, to the observation that directives are essentially rights without remedies.)

§ 7.10 Critique of Case Study

As alluded to at the end of Chapter 6, the *Cruzan* case actually was a double tragedy.

Nancy's father, Lester ("Joe") Cruzan, Jr., surely swept up in riptides of emotion as he sat at his daughter's bedside, at one point could hear and see demonstrators as they railed outside in cold weather against his efforts to let her die.

Joe's magnanimous response was to go to a local store, purchase a coffee maker and an extension cord, and brew and carry hot cups to those who literally shivered in opposition to him.

The court decisions eventually came down. Nancy died. The searing lights of publicity winked off.

Perhaps the lights in Joe's life flickered out at about the same time.

"Survivors," it turns out, don't necessarily survive. On August 17, 1996, a severely depressed Joe Cruzan hung himself. He was sixty-two years old.

§ 7.11 Conclusion

Advance health care directives may be the most important legal documents any of us will ever sign. They have become an integral part of everyone's personal planning. You do your clients—and your profession, and yourself— an enormous service by encouraging and facilitating their use.

Notes

1. Cruzan v. Director, Mo. Dep't of Health. 497 U.S. 261, 111 L Ed 2d 224, 110 S Ct 2841 (1990).
2. Griswold v. Connecticut, 381 U.S. 479 (1965).
3. Roe v. Wade, 410 U.S. 113 (1973).
4. *Cruzan*, 479 U.S. at 269, 111 L Ed 2d at 236, 110 S Ct at 2846.
5. *Id.* at 270, 111, L Ed 2d at 236, 110 S Ct at 2847.
6. *Id.* at 269, 111 L Ed 2d at 236, 110 S Ct at 2846 (quoting the Supreme Court of Missouri in *Cruzan v. Harmon*, 760 S.W. 2d 408, at 425).
7. *Id.* at 289, 111 L Ed 2d at 249, 110 S Ct at 2857.
8. Oregon's Death with Dignity Act, OR. REV. STAT. §§ 127.800 *et seq.*
9. E. Gamble et al., *Knowledge, Attitudes, and Behaviors of Elderly Persons Regarding Living Wills*, 151 ARCHIVES INTERNAL MED. 277 (1991).
10. Values history developed by the Institute for Public Law at the University of New Mexico; *see* Appendix D.
11. Illustrative programs are Vial for Life and File for Life.

CHAPTER 7 APPENDIX
Drafting Checklist

1. Review state statute and available forms. Consider alternatives:
   (a) Health care proxy (or durable power of attorney for health care)
   (b) Living will (or declaration)
   (c) Organ and tissue donation
   (d) Declaration of preferences for mental health treatment (where available) or other mental health treatment protocols
   (e) Do-Not-Resuscitate orders (DNRs) or directives or protocols
   (f) Other applicable statutory provisions (e.g., delegation of health care of minors, life prolonging procedures declaration)
2. Review statutes and case law for nuances. Some possible issues:
   (a) Are the forms contained in statute suggested or compulsory?
   (b) Does one style of form obviate another or conflict with another? (Do proxies supercede living wills?)
   (c) Are there prohibitions on withdrawal of hydration and nutrition, irrespective of the maker's stated wishes? Or might directives be suspended or invalid during pregnancy?
   (d) Are co-agents or co-proxies permitted or prohibited?
   (e) Are thresholds of capacity defined?
3. Just who is the client? Remember, even though a third party (e.g., an adult child) may be paying your bill, a *nonpaying* person (e.g., an elderly parent) actually may be your client. As well meaning as all parties probably are, make it clear in your own mind—*and abundantly clear to all concerned* (in writing, if need be)—just whom it is you will represent. Carefully think through the ramifications of your prior or ongoing representations (e.g., of other family members). Avoid dual representation with directives. If in doubt, refer the matter elsewhere.
4. Does the client have sufficient capacity to execute directives? At times, this critical question can be exceedingly difficult to answer. First, check the statute on directives and determine if capacity to execute directives is defined. If the client lacks the statutory definition of capacity, or if there is no definition, or if you have reasons to doubt client capacity, STOP and observe the rule of thumb: No capacity? Then no directives. Proceed very cautiously and very conservatively. Review Chapter 4 ("Competence and Incompetence") for ideas about next steps. Although legal definitions of capacity do not necessarily comport with medical definitions, it probably is a good idea to obtain a medical doctor's independent evaluation. Also, always remember that capacity rarely is a simple "yes or no" issue. Individuals with diminished capacity still may be able to express some treatment preferences suitable for memorialization.
5. Be on guard for undue influence, inadvertent or otherwise. If family members—or (especially) unrelated informal caregivers—are involved, be certain to conduct at least part of the interviews privately and one-on-one,

irrespective of the seeming well meaning and good intentions of all concerned. Probe carefully. Admonish if you think it prudent. Make inquiries of
third parties if you are suspicious. Withdraw altogether if you must. In the
unlikely event you sense exploitation, contact appropriate authorities.

6. As necessary or appropriate, elicit (and either attach to a directive, or incorporate by reference) a general values history or similar ancillary and expansive
   statement (see Appendix D):
   (a) Overall attitude about personal health
   (b) Overall attitudes about life and death
   (c) Philosophical/ethical/moral points of view
   (d) Spiritual or religious values (if any)
   (e) General attitudes toward delivery of health care and treatments

7. Does the client have a chronic health condition (or conditions) that may,
   in effect, drive the directives? In other words, is the client suffering from
   cancer, heart disease, dementia, renal failure, pulmonary disease, AIDS, or
   another chronic or terminal condition? Accordingly, is there a likely course
   of medical treatments that the directives should address? If so, the advice
   of an attending physician should be sought as to prognosis and types (and
   scopes) of possible treatments, both conventional and experimental. Directives should be tailored accordingly.

8. Are there any treatments that the client specifically wants included or excluded? Be reluctant to serve as scrivener for categorical statements—for
   example, "no ventilator." What if a "vent" is needed only briefly after, say,
   an emergency appendectomy?

9. What are the client's wishes regarding specific conditions and procedures?
   (a) Cardiopulmonary Resuscitation (CPR)
   (b) Do-Not-Resuscitate orders (DNRs)
   (c) Dialysis
   (d) Respirators
   (e) Artificial hydration and nutrition
   (f) Organ/tissue transplantation and/or donation
   (g) Blood transfusions
   (h) Psychotropic medications/electroconvulsive therapies/psychosurgeries
   (i) Amputations
   (j) Client's definition as to when (if at all) life-sustaining measures should
       be withheld

10. Who are the client's nominees as proxy/agent (and successors or
    alternates)?
    Name: _____
    Name: _____

11. Screen the client's nominees as proxy/agent (and successors):
    (a) How long/how well have they known the client?
    (b) Are there any possible conflicts of interest (e.g., is a candidate financially
        liable for the client's health care? Is the client a creditor of a candidate, or
        vice versa? Does a candidate have an expectancy, either real or imagined,
        in the client's property?)

(c) Has the client discussed health care preferences with the nominees?

(d) Are the candidates sympathetic to the client's general philosophies and wishes? Are they able to exercise substituted judgment, i.e., impute and extrapolate and then impart the values of the client/principal to surrogate decision-making, and not superimpose their OWN personal values?

(e) What is the client's comfort level with "letting go" their personal decision-making to any of the candidates?

(f) Are the nominees capable of making end-of-life decisions for another, i.e. the client/principal? Or might they quail or falter at such a prospect?

12. Nominate the agent/proxy. (Impart to the client that **this is the most important decision to be made** in executing an advance directive.) Then nominate successor agents/contingent proxies, as statute may provide or permit. Include as much information as possible about how to reach those so named:

Addresses: Pager:
Residence phones: FAX:
Business/work phones: E-Mail:
Wireless/cellular:

13. Select generalized level of preferred treatments, as statute/forms may permit or suggest—e.g., continue all treatments irrespective of cost or prognosis, or discontinue heroic treatments if costs outweigh benefits, or discontinue heroic treatments if the principal is in an irreversible coma or persistent vegetative state.

14. Control implementation. As statute may permit, choose when the directive becomes effective:

(a) Immediately upon execution.

(b) A specified "sunrise" date some time in the future (e.g., "January 1, 2005").

(c) A "springing" power or proxy (e.g., "This directive becomes effective upon the written determination of (one or two) medical doctor(s) that I am no longer capable of making personal decisions.")

(d) Upon a given circumstance (e.g., administration of anesthesia).

(e) A directive without restriction as to effective date but deposited with a third party for delivery to the agent/proxy upon an indicated circumstance.

15. Control termination. As statute may permit, choose:

(a) Upon a given circumstance (e.g., recovery from anesthesia).

(b) Written revocation (or "tearing, cutting, obliterating, or burning").

(c) Oral revocation.

(d) Upon death.

(e) "Beyond death", e.g., allow the proxy/agent to consent to autopsy, or to organ and tissue donation, or to disposition of remains, as the client/principal may direct.

(f) A specified "sunset" date (e.g., "December 31, 2006"). Be aware that some states provide for effectiveness beyond sunset dates if the principal is incapacitated at that point.

16. Execute in accordance with required formalities (signature/witnesses/notary, as required; record or deposit with registry if required or requested.)

17. Make plenty of photocopies, or execute duplicate originals or make conformed copies, as appropriate. Impart to the client the fact that directives are *worthless* if others don't know about them or where they can be found. Describe the "good footprints" approach: the client (or the lawyer, upon direction) should distribute executed directives to the agent/proxy and successors, family members, attending physicians, institutions (e.g., residential facility), and so forth, with attached written notations indicating where the original may be found. (A safe deposit box generally is *not* a good idea, given restrictions to access that may be presented. If your jurisdiction provides that photocopies are as valid as originals, then measures to assure access to originals may of course be of little consequence.) Copies also should be kept at home and at work in places (e.g., top desk drawers, bulletin boards) where emergency personnel are likely to look. There are even programs that promote the keeping of important records in the refrigerator.[11] Provide a notification card to be carried in a wallet or purse. Some clients may wish to procure a bracelet or medallion. Consider use of a local or statewide or online registry for directives. (See the sidebar in Chapter 5.)

18. If the client is receptive to organ and/or tissue donation, offer to serve as an on-the-spot witness for a driver license or similar statement. (Be certain that a statement so made is consistent with concurrently executed directives.)

19. Consider the big picture. Advance health care directives are contingency plans for personal decision making *only*. Finances need to be addressed as well. As appropriate, suggest preparation (or review) of an estate plan, or drafting of a will, or development of an intervivos trust, or execution of a companion statutory durable power of attorney for *property*.

Much thought goes into the preparation of advance health care directives. Careful planning and a skillful interview can deliver to clients the "extra value" you want them to have—and also inculcate in them an abiding respect for and pride in *you* as an astute and compassionate lawyer. It is a great feeling to have a well-served client stand up from the signing table with a broad smile and a heartfelt handshake for you—especially given the solemnity and moment of the subject. You are helping people make some of the toughest decisions of their lives. You have every right to stand proud.

CHAPTER 8

The Health Care
Provider Perspective

§ 8.01 Introduction

Mirth Green is a 72-year-old female with a medical history of emphysema. Occasionally assisted by a home health aide, she lives alone and leaves her home only for doctor's appointments. Limited physically, Ms. Green experiences severe shortness of breath with minimal exertion. The patient has no close relatives and relies on informal assistance from neighbors.

Over the past year, Mirth has been hospitalized twice for her worsening chronic lung disease. On both occasions, aggressive management resulted in stabilization of her medical condition. During her last hospitalization, a lung specialist was called in on consult. He agreed with the treating physician's management plan and felt that the condition was end-stage.

Ms. Green never executed an advance health care directive. During the second hospitalization, the primary care physician asked her if she would consider the use of a mechanical ventilator for aid in breathing if her condition worsened. He explained that this might become the only measure available to keep her alive. Although clearly reluctant to decide about the "vent," or to talk about a living will or durable power, Mirth said she would "think about it," and let the doctor know her decision "in the next couple of days." The treating physician, sensing her hesitation, did not press. No decision ever was made, and Green was discharged without event.

During an influenza outbreak three months later, Ms. Green developed pneumonia. She was brought to the local hospital emergency room in respiratory failure and was intubated and placed on a ventilator. Plainly in great anguish and distress, Mirth sought to see her primary care physician the next day. Unable to speak because of the tube, she wrote the doctor a note: "Why did you let them do this to me? I never wanted this. I would rather die than live like this." Days later, die she did—on the ventilator she seemingly never wanted.

§ 8.02 The Patient–Physician Relationship

A discussion of advance health care directives from a physician's standpoint begins, most logically, with some historical insight into the patient–physician relationship.

Prior to the past half-century's sweeping advances in medical technology, the physician was, for the most part, the undisputed "broker" of health knowledge. There were but limited treatment alternatives, and the physician could be relied upon to faithfully follow the maxim of "do no harm" and act almost unilaterally in the patient's best interests.

Given the stunning technological advances, however, more choices have come to exist. Although the physician may still wish to "do no harm," it has become far more difficult to gauge patient preferences. In a profound change, patients are also consumers who are often impressively well-educated about treatment alternatives.

In this environment, patient participation—indeed, direction—in health decisions becomes a daily fact rather than a choice. Despite this growing consumerism, however, patients still expect their health care provider to initiate discussions about advance health care directives.[1]

Furthermore, physicians commonly work in teams with other health care providers. Consensus among various physicians, nurses, and medical social workers becomes increasingly more important, especially in the care plans of medically and socially complex patients.

Because of their involvement with patients during medical crises, health care providers (including doctors, nursing professionals, clinical ethicists, psychologists, medical social workers, palliative caregivers, and therapists) often are seen as key professional contacts on the subject of advance health care directives. Although it is true that many health professionals regularly deal with these documents, not all are comfortable with them. Some are not fully knowledgeable. Given time constraints, others are disinclined to assist in their preparation and execution.

Health care providers, like clients, may share the same opposition on philosophical grounds, or share the same gaps in knowledge. These may influence the health care provider's interest or ability to educate and facilitate the client's interest in completing a directive. In addition, physicians may not be naturally inclined or trained to collaborate with other professionals who also are involved with the client's interest to complete a directive. They may defer to other professionals to initiate and complete discussion of directives.

§ 8.03 Review of Literature

Health providers have a very valuable role in initiation and interpretation of patient education on directives. The following literature review and discussion scrutinizes the barriers health care providers face in incorporating this discussion into their practice environments. Suggestions for making this discussion an integral part of the patient encounter also are presented.

It is not surprising that some health care professionals find advance health care directives difficult to approach. They involve, of course, complex ethical, legal, and medical issues.

§ 8.04—Finding the Facts

Some practitioners are uncertain about the facts concerning advance directives, or are perturbed by perceived medical–legal ramifications. Others may be guided strongly by the "do no harm" premise of medicine, which some interpret as keeping the patient alive at all costs. Despite perceived misgivings about advance directives, surveyed physicians generally seem to favor the withdrawal of life support systems in hopeless situations.[2] Nurses also have expressed considerable support for the concept of advance health care directives.[3]

§ 8.05—Discussing the Issues

Compelled to conform to the mandates of the federal Patient Self-Determination Act (PSDA) (see Appendix A), some medical caregivers have found their roles in implementation to be satisfying. Among nurses and physicians, experience dealing with terminally ill patients has been correlated with increased professional ease and comfort in discussing directives with patients.[4]

Furthermore, other health care delivery providers are comfortable with discussion of the use of directives. Investigators have demonstrated that hospital social workers and nurses were knowledgeable about advance directives and were implementing programs required as part of the PSDA.[5] Surveys of home health agencies, dialysis staff, hospital administrators, and cardiovascular and pulmonary rehabilitation directors all acknowledge the value of advance directives in patient care.[6]

Barriers to patient discussion at that time included lack of professional knowledge and understanding—strong deterrents to employment and use.[7] Doukas determined that one-fourth of health professionals who never initiate discussions with their patients about directives attribute this behavior to lapses in their own knowledge. Doukas also concluded that those professionals who *are* knowledgeable are more likely to introduce directives in their practices.[8] Studies of resident physicians in training also have shown deficiencies in knowledge about use of directives.[9]

§ 8.06—Executing the Directives

Some investigators have found that physicians as a group are no more likely than the population as a whole to personally execute directives.[10] However, those physicians surveyed described a preference for limiting medical interventions for themselves in the event of serious or life threatening illnesses.[11]

Recent investigation indicates that preferences of physicians for their own end-of-life care mirror that of patients grouped culturally and ethnically: African American physicians were more likely to select life prolonging treatments than were white physicians.[12] Despite seeming acceptance of the general concept of advance directives, surveys have shown that physicians infrequently initiate this discussion with patients.[13] When discussions do occur, most are with the elderly or demented.[14]

The notion that "doctors know what their patients want" also has come under question. Studies have shown that in the absence of directives, physicians actually may misconstrue or poorly impute patient wishes. Bedell[15] showed that among survivors of cardiopulmonary resuscitation (CPR), physician judgment that patients would have requested resuscitation often was inaccurate.

Scenario studies have examined patient and physician decisions among patient–physician pairs and have found that physician decisions do not correlate with patients.[16] Schneiderman's review indicates that physicians would choose fewer treatments; furthermore, treatment preferences for patients correlated not with patient views but rather with their *own* desires in identical situations.[17]

Starr found that doctors also tend to underestimate preferences for treatment utilizing quality of life judgments. Starr also determined that physicians evaluate quality-of-life based on medical criteria, while their patients base it more on factors such as self-esteem and relationships.[18] In all cases, there seems to be a significant potential for physicians to misunderstand, misconstrue, or underestimate patient preferences.

Additional studies have shown that physicians will make treatment decisions based on precepts *other* than those contained in a patient's previously executed directive. Among nursing home patients, Danis[19] found that the care was consistent with directives only 75 percent of the time.

§ 8.07—Improving Provider Participation

Several interventions designed to improve provider participation in the use of advance directives have shown positive responses. Reilly[20] establishes that a regimen of physician education, reminders, and feedback elicit greater numbers of advance directives from hospital inpatients. Markson shows that education, improved patient discussions, and critique of performance increases physician performance in discussing directives.[21] Similarly, educational interventions with primary care doctors in residency training have successfully increased knowledge about (and comfort in discussing) end-of-life care.[22]

Other interventions designed to improve provider participation have not been as successful. The most notable has been the SUPPORT ("Study to Understand Prognosis and Preferences for Outcomes and Risks of Treatment")[23] project, sponsored by the Robert Wood Johnson Foundation. To learn more about end-of-life care, 10,000 seriously ill patients were followed during the early 1990s in five hospitals. Investigators worked with physicians who received information from a nurse facilitator about patient prognosis, the existence of directives, and the attitudes of both patients and proxy decision-makers about use of medical services. Despite this information, physicians were slow to respond to patient requests for "Do–Not-Resuscitate" (DNR), resulting in more days in the intensive care unit (ICU) and more aggressive treatments than patients and their proxies wanted. The SUPPORT study indicates that physician education (and the enhancement of communication between patients and doctors) may not be sufficient to ensure physician compliance with patient preferences.

Other factors not included in the SUPPORT study may have significant influence on physician decision-making. Critics recommend additional inquiry.[24]

Investigators involved in the SUPPORT and supplemental HELP ("Hospitalized Elderly Longitudinal Project") projects recently published detailed findings and conclusions.[25] Their final data supports earlier impressions: physicians often misinterpret the resuscitation preferences of seriously ill hospitalized patients, suggesting that health providers infer preferences without asking the patient.[26] Researchers concluded that (1) physicians often are unaware of the preferences of seriously ill patients and (2) care provided is not consistent with patient preferences or prognosis. They suggest that systematic approaches (rather than the simple interventions attempted in the SUPPORT project) are needed to change physician behaviors.[27]

Studies examining the employment of DNR practices in the intensive care setting show that over the past decade, physicians and families are tending to set limits for patients with poor outcomes,[28] while other studies have shown that life-sustaining care is infrequently withdrawn in ICUs. Nevertheless, such decisions are responsible for half of the deaths in ICUs.[29] Other inquiries have shown that in a university hospital setting, DNR orders are entered in an increasing number of patients, although often just prior to death.[30] Others have shown that patients often are admitted from the emergency room to intensive care units without regard to patient preferences because advance directives are lacking.[31]

Administrative changes can lead to improvements. "The Breakthrough Series Collaboration" (sponsored by the Center to Improve Care of the Dying and the Institute for Healthcare Improvement) brought together teams of individuals from a variety of health care settings to work on quality improvement (QI) activities designed to improve end of life care (including advance planning). Remarkable improvements using the PDSA cycle ("Plan-Do-Study-Act") support the validity of QI processes to stimulate change.[32]

Increasingly, medical practitioners are involving hospital ethics committees to help with difficult cases.[33] This process may help practitioners grapple with issues more effectively. For discussion, see Chapter 10, "Alternatives in the Absence of Directives."

§ 8.08 Common Professional Misconceptions

On a personal level, health care professionals may have the same misconceptions about the use of advance health care directives as do their patients (see Chapter 5, "Client Issues"). In addition, caregivers may have other knowledge gaps that relate to their professional roles. Such misconceptions often influence a professional's acceptance of the utility of directives.

Many practitioners feel that advance health care directives are legal documents that must be reviewed by an attorney to be valid. Quite the contrary: directives *may* be initiated and completed without the involvement of a lawyer. However, when confronted with client questions relating to the specific legislation, language, or relationship to other estate planning documents, the prudent medical practitioner is wise to refer the patient to his/her personal attorney.

Note well that in some states (Alabama, California, Connecticut, Georgia and Kansas, for example), attending physicians, other health care providers, and officers and employees of care facilities may be specifically prohibited from serving as agents or proxies under health care powers. However, a doctor may serve as an agent or proxy if not serving simultaneously as a care provider. (Example: a physician not involved in care may serve as proxy for, say, a relative or family friend.) Even if state statue is silent on this point, wise practitioners know that a proxy or agent can provide valuable third party objectivity and perspective. As a general rule, providers should be disinclined to serve as agents or proxies under health care powers.

§ 8.09 Barriers to Acceptance among Medical Professionals

Health care providers may have ethical or personal beliefs or experiences that conflict with advance health care directives. In addition, the following professional concerns may interfere with the practitioner's wholehearted acceptance of these documents.

Some practitioners believe that advance directives connote patient abandonment. Accordingly, some fear medical malpractice action: they worry that patients may think that their doctors are "giving up" on them.

From the first day of their medical training, doctors are taught to "do no harm." Some may interpret this as doing all that technically can be done for a patient, irrespective of the personal, economic, or emotional burdens of treatment. Some practitioners may have little professional experience with value judgments about the burdens of treatment.

Some practitioners may be of the opinion that patients (and their agents or proxies or surrogates) lack the technical knowledge and experience necessary to intelligently direct critical medical decisions. Although this opinion does not appear to be openly held by a majority of physicians, a minority may feel that medical decisions and judgments are better left solely to trained professionals. By implication, directives are to be overridden.

§ 8.10 Barriers to Implementation within the Medical Profession

§ 8.11—Professional Education

Lack of professional education appears to be a principal impediment to advance directives. Physicians with but a nodding acquaintance are less likely to educate patients than those who take the time to gain command of the subject. Some may not have sufficient training to distinguish subtle differences between various directives and may not be confident enough to educate patients. Although most physicians are well aware of the importance of directives, it appears that most can answer at best only very basic questions.

Advance directives are of course at their core legal documents. Designs vary by state. Some directives may contain obtuse phrasing or jargon; others have precise requirements for types of documentation required or allowed. Some practitioners have not studied statutorily suggested forms sufficiently to help patients effectively complete directives.

Fortunately, new Internet resources help ameliorate these difficulties. The EPEC Project ("Education for Physicians on End-of-Life Care"), which is supported by the Robert Wood Johnson Foundation and sponsored by the American Medical Association, may be accessed at www.epec.net. A similar effort, the End of Life Physician Education Resource Center (EPERC), bills itself as "a central repository for educational materials and information about end of life (EOL) issues." A joint project of the Robert Wood Johnson Foundation and the Medical College of Wisconsin, this may be viewed at www.eperc.mcw.edu.

A superb pamphlet, "Advance Care Planning: Raising End-of-Life Issues—A Communication Pocket Guide for Physicians," is sold by the Chicago-based Park Ridge Center for the Study of Health, Faith, and Ethics (www.parkridgecenter.org).

An intensive educational program sponsored by the Harvard Medical School's Center for Palliative Care promotes expertise in clinical practice and teaching of end-of-life care. Details are available through www.hms.harvard.edu/cdi/pallcare.

§ 8.12—Available Time

Another frequent impediment is lack of time. Regrettably, discussion of directives is inherently awkward and time consuming. Most will agree that the worst time for this discussion is when the patient is critically ill and in the hospital. On the other hand, clinical demands and scheduling pressures may combine to effectively preclude discussion during office visits.Perhaps discussion of directives is most appropriately couched within the context of questioning common for a general physical examination. With this type of interview, practitioners also may have more time to provide basic education.

The One-Minute Patient Intervention

Without doubt, it's exceedingly difficult to find the time to work discussions about advance health care directives into a busy clinical practice. Here's a way, perhaps, to "make the time": a one-minute patient intervention.

The key to accomplishing this is to completely skip theory and explanation while in the exam room. That's right—*don't* go by this (or any other) book. *Get straight to the main question: "Who is your health care 'deputy'?"*

Use (and adapt and modify) the following questions for this "icebreaker" intervention with patients:

- "Do you have a living will or health care power?" (The answer probably will be no. If yes, ask the patient to bring it in next time so that it can be copied or scanned for the chart.)
- "Do you have someone in mind who can make health care decisions for you if you can't?"
- "Have you spoken with that person (or anyone else) about your intentions?"
- "If you don't designate a 'deputy' to make health decisions for you, someone you don't want might step in and choose for you."
- "If you don't write down your intentions and ideas, your loved ones might end up clueless about what you want."
- "Here's some information on advance directives for you and your family to read." (Provide suitable brochure or other patient education materials.)
- Suggest attendance at an upcoming "one hour meeting": a hospital or office or video or community presentation on advance health care directives. (See Appendix K.)
- "Bring the form in next time and we (or patient with other staff) will discuss it again."
- Subsequently document substance of conversation in the patient's chart.

There you have it—the one minute intervention. Try it on just a few patients at first to gauge reactions and get a rhythm. Introduce it on a "rolling" basis: the available time for a patient encounter (and, of course, the substance of the encounter itself) dictate suitability.

It's done with all the verve and fanfare and excitement of standing around and watching cold water slowly come to a boil. But squeezing in these sixty second patient interventions—one at a time, over months and years—probably is the surest way to get directives to "take" among your patients.

Even within the context of a comprehensive health care interview, few practitioners will have sufficient time to discuss fully all facets of advance directives: the detailed explanations required, plus the attendant (and weighty) philosophical and values discussions, preclude it. By at least introducing the topic and sketching out some of the ramifications, patients may come away with greater awareness. Directives may, if desired, also be discussed in stages over a course of visits. (See sidebars, "One Minute" and "Ten Minute Patient Interventions," this chapter.)

§ 8.13—Opportunities for Patient Education

Make a point of providing patients with forms and instructions. Medical societies, hospitals, and bar associations are excellent sources for brochures that are at once thoughtful, tasteful, and authoritative. Keep a supply with patient education materials. Maintain a display in the patient reception area. For that matter, exhibit brochures in exam rooms. If a patient has one in hand upon your arrival for a consultation, it is an obvious cue.

A comprehensive conversation about advance health care directives—from introduction to a line-by-line discussion of a document to execution—may take upwards of an hour. Physicians are not accustomed to performing or billing for this level of detailed health education. Let's be realistic: insurers and other indemnitors (Medicare, Medicaid) won't pay for it either. Practitioner time can be utilized more effectively by arranging group presentations and by training staff to provide one-on-one discussions. Distributing brochures and forms in advance will help.

Most health care powers and proxies afford patients an option to specify medical treatments they want or don't want. Those desiring this feature may require extra coaching and education from their health care provider. For example, a patient wishing to avoid long-term ventilator care probably should *not* write in a categorical exclusion of "vents." What if short-term ventilator treatment is later required for a self-limiting condition like post-operative recovery? The same can be said for short-term dialysis, tube feedings, and minor surgery.

Practitioners may find patients to be ambivalent about directives. This ambivalence may stem from misconceptions about their use (e.g., "If I have a directive, does that mean there's no hope for me?"). Again, education by stages may be the most effective approach. Providing increments of information and encouraging patients to revisit the issue at a future time may be all that is required. The goal is not to talk patients out of their values or convictions—it is to provide them with adequate information to make informed decisions. Remember, there is no "right way" with advance directives. Help patients tailor-make medical instructions that mirror *their* personal values.

The undercurrents of emotion accompanying discussion of advance directives—and the cultural and ethnic differences in perception described in Chapter 5 and mentioned below—make group presentations problematical enough. Don't compound the difficulty by inadvertently alienating audiences with medical and legal jargon. An overview of the rationale for use of directives, coupled with a "walk through" of pertinent documents, makes for a good basic presentation. After a break, reconvene for those who want to stay and fill out directives step-by-step. Answer audience questions as you go

---

The Ten-Minute Patient Intervention

Once again, it's counterintuitive—but the ten-minute patient intervention probably works best *after* both the one minute and one hour (i.e., community education on advance directives—Appendix K) interventions. Fit in this final step as scheduling permits.

There are two types of ten-minute interventions: one where the patient brings in a completed directive, and one where the directive is not yet finished.

A.   Patient Brings in Directive
- Is it complete? If not, the patient should fill in blanks and check off appropriate boxes. Guide and advise.
- Clarify the level of care requested. If more detail is indicated or required, provide a values history form such as the one in Appendix D.
- Has the patient discussed the directive with the designated agent or proxy and shared a copy?
- Admonish the patient about "good footprints." (See the sidebar on page 61).
- Make multiple copies for the patient and retain one for the patient's chart.
- Provide a pocket card (Appendix O).
- Raise the possibility of organ donation. Offer to witness "on the spot" the signing of the back of a driver's license.
- Point out that directives typically run *only* to health care decisions and that patients also need to consider how *financial* decisions are to be made in the event of incapacity. Suggest that they contact their lawyers if they have questions about this.
- Document discussion in the chart.

B.   Directive Not Completed
- Answer questions and guide discussion about the nature of directives. Probe for misconceptions.

(continued)

along. (See Appendix K for a suggested outline for a community education presentation.)

§ 8.14—Questions about Capacity

Note well that decisionally-incapacitated patients are *not* candidates for advance health care directives. Patients who have marginal mental capacity or who have been adjudicated as decisionally impaired may or may not be

---

- Explore possible barriers to implementation (cultural, religious, etc.) and address if possible.
- Assist with completion if requested. If unsigned, procure a disinterested witness or witnesses. As above, retain one copy and provide the patient with extras for "footprints."
- Schedule follow-up as needed. Pointedly channel issues and questions for future consideration and provide these to the patient (in writing, if possible) to minimize chances for redundant or open-ended discussions.
- As appropriate, encourage the assistance of family, friends, clergy, lawyers and any concerned others.
- A reminder: some states forbid attending physicians—and, in some instances, other health care providers and their employees—from personally serving as agent or proxy (or as a witness to a power or proxy), even if the patient pointedly requests it. Check applicable statutes. Even if this is not the case in your jurisdiction, consider both the appearances and the pragmatics: an independent third party can provide exceedingly valuable perspective in considering treatment options for an uncomprehending patient. In other words—shy away from even the appearance of a possible conflict of interest, and refrain from serving simultaneously as proxy and provider.
- Document the encounter in the chart.

These ten minute interventions are *extra investments of time* in your patients. Make certain that they understand and respect this. Use appropriate subtle (and, if necessary, not-so-subtle) cues to indicate that this is all the time you can personally "ration" for them on the subject. During the one minute and one hour interventions (as well as at the outset of the ten minutes themselves), raise the specter of limited time allotment so that patients can anticipate and budget accordingly.

Advance health care directives require a lot of thought. "Incubate" patient thinking with one minute, one hour, and, finally, ten minute interventions.

candidates, depending on the consistency of their interest, the practitioner's knowledge of their prior health care decisions and values, and governing statutory and case law. (See Chapter 4, "Competence and Incompetence.")

Marginally capable individuals (including maturing minors) should participate to the greatest degree possible in decisions regarding their own health care. When in doubt about a patient's capacity to render informed consents, seek second opinions from other practitioners. Family members and friends may provide valuable perspective.

If a patient has a judicially appointed guardian, it may be necessary to petition a court for authorization for the guardian to consent to care. This is particularly likely if invasive treatments are contemplated. Note the nuance here. Typically, a judge will not directly order doctors to treat. The court will instead empower the guardian: she or he will be authorized to consult with physicians and consent, if warranted, to recommended treatments.

§ 8.15—Cultural/Ethnic/Spiritual Barriers

Research has established the existence of cultural and ethnic differences in both the understanding of and approach to advance health care directives. Practitioners do well to gain as much information as possible about cultural variations within their communities (see Chapter 5, "Client Issues" and Chapter 9, "Involvement of Spiritual Advisors"). Properly approached, misconceptions might be better addressed and concerns resolved. Recent studies of white, African American, and Hispanic individuals show that disinclination to complete health care directives may be influenced by (1) lack of knowledge and (2) perceived irrelevance of need for a health proxy if family is involved. Education specifically addressing these issues may result in increased completion of health care proxies.[34]

§ 8.16—Conflicts

Not all medical professionals are alike in their recognition of the value of health care directives. If a primary care physician, primary support staff, and specialty providers do not agree with the concept or implementation of a directive, the care may be at best fragmented and confusing to the patient and the family.

For example, some surgical teams (anesthesiologists in particular) compel patients to stipulate in writing that any DNR instructions contained in a directive are to be overridden or held in abeyance until after the patient has recovered. Team conferences may help bring issues into the open for full discussion. In situations where unresolved conflict exists among health care providers, ethics consultation may be an appropriate solution.

Fearing that they may be required to perform acts contrary to their religious or moral convictions, some practitioners may be understandably reluctant to initiate discussions about advance directives. Many state statutes anticipate this contingency. A doctor need not take steps (e.g., remove life support) that are contrary or repugnant to her or his personal beliefs. A physician may instead resign or withdraw from care once a willing successor is found. (Note well that unless a willing successor physician is first procured, discontinuation of care could be construed as patient abandonment.)

In a similar vein, practitioners who have had long standing relationships with patients and families may find it difficult to remain detached from or objective about a patient's decision to withdraw from aggressive treatment. When a practitioner's emotions conflict with a patient's stated preferences, the provider should offer to withdraw.

Other conflicts may arise within the patient–physician relationship. Doctors must not honor requests for euthanasia: the practice is categorically outlawed in all U.S. jurisdictions. See Appendix I regarding the limited and highly controlled "carveout" of the Oregon Death with Dignity Act.

Likewise, practitioners may object to patient, agent, proxy, or surrogate requests or recommendations for patently futile medical treatments. Professional ethics do not compel a physician to provide futile care. The American Medical Association Code of Medical Ethics suggests "Denial of treatment should be justified by reliance on openly stated ethical principles and acceptable standards of care . . . not on the concept of 'futility' which cannot be meaningfully defined."[35] Conflicts relating to patient and family requests for futile care are more often related to miscommunication or lack of knowledge.

Know that many jurisdictions have prospectively addressed the issue of medical futility and medically ineffective treatment in their statutes. Examples include:

- California. "A health care provider or health care institution may decline to comply with an individual health care instruction or health care decision that requires medically ineffective health care or health care contrary to generally accepted health care standards applicable to the health care provider or institution."[36]
- Maryland. Subject to a caveat regarding pendancy of provider withdrawal from care, ". . . nothing in this subtitle may be construed to require a physician to prescribe or render medically ineffective treatment."[37]
- Nevada. Applicable sections of Nevada law ". . . do not require a physician or other provider of health care to take action contrary to reasonable medical standards."[38]

When conflicts occur, practitioners may make use of hospital ethics committees to mediate discussions and arbitrate differences. If not resolved, a doctor may state preferences and withdraw from treatment as soon as another physician may be substituted.

Prior to withdrawal, practitioners should state their inability or disinclination to carry out patient or proxy wishes and allow open discussion about why they could not or would not comply or conform. Appropriate chart notations indicating formal withdrawal and substitution—ideally consented to and countersigned by the patient or agent or surrogate, or by a witness observing oral consent—should be made. Naturally, the "old" physician should, with patient/proxy consent, brief the "new" doctor and provide copies of all pertinent clinical information, including reports of laboratory and diagnostic tests.

Conflict with and among patient families may present the most challenging obstacle to implementation of a directive. During a health care crisis, latent hostilities may accelerate into venal and vicious arguments, leading family members to challenge the validity of a directive or the authority of a designated agent or proxy. A doctor may unwittingly become the focus for transference of pent up rage or guilt by grieving (or, worse, conniving and manipulative) family.

Practitioners must be alert to those who may be exerting influence (unintentionally or otherwise) in the initiation and design of another's health care directive. Remember, it is the patient—not an adult child or other third party who may be accompanying the patient—who needs to direct the terms of the document. More often than not, a family member has only the best of motivations: he or she wants a loved one to give written expression and effect to the patient's own health care wishes. Make a point, however, of visiting with the patient privately to ascertain or verify intentions.

When confronted with family strife, health care providers do well to make use of social service professionals and clergy to help negotiate conflict. Resort to legal processes (such as judicial construction of a directive, or appointment of a guardian) *only* when all other attempts at resolution have failed.

§ 8.17—Weaknesses of the Patient Self-Determination Act

The federal Patient Self Determination Act (Appendix A) mandates that patients in Medicare/Medicaid-funded entities (e.g., hospitals, nursing facilities, hospices, home health care) be provided at the time of contact with information about content and availability of state-specific directives. This is a start toward implementation. From a practical standpoint, it may be, unfortunately, a false start. There are many procedural barriers to implementation.

The first barrier is haphazard implementation of the law. Often, the task falls to admissions personnel who may, through no fault of their own, have but cursory instruction on the subject from superiors. Directives sometimes are included in myriad admissions documents without explanation and end up being put aside. Staff may be utterly misinformed: completion of directives is *not* compulsory and is *not* a federally-mandated condition for admission to a facility. Occasionally, executed directives do not get tagged for inclusion in the chart and end up "lost," thereby rendering the exercise pointless and futile.

Another principal barrier is the condition of the patient. Presentation of directives at admission may be the absolutely worst time: the patient may be in shock or delirious with pain, or judgment may be temporarily impaired or clouded by medications or the underlying illness or injury itself. On occasion, no administrative mechanism exists for going over directives with a stabilized patient later during the hospital stay: if directives aren't introduced at admission, they aren't introduced at all.

§ 8.18—Difficulty Determining Prognosis

The lack of reliable prognostic factors to identify with certainty those patients who are terminally or critically ill can be another impediment. For some patients, the initiation of discussion about directives will be based only on the physician's estimate of prognosis. Practitioners may be uncomfortable with limited data available to define prognosis for each individual and, therefore, may not be willing to discuss directives with patients unless prompted by their questions or concerns. Christakis and Lamont indicate that physician assessments of prognoses for terminally ill patients often are inaccurate—and, generally, optimistically so.[39] Furthermore, physicians reported that they offer frank estimates only 37% of the time.[40] The previously discussed SUPPORT and HELP interventions[41] have prompted calls for future investigations utilizing prognostic models for survival and functional status.

§ 8.19—Limited Use of Protocols for Providers

Staff education—specifically, the lack of it—may be the most imposing barrier of all. Most institutions do not require that practitioners follow a guideline or protocol for initiation or implementation of directives. There may be little in the way of formal direction, education, or support for providers assigned with the task.

§ 8.20—Poor Footprints

Perhaps the most exasperating barrier is the "no footprints" phenomenon, when a patient purportedly has directives but no one knows their whereabouts. Incredibly, family and friends sometimes know about directives but fail to either mention them or present them to the medical team. (The moral? Ask if they exist.) Properly executed directives may not make it to the hospital when the patient is transferred from home or a nursing home (and vice versa).

Impress upon patients that medical professionals, family, caregivers, and emergency personnel are not mind readers, and that the best-crafted directives are utterly worthless if the patient fails to leave good footprints. Patients need to take some or all of the following protective steps:

- Provide copies to treating physicians and institutions
- Provide copies to the agent or proxy
- Tell family and friends that directives have been executed and where they are
- Carry a card in a wallet or purse, or wear a medallion or bracelet that indicates the existence of directives and where they are
- Keep copies at home and work where they may be easily found
- Use a registry service (hospital, nonprofit agency, governmental agency, and/or online service)
- Implement better designed charting systems and patient databases that electronically flag the existence of directives (see Chapter 11, "The Future of Advance Directives").

Please refer to the Chapter 5 sidebar "Leaving Good Footprints" (page 60).

§ 8.21 Legal Issues

Directives are, at their core, legal documents. Note, however, an intriguing dichotomy: advance health care directives are much more commonly seen in medical settings than in courts.

This is as it should be—medical decisions are intensely private matters and are best left to patients, *assisted by* physicians. Proxies, agents, surrogates, and families stand by to "step into patient shoes" in the event of decisional or communicative incapacity. If anything, the courts are ill-equipped to handle high volumes of health care decision-making cases.

Health care providers should always keep in mind that even in the most conflicted treatment situation, judicial processes are *invariably* the last resort. The emotional and financial tolls can be enormous. The delays can be significant. Considerable clinical time may be lost to testifying in court. The legal remedies (even if achieved) may be clumsy, intrusive, overbearing, and counterproductive. Litigation may be harmful to a patient, who may inadvertently be subjected to unnecessary pain and suffering as the proceedings take their course. Doctors don't want to litigate health care. Patients don't want it. And guess what—lawyers and judges probably don't want it, either.

If compelled to file a court case to have a judge construe a health care power or proxy, or to have a guardian appointed for a patient, or if subpoenaed or called as a witness, or if sued, here is what to do:

- Don't speak with *anybody* until you've spoken with counsel.
- Tell *all* to your lawyer . . . in private.
- Don't volunteer anything to anyone else . . . ever.
- Be polite to all parties . . . even when it hurts.
- Make yourself fully available at all times to your legal team.
- Conserve clinical time by suggesting to your attorney sworn affidavits or in-office depositions in lieu of court testimony.

§ 8.22 Countermanding or Overriding Patient Directives or Instructions of Agents

In a word—DON'T. Your patient (and/or family) will have grounds to sue you for battery and intentional infliction of severe emotional distress, among other things. (See the discussion in Chapter 7, "The Lawyer Perspective").

If you disagree with the treatments specified in a patient directive, or with the course of action requested by an agent or proxy or surrogate or family, find a willing successor physician first and then resign. Never take it upon yourself to unilaterally treat contrary to patient (or agent/proxy) wishes. Ethics committees are especially helpful in this situation.

It is very important to observe that a physician must first procure a willing successor acceptable to the patient before withdrawing. Absent continuity of care, the resigning doctor risks a claim of patient abandonment. Prepare a one page resignation—and go easy on the reasons (if you must state reasons at all). Leave room for the "new" doctor to acknowledge by signature acceptance of the case and for the patient (or agent/proxy) to sign in consent. Perhaps this can be done directly in the chart.

§ 8.23 Tailoring Clinical Situations to Directives

Doctors can perform an invaluable service by helping patients with chronic conditions develop directives that are clinically correlated with their illnesses.

In other words, the disease can dictate the directive. A patient in renal failure needs to focus on desired parameters for dialysis. Pulmonary patients need to articulate the terms and scope of ventilator treatments, and so forth.

Here is a partial list of illnesses, along with some of the treatments that might be addressed in a directive. Detailed statements of desired treatment parameters need not be written into a directive. As an alternative, these expressions may be made part of an accompanying values history or other statement, and expressly incorporated by reference into the advance health care directive (see Appendix D and Appendix E):

- **Cardiac conditions**: Pacemaker? Cardiopulmonary resuscitation?
- **Cancer**: Radiation? Chemotherapy? Surgery at end-stage? Bone marrow transplantation? Mastectomy/lumpectomy? Hydration? Transfusions?
- **Renal disease**: Dialysis?
- **Mental illness:** Psychotropic medications? Electroconvulsive therapy? Institutionalization?
- **Pulmonary illness**. CPR? Ventilator? Intravenous antibiotics?
- **Alzheimer's Disease and other dementing illnesses**: Consent to trials of new medications? Artificial hydration/nutrition at end stage?
- **Neurological conditions:** (Parkinson's, multiple sclerosis, amyotrophic lateral sclerosis, etc.), Artificial hydration/nutrition? Respiratory support?

Although specific information can be helpful to surrogate decision-makers, patients should not articulate their preferences dogmatically. Details should be used to illustrate general values or philosophy. The patient may add an additional statement encouraging the agent to make use of the information and later modify it in accordance with changes in health status that might not be foreseen.

Tips for Practitioners

Here's a short list of important considerations for health care professionals on the subject of advance health care directives:

- Explore your own understanding and attitudes concerning advance health care directives. Directives may or may not appeal to you personally. But now you arguably have some obligation to your patients on the subject. Either become somewhat conversant about directives, or be able to readily refer questions and discussion to a knowledgeable source. The more educated practitioners become about directives, the more likely they are to talk about them. And the more they get talked about, the more likely patients are to commit to having them.
- For better or worse, studies show that patients look to their doctors and other health care professionals to initiate discussions about directives. You're an authority figure. Your say-so or assertion about the value of directives may be just the bit of impetus patients need—indeed, want—to go ahead and execute them.
- Select the right patient. Directives aren't for everyone: don't proselytize. Know, too, that cultural and ethnic issues abound; work to become sensitive about them. The next (and dispositive) issue is capacity. Simply put, it's this: no capacity, no directives. Advance health care directives may *only* be prepared contemplatively, by a person of legal or statutory age who is cognizant of the choices at hand. That said, be ever mindful of the expressions (limited as they may be) and needs of the decisionally impaired who are for whatever reason foreclosed from employing directives. To the extent that these individuals can (with the assistance of a surrogate or guardian) articulate some choices, strive very hard to accommodate and honor them to the greatest extent possible.
- In addition to selecting the right patient, assess the patient. Does she or he understand a given prognosis? What are the patient's life values? Does the patient have trust in the provider relationship?
- Select the right tone. Emphasize the patient autonomy aspect of directives: they are tailor-making personal contingency plans on their own

(continued)

§ 8.24 The Ever–Changing Continuum of Health Care Directives

Here are two final thoughts about advance health care directives from a clinical standpoint.

First, directives are not forever. Patient interests, attitudes, and needs change. Prognoses can change. At some future time, medical advances may

---

terms. Suggest in turn that patients take special care to select the right agent or proxy: this choice can literally make or break a directive.

- Select the best time and place. It's very difficult to work discussions about directives into a busy medical practice. A complete physical may present the most opportune clinical setting. Otherwise, initiate and conduct discussions in increments over a series of consultations; refer details to staff.
- Select patient education opportunities. Get on the local public service "lecture circuit": hospitals, libraries, clubs, adult education programs, senior centers, municipal governments, and the like always are looking for prescient presentations—and they know that health professionals draw audiences! Offer to be interviewed on local radio and television. Get the word out in writing, too—waiting and examination room pamphlets, inserts in bills and other mailings, discussions in office or hospital newsletters and websites, patient education materials, newspaper columns, and so forth. How about a video for the waiting room? If you are committed to directives—spread the word.
- Select an education strategy. Directives are tricky; begin by providing the pros and cons of the directives available in your state. "Walk through" the general layouts of state-suggested forms. Discuss briefly areas where documents may be customized (such as general values statements, specific information and instructions on treatments to be provided or withheld, and selection of agent or proxy). Emphasize the "good footprints" principles: list all telephone numbers, etc., for reaching the proxy and disseminate data on where directives may be found. (See the sidebar in Chapter 5.) Send the patient out with written materials, including draft forms for directives. Follow up on status of the document at the next visit. For details and ideas on patient education and community presentations, refer to Appendix K.
- Legal issues? Once all medical questions and issues have been addressed, be exceedingly conservative: suggest that patients retain knowledgeable counsel if they need it.
- By the way—have you filled out your OWN directives yet?

altogether obviate certain treatments—or may yet curb or mitigate or even cure given illnesses.

Accordingly, it is perfectly appropriate for patients to revoke directives from time to time and write new ones. Encourage (rather than discourage) this, especially among patients who have encountered a profound change in their circumstances—a pronounced deterioration (or improvement) in medical condition, or the loss of a trusted agent or proxy, or a divorce or other life change.

In such instances, encourage patients to locate and destroy copies of all "old" directives. Also suggest the insertion of a line in the "new" directive to this effect: "I hereby revoke all other advance health care directives I have previously made." In short, revocation and re-execution of directives probably should, over time, be considered the norm rather than the exception.

The second point is the occasional need for agents and proxies to extrapolate or interpolate patient wishes. It is utterly impossible to anticipate every medical contingency. What is to be done when the clinical issue at hand does not fit the directive, or if the directive is altogether silent on an important treatment issue?

Many form or statutory directives contain a section that permits a patient to pick a generalized or thematic level of treatment. These "elastic clauses" are one of the most important aspects of the document: agents/proxies can discern or divine from it at least some of the direction they need. (The rest may come from personal knowledge, values histories, recollections of family and friends, and the like.)

One of the most kind and gracious services a clinician can provide in such a circumstance is guidance to an agent on how a decisionally-incapacitated patient's "elastic" statement comports with various treatment possibilities. Don't inadvertently make the agent render awkward (if not excruciatingly difficult) treatment decisions in a clinical vacuum. If anything, an agent or proxy or surrogate likely is engulfed in an undertow of emotions, especially if end-of-life decisions are about to be made. Advise, sympathize—and gently encourage.

§ 8.25 Critique of Case Study

There are no easy answers for Mirth Green's plight. Her primary care doctor might have been of more help in gently and diplomatically raising the issue from time to time – particularly with each hospital admission. ("Mirth, you *will* have a clinical crisis at some point—what do you want done when it happens?") Similarly, the pulmonologist might have raised the "future crisis" idea. Try posing the issue in as neutral a way as possible: "Mirth, if things go downhill really fast—that's IF—what would you think of the idea of having a machine help you breathe? What if the machine—the ventilator—was to help just for a little while? What would you want if the only way we could keep you breathing was with the ventilator full time?"

§ 8.26 Conclusion

Many patients wish to articulate their concerns about end-of-life care to their health care providers. However, practitioners are constantly under pressure to function under conflicting mandates: they are to provide increasingly efficient, more comprehensive, higher quality care while simultaneously minimizing medical time and resources. Indeed, compressed or rationed time allotments for myriad clinical issues (be they acute, chronic, psychosocial, environmental, or preventive) can effectively defer (if not altogether foreclose) discussions with patients about advance directives.

To the extent that these organizational and programmatic difficulties can be overcome, practitioners will find that exploration of patient preferences for end-of-life care—and attendant employment of advance health care directives—can offer illuminating opportunities to learn and share in the values, goals and vulnerabilities of their charges. In the intimacy of the clinical setting, many dedicated practitioners may yet come to more fully experience the privileges and pleasures of being healers—and will with quiet delight come to rekindle some of the reasons why they came to the healing professions in the first place.

Notes

1. E. Gamble, P. McDonald, & P. Lichstein, *Knowledge, Attitudes, and Behaviors of Elderly Persons Regarding Living Will*, 151 ARCHIVES INTERNAL MED. 277 (1991).
2. K. Davidson et al., *Physician Attitudes on Advance Directives*, 262 JAMA 2415 (1989); L. Brunetti, S. Carperos, & R. Westlund, *Physicians Attitudes Toward Living Wills and Cardiopulmonary Resuscitation*, 6 J. GEN. INTERNAL MED. 323 (1991).
3. M. Gillick, K. Hesse, & N. Mazzapica, *Medical Technology at the End of Life: What Would Physicians and Nurses Want for Themselves?* 153 ARCHIVES INTERNAL MED. 2542 (1993).
4. *Id.*; J. Stechmiller, M. Conlon, & G. Cranston Anderson, *Selected Characteristics of Nurses and Physicians Who Have Living Wills*, 15 DEATH STUDIES 119 (1991).
5. M. Mezey et al., *Implementation of the PSDA in Nursing Homes in New York City,* 45 J. AM. GERIATRICS SOC'Y 43 (1997); H. Silverman, S. Fry, & N. Armistead, *Nurses' Perspective on Implementation of the Patient Self-Determination Act,* 5 J. CLINICAL ETHICS 30 (1994).
6. C. Klem, *Attitudes of Direct Care Staff in Home Healthcare Toward Advance Directives,* 12 HOME HEALTHCARE NURSE 55 (1994); E. Perry et al., *Dialysis Staff Influence Patients in Formulating Their Advance Directives,* 25 AM. J. KIDNEY DISEASES 262 (1995); J. Davitt & L. Kaye, *Supporting Patient Autonomy: Decision Making: Decision Making in Home Health Care,* 41 SOCIAL WORK 41 (1996); J. Heffner, B. Fahy, & C. Barbieri, *Advance Directive Education During Pulmonary Rehabilitation,* 109 CHEST 373 (1996); J. Heffner & C. Barbieri, *Involvement of Cardiovascular Rehabilitation Programs and Advance Directive Education,* 156 ARCHIVES INTERNAL MED. 1746 (1996).

7. R. Morrison, E. Morrison, & D. Glickman, *Physician Reluctance to Discuss Advance Directives an Empiric Investigation of Potential Barriers,* 154 ARCHIVES INTERNAL MED. 2311 (1994).
8. D. Doukas, D Gorenflo, & S. Coughlin, *The Living Will: A National Survey,* 23 FAMILY MED. 354 (1991).
9. G. Gordon & S. Tolle, *Discussing Life-Sustaining Treatment: A Teaching Program for Residents,* 151 ARCHIVES INTERNAL MED. 567 (1991).
10. L. Brunetti et al., *supra* note 2.
11. *Id.*; L. Schneiderman et al., *Do Physicians' Own Preferences for Life-Sustaining Influence Their Perceptions of Patients' Preferences?,* 4 J. CLINICAL ETHICS 28 (1993).
12. E. Mebane et al., *The Influence of Physician Race, Age, and Gender on Physician Attitudes Toward Advance Care Directives and Preferences for End-Of-Life Decision Making,* 47 J. AM. GERIATRICS SOC'Y 5 (1999).
13. L. Brunetti et al., *supra* note 2; S. Dorr Goold, R. Arnold, & L. Siminoff, *Discussion About Limiting Treatment in a Geriatric Clinic,* 41 J. AM. GERIATRICS SOC'Y 277 (1993); R. Morrison et al., *supra* note 7.
14. Dorr Goold, Arnold, & Siminoff, *supra* note 13; L. Blackhall, J. Cobb, & M. Moskowitz, *Discussions Regarding Aggressive Care with Critically Ill Patients,* 4 J. GEN. INTERNAL MED. 399 (1989).
15. S. Bedell & T. Delbanco, *Choices About Cardiopulmonary Resuscitation in the Hospital: When Do Physicians Talk with Patients?,* 310 NEW ENG. J. MED. 1089 (1984).
16. J. Teno et al., *Preferences for Cardiopulmonary Resuscitation: Physician-Patient Agreement and Hospital Resource Use,* 10 J. GEN. INTERNAL MED. 179 (1995); L. Schneiderman et al., *supra* note 11; T. Starr, R. Pearlman, & R. Uhlmann, *Quality of Life and Resuscitation Decisions in Elderly Patients,* 1 J. GEN. INTERNAL MED. 373 (1986).
17. L. Schneiderman et al., *supra* note 11.
18. T. Starr et al., *supra* note 16.
19. M. Danis et al., *A Prospective Study of Advance Directives for Life-Sustaining Care,* 324 NEW ENG. J. MED. 882 (1991).
20. B. Reilly et al., *Can We Talk? Inpatient Discussions About Advance Directives in a Community Hospital,* 154 ARCHIVES INTERNAL MED. 2299 (1994); B. Reilly et al., *Promoting Inpatient Directives About Life-Sustaining Treatments in a Community Hospital,* 155 ARCHIVES INTERNAL MED. 2317 (1995).
21. L. Markson et al., *Implementing Advance Directives in the Primary Care Setting,* 154 ARCHIVES INTERNAL MED. 2321 (1994).
22. G. Gordon & S. Tolle, *supra* note 9; J. Kvale et al., *Factors Associated with Residents' Attitudes Toward Dying Patients,* 31 FAMILY MED. 10 (1999).
23. SUPPORT Principal Investigators, *A Controlled Trial to Improve Care for Seriously Ill Hospitalized Patients,* 274 JAMA 1591 (1995).
24. J. Teno et al., *Do Formal Advance Directives Affect Resuscitation Decisions and the Use of Resources for Seriously Ill Patients?,* 5 J. CLINICAL ETHICS 23 (1994); J. Sugarman, *Outcomes Research and Advance Directives,* 5 J. CLINICAL ETHICS 60 (1994); D. Brock, *Advance Directives: What Is Reasonable to Expect from Them?,* 5 J. CLINICAL ETHICS 57 (1994).
25. R. Phillips et al., *Findings from SUPPORT and HELP: An Introduction,* 48 J. AM. GERIATRICS SOC'Y S1 (2000).

26. N. Wenger et al., *Physician Understanding of Patient Resuscitation Preferences: Insights and Clinical Implications,* 48 J. Am. Geriatrics Soc'y S44 (2000).

27. K Covinsky et al., *Communication and Decision-Making in Seriously Ill Patients: Findings of the SUPPORT Project,* 48 J. Am. Geriatrics Soc'y S187 (2000).

28. R. Jayes et al., *Do-Not-Resuscitate Orders in Intensive Care Units Current Practices and Recent Changes,* 270 JAMA 2213 (1993).

29. N. Smedira et al., *Withholding and Withdrawal of Life Support from the Critically Ill,* 322 New Eng. J. Med. 309 (1990).

30. K. Gleeson & S. Wise, *The Do-Not-Resuscitate Order: Still Too Little Too Late.* 150 Archives Internal Med. 1057 (1990).

31. L. Hanson & M. Danis, *Emergency Triage to Intensive Care: Can We Use Prognosis and Patient Preferences?,* 42 J. Am. Geriatrics Soc'y 1277 (1994).

32. J. Lynn et al., *Improving Care for the End of Life,* Oxford University Press, New York, 2000, pp. 73–90.

33. Brennan, *Ethics Committees and Decisions to Limit Care,* 260 JAMA 803 (1988); H. Perkins, *Clinical Ethics Consultations: Reasons for Optimism but Problems Exist,* 3 J. Clinical Ethics 133 (1992); J. La Puma et al., *How Ethics Consultation Can Help Resolve Dilemmas About Dying Patients,* 163 West J Med 263 (1995).

34. R. Morrison et al., *Barriers to Completion of Health Care Proxies: An Examination of Ethnic Differences,* 158 Archives Internal Med. 2493 (1998).

35. American Med. Ass'n Council on Ethical & Judicial Affairs, Code of Medical Ethics, Current Opinions with Annotations § 2.035 (1997).

36. Cal. Probate Code § 4735

37. Md. Health Code Ann. § 5-611(b).

38. Nev. Rev. Stat. § 449.670

39. N. Christakis et al., *Extent and determinants of error in doctors' prognoses in terminally ill patients: prospective cohort study,* 320 British Medical Journal 469 (2000); *N. Christakis, Death Foretold: Prophecy and Prognosis in Medical Care,* University of Chicago Press, Chicago, 2000, pp. 84–134.

40. E. Lamont et al., *Prognostic Disclosure to Patients with Cancer near the End of Life,* 134 Annals Internal Med. 1096 (2001).

41. A.W. Wu et al., *Predicting Functional Status Outcomes in Hospitalized Patients 80 Years and Older,* 48 J Am. Geriatrics Soc'y S6 (2000); J. Teno et al., *Prediction of Survival for Older Hospitalized Patients: The HELP Survival Model,* 48 J. Am. Geriatrics Soc'y S16 (2000).

CHAPTER 9

Involvement of Clergy and Spiritual Advisors

§ 9.01 Introduction

On the night of April 15, 1975, for reasons still unclear, K.Q. ceased breathing for at least two 15 minute periods. She received some ineffectual mouth-to-mouth resuscitation from friends. . . . (E)xpert physicians who (subsequently) examined her characterized K.Q. as being in a "chronic persistent vegetative state." . . .

The record bespeaks the high degree of familial love which pervaded the home of K.Q.'s father, J.Q., and reached out fully to embrace K.Q., although she was living elsewhere at the time of her collapse. The proofs showed him to be deeply religious, imbued with a morality so sensitive that months of tortured indecision preceded his belated conclusion (despite earlier moral judgments reached by the other family members, but unexpressed to him in order not to influence him) to seek the termination of life-supportive measures sustaining K.Q. A communicant of the Roman Catholic Church, as were other family members, he first sought solace in private prayer looking with confidence, as he says, to the Creator, first for recovery of K.Q. and then, if that were not possible, for guidance with respect to the awesome decision confronting him.

To confirm the moral rightness of the decision he was about to make he consulted with his parish priest and later with the Catholic chaplain of S.C. Hospital. He would not, he testified, have sought termination if that act were to be morally wrong or in conflict with the tenets of the religion he so profoundly respects. He was disabused of doubt, however, when the position of the Roman Catholic Church was made known to him as it is reflected in the record in this case.

[The amicus brief of Bishop C.]. validated the decision of J.Q.:

(T)he decision of J.Q. to request the discontinuance of this treatment (of K.Q.) is, according to the teachings of the Catholic Church, a morally correct decision.

The right to a natural death is one outstanding area in which the disciplines of theology, medicine and law overlap; or, to put it another way, it is an area in which these three disciplines convene.

Medicine with its combination of advanced technology and professional ethics is both able and inclined to prolong biological life. Law with its felt obligation to protect the life and freedom of the individual seeks to assure each person's right to live out his human life until its natural and inevitable conclusion. Theology with its acknowledgment of man's dissatisfaction with biological life as the ultimate source of joy... defends the sacredness of human life and defends it from all direct attacks.

These disciplines do not conflict with one another, but are necessarily conjoined in the application of their principles in a particular instance such as that of K.Q. Each must in some way acknowledge the other without denying its own competence. The civil law is not expected to assert a belief in eternal life; nor, on the other hand, is it expected to ignore the right of the individual to profess it, and to form and pursue his conscience in accord with that belief. Medical science is not authorized to directly cause natural death; nor, however, is it expected to prevent it when it is inevitable and all hope of a return to an even partial exercise of human life is irreparably lost. Religion is not expected to define biological death; nor, on its part, is it expected to relinquish its responsibility to assist man in the formation and pursuit of a correct conscience as to the acceptance of natural death when science has confirmed its inevitability beyond any hope other than that of preserving biological life in a merely vegetative state.

It is both possible and necessary for society to have laws and ethical standards which provide freedom for decisions, in accord with the expressed or implied intentions of the patient, to terminate or withhold extraordinary treatment in cases which are judged to be hopeless by competent medical authorities, without at the same time leaving an opening for euthanasia. Indeed, to accomplish this, it may simply be required that courts and legislative bodies recognize the present standards and practices of many people engaged in medical care who have been doing what the parents of K.Q. are requesting authorization to have done for their beloved daughter.

(W)e feel it essential to reiterate that the "Catholic view" of religious neutrality in the circumstances of this case is considered by the Court only in the aspect of its impact upon the conscience, motivation and purpose of the intending guardian (of K.Q.), J.Q., and not as a precedent in terms of the civil law.

If J.Q., for instance, were a follower and strongly influenced by the teachings of Buddha, or if, as an agnostic or atheist, his moral judgments were formed without reference to religious feelings, but were nevertheless formed and viable, we would with equal attention and high respect consider these elements, as bearing upon his character, motivations and purposes as relevant to his qualification and suitability as guardian (of his daughter, K.Q.)

By now, many readers will have guessed correctly: the foregoing was adapted from *Matter of Quinlan*, 355 A.2d 647, 70 N.J. 10, cert. denied *sub nom, Garger v. New Jersey*, 429 U.S. 922 (1976). K.Q. refers to Karen Ann Quinlan and J.Q. to her father Joseph.

Few recall today that the case was inured with achingly poignant moral and religious questions. Readers surely will agree that the amicus brief cited above, as extensively quoted by the Supreme Court of New Jersey in its decision, still rings clear. It was submitted by Bishop Lawrence B. Casey of the New Jersey Catholic Conference.

§ 9.02 The Benefits of a Multidisciplinary Approach

Decisions related to death and dying—and the advance health care directives that may contemplatively come to mirror these decisions—are significantly affected by closely held philosophical and spiritual beliefs.

Patients and clients grappling with directives likely need more assistance than health practitioners and lawyers alone are able to provide: many may wish to have help from spiritual advisors, clergy, social workers, palliative caregivers, mental health providers, and others.

A multidisciplinary approach to directives can result in remarkable intrinsic benefits for all concerned. Patients and clients may become more comfortable with advance health care directives if they are correlated to a system of beliefs or values, or placed in a spiritual context, or related to applicable religious tenets. In the process, professionals—no, let's now call ourselves artisans—from all three of the noble walks (law, medicine, and divinity) can gain better understandings of the barriers and breakthroughs to implementation of directives. In so doing, we artisans collectively become more deft and astute in broaching and handling the subject. We artisans come to full measures of comprehension and affinity, respect and compassion for the turmoils and agonies of our patients, clients, and charges. We all blossom in devotion.

Law cannot fathom the mysteries of life. Yet case law now seems to establish that state interest in preserving it has both a start and finish: it commences at the time a fetus becomes viable (*Roe v. Wade*[1]) and ends when a competent patient declines treatment (*Cruzan*,[2] *Vacco*,[3] *infra*.)

Many religious, spiritual, and philosophical movements gratefully accept the healing hand of the physician and regard medical interventions and relief of physical burdens as extensions of faith. Others may view medical practices as being at variance with their precepts.

In dealing with hopeless medical scenarios, some faiths accept the futility of prolonged treatment while others reject withdrawal of life supports. The sanctity of human life is a postulate for many religious groups. Others do not view preservation of human life at any cost as a core belief.

§ 9.03—Religious/Spiritual Leaders and End-of-Life Issues

Many clergy and spiritual advisors wish to become more involved with end-of-life issues but find obstacles to their participation. As part of a community-based strategy to provide better spiritual care to the community's dying, the Midwest Bioethics Center has developed *Compassion Sabbath*, "a community-based, interfaith initiative to help clergy and religious educators address the spiritual needs of dying people and their families." Launched in 1999, the project is said to have markedly improved the quality of ministry to both critically and terminally ill individuals.[4]

Some movements and denominations lack explicit statements or policies on end-of-life care, leaving some clergy uncertain on how to advise their charges. This uncertainty often comes to be mirrored in those adherents struggling with end-of-life issues.

Given the diversity and complexity of religious and philosophical thought, artisans of spirit may face considerable variation in attitudes toward advance health care directives. Lay and spiritual advisors may hold widely disparate views; it is of course essential that we collectively force into transparency our personal perceptions and faiths and opinions as we help others articulate their wishes.

Of all advisors, it may well be that spiritual and religious artisans in particular are the most adept at assuaging doubt and turmoil and fear about advance health care directives, and the most caring and astute about giving directives voice. Doctors and lawyers should encourage this participation. Clergy, make your authority known.

§ 9.04 Religious and Spiritual Precepts about Advance Directives

In 2000, Gallup survey data demonstrated that 57 percent of the adults surveyed feel that religion is very important in their lives. Forty percent attend religious services weekly.[5] As recently as 1999, 45 percent of ambulatory outpatients felt that religious beliefs would influence health care decisions, and 94 percent of patients who held these beliefs felt that a physician should inquire into their belief system. Forty-five percent of those who do not believe in the importance of spirituality in healing also believed that physicians should inquire into the spiritual convictions of patients.[6] A 2001 study confirms that patients are receptive to physician inquiries about their support and coping mechanisms, including spiritual preferences; further, patients want their physicians to discuss these matters with empathy and respect.[7] Several authors have demonstrated a relationship between spirituality and psychological resilience and the ability to cope.[8] Caregivers also use spirituality to help them deal with challenges in their caregiving roles.[9] From these studies, it appears that religious affiliation may significantly impact how individuals view ethical issues relating to advance health care directives.

Ethnicity and nationality never are dispositive of religious, spiritual, or philosophical affiliations. Consider the constellations of Christian denominations here in the United States, which are but parts of the galaxy of religious movements and spiritual thinking to be found in this land. India, though predominately Hindu, is home as well to Muslims, Sikhs, and Jains, among others. The Jewish state of Israel has a sizeable Muslim minority. China is replete with Buddhists, Confucianists, Taoists—and Christians.

The following is a summary of the positions taken by some faiths and denominations on the subjects of end-of-life care and (where specified) advance health care directives. In some instances, positions on directives are not explicit but may be adduced or deduced from tenets and core beliefs. Some denominations offer specific and detailed instructions or recommendations; others are purposely vague, leaving issues open to personal choice.

Given the recent swelling of interest in end-of-life care, some movements may be formulating or restating their positions. Recent scholarship has discerned a general consensus on tissue and organ donation and transplantation: most faiths and movements accept these practices as acts of charity.[10] No companion work yet exists on advance health care directives, although scholarship in this area appears to be developing.

Some caveats: the summary that follows is but a sample of positions taken by various faiths, movements, and denominations, meant merely to illustrate some of the diversity that exists in thought and feeling about end-of-life care. It is not at all definitive or dispositive. It most emphatically is *not* advice. Contact appropriate clergy, practitioners, or advisors for elaboration, refinements, and current information.

§ 9.05—Buddhism

Given three streams of thought (Theravada, Mahayana, and Vajrayana), Buddhist approaches to health care may differ. Accordingly, generalizations may be misleading.

In Buddhist thinking, existence is a cycle of birth and rebirth; one's thoughts and actions are part of this pattern. Deliberate taking of life is anathema to adherents of Buddhism. Phillip Lesco's writing from the Tibetan Buddhist perspective concludes that for this reason, hospice care is advocated over euthanasia.[11]

Keown offers one Buddhist view on contemporary treatments: "There is no obligation . . . to connect patients to life-support machines simply to keep them alive. . . . In the case of PVS (persistent vegetative state) patients who have not been declared dead on the criteria of brainstem death, the provision of food and hydration should be continued. There would, however, be no requirement to treat subsequent complications (such as pneumonia). . . . . ."[12]

§ 9.06—American Baptist

"Imperfect as they may be, living wills do provide an invaluable record of a person's informed choices." Some long-term care facilities operated by American Baptists have adopted crisis care policies to encourage contemplative choices. The American Baptist church and related organizations are to "familiarize themselves with the statutes within their states regarding living wills, the durable power of attorney and natural death act and where appropriate lobby for legislation that enhances and facilitates the individual's right to make his/her own decisions regarding life sustaining treatment or measures."[13] The website for American Baptist Churches USA is www.abc-usa.org.

§ 9.07—The Church of Christ, Scientist (Christian Science)

Generally, followers of Christian Science neither consult with medical doctors nor avail themselves of clinical interventions. Adherents believe that illness may be addressed through better understanding of the divine. Members pray for their own healing; they also may obtain assistance from Christian Science practitioners who act as intercessors with God.

Christian Science adherents may execute advance directives. In so doing, they may express a preference for Christian Science practices. Since Christian Scientists do not generally avail themselves of aggressive medical interventions, declination of end-of-life clinical interventions typically poses no theological implications or issues.

It appears that members are free to give rein to their own moral proclivities when making choices between the applicability of traditional medical practices and Christian Science approaches to healing.[14] Additional information may be had from www.tfccs.com.

§ 9.08—Jehovah's Witnesses

Jehovah's Witnesses do not reject contemporary medicine, but do forbid use of blood and some blood products. Assertions of adherents for autonomy in medical decision-making have led to many court cases, several upholding the right to refuse treatments.[15]

Generally, it appears that heroic medical efforts may be foregone if death is imminent. There is no absolute prohibition against organ transplantation: this decision is left to individual choice. Euthanasia is forbidden.[16]

Jehovah's Witnesses may carry Medical Document Cards stating convictions about treatments; these cards also may contain the names of designated surrogate decision makers. Additionally, adherents in many cities have established hospital liaison committees that afford referrals to health care providers who are sensitive to their needs. A call to national headquarters (718-560-5000) may provide a local committee contact. The denomination's website is www.watchtower.org.

§ 9.09—Evangelical Lutheran

"Patients have the right to refuse unduly burdensome treatments which are disproportionate to the expected benefits. . . . This is also the case for patients who are incompetent, but who have identified their wishes through advance directives, living wills, or conversations with family or designated surrogates. . . . Advance Directives are welcome means to foster responsible decisions at the end of life. . . . Communities of faith should, can, and often do provide holistic ministry to prepare people for end of life decisions. They can invite (those) knowledgeable about advance directives to help them consider the topic's many dimensions."[17] More data may be had from www.elca.org.

§ 9.10—The Lutheran Church—Missouri Synod

"Christians will seek prayerfully to prepare advance directives in ways that will express our commitment never to aim at death. . . . Disagreement exists among Christians concerning difficult questions. . . Therefore, we will expect to find Christians conscientiously taking different positions on what can be included in an advance directive. . . .[Individuals are encouraged to] ask legal and medical professionals to acquaint [one] with typical examples of advance directives in use in the community and with the laws that govern them."[18]

§ 9.11—Roman Catholic

The May, 1980 Vatican Document on Euthanasia provides, in part:

> When inevitable death is imminent in spite of the means used, it is permitted in conscience to take the decision to refuse forms of treatment that would only secure a precarious and burdensome prolongation of life, so long as the normal care due to the sick person in similar cases is not interrupted. In such circumstances the doctor has no reason to reproach himself with failing to help the person in danger.
>
> It is also permissible to make do with the normal means that medicine can offer. Therefore one cannot impose on anyone the obligation to have recourse to a technique which is already in use but which carries a risk or is burdensome. Such a refusal is not the equivalent of suicide; on the contrary, it should be considered as an acceptance of the human condition, or a wish to avoid the application of a medical procedure disproportionate to the results that can be expected, or a desire not to impose excessive expense on the family or the community.[19]

The Catholic Health Association of the United States concurs that no extraordinary treatments are required in hopeless situations. However, means to hasten death are prohibited.[20] The organization has promulgated a "Durable Power of Attorney for Healthcare," available from its national headquarters at 4455 Woodson Road, St. Louis, MO 63134 (314-427-2500). Also refer to Appendix F for Catholic directives developed by the National Catholic Bioethics Center.

§ 9.12—United Church of Christ

In 1973, the general synod of the United Church of Christ, in its resolution titled. *The Rights and Responsibilities of Christians Regarding Human Death*, affirmed the right of individuals to "die rather than suffer unnecessarily through heroic measures frequently used to keep the terminally ill alive." They called for more collaboration of all concerned in end-of-life decisions.[21] The Council for Health and Human Services Ministries of the United Church of Christ, in association with the United Church of Christ Chaplains in Health Care, have issued a member resource entitled: *Making End-Of-Life Decisions: the United Church of Christ Perspective*. The document states that "In our time, it is equally imperative we set our affairs in order while we are healthy and competent . . . One can protect this right of privacy and control over one's medical care while one is still competent by writing legal documents (such as the Living Will and Durable Health Care Power)."[22] Additional data is at www.ucc.org.

§ 9.13—Hinduism

Hindu interpretations of end-of-life issues are rooted in ancient scriptures. Desai indicates that ". . .in Hindu consciousness, death is not the opposite of life/it is the opposite of birth. The two events simply mark a passage. . . . ."[23] Similarly, "(T)he cycle of birth, death, and rebirth as well as that of health and disease is governed by the laws of karma."[24]

Desai also observes that Hindus ". . .do not passively wait for their karma to manifest itself. Karma is more often invoked as an explanation after the fact; the failure of incurable illness is explained by unseen karma."[25]

Hindu-oriented medicine is based in the discipline of Ayurvedic medicine, which arose in the fifth century and which grew in tandem with spiritual practices. Ayurvedic physicians may be called on to support dying patients and encourage their wills to live. However, Ayurvedic texts discourage heroic efforts to prevent the inevitable.[26]

Desai's scholarship summarizes the Hindu tradition of "will death," whereby those at the end of life may reject food and water and other supports to allow inevitable death.[27] Interestingly, this concept has similarities to (and, of course, considerably predates) statutory provisions for living wills (or declarations) in the United States. With the introduction of new medical technologies, views on end of life issues may require reexamination.

§ 9.14—Islam

Islam means "submission to Allah;" a Muslim is an adherent who "submits to Allah." The Islamic movement represents the world's second largest religious tradition.

Doctrine and practice are outlined in two major writings, the Qur'an and the Sunna. With respect to the issues at hand, disease is part of existence, and death an expected outcome. Life on this earth is meant for the service of Allah.

Rahman states that "prolongation of artificial life supports would be strongly disapproved of by the Qur'an. But improvements of the quality of life, along with its prolongation, can only earn the approval of Islam."[28] Athar observes: "While Islam gives importance to saving lives. . . .it makes it clear that dying is part of the contract (with Allah), and the final decision (of term) is up to (Allah)." Athar also stresses that the ". . . quality of life is equally or more important than the duration of living."[29]

The website maintained by the Islamic Medical Association of North America's Medical Ethics Committee (www.islam-usa.com) offers information for health care providers engaged in aiding Muslim patients.[30] Some points include:

- Autopsy is not permitted unless required by law.
- Maintaining a terminal patient on artificial support for a prolonged period of time in a vegetative state is not encouraged.
- Transplantation is generally allowed with some restrictions.
- Muslims can have a living will or a case manager.

§ 9.15—Church of the Brethren

According to its 1996 Annual Conference statement, the Brethren tradition endorses stewardship and simplicity as death approaches. "Advance care directives, a living will and durable power of attorney, for example, instruct care providers about preferred treatment choices, especially when a person is too ill to state his or her wishes. Choosing to donate organs and/or tissues at the time of death is another act of stewardship, which serves others who have special needs." They further recommend that congregational files of end-of-life documents such as advance health care directives be maintained by pastors and/or deacons.[31] For information, visit www.brethren.org.

§ 9.16—United Methodist Church

The following resolution was passed by the United Methodist General Conference at Cleveland, Ohio, in May, 2000: "Religious institutions make a unique and significant contribution to human life. Living involves ethical issues and value decisions. Therefore, a religious presence is important to the quality of total community life . . . Our society is called upon to respond to basic human right of the elderly: the right to faithful care in dying and to have personal wishes respected concerning the number and type of life-sustaining measures that should be used to prolong life. Living wills, requests that no heroic measures be used, and other such efforts to die with faithful care should be supported. . . . The church understands itself as called by the Lord to the holistic ministry of healing: spiritual, mental and emotional, and physical.

Health in this sense is something beyond, but not exclusive of, biological well-being. In this view, health care is inadequate when it fixes its attention solely on the body and its physiological functions, as is any religion that focuses its interest entirely on the spirit . . . forms of counseling should be available to all patients and families . . . concerning use of extreme measures to prolong life . . . and death with dignity".[32] The denomination's website is www.umc.org.

§ 9.17—Presbyterian Church (U.S.A.)

In their booklet and video *Stewardship of Life: Preparing an Advance Directive*, the Board of Pensions of the Presbyterian Church (U.S.A.) endorses literature and forms promulgated through the combined efforts of the American Bar Association (ABA), the American Medical Association (AMA), and the American Association of Retired Persons (AARP) and modified with their collective permission. The booklet provides contains a preparation guide, forms, and state law requirements.[33] Visit www.pcusa.org for more.

§ 9.18—Mennonites

The Mennonite Mutual Aid organization serves a large body of church members from 25 denominations representing the Anabaptist tradition. Although they do not represent all Mennonite traditions and do not claim to be representing official church policy, the group has issued a guide for creating advance medical directives. The following passage comes from the booklet *Making Your Wishes Known: Guidelines for Creating Your Advance Medical Directives:* "The way the Anabaptist faith community views life, death, the resurrection, and stewardship helps shape decisions about advance directives. Agreement on the basic theology regarding life and death issues does not necessarily mean we will apply our beliefs uniformly. . . . A differentiation needs to be made between intentionally taking the life of another and withholding treatment to permit a person to complete the dying process. Because the dying process *can* be stopped does not necessarily mean that it *should* be stopped. We can love, respect, and revere persons both in prolonging their life and permitting dying. . . . Making decisions about end-of-life medical treatment helps you identify your beliefs about life and death. Completing a living will and appointing a proxy allows people to choose treatment based on their Christian faith rather than giving that responsibility to those who may not hold similar faith values."[34] These precepts may not fully apply (if at all) to certain Mennonite groups. Advice of adherents is recommended.

§ 9.19—Navajo

Navajo philosophy and spiritual direction may be incongruent with the notion of advance directives. Like many Eastern religions, the concept of autonomy is secondary to the needs of the tribal community. Future planning for health care needs is not necessarily a priority. In addition, anticipation of illness and open discussion of death may conflict with visions of harmony and oneness.[35] Other Native American tribes may take different positions.

§ 9.20—Judaism

It appears that both conservative and reform Jews are receptive to advance health care directives. Here is an excerpt from a May 15, 1989 policy statement of the American Jewish Congress on life-sustaining treatments:[36]

> (T)he American Jewish Congress supports public policies to enable individuals to create advance directives, such as living wills and health care proxies. Typically, patients lack decision-making capacity at the time life-sustaining treatment decisions must be made. Thus, our commitment to patient self-determination necessitates recognition of advance directives. Without such device, patients have little assurance that their wishes about life-sustaining treatment will be honored.

Orthodox Jews appear to assert the sanctity of life, irrespective of perceived impairment, suffering, or pain. Under strictly delineated circumstances, however, the withholding (as opposed to withdrawal) of life-sustaining treatments may be permitted. Seek rabbinical guidance.

> Although euthanasia in any form is forbidden and the hastening of death, even by a matter of moments, is regarded as tantamount to murder, there is one situation in which treatment may be withheld from the moribund patient in order to provide for an unimpeded death. While the death of a *goses* may not be speeded, there is no obligation to perform any action which will lengthen the life of a patient in this state. This distinction between an active and passive act applies only to a *goses*. When a patient is in the death process, there is no obligation to heal.[37]

Halachic (i.e., in accordance with Orthodox Jewish law and custom) living wills, durable powers of attorney for health care (including some state-specific powers), wallet cards, and related materials are available from Agudath Israel of America, 84 William Street, New York, NY 10038 (212-797-9000). See Appendix F for a sample.

§ 9.21—Unitarian Universalist Association

The Unitarian Universalist Association (UUA) " . . . supports the right of all adults to use living wills, health-care proxies, or advance medical directives to consent or refuse consent to medical treatment. We believe that all people have the right to make their own medical decisions, even if death results."[38] Unitarian Universalists usually do not ascribe to tenets of reincarnation or resurrection; accordingly, neither intentional nor assisted suicides are categorically forbidden, although they appear to be viewed with considerable misgiving and apprehension. In 1988, the organization's General Assembly resolved that all individuals have " . . . the right to self-determination in dying with release from civil or criminal penalties of those who, under proper safeguards, act to honor the right of terminally ill patients to select the time of their own deaths." Some UUA members do not abide by this policy statement, however.[39] More information is located at www.uua.org.

§ 9.22—Eastern Orthodox

Although the Eastern Orthodox Church is opposed to any form of active euthanasia, there is a tolerance for allowing natural death. Church members may consider hospice care and living wills to prevent extraordinary care from being imposed.[40]

§ 9.23—The Church of Jesus Christ of Latter-day Saints (LDS); Community of Christ (formerly Reorganized Church of Jesus Christ of Latter Day Saints—RLDS) (Mormons)

Note that two lines are associated with the Mormon tradition: the larger LDS (headquartered in Salt Lake City), and the smaller Independence, Missouri-based Community of Christ. Although nuanced at times, there are differences between the two.

According to Campbell, LDS theology stems from the sovereignty of God, who controls life and death. Stewardship requires that members care for the needs of others; moral agency entails respect for the decisions that others may make. LDS policy confirms that "when dying becomes inevitable, it should be looked upon as a blessing and purposeful part of eternal existence." Family members become the ultimate decision makers and are called on to obtain "competent medical advice and seek divine guidance through fasting and prayer."[41]

In its 1995 monograph, the Park Ridge Center reported that the Community of Christ (known as RLDS at that time) condones the prerogative of all individuals to decline life-sustaining treatments on the basis of self-determination. Additionally, the group's Standing High Council "supports the patient's right to execute a living will indicating that no resuscitation be attempted in the case of specified circumstances. It further supports the concept that the family, in the absence of such indication by the patient and in case the patient is unable to indicate his or her wish for whatever reason, has the right to request no resuscitation if in their judgment the condition is hopeless, provided such indicated order is legal in the state in which the hospital is licensed."[42]

Information about the LDS may be viewed at www.lds.org. For more on the Community of Christ, go to www.cofchrist.org.

§ 9.24—Anglican Church

The Anglican Church endorses a ministry that "affirms the body's natural powers of healing . . . and the use of medical knowledge . . . to assist restoration or relieve pain and to establish peace as we acknowledge that we are mortal and yet are born for eternity." In the 1998 Lambeth Conference, the Standing Commission on Human Affairs and Health commented that the use of directives can be helpful to document willingness to donate organs or tissues and guide caregivers as to the individual's wishes for terminal care.[43] Visit www.episcopalchurch.org or www.cofe.anglican.org.

§ 9.25—Seventh-day Adventists

Seventh-day Adventists believe that health is a gift from God, which adherents are responsible to maintain. They do so, in part, through prudent personal practices (dietary restrictions, prohibitions against alcohol and tobacco). Spiritual tenets allow both individual health care choices and the designation of surrogate decision makers who understand patient preferences. Formal health care planning should be in accordance with legal requirements.[44] Learn more at www.adventist.org.

§ 9.26 Barriers to Acceptance

With or without religious, spiritual, or philosophical constructs, patients, family members, and advisors may ascribe to beliefs or tenets that may influence receptivity to or acceptance of advance health care directives.

- **Spiritual tenets supporting preservation of life at any cost.** Some faiths or beliefs see life as a gift from God, which should be preserved at all costs. Advance health care directives, often simplistically misconstrued as "pull the plug" documents, might be rejected.
- **Subjugation of personal autonomy to spiritual postulates or teachings.** Personal autonomy and self-determination are not universally valued. Many faiths promote the good of all over the requirements of the individual.
- **Relationship of suffering and redemption.** The quality of experience at the end of life may not be meaningful for all religions. Some view suffering and redemption as a continuum—one necessary for the evolution of the other.
- **God will provide; people should not interfere.** Some religious organizations minimize human contributions and importance and defer to higher powers for important issues.
- **Preplanning medical contingencies may conflict with God's intervention.** For some with severe illness, divine intervention and guidance must be sought through prayer and meditation. Preplanning makes no sense in this context.
- **Construction of advance health care directives as euthanasia or mercy killing.** End-of-life issues invariably turn, if only fleetingly in some instances, to the issues of passive and active euthanasia. Complicity in the taking of a life in any context is strictly prohibited by

some organizations. Advance directives will be rejected if seen as a tool (or ruse) for euthanasia.

• **Moral obligation for family and loved ones to continue providing care.** Care of the sick and dying is an ethical and moral obligation. Minimizing care might lead to guilt and a sense of failure.

§ 9.27 Barriers to Implementation

Barriers to implementation relate primarily to lack of knowledge, miscommunication, and missed opportunities.

• **Lack of knowledge on part of clergy or spiritual advisors.** Clergy or spiritual advisors may lack specific training or knowledge relating to the importance (and implementation) of advance directives. Few interventions have been directed toward this key group even though those attempted have been successful.[45]

• **No policy statement or exploration of end-of-life issues.** Some movements, faiths, and denominations are vague or silent on end-of-life issues. Others may opt for open-ended statements on "individual consciousness" which renders interpretation and advice difficult.

• **Lack of opportunity to discuss with clergy or spiritual advisors.** Advance health care directives are not pressing issues for many patients. A medical crisis may be the one factor that will prompt discussion with clergy or a spiritual advisor. Unfortunately, this may be the least opportune time.

• **Lack of participation of clergy and spiritual advisors in the acute care setting.** Clergy or a spiritual advisor may not be able to tend to a patient's needs during a hospitalization or other medical crisis. Geographic barriers, time, and the hospital culture itself may minimize the involvement of the primary spiritual provider. Lack of experience with acute care settings may create discomfort for both the patient and the advisor.[46]

• **Conflict/biases between legal, medical, and spiritual systems.** The independent recommendations of professional advisors may be confusing to family—or be in outright conflict. Participation of allied professionals is, in practice, only occasionally recommended—and even then often is left to the judgment of the patient. Many such difficulties might be alleviated through better communication and coordination.

• **Lack of understanding among family, patient, and clergy or spiritual advisor.** As with any other profession, interactions between patient/family and clergy or spiritual advisor may fall prey to misunderstanding and miscommunication. Patients may see a discussion of directives as God "giving up on them." Others may not see a connection between medical and spiritual issues and may categorically reject the involvement of a spiritual advisor in decisions about end of life.

§ 9.28 Accomodation of Faith

It is important to note that in some states, accommodation of faith is embodied in the enabling statutes for advance directives. In other words, medical arts do not foreclose other practices. Some examples:

- Delaware. "Notwithstanding this chapter, an individual who elects to have treatment by spiritual means in lieu of medical or surgical treatment shall not be compelled to submit to medical or surgical treatment."[47]
- Indiana. "This section does not prohibit an individual capable of consenting to the individual's own health care or to the health care of another from consenting to health care administered in good faith under the religious tenets and practices of the individual requiring health care."[48]
- Kansas. "Nothing in this act shall be construed as prohibiting an agent from providing treatment by spiritual means through prayer alone and care consistent therewith, in lieu of medical care and treatment, in accordance with the tenets and practices of any church or religious denomination of which the principal is a member."[49]

§ 9.29 Critique of Case Study

Lest we forget, the sorry story of Karen Ann Quinlan served as more than a landmark legal case. It eloquently established that the involvement of allied professionals—clergy and spiritual advisors in particular—is indispensable. In order to succeed—indeed, if they are to any chance at all of succeeding—advance health care directives must be predicated on a multidisciplinary approach.

§ 9.30 Conclusion

The religious, spiritual, and philosophical sides of an individual are intricately intertwined with his/her physical nature. A holistic approach provides opportunities for more meaningful discussions of end-of-life care, including the completion and use of advance directives. Unfortunately, clergy and spiritual advisors frequently are not asked to participate in the crafting and implementation of advance directives, even though many denominations have deeply held beliefs about end-of-life care. Clergy and other practitioners clearly welcome—and, indeed, command authority—to participate within a team of professionals.

May Bishop Carey's elegant admonition for each profession to "acknowledge the other" inspire us all to approach directives holistically. In so doing, we help each of our patients and clients and charges give soaring and sonorous voice to the fullest measure of individual expression. And in so doing, we become the noblest of servants. We become forever proud supplicants of fealty and devotion.

Notes

1. Roe v. Wade, 410 U.S. 113 (1973)
2. Cruzan v. Missouri Dep't of Health, 497 U.S. 261 (1990)
3. Vacco v. Quill, 117 S.Ct. 2293 (1997).
4. Wurth, JoEllen. Compassion Sabbath: Summary of Year One. Available from Midwest Bioethics Center. 1021–1025 Jefferson Street. Kansas City, MO 64105. www.midbio.org
5. Gallup Poll: Religion, the Gallup Organization. As reported at www.gallup.com/poll/indicators/indreligion.asp. October, 2000.
6. J. Hansen-Flaschen, et al. Do Patients Want Physicians to Inquire about their Spiritual or Religious Beliefs if They Become Gravely Ill? Archives Internal Medicine, 1999. Vol. 159, pp. 1803–1806.
7. R. Herbert, M. Jenckes, D. Ford, et al. Patient Perspectives on Spirituality and the Patient—Physician Relationship. Journal General Internal Medicine, 2001. Vol. 16, pp. 685–692.
8. DD. Coward, Self-Transcendence and Emotional Well-Being in Women with Advanced Breast Cancer. Oncology Nursing Forum 1991; Vol. 18. No. 5, pp. 857–63. Gurklis, JA. & Menke, EM. Identification of Stressors and Use of Coping, Methods in Chronic Hemodialysis Patients. Nursing Research 1988. Vol. 37(4) pp. 236–239. Block, Susan. Psychological Considerations, Growth, and Transcendence at the End of Life. JAMA. Vol. 285. No. 22, 2001, pp. 2898–2906.
9. K. Herth, Hope in the Family Caregiver of Terminally Ill People. Journal of Advanced Nursing 1993; Vol. 18(4) pp. 543. Kaye, J. & Robinson, KM. Spirituality Among Caregivers IMAGE 1994; Vol. 26, pp. 218–221.
10. ML. Cooper Hammon, & G. Taylor, Organ and Tissue Donation: A Reference for Clergy 4th Edition SEOPF/UNOS 2000, pp. V1–V11.
11. P. Lesco, Euthanasia: A Buddhist Perspective. Journal of Religion and Health, 1986 25.1. pp. 51–7.
12. Keown, Damien. Buddhism and Bioethics. Palgrave, New York 2001. p. 167.
13. American Baptist Church homepage (www.abc-usa.org). Resolution on Death and Dying Adopted by General Board of American Baptist Church, Dec. 1990 (modified 1992, 1996) General Board reference number 8182:6190
14. D. Harris-Abbott, The Christian Science Tradition: Religious Beliefs and Health care Decisions. Published by the Park Ridge Center for the Study of Health, Faith, and Ethics, 1996. pp. 1–10.
15. Jehovah's Witnesses The Surgical Ethical Challenge. JAMA 1981; Vol. 246 (21) pp. 2471–2472.
16. E. DuBose, The Jehovah's Witness Tradition: Religious Beliefs and Health Care Decisions. From the Religious Traditions and Health Care Decisions:

A Quick Reference to Fifteen Religious Traditions and Their Application in Health Care. The Park Ridge Center for the Study of Health, Faith, and Ethics. 211 E. Ontario, Suite 800, Chicago, IL 60611. 1995. pp. 1–10.

17. A Message on End of Life Decisions. Evangelical Lutheran Church in America, 1992. Statement draws upon "Death and Dying" statement of predecessor church body which was first issued in 1982 and adopted by the Lutheran Church in America.

18. Christian Care at Life's End: Report of the Commission Theology and Church Relations of the Lutheran Church—Missouri Synod. Feb. 1993.

19. Taken from the release of the office of communications of Roman Catholic Archdiocese of New York. (No date specified.)

20. The Catholic Health Association of the US. Advice on Advance Directives: Helping You Prepare for Your Health Care. Revised 1995.

21. A. Nehring, United Church of Christ Religious Beliefs and Healthcare Decisions.1999 The Park Ridge Center for the Study of Health, Faith, and Ethics. 211 E. Ontario, Suite 800, Chicago, IL 60611. http://www.prchfe.org

22. The Council for Health and Human Service Ministries of the United Church of Christ & United Church of Christ Chaplains in Health Care. Making End-of-Life Decisions: United Church of Christ Perspective. 1997. United Church of Christ, 700 Prospect Avenue Cleveland, Ohio 44115. (216) 736-2250.

23. Desai, Prakash. Health and Medicine in the Hindu Tradition: Continuity and Cohesion. Crosswood Publishing Company, 1989. New York. p. 93.

24. Reich, Warren (Editor in chief) Desai, Prakash (contributor) Encyclopedia of Bioethics. Simon and Schuster Mac Millan, 1995 New York. p. 1477.

25. Desai, Prakash. Health and Medicine in the Hindu Tradition: Continuity and Cohesion. Crosswood Publishing Company, 1989. New York. pp. 94–95.

26. Reich, Warren (Editor in chief) Desai, Prakash (contributor) Encyclopedia of Bioethics. Simon and Schustr Mac Millan, 1995 New York. p. 1475.

27. Ibid, p. 1475.

28. Rahman, Fazlur. Health and Medicine in the Islamic Tradition. Crossroad Publishing Company 1987 New York. p. 109.

29. Athar, Shahid Health Concerns for Believers Contemporary Issues. Library of Islam, 1995. South Elgin, Illinois. p. 71.

30. Athar, Shahid. Information for Health Care Providers When Dealing with a Muslim Patient Islamic Medical Association of North America. Downers Grove, Illinois. 630-852-2122. www.islam-usa.com/e40.html

31. Church of the Brethren, End-of-Life Decision-Making Statement, 1996 Annual Conference. http://www.brethren.org/ac/ac_statements/endolife.htm

32. United Methodist General Conference. United Methodist Resolutions Related to Advance Directives, Health Care Powers of Attorney, Health Care Proxies, Living Wills, Organ Donation, as passed by the United Methodist General Conference, Cleveland, Ohio, May 2000. Copied from pre-publication draft materials, United Methodist Book of Resolutions, to be released early 2001.

33. The Board of Pensions of the Presbyterian Church (U.S.A.) Stewardship of Life: Preparing an Advance Directive Study Guide. 1999. 2000 Market Street, Philadelphia, PA 19103-3298 (800) 773-7752.

34. Mennonite Mutual Aid. Making Your Wishes Known: Guidelines for Creating Your Advance Medical Directive. 1995. 1110 North Main Street, Post Office Box 483, Goshen, IN 46527. (800)533-9511.

35. J. Carrese, & L. Rhodes, Western Bioethics on the Navajo Reservation. JAMA 1995; Vol. 274:826-829. Mercer S. Navajo Elderly People in a Reservation Nursing Home: Admission Predictors and Culture Care Practices. Social Work 1996; Vol. 41:181–189.

36. Policy statement 1989, American Jewish Conference.

37. Meier Jewish Values in Bioethics, ed. Levi Meier (New York) Human Service Press, 1986.

38. R. Mero, Choices in Dying Unitarian Universalist Association. 1997.

39. Id

40. Harakas, Stanley Samuel. Eastern Orthodox Bioethics. Bioethics Yearbook 1988–90; Vol. 1: 85–101.

41. S. Campbell Courtney, The Latter-Day Saints and Medical Ethics. Bioethics Yearbook 1988–90; Vol. 1:31–40.

42. Harris-Abbott, Deborah. The Latter-day Saints Tradition: Religious Beliefs and Health Care Decisions. From Religious Traditions and Health Care Decisions: A Quick Reference to Fifteen Religious Traditions and Their Application in Health Care. Park Ridge Center for the Study of Health, Faith, and Ethics, 211 E. Ontario, Suite 800, Chicago, IL 60611. 1995. pp. 1–20.

43. Anglican Church. 1998, Lambeth Conference. Report of the Anglican Consultative Council and the Standing Commission on Human Affairs and Health.

44. The Seventh-day Adventist Church. Focuses on Ethical Issues. The Christian View of Human Life Committee, 1995. General conference in Silver Spring, Maryland.

45. Wurth, JoEllen. Compassion Sabbath: Summary of Year One. Available from Midwest Bioethics Center. 1021–1025 Jefferson Street. Kansas City, MO 64105. www.midbio.org

46. Ibid.

47. DEL CODE ANN tit 16 2515

48. IND CODE ANN 30-5-5-16

49. KAN STAT ANN 58-629(b)

CHAPTER 10

Alternatives in the Absence of Directives

§ 10.01 Introduction

What can be done in a difficult health care situation when there are no advance directives?

Fortunately, there are some alternatives and fallbacks—"diversions," as they might be called. Note well, however, that some may be severely limited in their usefulness; at best, they can only mitigate or ameliorate—or, more bluntly, salvage—difficult treatment situations. It is important to once again stress the oft-repeated refrain: the best individual approach is to have thorough, tailor-made, contemplative directives executed and ready.

§ 10.02 Diversions

The general diversions for use in the absence of advance health care directives—not all of which are statutorily condoned—are:

- Informal practice
- Surrogacy statutes
- "Do Not Resuscitate" (DNR) statutes
- Guardianship and conservatorship
- Health care ethics committees

§ 10.03—Informal Practice

For better or worse, informal practice probably represents the principal diversion. It seems unlikely that we will ever accurately know its incidence or prevalence.

Most readers will have an anecdote or two about grieving family gathered at bedside and bringing themselves to finally directing—or consenting to—the withdrawal of life support. The professional who takes up (or is thrust into) service as a facilitator will find that the emotional dimension alone ranges from uplifting to harrowing.

It also is a perilous role: the potential for professional liability is rife. Be especially cautious. Generally, it is best to shun informal involvement if other diversions are possible. Do not blunder into a fractious family situation, or inadvertently become the focus for transferred rage or grief.

§ 10.04—Surrogacy statutes

Twenty-nine U.S. jurisdictions[1] have anticipated that some individuals will not, for whatever reason, execute advance directives. Accordingly, they have enacted surrogacy (or similarly titled) statutes. Where available, these laws authorize physicians to turn to a hierarchy of substitute decision-makers (such as court-appointed guardians, spouses, parents, adult children, adult siblings, and so forth) for authority to treat those who are near the end of life and incapable of giving consent.

Typically, surrogacy acts do not apply when a patient can render informed consents or has previously executed a living will or durable health care power or proxy. Such laws also may be sharply limited to carefully controlled and specifically defined circumstances of terminal illness or injury, sometimes referred to statutorily as "qualifying conditions".

Some jurisdictions (Illinois for one) are more expansive: they permit a surrogate to render broad treatment decisions for an uncomprehending patient without "end-of-life only" limitations. Consult appropriate state statutes.

Surrogacy laws, however, may be *detrimental* to the interests of a patient: the statutory hierarchy may identify as decision-maker a person the patient may not have wanted (for example, an estranged spouse). Similarly, members of a class of equally entitled decision-makers (e.g., adult children) each may have entirely different ideas and wishes as to treatment of, say, a parent; invocation of an applicable surrogacy statute may only compound the problem. (Does "majority rule" apply in this circumstance? Or is the prospect of surrogate decision-making lost altogether—and choices inadvertently rendered far more difficult—due to deadlock or stalemate among equally entitled decision-makers?) Impress on patients/clients/principals that these reasons combined make a persuasive argument for contemplatively drawn advance directives.

With their limited applicability and restrictive requirements, health care surrogacy acts usually do not provide the preferred course of action. Still, they may be a useful diversion in the absence of advance directives.

§ 10.05—"Do Not Resuscitate" (DNR) Protocols

In recent years, 44 states and the District of Columbia have established, by statute or other mechanism (e.g., regulation), the circumstances under which a so-called DNR is permitted. (Six jurisdictions lack such provisions:

Iowa, Mississippi, Nebraska, North Dakota, Pennsylvania, and Vermont).[2] Carefully study both statute and attendant case law before resorting to this diversion: there may be significant differentiations between out-of-hospital and in-hospital DNR protocols. It may be that some sort of oversight (concurrence of additional physicians, institutional ethics committee, familial consent, judicial review) and/or a waiting period are required.

§ 10.06—Guardianship

Another health care decision-making diversion is judicial appointment of a guardian of the person (or similarly titled functionary), charged in part with consulting with physicians and consenting to medical treatments of an adult adjudicated as mentally disabled (or incapacitated, or incompetent). Similarly, a guardian of a minor's person may be designated to oversee, in part, the health care decisions made on behalf of a child.

§ 10.07—Proceedings

To the uninitiated—and unwary—guardianship surely must seem an alluring way of resolving a conflicted or convoluted treatment situation. After all, an outside decision-maker (usually a judge) will sort out the rights of contesting parties and render determinations in the best interests of a patient; a court-appointed guardian will become the sole (and, presumably, definitive) decision-maker for an individual incapable of providing medical consents.

In many states, guardianship is a rather simple proceeding to initiate: a one or two page petition filed with the clerk of court may be all that is required. However, enormous complexities can stem from such a seemingly simple and beguiling beginning. Inappropriate use of guardianship can have the unintended effect of rendering a tricky set of circumstances vastly more difficult.

Because guardianship amounts to a curtailing—or even a taking—of an individual's right to make her or his own decisions about health care, living arrangements, and finances, it should be used sparingly. Consider guardianship to be the "last resort" among the diversions discussed in this section. It is most appropriately used in contested situations (e.g., adamant disagreements and deadlock among family members as to care choices for an uncomprehending patient). Guardianship can be a time-consuming, cumbersome, expensive, exasperating, and, at times, overbearing and oppressive proceeding.

In any guardianship, the burden of proof always is on the party bringing the case (the "petitioner" or similarly styled functionary). As a matter of law, there is a presumption that any individual reaching majority is entirely capable of making his or her decisions. Accordingly, most guardianship courts will, at least in theory, be favorably disposed to any subsequent motion to dismiss.

Hence this counterintuitive caution about cavalierly filing a guardianship case: it may *not* be possible to obtain summary dismissal of a case if circumstances change (for example, if the family members decide they no longer want to proceed, or if the doctors subsequently feel that other health care decision-making mechanisms may be used). If a condition or disability was serious enough to warrant a petition for guardianship in the first place, then a court often will not yield its jurisdiction unless and until it is satisfied that the subject is able to once again render informed consents. This may require presentation of a physician's written report—or even entail testimony in court—refuting for the record the allegations of decisional or communicative impairment contained in the petition.

If the refuting evidence or documentation or testimony is deemed insufficient, a judge may *deny* a motion to dismiss: a petitioner's subsequent reticence to come ahead with the case will hardly ever suffice as a reason. Be absolutely certain to brace a family or doctor or care facility for this possibility. Once a guardianship case is filed, counsel may be compelled to try it on the merits, no matter what the cost or effort.

§ 10.08—Limitations

Be aware, too, that when there are profound health issues at hand—for example, invasive medical procedures, or end of life medical decisions—a duly appointed guardian of the person, by counsel, should (or even must) formally petition a judge for instructions. Typically, the court itself will not direct the course of care: rather, it will authorize (or refuse to authorize) the guardian to consent to contemplated treatments. Draft motions or petitions with this precept in mind. Carefully explain this nuance to all concerned.

A guardian of the person can, with relative ease, consent to such death-delaying treatments as cardiac life support, ventilators, artificial hydration and nutrition, and the like. Once started, however, these medical procedures sometimes cannot be stopped by the guardian without judicial permission. Statute and case law may impose very high burdens of proof upon counsel seeking judicial authorization for a guardian to consent to the withdrawal of a ward's life support. Similarly, a guardian should not (or, indeed, may not) agree to a DNR order, absent statutory authority or judicial approval. The burden of proof for judicial authorization to consent to a DNR also may be daunting (e.g., one or more treating physicians testifying in court).

Know that guardianship often presents as a bifurcated proceeding: in addition to a guardian of the person (for health care and living arrangements), a conservator (or guardian of the estate) may or may not be necessary to handle financial matters.

§ 10.09—Avoiding Guardianship

A properly executed (and sufficiently broad) health care power or proxy almost always obviates the need for guardianship of the person. Similarly, an intervivos trust (commonly known as a "living trust"), or a *durable* power of attorney for property can preclude the need to seek a conservatorship or a guardianship of the estate. It is exceedingly important to note that in some jurisdictions (Hawaii and Illinois, for example), principals need to execute *both* health care *and* property powers in order to stave off these two different forms of guardianship.

Few laypersons recognize that guardianship commonly is a probate proceeding. If a client clings to the widespread and simplistic notion that probate of a deceased's estate is repugnant, then galvanize her or him in this fashion: guardianship is worse. Guardianship is "living probate," and "living probate" is what happens to those of us who don't have directives. Guardians, empowered as agents of the court, step in and render care decisions *instead*. And the health care decisions so rendered may be diametrically opposed to what the patient may have wanted. Compelling reason, indeed, to contemplatively prepare advance health care directives.

For more on guardianships, consult a state-specific source. A generalized treatment may be found in: *Guardianship and Conservatorship: A Handbook for Lawyers,* by Scott K. Summers (American Bar Association, 1996).

§ 10.10—Health Care Ethics Committees

There may be times when the diversions (or variants) previously described do not readily lend themselves (if at all) to resolving issues of medical ethics. Larger hospitals and long-term care institutions generally have committees of physicians and other professionals to review difficult "life and death" treatment situations. An in-house consultative group (i.e., an ethics service) may make hospital rounds and can provide more frequent assistance than might a committee. These entities may provide requisite guidance to satisfy all concerned.

In the case of Karen Quinlan,[3] the New Jersey court viewed with favor the use of ethics committees. Since that time, ethics committees across the country have explored what should and can be done in difficult treatment situations. Ethics committees typically give families and health care providers sufficient perspective, context, and insight to proceed in otherwise difficult or fractious situations without necessarily resorting to judicial review. For an excellent discussion, see *Health Care Ethics Committees: The Next Generation.*[4]

In addition to the hospital setting, ethics committees now are fairly common in long-term care environments such as nursing homes and rehabilitation centers.[5]

Ethics committees usually are drawn from a variety of professional walks and tend to be rich both in talent and experience. Physicians, nurses, social workers, clergy, attorneys, ethicists, and mental health specialists often are involved. Participants usually have had first hand experience with ethical dilemmas in clinical practice; they also should have training in the field of medical ethics.[6] Whenever possible, members should reflect cultural and ethical backgrounds of the populations served by the institution.

An ethics committee often will be asked to assist with decisions for an incompetent or decisionally incapacitated individual (typically one without advance directives), and with no family or friends to serve as surrogate decision-makers, or with a conflicted family quarreling about care. Beneficence (see Chapter 3) guides most such decision-making.[7]

At times, an ethics committee will have to grapple with the requests of a competent patient (or authorized surrogate) for patently futile care or (conversely) for imposition of unreasonable care limitations or restrictions. In either case, a committee will facilitate communication and offer insight. Note that an ethics committee rarely has binding authority. In instances where patients, surrogates, or providers cannot agree, judicial review may be the only option.

Absent a directive, or an appropriate surrogate, or agreement among care providers and surrogates, many types of unresolved issues may present for committee review:

- Limitations on care for the terminally ill
- DNR orders
- Withdrawal of care/termination of life support
- Requests for futile or medically ineffective care
- Conflict about or misunderstanding of treatment goals between providers and patient/family
- Conflict about or misunderstanding of treatment goals among family members

Although often a useful institutional resource, ethics committees cannot resolve all treatment dilemmas. Accordingly, they cannot be viewed as a uniformly effective substitute for advance health care planning. Perkins outlines concerns about their use (particularly the ethics of ethics consultants giving pointed treatment recommendations).[8]

§ 10.11—A Word about Euthanasia or "Mercy Killing" or "Assisted Suicide"

Make no mistake about it: euthanasia and mercy killing and assisted suicide are *not* diversions. They are *illegal acts* in all U.S. jurisdictions (the limited "carveout" being the Oregon Death with Dignity Act—Appendix I).

In recent years, Michigan has been embroiled in an assisted suicide controversy, precipitated by a physician who has (with varying degrees of openness) ostensibly made it possible for profoundly ill patients to end their own lives. Prosecution of the practitioner has yielded varying results, from a series of acquittals to a conviction (and prison sentence) for second-degree murder. The issue is—to mince words—unsettled.

Absent directives and consensus of immediate family, it is reported[9] that some medical practitioners unilaterally—surreptitiously, perhaps—resort to approaches that come right up to the line of passive euthanasia: "slow codes" (also known as "Hollywood Codes" or "Light Blue," among other euphemisms), where health care providers go through the motions of heroic interventions. These are highly risky practices unlikely to be condoned by statute.

One school of thought holds that advance health care directives—and any diversions to directives—are themselves tantamount to passive euthanasia. Agree or not, the position must be afforded thoughtful deference and respect: as the authors have observed, there is no right way. To some, there may be no such thing as a diversion to directives, because the entire concept of directives is itself repugnant.

Once again—with the sole (and carefully limited) exception of Oregon, euthanasia and assisted suicide are most emphatically *not* options or alternatives or diversions. Oregon, too, prohibits outright mercy killing and suicide.[10]

Professionals drawn to the flickers of these flames may place their careers at peril.

§ 10.12 Conclusion

All is not lost in the absence of directives, even in difficult treatment circumstances or conflicted family situations. Employ these diversions as figurative lifeboats—and help steer people through.

Notes

1. States included: Alabama, Arizona, Arkansas, Colorado, Connecticut, District of Columbia, Delaware, Florida, Hawaii, Illinois, Indiana, Iowa, Kentucky, Louisiana, Maine, Maryland, Mississippi, Montana, Nevada, New Mexico, North Carolina, Ohio, Oregon, South Carolina, Texas, Utah, Virginia, West Virginia, and Wyoming. *End-of-Life Law Digest*, "State Statutes Governing Surrogate Decisionmaking", Partnership for Caring, Inc., Washington, DC (March, 2001).
2. *End-of-Life Law Digest*, "State Statutes and Protocols Governing Nonhospital Do-Not-Resuscitate Orders", Partnership for Caring, Inc., Washington, DC (March, 2001).
3. *In re* Quinlan, 355 A.2d 647, 70 N.J. 10 (1976).
4. J. ROSS ET AL., HEALTH CARE ETHICS COMMITTEES: THE NEXT GENERATION (1993).
5. P. Winn et al., *Ethics Committees in Long Term Care: A User's Guide to Getting Started*, 8 ANNALS OF LONG TERM CARE 1 (2000).
6. K. Simpson, *The Development of a Clinical Ethics Consultative Service in a Community Hospital*, 3 J. CLINICAL ETHICS 2 (1992).
7. T. Brennan, *Ethics Committees and Decisions to Limit Care: The Experience at Massachusetts General Hospital*, 260 JAMA 6 (1988).
8. H. Perkins, *Clinical Ethics Consultations: Reason for Optimism but Problems Exist*, 3 J. CLINICAL ETHICS 2 (1992).
9. *The Slow Code—Should Anyone Rush to Its Defense?* 338 NEW ENG. J. MED. 7 (1998).
10. OR. REV. STAT. § 127.570.

CHAPTER II

Special Circumstances

§ 11.01 Introduction

There are several "special issue" circumstances that can have a bearing on advance health care directives. Here is a synopsis:

§ 11.02—Anencephalic Infants

A child so afflicted is fatally deformed: she or he completely lacks cortex (upper brain) and usually dies within hours or days of birth. The prospect of organ and tissue donation may become highly charged, both emotionally and ethically. Proceed with utmost caution, care, and sensitivity; ethics committee involvement (where available) and spiritual bereavement counseling may be prudent. A suggested donor protocol (not necessarily endorsed by the authors or by the ABA) may be found at http://www.med.miami.edu/OPO/organ.htm. Be aware that the "Baby Jane Doe" regulations[1] require that these infants receive "appropriate" nutrition, hydration, and medication. Refer to the section on "Minors" (below) and the discussion on organ donation (page 13) for related information.

§ 11.03—Anatomical Donation

This may be a limited postmortem function that falls to an agent or proxy under the terms of an advance directive. If a body is to be donated for medical study, organ donation (other than eyes) typically is precluded. Other restrictions apply; contact a nearby medical school, or the office of the local coroner or medical examiner, for more information.

Arrangements are best made contemplatively and in advance. Be certain to make alternative plans for disposition of remains in the event the donation is refused for some reason (e.g., communicable disease). For a listing of medical school donor programs throughout the U.S., set your browser to http://www.livingbank.org/wholebody.htm.

§ 11.04—Autopsy

Consent to the autopsy of the principal is another limited postmortem function that may be covered by a health care power or proxy: California, Illinois, and North Carolina are among the states so providing. Consult applicable statute.

Be alert for spiritual and religious imperatives and precepts. Buddhists, for example, believe in the slow release of consciousness from the body; accordingly, autopsy (if required at all) should be delayed for at least three days.[2]

§ 11.05—Cord Blood

Until recently, umbilical cords and placentas were routinely destroyed after birth. Therapies using stem cells derived from cord blood now are showing extraordinary promise for treatment of leukemia, Hodgkin's lymphoma, sickle cell anemia, and other conditions. Expectant parents should be counseled to donate. Donation is painless (apart from delivery, of course!) and is without cost to the donors. Similarly, it is possible to privately bank (for a fee) the few ounces of blood so obtained and retain it for future familial use. Note that application and requisite testing must commence approximately two months before delivery. Note, too, that geographic and other limitations may curb participation, at least for the present. Individuals in their childbearing years may wish to include instructions in an advance directive. One information source (not necessarily endorsed by the authors or the ABA) is a for-profit entity, the Cord Blood Banking Registry. Staff may be reached through http://www.cordblood.com or 1-888-CORDBLOOD. The National Marrow Donor Program (NMDP) also is an information source (1-800-MARROW-2). Refer to the NMDP's website (http://www.marrow.org) for a listing of the roughly two dozen public cord blood banks in the U.S.

§ 11.06—Cryonics

This is the concept (fanciful, perhaps, to some) of deep-freezing a body at or near the instant of death on the premise or hypothesis that one might be resuscitated and reanimated at some future date through yet-to-be-developed cures or treatments. In jurisdictions permitting instructions for disposition of remains, terms or instructions conceivably might be contained in an advance directive. Be aware that one court has determined that there is no constitutional right to *pre*-mortem cryogenic suspension because it is tantamount to assisted suicide.[3]

§ 11.07—Defective, Inoperative, or Stale Directives

What if an advance directive is defective on its face—if, say, the principal mistakenly signed on the witness line and a witness signed as the principal?

What if the designated agent or proxy has predeceased or declines to act and no successor is named? What if a sunset date was incorporated into the directive and it has already expired?

Practitioners probably will have little choice but to turn to available diversions in the absence of directives (see Chapter 10). All may not be lost, however. The authors believe that defective, stale, or otherwise inoperative directives may have some limited value as the "prior expressions of intent" called for in the *Cruzan* decision (*supra*). Note that state statute may expressly give effect to a seemingly expired directive if the principal lost decisional capacity prior to the expiration date: Oregon, for example, so provides.

Although now arguably in eclipse in most states due to its limited scope,[4] a living will or declaration may have value in such circumstances as a contingency document for a failed health care power of attorney or proxy. Check state law carefully before proceeding to execute both a health care power and a living will. Some jurisdictions (e.g., Georgia, Illinois) address the possibility directly: if both are executed, the power (or proxy) takes precedence over the living will. Others are silent on this point. Accordingly, having both a power/proxy and a living will may inadvertently cause difficulty.

§ 11.08—Divorce or Dissolution or Annulment of Marriage; Termination of Domestic Partnership

If a principal names a spouse as agent in an advance health care directive and the couple subsequently divorces, the former spouse *may* be considered (for the purposes of the directive) to have predeceased the principal. Accordingly, she or he will be unable to act as agent or proxy. If no backup or successor agents are named, the divorce or dissolution or annulment may have the unintended effect of rendering directives useless or moot. Among the states so providing are Alabama, California, Colorado, Connecticut, Delaware, Hawaii, Idaho, Massachusetts, Michigan, Mississippi, New Jersey, New York, North Carolina, North Dakota, Texas and West Virginia. In New Hampshire, the *filing* of a case revokes the directive, unless an alternate is designated. In Minnesota, a directive also is revoked upon commencement of an action for termination of a principal's registered domestic partnership. To retain the former spouse as proxy or agent, consider re-executing applicable directives after the divorce becomes final. Review applicable statutes.

§ 11.09—Domestic Partners/Companions

An adult (married or unmarried) wishing to have a partner or companion or enduring friend or other traditionally unrelated individual render health care consents is particularly well-advised to execute pertinent advance directives: virtually all of the diversions referred to in Chapter 10 are heavily predicated on surrogates of the closest kindred or degree, either by blood or marriage.[5] In order to head off possible confusion or ill will or anger on the part of family members, they (and health care providers) should be prospectively (and, perhaps, pointedly) advised well in advance that the companion or partner or friend has been designated as agent or proxy. It may be advisable for family members to be provided with copies of the document appointing the partner or companion. Note well that in the absence of directives, a partner or companion or friend may be *summarily precluded* from direction of or participation in health care decision-making for the esteemed other.

§ 11.10—Embryos, Ova, and Sperm

Embryos, ova and sperm may be banked indefinitely. Written stipulations as to use may be a prerequisite to either infertility treatments or banking; although not likely contemplated as such at execution, these private contractual agreements may be logically considered a style of advance directives. Conceivably (no pun intended), instructions for disposition of embryos, ova and sperm could be formally included in an all-encompassing directive. In this event, be careful that instructions are stated consistently in all related documents. Also check to see if there is statute or case law on this point.

§ 11.11—Expressions by Decisionally Incapacitated

An individual already subject to guardianship may retain sufficient ability to participate to some degree in his health care decisions. As with mature minors (below), guardians and doctors will do well to carefully solicit and then weigh all cogent expressions a decisionally incapacitated individual may make. As necessary, seek judicial instruction if a guardianship is in place. (See following.)

§ 11.12—Guardianship and Conservatorship and Directives

If a guardian is appointed, what becomes of a directive? Some state statutes govern this eventuality; those that do vary considerably in application. In North Dakota, the terms of a pre-existing directive take precedence over the functions of a guardian. Kansas provides that a guardian assumes the same power to revoke or amend a health care document that the principal would have had. A health care power ceases altogether upon appointment and qualification of a guardian in North Carolina. Given the divergence of these three illustrations, check statutes and case law with extra care. Refer to the discussion of guardianship in Chapter 10.

§ 11.13—Foreign Nationals

Of all the states, only New Jersey appears to have prospectively and specifically addressed the needs of foreign nationals travelling or living in the U.S.: "An advance directive executed in a foreign country in compliance with the laws of that country or the State of New Jersey, and not contrary to the public policy of this state, is validly executed for purposes of this act."[6] See the reciprocal issue of "International Travel," below. Parenthetically, other nations taking initiatives with advance directives include Australia, Canada, Denmark, Finland, Germany, Japan, the Netherlands, and the United Kingdom. Palliative care (i.e., comfort care of the terminally ill) movements now are found in countries throughout the world.

§ 11.14—Health Care Providers Serving as Agents or Proxies

Generally, this is not a good idea, if only because it may engender the appearance (if nothing else) of a conflict of interest. Alabama, Connecticut, and Georgia are among the states that have laws prohibiting a patient's attending physician from serving as health care agent or proxy. California and Kansas are examples of states that additionally exclude operators or employees of certain care facilities from service. Check applicable statute.

§ 11.15—International Travel

There is no uniform international law or convention or treaty on the subject of advance health care directives. They are unheard of in some nations.

Depending on the country, directives may be either honored or utterly useless. They likely will elicit reaction ranging from acceptance to puzzlement and bewilderment to, perhaps, disdain, derision, and outright rejection. Travelers and permanent overseas residents alike need to brace accordingly. In the event the host nation provides for advance directives in some form, American citizens residing abroad should consult foreign lawyers for advice. U.S. nationals will do well to carry copies of their directives. They cannot, however, count on other countries to give them the least bit of force or effect. Embassies and consulates may be unable to render much help. From this stems a disturbing scenario: must a patient be physically removed from a nation or state back to the state governing the directive in order to permit the agent to act (e.g., discontinue life support)? Also see "Foreign Nationals" (above) and the Chapter 12 subsection "Forum Shopping" (page 156).

§ 11.16—Military Personnel on Active Duty

Refer to 10 U.S.C.A. 1044c (reproduced in Appendix A). Of all the states, only Louisiana appears to have a "Military Advance Medical Directive"[7] predicated on the federal statute. The illustrative Louisiana form is contained on the accompanying CD-ROM.

§ 11.17—Minors

Minor children in the U.S. typically do not possess authority to consent to or refuse or delegate health care. However, many (particularly those approaching maturity and emancipation) can express astute choices. Accommodate their participation to the greatest extent possible.

What should be done if the articulations of a minor are sharply at variance with parental or medical suggestions? Parents/guardians and care providers are best advised to take a child's wishes into careful consideration before consents are rendered. Keep an open mind. Ideally, some sort of consensus will be attained.

In the event of profound disagreement, guardianship proceedings might be considered as a last resort. Note well, however, that a "cramdown" of this nature may only make matters worse: the child might become even more intractable toward a suggested course of treatments, irrespective of authorizations a guardian may obtain from a judge.

Check state statutes about consents to health care: some may have provisions governing minors. Although rarely used, many states provide for emancipation of mature minors (for example, at age 16). In the event of serious or terminal illness, it might be possible for a minor to be formally emancipated and then execute advance health care directives, thereby taking complete control of her care. If this avenue is followed, seek a concurrent judicial order specifically authorizing the newly emancipated individual to execute directives.

Seven states (Arkansas, Connecticut, Illinois, Indiana, Louisiana, New Mexico, and Texas) have either an advance directive or surrogate law that allows parents (or others with standing) to authorize withdrawal of life sustaining treatments from minors. Appellate court decisions with similar scope and impact have been rendered in Georgia, Maine, Michigan,[8] Missouri, and Virginia. The remaining 38 states and the District of Columbia have not addressed the issue of end-of-life decisions for minors.[9] Also refer to the section on anencephalic infants (above).

§ 11.18—No Agent or Proxy or Surrogate

This circumstance may present with disconcerting frequency in institutional settings, particularly among the very elderly: some patients quite literally come to outlive all of their immediate family members and friends. As appropriate, this augurs for execution (where appropriate and available) of a living will or declaration. This style of directive represents an end-of-life instruction to treating physicians and does not require the designation of an agent or proxy.

A bit of calling and checking may identify a remote cousin or nephew or niece, or a neighbor or other acquaintance, or clergy. Inquire of local social service organizations or agencies on aging or senior citizen centers or former neighbors: a person knowledgeable about a patient's habits and treatment preferences may be located in this fashion. If the patient has an uncommon surname, check regional phone books or online "people finder" functions: similarly surnamed individuals may be surprisingly helpful. (Be tactful. A person so contacted may be greatly taken aback to learn that the patient— whom they indeed may know or to whom they may be related—is ill or in crisis. Also, take care not to inadvertently blunder into old family feuds and animosities.) Here is another idea, albeit a bit of a longshot: genealogists now are posting family trees widely on websites. Try searching for uncommon names in this fashion as well.

As a last resort—and only as a last resort—work with counsel to obtain court appointment of a guardian to render requisite health care consents. Refer to the Chapter 10 discussion on guardianship.

§ 11.19—Organ Donation

See the discussion on page 13.

§ 11.20—Out of State Travel or Relocation

What happens if a resident of State Q executes directives there and is grievously injured in a State R car accident while enroute to a vacation in State S? Do State Q directives apply in State R?

Fortunately, the majority of states have provided for reciprocity. The following 33 give statutory credence to the living wills of others: Alabama, Alaska, Arkansas, Arizona, California, Delaware, Florida, Hawaii, Illinois, Iowa, Louisiana, Maine, Maryland, Minnesota, Montana, Nebraska, Nevada, New Hampshire, New Jersey, New Mexico, North Dakota, Ohio, Oklahoma, Oregon, Rhode Island, South Carolina, South Dakota, Tennessee, Texas, Utah, Virginia, Washington, and West Virginia. Reciprocity in recognition of living wills is not addressed in Colorado, Connecticut, District of Columbia, Georgia, Idaho, Indiana, Kansas, Kentucky, Mississippi, Missouri, North Carolina, Pennsylvania, Vermont, Wisconsin and Wyoming. Three states (Massachusetts, Michigan, and New York) do not provide for living wills.[10]

Reciprocity is extended to out of state health care agencies and proxies by 33 states: Alabama, Arkansas, Arizona, California, Colorado, Delaware, Florida, Hawaii, Indiana, Iowa, Kansas, Maine, Maryland, Massachusetts, Minnesota, Nebraska, New Hampshire, New Jersey, New Mexico, New York, North Dakota, Ohio, Oklahoma, Oregon, Rhode Island, South Carolina, Tennessee, Texas, Utah, Vermont, Virginia, Washington, and West Virginia. This contingency is not contemplated in the laws of Connecticut, District of Columbia, Georgia, Idaho, Illinois, Kentucky, Louisiana, Michigan, Mississippi, Missouri, Montana, Nevada, North Carolina, Pennsylvania, South Dakota, Wisconsin and Wyoming (17 total). Alaska does not have a law on health care agency.[11]

In instances where reciprocity is not expressly provided for by statute, one conceivably might assert that the full faith and credit clause of Article IV of the U.S. Constitution compels one state to honor the advance health care directive of another.

Individuals who permanently relocate from one jurisdiction to another will do well to destroy directives from their "old" state of residence and re-execute them with the suggested language and formalities of the "new" state.

The "Five Wishes" document (which incorporates a values history) attempts to overcome the balkanization of advance directives: it purports to be valid in thirty-five states and the District of Columbia. It may be viewed (and, if desired, purchased) through www.agingwithdignity.org/5wishes.html.

§ 11.21—Pregnancy

Perhaps a pregnant woman is in an irreversible coma due to, say, a severe head injury. What if she has a pre-existing advance directive that pointedly calls for the termination of "high tech" life support or the withdrawal of artificial hydration and nutrition in such a circumstance?

Thirty-one states suspend or curtail the application of living wills to pregnant patients: Alabama, Alaska, Arkansas, Colorado, Connecticut, Delaware, Georgia, Idaho, Illinois, Indiana, Iowa, Kansas, Kentucky, Massachusetts, Missouri, Montana, Nebraska, Nevada, New Hampshire, North Dakota, Ohio, Oklahoma, Pennsylvania, Rhode Island, South Carolina, South Dakota, Texas, Utah, Washington, Wisconsin and Wyoming. In Arizona, Maryland, Minnesota, and New Jersey a pregnant woman may refuse life support pursuant to a living will. In California, the District of Columbia, Florida, Louisiana, Maine, New Mexico, North Carolina, Oregon, Tennessee, Vermont and West Virginia, living will statutes make no reference to pregnancy. Living wills do not exist in Massachusetts, Michigan and New York.[12]

With respect to laws on health care agencies and proxies, 15 states—Alabama, Arkansas, Connecticut, Delaware, Kentucky, Michigan, Montana, Nebraska, New Hampshire, Ohio, Oklahoma, Pennsylvania, South Carolina, South Dakota and Utah—expressly prohibit agents or proxies from withdrawing or withholding life supports from pregnant patients. An agent or proxy may choose whether to withhold or withdraw life supports from a pregnant principal in Florida, Maryland, Minnesota, New Jersey, and Wisconsin. Alaska lacks a statute on health care agency. The District of Columbia and the remaining 29 states are silent on the issue of pregnancy and health care agency at the end of life.[13]

Presumably, directives regain effect when pregnancy ends. Check applicable statutes. Once again, the involvement of ethics committees may be particularly helpful.

§ 11.22—Prisoners

Prisoners may represent a suspect class of individuals—but this does not mean that the right to express treatment preferences in the form of advance health care directives is necessarily abridged or extinguished. Authority on this issue is scant. The Nevada attorney general has opined that a prisoner may sign a directive. However, that state's Department of Prisons may elect to disregard it for legitimate penological reasons.[14]

Although but tangential to the subject of advance directives, it has been held that a prisoner (if competent) may refuse medical interventions and forego life saving medical procedures.[15]

§ 11.23—Revocation of Directives

It is particularly important to observe that directives are predicated only upon ephemeral consents. Easily given, they also may be exceedingly easy to revoke. Examine state statute.

Revocation may be had in any of the fashions long associated with last wills and testaments: cutting, tearing, obliterating, or burning. However, in some jurisdictions (for example: Alabama, Arizona, Colorado, Connecticut, District of Columbia, Florida, Idaho, Illinois, Maryland, and Nebraska), they also may be *orally* revoked (generally in the presence of a competent witness, who subsequently must attest to the oral revocation through some sort of written formality). On this basis, the faintest murmur or whisper—sometimes even from a decisionally incapacitated patient—summarily ends the operation of a directive. Incongruous or disconcerting as this may be to an agent or proxy or medical practitioner, an oral revocation (where permitted) must be scrupulously and faithfully honored. If a directive is revoked in any fashion, practitioners have little choice but to resort to the diversions outlined in Chapter 10.

§ 11.24—Spiritual or Religious or Philosophical Imperatives

Refer to Chapter 9 and Appendix F.

§ 11.25 Conclusion

The foregoing are but some of the special circumstances and situations that may come to involve advance health care directives. If in doubt about any of the foregoing, or if confronted with an entirely different topic or issue, be *certain* to consult knowledgeable counsel.

Notes

1. 45 C.F.R § 1340.15.
2. Numrich, PD. "The Buddhist Tradition: Religious Beliefs and Healthcare Decisions." The Park Ridge Center, Chicago, 2001. p. 10.
3. *Donaldson v. Van De Kamp*, 4 Cal. Rptr. 2d 59 (Ct. App. 1992).
4. Forty-six states and the District of Columbia provide for both living wills and health care agents or proxies. MA, MI, and NY authorize the appointment of health care agents (only). Alaska provides only for the living will. Source: *End-of-Life-Law Digest*, "State Statutes Governing Living Wills and Appointment of Health Care Agents", Partnership for Caring, Inc., Washington, DC (March, 2001).

5. See the Minnesota reference in the section immediately above. Additionally, Vermont's recent initiative with civil unions may possibly contravene this premise.

6. N. J. STAT. ANN. § 25:2H-77.

7. LA. REV. STAT. §§ 1299.60 *et seq.*

8. "The advance directive of a mature minor, stating the desire that life-sustaining treatment be refused, should be taken into consideration or enforced when deciding whether to terminate the minor's life-support treatment or refuse medical treatment. (Citations.)" *In re Rosebush*, 491 N.W.2d 633, 634 (Mich.App. 1992).

9. *End-of-Life Law Digest*, "State Law Addressing Minors and End-of-Life Decisionmaking", Partnership for Caring, Inc. Washington, DC (Mar. 2001).

10. *End-of-Life Law Digest*, "Reciprocity Provisions in Living Will Statutes", Partnership for Caring, Inc., Washington, DC (March, 2001).

11. *End-of-Life Law Digest*, "Reciprocity Provisions in Statutes Authorizing Health Care Agents", Partnership for Caring, Inc., Washington, DC (March, 2001).

12. *End-of-Life Law Digest*, "Pregnancy Restrictions in Living Will Statutes," Partnership for Caring, Inc., Washington, DC (March, 2001).

13. *End-of-Life Law Digest*, "Pregnancy Restrictions in Statutes Authorizing Health Care Agents", Partnership for Caring, Inc., Washington, DC (March, 2001).

14. Op. Nev. Att'y Gen. 95-02 (Feb. 23, 1995).

15. *Singletary v. Costello*, 665 So. 2d 1099 (Fla. Dist. Ct. App. 1996).

CHAPTER 12

The Future of Advance Health Care Directives

§ 12.01 Introduction

The future of advance health care directives is virtually impossible to discern.

It seems safe to say, however, that directives as we know them today likely will become "extinct"—remembered dimly as crude harbingers and recounted as the first timid individual expressions of how we "ancestors" wanted to be cared for in the event of decisional or communicative incapacity.

It is, of course, the staggering advances of medicine and science that will drive today's directives to oblivion.

Consider the progress of recent decades. Sophisticated machinery now staves off clinical death so effectively that we are sore pressed to decide whether the life it sustains be miracle or abomination.

§ 12.02—Questions to Ask

Humans may be conceived in laboratories; embryos so resulting may be frozen and preserved indefinitely. (And if they be life, just whose lives are those, anyway?)

Human organ transplantation now is almost routine. Successful xenotransplantation—from animals into humans, perhaps using genetically modified organs—cannot be far behind. Mechanical "spare parts?" Blood and tissue substitutes? Why not?

Animals have been cloned. Dare we now dabble in human cloning for the sole purpose of producing therapeutic stem cells? Deplorable and despicable as many of us may think it to be, it is merely a matter of time before some renegade team reproduces a human as a clone. What then?

And here's one more. We recently reached what may yet prove to be one of history's major milestones: the mapping of the human genome. The implications—to the extent we now can feebly discern them—are stupefying.

Genetic markers as precursors of disease? We'll come to know them all. Genetic manipulation to mitigate or stave off or even cure diseases? Who can argue? Facilitate recovery from addictions—or blunt or even block addictions altogether? Terrific! Genetically "preselect" or "prefabricate" a baby? What's to stop us? Culture and bank our own "spare" organs? Arrest the aging process? Miraculous—perhaps.

§ 12.03—Ethical Issues

There's a dark side, of course—and a fiendishly dark side, at that. Genetic discrimination in education and employment and insurance? Outlawed—for now, perhaps. "Outbreeding" of the genetically "infirm" by selectively forbidding reproduction—in any form? Or cultivating a genetically "superior" species to supplant the "inferior" human race? Talk about sinister!

And what about the seemingly (until now, perhaps) science fiction idea of cryonics, where people are frozen upon death to await thawing, resuscitation, and subsequent "cure" and reanimation by unknown future means?

Alice in Wonderland possibilities abound. Would a genetically manipulated (or, perhaps, concocted?) child actually even have parents? Just what will be the status of children conceived of the sperm and ova of dead parents? Heirs? Orphans? Neither? (And say, lawyers—what might become of the Rules Against Perpetuities?) Would a woman carrying the implanted male embryo of, say, her own biological parents end up bearing a brother or a son— or both? Will a human clone be offspring, or self, or some entirely new legal entity (or fiction)? What about carrying to term an embryo selected solely for purposes of conscription as an involuntary blood or marrow (or lung or liver or kidney?) donor for a living relative? (Might the fetus have the right to a guardian ad litem or similar functionary to object in court? Might the parents and doctors and prospective recipient actually be engaged in planning or commissioning some kind of assault or tort? Or imposing some form of involuntary servitude?) The hundreds of dizzying hypotheticals—some of which surely will come to pass—eventually will make Aldous Huxley's *Brave New World* read like a quaint little nursery rhyme.

It is a certainty that the law—and ethics, and spiritual and religious thinking—will be sorely pressed to keep up with (much less interpret) these medical developments.

What will advance health care directives be able to do about any of this? Simply put—absolutely nothing, as we presently know directives to be.

§ 12.04—The Future of Directives

But maybe the "descendents" of directives will be structured to accommodate some or all of these scenarios—plus the many we surely cannot now foresee. Perhaps the disposition of embryos might someday be addressed in a directive—as might cloning, or manipulation of genes, or "ownership" of banked organs and tissue, or stewardship (if not ownership) of one's own genetic sequencing. Surely we all hope for the best of outcomes. Surely we all hope that individual expression on matters so personal will forever hold sway. Surely we all hope to adapt or devise variants of advance directives that can rise to the enormous challenges ahead.

So whither directives? What can be done—indeed, if anything can be done at all—to improve the paltry incidence of use? What can be done to propel (rather than drag) directives into the future?

§ 12.05 Better Methods of Implementation

§ 12.06—Details, Details

One drawback to health care powers and proxies in some jurisdictions is that they are perceived as downright intimidating: the "one size fits all" form prescribed by statutes can be multiple pages long. The dilemma is that the "one size" form can at the same time be, by necessity, inordinately general; additional detail may be of enormous help to a proxy/agent and the doctors. A partial solution might be the use of forms, templates, or adaptive software that can prompt differing lines of thinking and decision-making. This would be especially useful if a patient/client suffers from a chronic disease or condition: the choices of, say, an individual with pulmonary disease may be dramatically different from those of a heart or renal or dementia or cancer patient. Also, religious, spiritual, or philosophical affinities may trigger wholly different treatment preferences and might be similarly prompted and accommodated. As an alternative, wider use of values histories (Appendix D) to augment and supplement directives should be considered.

§ 12.07—Palliative Care and Hospices

Upon reflection, many of us will agree that advocating for and aiding a terminally ill person—providing comfort care, solace, encouragement, and a modicum of decency and dignity for the final days, hours, and moments—is a function that is desperately needed in our society. As the hospice movement becomes more engrained in our social consciousness, assistance with dying and support while living the final days may become a realistic priority for all. Within the hospice environment, prioritizing health and personal needs and relating these to quality of life and final days is consistent with the concept of advance health care directives. The multidisciplinary team assembled for hospice care can be an extra set of eyes and ears assuring that advance directives are carried out as the principal intended. Much insight has been gained by pioneers in this field, as well as continuing support for consumer and professional education. For more information, refer to the authors' website (http://www.AdvanceHealthCareDirectives.com).

§ 12.08—Quality Improvement

Quality improvement (QI) activities represent local efforts to optimize health care outcomes. Common in settings such as hospitals and nursing facilities,

QI is characterized by cycles of empirical study and monitoring, followed by recommendations, and then interventions which may include changes in institutional protocols. Examples of typical areas selected for study might include: rates of post-operative infections, or the timing of administration of medications for patients admitted to the hospital for pneumonia, or reducing the incidence of accidental patient falls out of bed.

Unlike formal clinical research studies, QI initiatives usually afford relaxed time frames, permit "mid-course corrections" (i.e., ongoing study refinements), and encourage widespread collaboration. Although they usually produce quantitative changes in localized clinical practices, QI studies are not bound by the rigorous study designs and statistical evaluations that characterize exhaustive medical research protocols. In short, QI activities are semi-formal institutional evaluations and "tweakings" designed to enhance and improve local delivery of health care services in manners consistent with broadly accepted standards.

It follows that quality improvement efforts also should encompass advance health care directives. Logical criterion (quality indicators) might include (1) presentation of state-specific documents to patients upon contact or admission, in fashions consistent with the Patient Self Determination Act, (2) incidences of execution of directives, (3) improved methods to incorporate copies into patient charts and records, (4) conversations about directives between patients (or, as appropriate, their agents) and health professionals, (5) steps to assure that directives are included in the paperwork accompanying patient transfers between facilities (e.g., nursing home to hospital and back), and (6) correlations of treatments actually rendered with the levels of care specified in directives.

In addition to aiding our collective empirical understanding about directives, QI efforts in this area are likely to lead to other enhancements, such as improved communications between patients and doctors. The "Breakthrough Series Collaborative", sponsored by the Center to Improve Care of the Dying and the Institute for Health Care Improvement, already has established that quality improvement activities in this respect lead to measurable improvements in care. (See Section 8.07.)

Impetus for QI in the area of advance health care directives may be forthcoming from oversight and regulatory entities in the very near future. (See Section 12.10.) Though subtle (if not altogether marginal) upon first regard, this development actually may come to have a marked impact—and a decidedly salutary effect—upon the incidence and use of directives.

§ 12.09—Ethics Consultants

A multidisciplinary approach to advance health care directives—generally, law, medicine, philosophy, and religion—is a core theme of this book. "Teams" of professionals should as necessary designate (perhaps from among themselves) an ethicist to take the lead. In larger hospitals and medical centers, bioethics committees may perform this function. The interests of patients/clients are perhaps best served when ethics is placed at the fore, with the various professions arrayed in support.

§ 12.10—Legislation, Regulation, and Other Oversight

For better or worse, legislative initiatives on advance health care directives are—and likely will continue to be—a state (rather than federal) function. To the extent that it is possible, states should adopt (or at least incorporate into their statutes precepts from) the model Uniform Health-Care Decisions Act (which the ABA approved in February, 1994.) (See Appendix C.)

New regulatory initiatives could give impetus to the Patient Self Determination Act (PSDA). Two avenues for change may be through the U.S. Department of Health and Human Services' Centers for Medicare and Medicaid Services (CMS—formerly known as the Health Care Financing Administration, or HCFA). For example, the Minimum Data Set (MDS) is a federally mandated assessment tool used to monitor quality issues for nursing home patients; at present, it is used in part to tabulate the existence (or nonexistence) of directives upon admission. The OASIS criterion track quality issues (including incidence of directives) among home health care patients. These are welcome first steps.

Similarly, the regional Quality Improvement Organizations (QIOs) contracted by CMS to provide Medicare quality oversight also could in the future promote review of health care decision making issues (including directives) in both hospital and long term care settings.

The Joint Commission on Accreditation of Healthcare Organizations (JCAHO) long has been involved with review and oversight of hospital performance. In recent years, this Oakbrook Terrace, Illinois-based nonprofit has expanded and taken on similar roles in long term care (e.g., nursing home) and home health care (including hospice) environments. Interestingly, advance health care planning now has become an additional compliance area to be evaluated as part of cyclical Joint Commission reviews. (See *Topics in Clinical Care Improvement: Advance Directives*, published by JCAHO in 1999. Copies may be purchased through www.jcaho.org.)

Future developments in legislation, regulation, and oversight (incremental though they may be) will, in aggregate, increase focus on advance health care directives—and increase their incidence of use.

§ 12.11—Saturation Marketing

As noted throughout, the federal Patient Self Determination Act (codified at 42 U.S.C.A. 1395cc (f)—reproduced in Appendix A) requires that state-specific directives be provided at the time of contact with Medicare and Medicaid-funded hospitals, nursing facilities, home health care agencies, and hospices. As modest a start as this is, and as well intended as this is, it simply does not carry the day: admission or contact may be the very worst time to be weighing directives, as patient judgment may be clouded or impaired. This introduction also imparts a highly unfortunate connotation and stigmatiza-tion: "I must *really* be sick if they want me to fill out directives."

Directives must be made ubiquitous. They should be included with drivers license and license plate renewals, or used as stuffers with utility bills, or printed from time to time in newspapers and magazines as public service advertisements, or passed out at polls on election days, or placed in literature racks in public places such as libraries or post offices or col-leges or municipal or state offices. Public service broadcast spots would also be immeasurably helpful. Directives are *good public policy* and should be encouraged accordingly.

Here is a thought: bind them into tax documents and offer a one-time "honorarium" tax credit of, say, $5 or $10, for filling them out and plac-ing them—plus organ donation instructions—with a designated registry.[1] Awareness of the federal Patient Self Determination Act (PSDA) might also be heightened through low-or-no cost federal "outlets": a special website ded-icated to the purpose, brochures at Social Security and post offices, mailings to Medicare recipients, literature at personnel offices for federal employees, and perhaps even through flyers or brochures with Internal Revenue Service materials.

§ 12.12—Technology

Pen-and-paper directives probably will forever be with us—but they soon will become anachronistic. Because health care providers and third party payers are rapidly converting to electronic record keeping, some form of electronic directives will have to be devised to match. Electronic directives[2] (or paper directives scanned into electronic systems) readily lend themselves to the "good footprints" admonition contained throughout this book: they are easily stored with physicians and hospitals and nursing homes, or in governmental or nonprofit registries, or on secure websites, or even encoded in full on the "smart" cards or pendants or similar devices that may yet become common in our wallets and purses or on our persons. Personal information such as directives may even come to be stored in subcutaneously embedded (i.e., implanted under the skin) chips.

Electronically stored directives are likely to be much more easily pro-duced in the event of an emergency. They also may reduce the incidence of "paper" directives being pressed on individuals of marginal capacity. Ad-mittedly, electronic directives will be a hard sell for some. But then again, personal computers, direct deposit, and automatic teller machines were once hard sells, too—and not so many years ago, either.

§ 12.13 Better Education

§ 12.14—Educating the Public

The idea of advance health care directives as prudent "personal contingency planning" must be inculcated in the public at large. It should be introduced (if only in passing) as early as grade school and surely by high school as part of public health or consumer curricula. For the present, adults probably are best reached through the "saturation marketing" ideas described above.

§ 12.15—Educating Professionals

Passing introduction (at least) should be made to directives in law, medical, divinity, and other corresponding professional schools. Continuing education forums also are appropriate venues. For lawyers, advance health care directives now should be considered an integral part of estate planning; they also should be introduced to clients who seek wills. (Better yet, directives should be prepared and executed contemporaneously *with* wills.) Disability planning may be far more important than "death planning" (i.e., a will). And remember—those without the personal contingency plans known as advance directives (and, similarly, those without contemplatively drawn property powers of attorney or trusts) run the risk of "living probate"—that is, a court-imposed guardianship or conservatorship (or both).

§ 12.16 Shifting Attitudes

Sensitive as they are, issues of race, culture, and ethnicity all affect the utility—as well as the incidence in use—of advance directives. To the extent that it is possible, the concept of directives must be adapted (or, better, made transparent) to these very human issues. In other words, race, culture, and ethnicity cannot—must not—be forced to conform to the idea. To be successfully presented, the idea of advance health care directives must be couched sensitively and in neutral terms.

Clients and patients look to lawyers, clinicians, and clergy and spiritual advisors for cues on any number of subjects (including advance health care directives). To the extent that professionals articulate and advocate the subject—indeed, work cooperatively in its promulgation—societal attitudes are bound to shift, if only by one individual at a time.

§ 12.17 Dilemmas

§ 12.18—Forum Shopping

Because advance health care directives do not appear to rise to a constitutional issue at the federal level, we have 51 jurisdictions (plus affiliated territories and entities) taking different approaches on the subject. This gives rise (if only in the abstract) to a disquieting possibility: might a principal and agent ever want to cross state lines to avail themselves of end-of-life decision-making mechanisms of another jurisdiction that they deem "desirable" or "more favorable?" As noted in Chapter 11, the majority of states have reciprocity provisions for advance directives. The full faith and credit clause of Article IV of the U.S. constitution arguably applies (at least in some form) to the rest. The only decidedly singular jurisdiction that might even possibly lend itself to "forum shopping" at present is, perhaps, Oregon because of its Death with Dignity Act (Appendix I). Note well, however, that the Oregon framers obviously anticipated—and moved to blunt—the "forum shopping" prospect by imposing a residency requirement.[3]

Might "forum shopping" ever go international? In January, 2002, the Netherlands became the first nation to legalize euthanasia. Observe, however, that the Dutch simultaneously foreclosed the forum shopping prospect. Upon passage of the enabling legislation in November, 2000, the Associated Press quoted a Dutch justice ministry official, Wijnand Stevens: "There is no possibility for foreigners to come here for euthanasia. The criteria call for a long-term doctor–patient relationship."

Another scenario—although surely rare—is if a U.S. national falls ill in a foreign nation (or vice versa). Might one have to return to his or her native land for treatments if the host country does not recognize (or declines to honor) a directive? Resolution of this possibility probably awaits some sort of future international protocol or convention or treaty. (See the Chapter 11 discussions of "Foreign Nationals" and "International Travel".)

§ 12.19—Utilization

Preservation of self-determination and maintenance of quality and dignity and comfort at the end of life are important reasons for promoting advance directives.

Unfortunately, end-of-life medical care can be very costly. In instances when lavish spending on care does not correspond with patient wishes, great waste (to both the individual and society) ensues. Whether performed in an intensive care unit of a hospital or in a home hospice setting, care for critically ill patients in precipitous medical and functional decline is labor intensive. Apart from some limited applications of robotics, plus enhancements to electronic, video, and computer-assisted monitoring and other interactive functions, this is not likely to change much. Who among us really wants to converse at length with a computer, or be cared for by a robot?

Even so, Emanuel believes that hospice care, coupled with the use of advance health care directives, can reduce health care costs in the range of 25 percent and 40 percent during the last month of life.[4] Similarly, recent studies of the implementation of advance care directives in nursing home populations have shown reduced utilization of costly services without affecting quality of care.[5] More definitive studies are necessary to pinpoint and quantify actual savings.

Cost containment at the end of life purely for economic reasons will never be widely accepted in our society. Carried to the extreme, ruthless or even brutish efforts to minimize health care costs might be construed by some as a form of euthanasia. Sharp limitations on, or reductions of, last care based strictly on precepts of equity or justice for society as a whole are not likely to win many adherents, either. On the other hand, few would argue with the notion of reducing medical waste when unwanted services run contrary to a patient's personal wishes for treatment.

Societal thinking in the U.S. (and, for that matter, throughout the world) over the next several decades undoubtedly will provoke sharp—and constant—controversy on personal autonomy versus justice in health care versus the common good. Dare we ration health care, particularly at the end of life? Or, at the other extreme, do we want to spend ourselves silly with grandiose health schemes and pour copious amounts of money into medical abominations that, to some, end up compromising and denigrating the very dignity of life itself? Will we ever find sensible limits or middle ground? Advance health care directives and end-of-life cost containment surely will be at the vortex of this fervent policy debate.

§ 12.20 One Last Look

Here's a final glimpse at the future. Pen and paper directives are becoming passé. Even electronic memorializations soon will be eclipsed—by biotechnology.

As it turns out, we humans (and our forebearers) have been carrying around a form of advance care directives—genes—for millions of years. With the completion of the genome project, we now can begin to decipher the directives within.

But for good or ill, we will do more than merely read human genetic code. We will write and edit it. And in so doing, we will come to express advance health care directives—at least in part—in a wholly new medium.

We will not write with ink. We will not write with the assistance of electronic devices. We will instead write our directives with tiny strands of DNA.

§ 12.21 Conclusion

Progress in the field of advance health care directives will result from incisive initiatives and improved education. We collectively must be astute enough to know that directives and their progeny will, as matters of public policy, have very short "half-lives" and will, by necessity, have to be constantly adapted or recast to accommodate futures we cannot possibly foresee.

We also must be astute enough to know that no matter how hard we try, some of the most nettlesome problems will forever defy complete solution. Issues of the timing of death, of competence and incompetence, of imputing what the decisionally incapacitated might really have wanted—and, most profoundly, the staggering and stupefying gravity of the justice and ethics of it all—will perpetually torment and befuddle us.

And so we resolve to band together, hang on to what is good and true and right, help those in need as best we can, and earnestly press into the trembling hands of the future our most sacred efforts. We dare do no less.

Notes

1. Examples of registries (not to be construed as endorsements by either the American Bar Association or the authors) include www.uslivingwillsregistry.com and the Medic Alert Foundation www.medicalert.com.
2. For a discussion, see J. M. Dumont, *The Electronic Living will and the Formalities of Execution* www.law.vill.edu/chron/articles/livingwi.htm.
3. OR. REV. STAT. § 127.860.
4. E. Emanuel, *Cost Savings at the End of Life: What Do the Data Show?*, 275 JAMA 24 (1996).
5. D.W. Molloy et al., *Systemic Implementation of an Advance Directive Program in Nursing Homes: A Randomized Controlled Trial*, 283 JAMA No 11 (2000) Pages 1437–1444.

AFTERWORD

Dear Friend

Dear Friend:

We are not kindred. We never will meet. Still we call you friend.

We write this day for people whom you surely number among your friends: your doctor, your lawyer, your religious or spiritual advisor, your caregivers. It is they who will help you grapple with some of the most intensely personal decisions of your life: advance health care directives.

In a dim and distant way, though, we speak to you through your advisor friends.

So just what are advance health care directives? Most commonly these are known as powers of attorney (or proxies) for health care. Living wills (or declarations), though still useful in some contexts, now are largely in eclipse.

Advance directives can be an excruciatingly difficult subject. You, like we, find the subject disquieting, disagreeable, and distasteful. Know that it's normal to feel that way.

The concept of the principal type of advance directives—health care powers or proxies—stems from the comfortable old idea of power of attorney. For example, if you wish to sell your car and must be out of town, you can, through a writing, appoint an agent and authorize her to show it, sell it, sign the papers, and collect the money for you. You can even direct some or all terms: the lowest selling price you will accept, payment by either cash or cashiers check, the date upon which the power expires, and so forth.

Health care powers are a fairly new variation on this theme. In the event you are unable to speak for yourself due to injury or illness, you can "deputize" someone else—an agent or proxy—to work with the doctors on your behalf. As with the authority you might give to sell your car, you may, if you wish, set general or specific terms for treatment: medical procedures you want or don't want, instructions on when (if at all) to withhold life sustaining procedures, start and stop dates for the agent's authority, and the like.

Forms will refer to you as the "principal" or "patient" or something similar. The person you designate (or "deputize") to make health care decisions for you will be referred to variously as the "proxy" or "agent".

Suggested or statutory forms probably represent the most broad and expansive delegations of health care decision-making authority. If that's what you want, fine. Know that most of these forms can be modified or adapted by filling in blanks or checking off boxes to define or limit scope of care or to include or exclude certain treatments. In other words, tailor-make directives by "chipping away" at the broad grants of authority likely contained in the form. Do it *your* way.

Although state law may permit you to write your own directive in your own words, consider using the statutory form at least as a point of departure. Care providers probably will recognize the state-suggested form and are comfortable working with it. A radically different presentation may give them pause.

An advance health care directive is not forever! As your interests and wishes change over the years, destroy old documents and execute new ones. In the event you move out of state, it is a good idea to re-execute the documents so that they comport with the laws of your new home.

The choice of agent or proxy is pivotal. Without a knowledgeable, astute, compassionate, and—yes—courageous person to step into you shoes and help the doctors decide, all your efforts with advance directives may be for naught.

It's downright impossible to anticipate all medical scenarios. That's another reason to give very careful thought to whom you name as your "deputy". At some point you—indeed, any of us—need to let go and trust the "deputy" to choose wisely and well in difficult circumstances. Give good guidance in your directives, and have confidence in your "deputy" to handle the unexpected. If upon reflection you don't have faith in that person, then you should—must, actually, for your own peace of mind—choose anew. Rip up your old directive and execute a new one. (Also, write in your new one that you are revoking the old. Specify the date of the former document. You don't want your updated wishes confused by stray old photocopies!)

In most states, you can control the timing of advance directives. Perhaps you can specify a start date, and even a stop or sunset date. In order to preserve your personal autonomy for as long as possible, consider a so-called springing power (one that sets triggering circumstances rather than a start date). An example might be "this directive take effect upon the independent determinations, in writing, of two medical doctors that I am totally incapable of making health care decisions."

Articulate the quality of life that you want. Do you desire comfort care only in the event of terminal illness? Do you think there comes a point where "high tech" medical interventions end up demeaning life? Do you want to be saved no matter what? Then say so. Write out just how you want it. Your deputy and family and friends and doctors are not mind readers.

Be wary of making blanket exclusions about treatments—for example, "no ventilator." It's one thing, perhaps, to decline ventilator treatment in the event of an irreversible coma or persistent vegetative state. But what are the doctors to do if you have, say, an emergency appendectomy and need a "vent" briefly as you recover from anesthesia?

If you suffer from a chronic condition, consider structuring directives along the lines of likely treatment scenarios for the specific illness.

If you anticipate arguments about your care in the event of your incapacity, try to articulate how decisions will be made. Avoid use of co-agents: they may disagree. (Some states expressly prohibit the use of co-agents in any event.) You don't want a quarreling family. You don't want a judge to have to appoint a guardian for you if family and agents and physicians end up deadlocked over your directives.

State any spiritual or religious preferences. Are certain treatments forbidden? Are there rites or rituals to be conducted? What beliefs govern disposition of remains?

Here's a really distasteful issue: the expense of care. Does there ever come a point where the costs of clinically maintaining you in a horribly compromised and denigrating way become financially ruinous for your family? (And what about the enormous *emotional* toll your suffering takes on your loved ones?) Can scarce health care dollars be put to better use? It's your call, perhaps, if you're a private pay patient. Can you bind third party payers? Should you? And what about medically futile care?

Give guidance on organ donation. If you are amenable, know that it is the very best gift any of us may ever make.

Be certain that directives contain more than merely the name and address of the agent or proxy. Provide both home and work telephone numbers. As appropriate, include wireless phone, pager, and fax numbers, as well as e-mail addresses. For that matter, list all appropriate numbers for successor or backup proxies or agents. You don't want to force emergency personnel to play sleuth on your behalf with directory assistance in a distant city. That could well be a waste of *your* precious treatment time! (Once again, don't force others to be mind readers.)

If you execute advance directives, leave good "footprints." Discuss your wishes with your agent or proxy. Give copies to your doctor and/or your care facility for inclusion in your medical records. Record them with a registry or possibly with an on-line service. Leave copies somewhere in your residence and workplace where emergency personnel may readily find them. Carry a card in your wallet or purse (or wear a bracelet or medallion) indicating that you have directives and where they may be found.

Consider this: you *want* advance health care directives. In the vernacular, you want 'em *bad*. Because if you don't decide how treatment choices— indeed, whether you are to live or die—are to be made if you cannot speak, then guess what? Someone *else* will decide for you. And that someone else may do something completely contrary to what you want. That's a really scary prospect!

Finally, this above all. There is *no* "right way" with advance health care directives. Your advisor friends will help you. But they cannot decide for you. Have the courage to call it as you see it. Set your course by the moral compass and spiritual stars that guide you all the days and nights of your life. Draw deeply upon your own very personal takes on ethics, philosophy, religion, righteousness, grace, and reason—and, yes, intuition and decency and common sense. You'll not go wrong.

Dear friend, we wish you well.

Carol Krohm and Scott Summers

Appendices

APPENDIX A
Federal Statutes

(i) The Patient Self Determination Act
42 USCA § 1395cc

- (f) Maintenance of written policies and procedures
  - (1) For purposes of subsection (a)(1)(Q) of this section and sections *1395i*-3(c)(2)(E), *1395l*(s), *1395w*-25(i), *1395mm*(c)(8), and 1395bbb(a)(6) of this title, the requirement of this subsection is that a provider of services, Medicare+Choice organization, or prepaid or eligible organization (as the case may be) maintain written policies and procedures with respect to all adult individuals receiving medical care by or through the provider or organization—
    - (A) to provide written information to each such individual concerning—
      - (i) an individual's rights under State law (whether statutory or as recognized by the courts of the State) to make decisions concerning such medical care, including the right to accept or refuse medical or surgical treatment and the right to formulate advance directives (as defined in paragraph (3)), and (ii) the written policies of the provider or organization respecting the implementation of such rights;
    - (B) to document in a prominent part of the individual's current medical record whether or not the individual has executed an advance directive;
    - (C) not to condition the provision of care or otherwise discriminate against an individual based on whether or not the individual has executed an advance directive;
    - (D) to ensure compliance with requirements of State law (whether statutory or as recognized by the courts of the State) respecting advance directives at facilities of the provider or organization; and
    - (E) to provide (individually or with others) for education for staff and the community on issues concerning advance directives. Subparagraph (C) shall not be construed as requiring the provision of care which conflicts with an advance directive.

- (2) The written information described in paragraph (1)(A) shall be provided to an adult individual—
  - (A) in the case of a hospital, at the time of the individual's admission as an inpatient,
  - (B) in the case of a skilled nursing facility, at the time of the individual's admission as a resident,

- (C) in the case of a home health agency, in advance of the individual coming under the care of the agency,
- (D) in the case of a hospice program, at the time of initial receipt of hospice care by the individual from the program, and

  (E) in the case of an eligible organization (as defined in section *1395mm*(b) of this title) or an organization provided payments under section *1395l*(a)(1)(A) of this title or a Medicare+Choice organization, at the time of enrollment of the individual with the organization.

- (3) In this subsection, the term "advance directive" means a written instruction, such as a living will or durable power of attorney for health care, recognized under State law (whether statutory or as recognized by the courts of the State) and relating to the provision of such care when the individual is incapacitated.
- (4) For construction relating to this subsection, see section *14406* of this title (relating to clarification respecting assisted suicide, euthanasia, and mercy killing).
  - (w) Maintenance of written policies and procedures respecting advance directives
    - (1) For purposes of subsection (a)(57) of this section and sections *1396b*(m)(1)(A) and 1396r(c)(2)(E) of this title, the requirement of this subsection is that a provider or organization (as the case may be) maintain written policies and procedures with respect to all adult individuals receiving medical care by or through the provider or organization—
      - (A) to provide written information to each such individual concerning—
        - (i) an individual's rights under State law (whether statutory or as recognized by the courts of the State) to make decisions concerning such medical care, including the right to accept or refuse medical or surgical treatment and the right to formulate advance directives (as defined in paragraph (3)), and
        - (ii) the provider's or organization's written policies respecting the implementation of such rights;
      - (B) to document in the individual's medical record whether or not the individual has executed an advance directive;
      - (C) not to condition the provision of care or otherwise discriminate against an individual based on whether or not the individual has executed an advance directive;
      - (D) to ensure compliance with requirements of State law (whether statutory or as recognized by the courts of the State) respecting advance directives; and

        (E) to provide (individually or with others) for education for staff and the community on issues concerning advance directives. Subparagraph (C) shall not be construed as requiring the provision of care which conflicts with an advance directive.

- (2) The written information described in paragraph (1)(A) shall be provided to an adult individual—
  - (A) in the case of a hospital, at the time of the individual's admission as an inpatient,
  - (B) in the case of a nursing facility, at the time of the individual's admission as a resident,
  - (C) in the case of a provider of home health care or personal care services, in advance of the individual coming under the care of the provider,
  - (D) in the case of a hospice program, at the time of initial receipt of hospice care by the individual from the program, and
  (E) in the case of a medicaid managed care organization, at the time of enrollment of the individual with the organization.

- (3) Nothing in this section shall be construed to prohibit the application of a State law which allows for an objection on the basis of conscience for any health care provider or any agent of such provider which as a matter of conscience cannot implement an advance directive.
- (4) In this subsection, the term "advance directive" means a written instruction, such as a living will or durable power of attorney for health care, recognized under State law (whether statutory or as recognized by the courts of the State) and relating to the provision of such care when the individual is incapacitated.
- (5) For construction relating to this subsection, see section *14406* of this title (relating to clarification respecting assisted suicide, euthanasia, and mercy killing).

42 USCA 14406

Sec. 14406. Clarification with respect to advance directives

Subject to section 14402(b) of this title (relating to construction and treatment of certain services), sections 1395cc(f) and 1396a(w) of this title shall not be construed—

- (1) to require any provider or organization, or any employee of such a provider or organization, to inform or counsel any individual regarding any right to obtain an item or service furnished for the purpose of causing, or the purpose of assisting in causing, the death of the individual, such as by assisted suicide, euthanasia, or mercy killing; or
- (2) to apply to or to affect any requirement with respect to a portion of an advance directive that directs the purposeful causing of, or the

purposeful assisting in causing, the death of any individual, such as by assisted suicide, euthanasia, or mercy killing.

Sec. 1395bbb.—Conditions of participation for home health agencies; home health quality

- (a) Conditions of participation; protection of individual rights; notification of State entities; use of home health aides; medical equipment; individual's plan of care; compliance with Federal, State, and local laws and regulations

    Federal, State, and local laws and regulations

The conditions of participation that a home health agency is required to meet under this subsection are as follows:
- (6) The agency complies with the requirement of section $1395cc$(f) of this title (relating to maintaining written policies and procedures respecting advance directives).

Sec. 1395l.—Payment of benefits

- (a) Amounts

    Except as provided in section $1395mm$ of this title, and subject to the succeeding provisions of this section, there shall be paid from the Federal Supplementary Medical Insurance Trust Fund, in the case of each individual who is covered under the insurance program established by this part and incurs expenses for services with respect to which benefits are payable under this part, amounts equal to—
    - (1) in the case of services described in section $1395k$(a)(1) of this title—80 percent of the reasonable charges for the services; except that
        - (A) an organization which provides medical and other health services (or arranges for their availability) on a prepayment basis (and either is sponsored by a union or employer, or does not provide, or arrange for the provision of, any inpatient hospital services) may elect to be paid 80 percent of the reasonable cost of services for which payment may be made under this part on behalf of individuals enrolled in such organization in lieu of 80 percent of the reasonable charges for such services if the organization undertakes to charge such individuals no more than 20 percent of such reasonable cost plus any amounts payable by them as a result of subsection (b) of this section.

- (s) Other prepaid organizations

    The Secretary may not provide for payment under subsection (a)(1)(A) of this section with respect to an organization unless the organization provides assurances satisfactory to the Secretary that the organization meets the requirement of section *1395cc*(f) of this title (relating to maintaining written policies and procedures respecting advance directives).

Sec. 1395mm.—Payments to health maintenance organizations and competitive medical plans

- (c) Enrollment in plan; duties of organization to enrollees
- (8) A contract under this section shall provide that the eligible organization shall meet the requirement of section *1395cc*(f) of this title (relating to maintaining written policies and procedures respecting advance directives).

(ii) Military Advance Medical Directive

10 USCA § 1044

Sec. 1044c. Advance medical directives of members and dependents: requirement for recognition by States

- (a) Instruments To Be Given Legal Effect Without Regard to State Law.—An advance medical directive executed by a person eligible for legal assistance—
  - (1) is exempt from any requirement of form, substance, formality, or recording that is provided for advance medical directives under the laws of a State; and
  (2) shall be given the same legal effect as an advance medical directive prepared and executed in accordance with the laws of the State concerned.
- (b) Advance Medical Directives.—For purposes of this section, an advance medical directive is any written declaration that—
  - (1) sets forth directions regarding the provision, withdrawal, or withholding of life-prolonging procedures, including hydration and sustenance, for the declarant whenever the declarant has a terminal physical condition or is in a persistent vegetative state; or
  - (2) authorizes another person to make health care decisions for the declarant, under circumstances stated in the declaration, whenever the declarant is incapable of making informed health care decisions.
- (c) Statement To Be Included.—(1) Under regulations prescribed by the Secretary concerned, an advance medical directive prepared by an attorney authorized to provide legal assistance shall contain a statement that sets forth the provisions of subsection (a).
  - (2) Paragraph (1) shall not be construed to make inapplicable the provisions of subsection (a) to an advance medical directive that does not include a statement described in that paragraph.
- (d) States Not Recognizing Advance Medical Directives.—Subsection (a) does not make an advance medical directive enforceable in a State

that does not otherwise recognize and enforce advance medical directives under the laws of the State.

- (e) Definitions.—In this section:
  - (1) The term "State" includes the District of Columbia, the Commonwealth of Puerto Rico, and a possession of the United States.
  - (2) The term "person eligible for legal assistance" means a person who is eligible for legal assistance under section 1044 of this title.
  - (3) The term "legal assistance" means legal services authorized under section *1044* of this title.

APPENDIX B
Glossary

(Note: the following generalized definitions may not suffice in all contexts. Refer as necessary to appropriate medical and legal resources. Some terms are explicitly defined in statutes and may be at variance among the states and with these descriptions.)

Advance health care directive. An instruction, usually in writing and usually witnessed, that either (1) directs the scope of care in the instance of terminal illness (i.e., a living will) or (2) appoints another individual to guide health care decisions (i.e., a health care proxy or agent under a health care power of attorney). See living will, directive, power of attorney for health care, health care proxy, declaration of preferences for mental health treatments, and organ donation. An advance health care directive may be executed only by an adult with requisite mental capacity. In almost all states, an onset of incapacity is required to put a directive into effect through the auspices of the designated third party "deputy" (i.e., agent, proxy). Virtually all U.S. jurisdictions provide for directives in some form. Note that each state approaches the subject differently.

Agent. An individual designated in a power of attorney for health care to make a health care decision for another individual (i.e., a principal or patient) granting the power. Synonymous with proxy, representative, attorney-in-fact, and some definitions of surrogate.

Anatomical gift. This is the donation of all or part of a human body upon death. It may be accomplished either through the signing of a donor card or driver's license, or in some jurisdictions by an agent or proxy acting under a power of attorney (or proxy) for health care. See organ donation.

Artificially provided nutrition and hydration. An invasive medical treatment consisting of the administration of food and water through a tube or intravenous line, where the recipient is not required to chew or swallow voluntarily. Artificially provided nutrition and hydration does not include assisted feeding, such as spoon or bottle feeding.

Assisted suicide. See euthanasia.

Attending physician. A licensed medical doctor or doctor of osteopathy who has the primary responsibility for a patient's medical care.

Attorney in fact. See agent.

Autonomy. Within the construct of advance directives, autonomy has become the principal ethical precept. As long as a competent patient can make her or his own health care decisions, deference is granted without ado. By their very nature, directives follow next in this track: health care proxies and living wills are styles of contemplatively given instructions for health care in the event a competent patient becomes unable to make or communicate medical decisions at some future time. These documents (and the state statutes that enable them) purport to preserve patient autonomy. Additionally, a third track— state laws establishing hierarchies of health care decision makers in the event of patient incapacity (i.e., health care surrogacy laws)—also endeavor to promote patient autonomy, even in the absence of directives. In short, the ethical tether of autonomy has come (through statute and case law) largely to eclipse the three other ethical precepts of nonmaleficence, beneficence, and justice.

Beneficence. As an ethical precept in the construct of advance directives, beneficence represents affirmative efforts to act for an uncomprehending patient in a positive fashion (i.e., "we *should* and *will* provide this medical treatment"). Refer to the related concept of nonmaleficence. The distinction between beneficence and nonmaleficence is a fine one: the former is couched as a duty to act, while the latter connotes a degree of passivity in making health care choices for another person.

Best interests. An ethical standard used to evaluate whether the benefits of a contemplated medical treatment for an uncomprehending patient outweigh the risks or burdens. Criterion include: effects of treatments, degrees of pain or discomfort, life expectancy, prognosis, and risks and side effects. Because these determinations are largely imputed by third parties who may have minimal or no knowledge of an incapacitated patient's values or wishes, they are more conservative in application and effect than the ethical standard of substituted judgment.

Brain death. The legal definition of death in most jurisdictions, brain death is the irreversible loss of all brain function.

Capacity. A patient's ability to understand the nature and consequences of proposed health care, including its significant benefits, risks, and alternatives, and to make and communicate a health care decision. See incapacity.

Cardiopulmonary resuscitation. CPR represents one or more "last ditch" techniques to revive a person who suffers cardiac or respiratory arrest. Procedures include cardiac compression, endotracheal intubation and other advanced airway management techniques, artificial ventilation, defibrillation (i.e., electric shocks to the chest area above the heart), injectable drugs to stimulate heart action, and other related life-sustaining procedures.

Comfort care. Treatment given in an attempt to protect and enhance the quality of life in terminal situations without artificially prolonging that life. This specifically includes measures to alleviate pain. See life sustaining treatment and palliative care.

Competence; competent. An individual possessing the ability, based on reasonable medical judgment, to understand and appreciate the nature and consequences of a treatment decision, including the significant benefits and harms of and reasonable alternatives to a proposed treatment decision. Synonym: capacity.

CPR. See cardiopulmonary resuscitation.

Declarant. See principal.

Declaration. A patient's voluntary statement (usually written) directing the withholding or withdrawal of medical treatment in the event she or he is in a terminal condition. However, comfort care and measures to alleviate pain typically cannot be withdrawn. Also often referred to as a living will.

Declaration of preferences for mental health treatments. This is an ancillary (or "special purpose") advance health care directive that exists in a minority of jurisdictions expressly for use by those who suffer from episodic mental illness. It is similar in form and function to durable powers of attorney (or proxies) for health care. However, these declarations are profoundly different in one exceedingly important respect: they may be ENTIRELY IRREVOCABLE if the principal is deemed to be in an active or acute phase of illness. It is, therefore, essential that this style of directive (where it exists) be employed with the utmost of sensitivity and care. Also known as advance instruction (or advance directive) for mental health treatment or declaration for mental illness treatment. Note that jurisdictions without this document still may provide for limited delegations of decision-making authority for mental health within the context of a health care proxy or power. See Appendix G.

DNR. See Do-Not-Resuscitate.

Do-Not-Resuscitate ("DNR"). A protocol variously established (e.g., statute, administrative regulation) in a majority of U.S. jurisdictions whereby cardiopulmonary resuscitation ("CPR") is withheld or withdrawn from prospectively identified patients in the event of cardiac or respiratory arrest. Differing standards and procedures may apply "in-hospital" (i.e., to physicians) and "out-of-hospital" (i.e., to certified emergency medical services personnel). Explicit requirements often exist and may vary considerably by state. Precise compliance (e.g., written physician certification, patient bracelets, forms on colored paper) is essential for effective implementation.

Durable medical power of attorney or durable power of attorney for medical care. At common law, powers of attorney lapse at the onset of a principal's decisional or communicative incapacity. This style of advance health care directive purports to outlast a principal's incapacity and permit the appointed agent or proxy to continue service. Some jurisdictions require that health powers and proxies be pointedly and explicitly cast as durable in order to successfully accomplish this. Synonym: health care proxy.

Durable powers of attorney for property. Strictly speaking, property powers (and related estate planning devices, such as trusts) are not advance health care directives at all: they pertain only to financial concerns. Directives, on the other hand, run solely to health care decision making in the event of decisional or communicative incapacity. A prospective—and holistic— contingency plan for incapacity should, however, include property matters *in addition to* advance directives. Note well that statutory devices for accomplishing these twin goals (i.e., property planning, health care planning) vary by state. Be aware that property powers (and, to a lesser degree, perhaps, health care powers) can become tools of abuse and exploitation if improvidently employed and applied. Refer to cautions expressed elsewhere in this book.

Ethics committees; institutional ethics committees. Larger hospitals and medical centers now commonly provide for these deliberative groups. They can assist with issues associated with advance directives (or the lack thereof). Although hardly panaceas, they represent an essential resource in assuring careful and forthright medical decision making on behalf of decisionally or communicatively incapacitated individuals. Additionally, immediate deliberative consultations may be found in some institutions through "on-call" staff ethicists.

Euthanasia. Euthanasia (or assisted suicide, or mercy killing) may be differentiated as active or passive. It is *categorically prohibited* in all U.S. jurisdictions. A highly controlled and carefully limited "carveout" is contained in the Oregon Death With Dignity Act. See Appendix I. Note well that even in this context, Oregon, too, expressly prohibits outright euthanasia: "Nothing . . . shall be construed to authorize a physician or any other person to end a patient's life by lethal injection, mercy killing or active euthanasia." (ORS 127.880). Of all the nations of the world, it appears that only the Netherlands condones euthanasia; however, it, too, attaches conditions and limitations.

Grantor. See principal.

Guardian. A judicially-appointed individual or entity having authority to make routine decisions about health care and living arrangements on behalf of either a minor or a decisionally or communicatively incapacitated adult. Depending on the jurisdiction, and depending on the gravity of a contemplated treatment (e.g., surgery), a guardian may be required to either (1) prospectively obtain judicial authority to consent to a procedure or (2) seek judicial ratification of invasive medical procedures rendered on an emergency basis. In any event, a guardian is almost universally charged with providing periodic reports to the court on the health care and living arrangements of a patient (i.e., a ward) who is the subject of a guardianship. Note that this function is distinguished from that of a guardian of the estate or a conservator, who may be separately appointed by a court to handle the property and financial matters of another person. Depending on the circumstances, a minor or a decision-ally incapacitated adult may require either a guardian or a conservator or both.

Health care. This refers to any procedure, treatment, or service to diagnose, treat, maintain, or provide for a patient's physical health, mental health, or personal care.

Health care decision. This encompasses informed consent, refusal of consent, or withdrawal of consent for any and all health care, including life sustaining treatment.

Health care representative. See agent.

Hospice. Hospice care typically is rendered to terminally ill people who have but months, weeks or days to live. It represents a patient's informed choice to forego either heroic "high tech" medical interventions or altogether futile treatments; similarly, it may be employed when the medical arts have nothing more to offer a patient. This style of palliative (comfort) care may be provided in either an institutional or home setting. Care providers may include medical professionals, physical therapists, clergy and spiritual advisors, family, friends, and volunteers. In addition to helping dying patients be as physically comfortable as possible, hospice workers also serve as advocates and counselors. Additionally, they may provide assistance and support to grieving family and friends.

Incapacity. A circumstance, either temporary or permanent, where a patient is physically or mentally unable to communicate a willful and knowing health care decision. Antonym: see capacity.

Incompetent. An individual lacking the ability to understand and comprehend the nature and consequences of a medical treatment decision, including the significant benefits and drawbacks of and alternatives to a proposed treatment decision. Antonym: see competent.

Informed consent. This is consent voluntarily given by a person after a sufficient explanation and disclosure of the subject matter involved to enable her or him to have a general understanding of the contemplated procedure (and alternatives, if any) and to make a knowing health care decision without undue influence or coercion.

Irreversible coma. A state in which higher brain functions are irreversibly destroyed.

Justice. A medical ethics construct applicable to the decisionally and communicatively incapacitated, justice turns on several issues: (1) a patient's inherent right to care; (2) the level of care afforded similarly situated patients; and (3) the degree of care sought on behalf of an uncomprehending patient (be it remarkably extraordinary or patently futile).

Living will. A prospective and contemplative statement (usually written and witnessed) which, when rendered, contains the express direction that no life-sustaining procedures be taken when the maker is in a terminal condition or is permanently unconscious, without hope of recovery. Note that comfort care and efforts to alleviate pain pointedly are to continue. In many jurisdictions, the removal of artificial hydration and nutrition is permitted; in some (e.g., Illinois, Missouri), this is expressly forbidden. A living will is also known in some jurisdictions as a declaration. Because living wills address only the contingency of non-curative or terminal illness, this style of advance health care directive now is largely in eclipse in many U.S. jurisdictions. Still, the fact that they require no third party (e.g., agent, proxy) to effectuate still may make them useful as ancillary or backup documents. Refer to cautions expressed elsewhere in this book.

Medically ineffective (or futile) life sustaining treatment. This means that, with a reasonable degree of medical certainty, a contemplated life sustaining medical procedure (1) will not prevent or reduce the deterioration of the health of a patient or (2) prevent the impending death of a patient. Statutes of a number of jurisdictions pointedly provide that physicians are not obligated to render ineffective or futile life sustaining treatment.

Mental health. See declaration of preferences for mental health treatments.

Mercy killing. See euthanasia.

Mini-Mental State Examination (MMSE) (the "Mini-Mental"). This widely known brief mental status exam (approximately ten minutes to administer) is but one tool used by medical professionals to *begin* to divine mental capacity: it is not of itself dispositive. Developed by Dr. Marshall Folstein, it has been translated into several languages and is available on the World Wide Web.

Nonmaleficence. A companion to the ethical construct of beneficence, this concept approximates the maxim that is the Hippocratic Oath: "First do no harm". In other words, no medical procedure *ought* to be undertaken on an uncomprehending patient which may prove to be deleterious to her or his overall well being. This idea connotes a degree of passivity in making medical choices for another. Contrast it with the related precept of beneficence, which imparts more of an affirmative duty to act on behalf of a patient.

Organ donation. This is a limited advance health care directive in which the maker consents to removal and donation of organs (and tissue, tendons, skin, bone, and/or corneas, as she or he may stipulate) upon death. This may be accomplished through a health care power or proxy, or with a donor card or similar declaration, or by signing the back of a driver's license before witnesses. Irrespective of donative intent, family members may be polled and asked to consent before organs are removed; accordingly, it is essential that a prospective donor affirmatively inform next of kin about her or his intentions.

Palliative care. This includes comprehensive measures taken by physicians, hospice staff, and other health care providers designed primarily to maintain and comfort a patient suffering from non-curative disease. Steps include, but are not limited to, pain management, hygiene, and the provision of nonartificial feeding and hydration. Pastoral or spiritual care for both patient and family is an exceedingly important component, as are bereavement and related counseling. See hospice.

Patient. See principal.

Permanent unconsciousness. A lasting condition (usually characterized by an absence of cerebral cortical functions) that, to a reasonable degree of medical certainty, will continue permanently, without improvement. Cognitive thought, sensation, purposeful action, social interaction and awareness of self and environment also are absent. This condition must be confirmed by a physician who is qualified and experienced in making such a diagnosis.

Persistent vegetative state. This is a condition characterized by a permanent and irreversible condition of unconsciousness in which a patient exhibits (1) the absence of voluntary action or cognitive behavior of any kind and (2) an inability to purposefully communicate or interact.

Principal. A competent adult executing an advance directive and on whose behalf health care decisions are made in the event of decisional or communicative incapacity. Often synonymous with grantor or declarant or patient.

Proxy. See agent.

Representative. See agent.

Substituted judgment. In the ethical construct of advance directives, this is the premise that a formerly competent patient has the right to exercise autonomy in health care decision making through the direction of a substitute (e.g., a proxy or agent or surrogate). This subsequent decision maker relies on recollections about the values of the patient and endeavors to impute medical choices that she or he believes to comport with what the patient, if competent, might have wanted.

Surrogate. There are two definitions for this term. One is synonymous with agent or proxy and is the person who may be called on to serve as a third party "deputy" under the terms of a durable power of attorney for health care (or similarly styled document). The other definition applies in those jurisdictions that have anticipated the contingency of no contemplatively-designated health care decision maker and have established a hierarchy of substitute decision makers (e.g., spouses, adult children) to step in and render health care consents on behalf of the decisionally incapacitated.

Terminally ill or injured patient. A patient whose death is imminent or whose condition, to a reasonable degree of medical certainty, is hopeless unless he or she is artificially supported through the use of life-sustaining procedures and which condition is confirmed by a physician who is qualified and experienced in making such a diagnosis.

APPENDIX C
Uniform Health-Care Decisions Act

Drafted by the

**NATIONAL CONFERENCE OF COMMISSIONERS
ON UNIFORM STATE LAWS**

and by it

**APPROVED AND RECOMMENDED FOR ENACTMENT
IN ALL THE STATES**

at its

ANNUAL CONFERENCE
MEETING IN ITS ONE-HUNDRED-AND-SECOND YEAR
IN CHARLESTON, SOUTH CAROLINA
JULY 30–AUGUST 6, 1993

WITH PREFATORY NOTE AND COMMENTS

Approved by the American Bar Association
Kansas City, Missouri, February 7, 1994

UNIFORM HEALTH-CARE DECISIONS ACT

The Committee that acted for the National Conference of Commissioners on Uniform State Laws in preparing the Uniform Health-Care Decisions Act was as follows:

MICHAEL FRANCK, 306 Townsend Street, Lansing, MI 48933, *Chair*
THOMAS P. FOY, SR., P.O. Box 2615, Silver City, NM 88062
M. KING HILL, JR., 6th Floor, 100 Light Street, Baltimore, MD 21202
MILDRED W. ROBINSON, University of Virginia, School of Law, Charlottesville, VA 22901
JOHN W. THOMAS, P.O. Box 100200, 10th Floor, 1441 Main Street, Columbia, SC 29202
RICHARD V. WELLMAN, University of Georgia, School of Law, Athens, GA 30602
W. JACKSON WILLOUGHBY, Placer County Municipal Court, 300 Taylor St., Roseville, CA 95678
DAVID M. ENGLISH, University of South Dakota, School of Law, 414 East Clark Street, Vermillion, SD 57069, *Reporter (1992–93)*
WILLARD H. PEDRICK, Arizona State University, College of Law, Tempe, AZ 85287, *Reporter (1991–92)*

EX OFFICIO

DWIGHT A. HAMILTON, Suite 600, 1600 Broadway, Denver, CO 80202, *President*
JOHN H. LANGBEIN, Yale Law School, 401A Yale Station, New Haven, CT 06520, *Chair, Division D*

EXECUTIVE DIRECTOR

FRED H. MILLER, University of Oklahoma, College of Law, 300 Timberdell Road, Norman, OK 73019, *Executive Director*
WILLIAM J. PIERCE, 1505 Roxbury Road, Ann Arbor, MI 48104, *Executive Director Emeritus*

REVIEW COMMITTEE

ROGER C. HENDERSON, University of Arizona, College of Law, Tucson, AZ 85721, *Chair*

MATTHEW S. RAE, JR., 34th Floor, 777 South Figueroa Street, Los Angeles, CA 90017

MARTHA TAYLOR STARKEY, 1800 One Indiana Square, Indianapolis, IN 46204

ADVISORS TO DRAFTING COMMITTEE

FRANCIS J. COLLIN, JR., *American Bar Association, Section of Real Property, Probate and Trust Law*
WALTER R. FUNK, *The First Church of Christ, Scientist*
JOHN H. PICKERING, *American Bar Association*
JAMES N. ZARTMAN, *American Bar Association*

OBSERVERS

SUSAN FOX BUCHANAN, *Choice in Dying*
JOHN L. MILES, *Catholic Health Association of the United States*
DAVID ORENTLICHER, *American Medical Association*
DAVID A. SMITH, *Choice in Dying*
HARLEY J. SPITLER, *State Bar of California, Section of Estate Planning, Trust and Probate Law*
ANNE F. VAIL, *American Medical Association*

© National Conference of Commissioners on Uniform State Laws.
Reproduced by permission.

Final, approved copies of this Act in printed pamphlet or computer diskette form (Word Perfect only) and copies of all Uniform and Model Acts and other printed matter issued by the Conference may be obtained from:

NATIONAL CONFERENCE OF COMMISSIONERS
ON UNIFORM STATE LAWS
676 North St. Clair Street, Suite 1700
Chicago, Illinois 60611
312/915-0195
www.nccusl.org

UNIFORM HEALTH-CARE DECISIONS ACT

PREFATORY NOTE

Since the Supreme Court's decision in *Cruzan v. Commissioner, Missouri Department of Health*, 497 U.S. 261 (1990), significant change has occurred in state legislation on health-care decision making. Every state now has legislation authorizing the use of some sort of advance health-care directive. All but a few states authorize what is typically known as a living will. Nearly all states have statutes authorizing the use of powers of attorney for health care. In addition, a majority of states have statutes allowing family members, and in some cases close friends, to make health-care decisions for adult individuals who lack capacity.

This state legislation, however, has developed in fits and starts, resulting in an often fragmented, incomplete, and sometimes inconsistent set of rules. Statutes enacted within a state often conflict and conflicts between statutes of different states are common. In an increasingly mobile society where an advance health-care directive given in one state must frequently be implemented in another, there is a need for greater uniformity.

The Health-Care Decisions Act was drafted with this confused situation in mind. The Act is built around the following concepts. *First*, the Act acknowledges the right of a competent individual to decide all aspects of his or her own health care in all circumstances, including the right to decline health care or to direct that health care be discontinued, even if death ensues. An individual's instructions may extend to any and all health-care decisions that might arise and, unless limited by the principal, an agent has authority to make all health-care decisions which the individual could have made. The Act recognizes and validates an individual's authority to define the scope of an instruction or agency as broadly or as narrowly as the individual chooses.

Second, the Act is comprehensive and will enable an enacting jurisdiction to replace its existing legislation on the subject with a single statute. The Act authorizes health-care decisions to be made by an agent who is designated to decide when an individual cannot or does not wish to; by a designated surrogate, family member, or close friend when an individual is unable to act and no guardian or agent has been appointed or is reasonably available; or by a court having jurisdiction as decision maker of last resort.

Third, the Act is designed to simplify and facilitate the making of advance health-care directives. An instruction may be either written or oral. A power of attorney for health care, while it must be in writing, need not be witnessed or acknowledged. In addition, an optional form for the making of a directive is provided.

Fourth, the Act seeks to ensure to the extent possible that decisions about an individual's health care will be governed by the individual's own desires concerning the issues to be resolved. The Act requires an agent or surrogate authorized to make health-care decisions for an individual to make those decisions in accordance with the instructions and other wishes of the individual to the extent known. Otherwise, the agent or surrogate must make those decisions in accordance with the best interest of the individual but in light of the individual's personal values known to the agent or surrogate. Furthermore, the Act requires a guardian to comply with a ward's previously given instructions and prohibits a guardian from revoking the ward's advance health-care directive without express court approval.

Fifth, the Act addresses compliance by health-care providers and institutions. A health-care provider or institution must comply with an instruction of the patient and with a reasonable interpretation of that instruction or other health-care decision made by a person then authorized to make health-care decisions for the patient. The obligation to comply is not absolute, however. A health-care provider or institution may decline to honor an instruction or decision for reasons of conscience or if the instruction or decision requires the provision of medically ineffective care or care contrary to applicable health-care standards.

Sixth, the Act provides a procedure for the resolution of disputes. While the Act is in general to be effectuated without litigation, situations will arise where resort to the courts may be necessary. For that reason, the Act authorizes the court to enjoin or direct a health-care decision or order other equitable relief and specifies who is entitled to bring a petition.

The Health-Care Decisions Act supersedes the Commissioners' Model Health-Care Consent Act (1982), the Uniform Rights of the Terminally Ill Act (1985), and the Uniform Rights of the Terminally Ill Act (1989). A state enacting the Health-Care Decisions Act which has one of these other acts in force should repeal it upon enactment.

UNIFORM HEALTH-CARE DECISIONS ACT

SECTION 1. DEFINITIONS. In this [Act]:

(1) "Advance health-care directive" means an individual instruction or a power of attorney for health care.

(2) "Agent" means an individual designated in a power of attorney for health care to make a health-care decision for the individual granting the power.

(3) "Capacity" means an individual's ability to understand the significant benefits, risks, and alternatives to proposed health care and to make and communicate a health-care decision.

(4) "Guardian" means a judicially appointed guardian or conservator having authority to make a health-care decision for an individual.

(5) "Health care" means any care, treatment, service, or procedure to maintain, diagnose, or otherwise affect an individual's physical or mental condition.

(6) "Health-care decision" means a decision made by an individual or the individual's agent, guardian, or surrogate, regarding the individual's health care, including:

    (i) selection and discharge of health-care providers and institutions;

    (ii) approval or disapproval of diagnostic tests, surgical procedures, programs of medication, and orders not to resuscitate; and

    (iii) directions to provide, withhold, or withdraw artificial nutrition and hydration and all other forms of health care.

(7) "Health-care institution" means an institution, facility, or agency licensed, certified, or otherwise authorized or permitted by law to provide health care in the ordinary course of business.

(8) "Health-care provider" means an individual licensed, certified, or otherwise authorized or permitted by law to provide health care in the ordinary course of business or practice of a profession.

(9) "Individual instruction" means an individual's direction concerning a health-care decision for the individual.

(10) "Person" means an individual, corporation, business trust, estate, trust, partnership, association, joint venture, government, governmental subdivision, agency, or instrumentality, or any other legal or commercial entity.

(11) "Physician" means an individual authorized to practice medicine [or osteopathy] under [appropriate statute].

(12) "Power of attorney for health care" means the designation of an agent to make health-care decisions for the individual granting the power.

(13) "Primary physician" means a physician designated by an individual or the individual's agent, guardian, or surrogate, to have primary responsibility for the individual's health care or, in the absence of a designation or if the designated physician is not reasonably available, a physician who undertakes the responsibility.

(14) "Reasonably available" means readily able to be contacted without undue effort and willing and able to act in a timely manner considering the urgency of the patient's health-care needs.

(15) "State" means a State of the United States, the District of Columbia, the Commonwealth of Puerto Rico, or a territory or insular possession subject to the jurisdiction of the United States.

(16) "Supervising health-care provider" means the primary physician or, if there is no primary physician or the primary physician is not reasonably available, the health-care provider who has undertaken primary responsibility for an individual's health care.

(17) "Surrogate" means an individual, other than a patient's agent or guardian, authorized under this [Act] to make a health-care decision for the patient.

Comment

The term "advance health-care directive" (subsection (1)) appears in the federal Patient Self-Determination Act enacted as sections 4206 and 4751 of the Omnibus Budget Reconciliation Act of 1990 and has gained widespread usage among health-care professionals.

The definition of "agent" (subsection (2)) is not limited to a single individual. The Act permits the appointment of co-agents and alternate agents.

The definition of "guardian" (subsection (4)) recognizes that some states grant health-care decision making authority to a conservator of the person.

The definition of "health care" (subsection (5)) is to be given the broadest possible construction. It includes the types of care referred to in the definition of "health-care decision" (subsection (6)), and to care, including custodial care, provided at a "health-care institution" (subsection (7)). It also includes non-medical remedial treatment such as practiced by adherents of Christian Science.

The term "health-care institution" (subsection (7)) includes a hospital, nursing home, residential-care facility, home health agency or hospice.

The term "individual instruction" (subsection (9)) includes any type of written or oral direction concerning health-care treatment. The direction may range from a written document which is intended to be effective at a future time if certain specified conditions arise and for which a form is provided in Section 4, to the written consent required before surgery is performed, to oral directions concerning care recorded in the health-care record. The instruction may relate to a particular health-care decision or to health care in general.

The definition of "person" (subsection (10)) includes a limited liability company, which falls within the category of "other legal or commercial entity."

Because states differ on the classes of professionals who may lawfully practice medicine, the definition of "physician" (subsection (11)) cross-references the appropriate licensing or other statute.

The Act employs the term "primary physician" (subsection (13)) instead of "attending physician." The term "attending physician" could be understood to refer to any physician providing treatment to the individual, and not to the physician whom the individual, or agent, guardian, or surrogate, has designated or, in the absence of a designation, the physician who has undertaken primary responsibility for the individual's health care.

The term "reasonably available" (subsection (14)) is used in the Act to accommodate the reality that individuals will sometimes not be timely available. The term is incorporated into the definition of "supervising health-care provider" (subsection (16)). It appears in the optional statutory form (Section 4) to indicate when an alternate agent may act. In Section 5 it is used to determine when a surrogate will be authorized to make health-care decisions for an individual, and if so, which class of individuals has authority to act.

The definition of "supervising health-care provider" (subsection (16)) accommodates the circumstance that frequently arises where care or supervision by a physician may not be readily available. The individual's primary physician is to assume the role, however, if reasonably available. For the contexts in which the term is used, see Sections 3, 5, and 7.

The definition of "surrogate" (subsection (17)) refers to the individual having present authority under Section 5 to make a health-care decision for a patient. It does not include an individual who might have such authority under a given set of circumstances which have not occurred.

SECTION 2. ADVANCE HEALTH-CARE DIRECTIVES.

(a) An adult or emancipated minor may give an individual instruction. The instruction may be oral or written. The instruction may be limited to take effect only if a specified condition arises.

(b) An adult or emancipated minor may execute a power of attorney for health care, which may authorize the agent to make any health-care decision the principal could have made while having capacity. The power must be in writing and signed by the principal. The power remains in effect notwithstanding the principal's later incapacity and may include individual instructions. Unless related to the principal by blood, marriage, or adoption, an agent may not be an owner, operator, or employee of [a residential long-term health-care institution] at which the principal is receiving care.

(c) Unless otherwise specified in a power of attorney for health care, the authority of an agent becomes effective only upon a determination that the principal lacks capacity, and ceases to be effective upon a determination that the principal has recovered capacity.

(d) Unless otherwise specified in a written advance health-care directive, a determination that an individual lacks or has recovered capacity, or that another condition exists that affects an individual instruction or the authority of an agent, must be made by the primary physician.

(e) An agent shall make a health-care decision in accordance with the principal's individual instructions, if any, and other wishes to the extent known to the agent. Otherwise, the agent shall make the decision in accordance with the agent's determination of the principal's best interest. In determining the principal's best interest, the agent shall consider the principal's personal values to the extent known to the agent.

(f) A health-care decision made by an agent for a principal is effective without judicial approval.

(g) A written advance health-care directive may include the individual's nomination of a guardian of the person.

(h) An advance health-care directive is valid for purposes of this [Act] if it complies with this [Act], regardless of when or where executed or communicated.

Comment

The individual instruction authorized in subsection (a) may but need not be limited to take effect in specified circumstances, such as if the individual is dying. An individual instruction may be either written or oral.

Subsection (b) authorizes a power of attorney for health care to include instructions regarding the principal's health care. This provision has been included in order to validate the practice of designating an agent and giving individual instructions in one document instead of two. The authority of an agent falls within the discretion of the principal as expressed in the instrument creating the power and may extend to any health-care decision the principal could have made while having capacity.

Subsection (b) excludes the oral designation of an agent. Section 5(b) authorizes an individual to orally designate a surrogate by personally informing the supervising health-care provider. A power of attorney for health care, however, must be in writing and signed by the principal, although it need not be witnessed or acknowledged.

Subsection (b) also limits those who may serve as agents to make health-care decisions for another. The subsection addresses the special vulnerability of individuals in residential long-term health-care institutions by protecting a principal against those who may have interests that conflict with the duty to follow the principal's expressed wishes or to determine the principal's best interest. Specifically, the owners, operators or employees of a residential long-term health-care institution at which the principal is receiving care may not act as agents. An exception is made for those related to the principal by blood, marriage or adoption, relationships which are assumed to neutralize any consequence of a conflict of interest adverse to the principal. The phrase "a residential long-term health-care institution" is placed in brackets to indicate to the legislature of an enacting jurisdiction that it should substitute the appropriate terminology used under local law.

Subsection (c) provides that the authority of the agent to make health-care decisions ordinarily does not become effective until the principal is determined to lack capacity and ceases to be effective should the principal recover capacity. A principal may provide, however, that the authority of the agent becomes effective immediately or upon the happening of some event other than the loss of capacity but may do so only by an express provision in the power of attorney. For example, a mother who does not want to make her own health-care decisions but prefers that her daughter make them for her may specify that the daughter as agent is to have authority to make health-care decisions immediately. The mother in that circumstance retains the right to later revoke the power of attorney as provided in Section 3.

Subsection (d) provides that unless otherwise specified in a written advance health-care directive, a determination that a principal has lost or recovered capacity to make health-care decisions must be made by the primary physician. For example, a principal might specify that the determination of capacity is to be made by the agent in consultation with the primary physician. Or a principal, such as a member of the Christian Science faith who relies on a religious method of healing and who has no primary physician, might specify that capacity be determined by other means. In the event that multiple decision makers are specified and they cannot agree, it may be necessary to seek court instruction as authorized by Section 14.

Subsection (d) also provides that unless otherwise specified in a written advance health-care directive, the existence of other conditions which affect an individual instruction or the authority of an agent must be determined by the primary physician. For example, an individual might specify that an agent may withdraw or withhold treatment that keeps the individual alive only if the individual has an incurable and irreversible condition that will result in the individual's death within a relatively short time. In that event, unless otherwise specified in the advance health-care directive, the determination that the individual has that condition must be made by the primary physician.

Subsection (e) requires the agent to follow the principal's individual instructions and other expressed wishes to the extent known to the agent. To the extent such instructions or other wishes are unknown, the agent must act in the principal's best interest. In determining the principal's best interest, the agent is to consider the principal's personal values to the extent known to the agent. The Act does not prescribe a detailed list of factors for determining the principal's best interest but instead grants the agent discretion to ascertain and weigh the factors likely to be of importance to the principal. The legislature of an enacting jurisdiction that wishes to add such a list may want to consult the Maryland Health-Care Decision Act, Md. Health-Gen. Code Ann. § 5-601.

Subsection (f) provides that a health-care decision made by an agent is effective without judicial approval. A similar provision applies to health-care decisions made by surrogates (Section 5(g)) or guardians (Section 6(c)).

Subsection (g) provides that a written advance health-care directive may include the individual's nomination of a guardian of the person. A nomination cannot guarantee that the nominee will be appointed but in the absence of cause to appoint another the court would likely select the nominee. Moreover, the mere nomination of the agent will reduce the likelihood that a guardianship could be used to thwart the agent's authority.

Subsection (h) validates advance health-care directives which conform to the Act, regardless of when or where executed or communicated. This includes an advance health-care directive which would be valid under the Act but which was made prior to the date of its enactment and failed to comply with the execution requirements then in effect. It also includes an advance health-care directive which was made in another jurisdiction but which does not comply with that jurisdiction's execution or other requirements.

SECTION 3. REVOCATION OF ADVANCE HEALTH-CARE DIRECTIVE.

(a) An individual may revoke the designation of an agent only by a signed writing or by personally informing the supervising health-care provider.

(b) An individual may revoke all or part of an advance health-care directive, other than the designation of an agent, at any time and in any manner that communicates an intent to revoke.

(c) A health-care provider, agent, guardian, or surrogate who is informed of a revocation shall promptly communicate the fact of the revocation to the supervising health-care provider and to any health-care institution at which the patient is receiving care.

(d) A decree of annulment, divorce, dissolution of marriage, or legal separation revokes a previous designation of a spouse as agent unless otherwise specified in the decree or in a power of attorney for health care.

(e) An advance health-care directive that conflicts with an earlier advance health-care directive revokes the earlier directive to the extent of the conflict.

Comment

Subsection (b) provides that an individual may revoke any portion of an advance health-care directive at any time and in any manner that communicates an intent to revoke. However, a more restrictive standard applies to the revocation of the portion of a power of attorney for health care relating to the designation of an agent. Subsection (a) provides that an individual may revoke the designation of an agent only by a signed writing or by personally informing the supervising health-care provider. This higher standard is justified by the risk of a false revocation of an agent's designation or of a misinterpretation or miscommunication of a principal's statement communicated through a third party. For example, without this higher standard, an individual motivated by a desire to gain control over a patient might be able to assume authority to act as agent by falsely informing a health-care provider that the principal no longer wishes the previously designated agent to act but instead wishes to appoint the individual.

Subsection (c) requires any health-care provider, agent, guardian or surrogate who is informed of a revocation to promptly communicate that fact to the supervising health-care provider and to any health-care institution at which the patient is receiving care. The communication triggers the Section 7(b) obligation of the supervising health-care provider to record the revocation in the patient's health-care record and reduces the risk that a health-care provider or agent, guardian or surrogate will rely on a health-care directive that is no longer valid.

Subsection (e) establishes a rule of construction permitting multiple advance health-care directives to be construed together in order to determine the individual's intent, with the later advance health-care directive superseding the former to the extent of any inconsistency.

The section does not specifically address amendment of an advance health-care directive because such reference is not necessary. Subsection (b) specifically authorizes partial revocation, and subsection (e) recognizes that an advance health-care directive may be modified by a later directive.

SECTION 4. OPTIONAL FORM. The following form may, but need not, be used to create an advance health-care directive. The other sections of this [Act] govern the effect of this or any other writing used to create an advance health-care directive. An individual may complete or modify all or any part of the following form:

ADVANCE HEALTH-CARE DIRECTIVE

Explanation

You have the right to give instructions about your own health care. You also have the right to name someone else to make health-care decisions for you. This form lets you do either or both of these things. It also lets you express your wishes regarding donation of organs and the designation of your primary physician. If you use this form, you may complete or modify all or any part of it. You are free to use a different form.

Part 1 of this form is a power of attorney for health care. Part 1 lets you name another individual as agent to make health-care decisions for you if you become incapable of making your own decisions or if you want someone else to make those decisions for you now even though you are still capable. You may also name an alternate agent to act for you if your first choice is not willing, able, or reasonably available to make decisions for you. Unless related to you, your agent may not be an owner, operator, or employee of [a residential long-term health-care institution] at which you are receiving care.

Unless the form you sign limits the authority of your agent, your agent may make all health-care decisions for you. This form has a place for you to limit the authority of your agent. You need not limit the authority of your agent if you wish to rely on your agent for all health-care decisions that may have to be made. If you choose not to limit the authority of your agent, your agent will have the right to:

   (a) consent or refuse consent to any care, treatment, service, or procedure to maintain, diagnose, or otherwise affect a physical or mental condition;
   (b) select or discharge health-care providers and institutions;
   (c) approve or disapprove diagnostic tests, surgical procedures, programs of medication, and orders not to resuscitate; and
   (d) direct the provision, withholding, or withdrawal of artificial nutrition and hydration and all other forms of health care.

Part 2 of this form lets you give specific instructions about any aspect of your health care. Choices are provided for you to express your wishes regarding the provision, withholding, or withdrawal of treatment to keep you alive, including the provision of artificial nutrition and hydration, as well as the provision of pain relief. Space is also provided for you to add to the choices you have made or for you to write out any additional wishes.

Part 3 of this form lets you express an intention to donate your bodily organs and tissues following your death.

Part 4 of this form lets you designate a physician to have primary responsibility for your health care.

After completing this form, sign and date the form at the end. It is recommended but not required that you request two other individuals to sign as witnesses. Give a copy of the signed and completed form to your physician, to any other health-care providers you may have, to any health-care institution at which you are receiving care, and to any health-care agents you have named. You should talk to the person you have named as agent to make sure that he or she understands your wishes and is willing to take the responsibility.

You have the right to revoke this advance health-care directive or replace this form at any time.

****

PART 1
POWER OF ATTORNEY FOR HEALTH CARE

(1) DESIGNATION OF AGENT: I designate the following individual as my agent to make health-care decisions for me:

_____

(name of individual you choose as agent)

_____

(address)   (city)   (state)   (zip code)

_____

(home phone)   (work phone)

OPTIONAL: If I revoke my agent's authority or if my agent is not willing, able, or reasonably available to make a health-care decision for me, I designate as my first alternate agent:

_____

(name of individual you choose as first alternate agent)

_____

(address)   (city)   (state)   (zip code)

_____

(home phone)   (work phone)

OPTIONAL: If I revoke the authority of my agent and first alternate agent or if neither is willing, able, or reasonably available to make a health-care decision for me, I designate as my second alternate agent:

_____

(name of individual you choose as second alternate agent)

_____

(address)   (city)   (state)   (zip code)

_____

(home phone)   (work phone)

(2) AGENT'S AUTHORITY: My agent is authorized to make all health-care decisions for me, including decisions to provide, withhold, or withdraw artificial nutrition and hydration and all other forms of health care to keep me alive, except as I state here:

_____

_____

_____

(Add additional sheets if needed.)

(3) WHEN AGENT'S AUTHORITY BECOMES EFFECTIVE: My agent's authority becomes effective when my primary physician determines that I am unable to make my own health-care decisions unless I mark the following box. If I mark this box [ ], my agent's authority to make health-care decisions for me takes effect immediately.

(4) AGENT'S OBLIGATION: My agent shall make health-care decisions for me in accordance with this power of attorney for health care, any instructions I give in Part 2 of this form, and my other wishes to the extent known to my agent. To the extent my wishes are unknown, my agent shall make health-care decisions for me in accordance with what my agent determines to be in my best interest. In determining my best interest, my agent shall consider my personal values to the extent known to my agent.

(5) NOMINATION OF GUARDIAN: If a guardian of my person needs to be appointed for me by a court, I nominate the agent designated in this form. If that agent is not willing, able, or reasonably available to act as guardian, I nominate the alternate agents whom I have named, in the order designated.

PART 2
INSTRUCTIONS FOR HEALTH CARE

If you are satisfied to allow your agent to determine what is best for you in making end-of-life decisions, you need not fill out this part of the form. If you do fill out this part of the form, you may strike any wording you do not want.

(6) END-OF-LIFE DECISIONS: I direct that my health-care providers and others involved in my care provide, withhold, or withdraw treatment in accordance with the choice I have marked below:

[ ] (a) Choice Not To Prolong Life

I do not want my life to be prolonged if (i) I have an incurable and irreversible condition that will result in my death within a relatively short time, (ii) I become unconscious and, to a reasonable degree of medical certainty, I will not regain consciousness, or (iii) the likely risks and burdens of treatment would outweigh the expected benefits, OR

[ ] (b) Choice To Prolong Life

I want my life to be prolonged as long as possible within the limits of generally accepted health-care standards.

(7) ARTIFICIAL NUTRITION AND HYDRATION: Artificial nutrition and hydration must be provided, withheld, or withdrawn in accordance with the choice I have made in paragraph (6) unless I mark the following box. If I mark this box [ ], artificial nutrition and hydration must be provided regardless of my condition and regardless of the choice I have made in paragraph (6).

(8) RELIEF FROM PAIN: Except as I state in the following space, I direct that treatment for alleviation of pain or discomfort be provided at all times, even if it hastens my death:

_____

_____

(9) OTHER WISHES: (If you do not agree with any of the optional choices above and wish to write your own, or if you wish to add to the instructions you have given above, you may do so here.) I direct that:

_____

_____

(Add additional sheets if needed.)

PART 3
DONATION OF ORGANS AT DEATH

(OPTIONAL)

(10) Upon my death (mark applicable box)

[ ] (a) I give any needed organs, tissues, or parts, OR

[ ] (b) I give the following organs, tissues, or parts only

_____

(c) My gift is for the following purposes (strike any of the following you do not want)
- (i) Transplant
- (ii) Therapy
- (iii) Research
- (iv) Education

PART 4
PRIMARY PHYSICIAN

(OPTIONAL)

(11) I designate the following physician as my primary physician:

_____

(name of physician)

_____

(address)   (city)   (state)   (zip code)

_____

(phone)

OPTIONAL: If the physician I have designated above is not willing, able, or reasonably available to act as my primary physician, I designate the following physician as my primary physician:

_____

(name of physician)

_____

(address)   (city)   (state)   (zip code)

_____

(phone)

****

(12) EFFECT OF COPY: A copy of this form has the same effect as the original.

(13) SIGNATURES: Sign and date the form here:

_____   _____

(date)   (sign your name)

_____   _____

(address)   (print your name)

_____

(city)   (state)

(Optional) SIGNATURES OF WITNESSES:

First witness   Second witness

_____   _____
(print name)   (print name)

_____   _____
(address)   (address)

_____   _____
(city)   (state)   (city)   (state)

_____   _____
(signature of witness)   (signature of witness)

_____   _____
(date)   (date)

Comment

The optional form set forth in this section incorporates the Section 2 requirements applicable to advance health-care directives. There are four parts to the form. An individual may complete all or any parts of the form. Any part of the form left blank is not to be given effect. For example, an individual may complete the instructions for health care part of the form alone. Or an individual may complete the power of attorney for health care part of the form alone. Or an individual may complete both the instructions and power of attorney for health care parts of the form. An individual may also, but need not, complete the parts of the form pertaining to donation of bodily organs and tissue and the designation of a primary physician.

Part 1, the power of attorney for health care, appears first on the form in order to ensure to the extent possible that it will come to the attention of a casual reader. This reflects the reality that the appointment of an agent is a more comprehensive approach to the making of health-care decisions than is the giving of an individual instruction, which cannot possibly anticipate all future circumstances which might arise.

Part 1 (1) of the power of attorney for health care form requires only the designation of a single agent, but with opportunity given to designate a single first alternate and a single second alternate, if the individual chooses. No provision is made in the form for the designation of co-agents in order not to encourage the practice. Designation of co-agents is discouraged because of the difficulties likely to be encountered if the co-agents are not all readily available or do not agree. If co-agents are appointed, the instrument should specify that either is authorized to act if the other is not reasonably available. It should also specify a method for resolving disagreements.

Part 1 (2) of the power of attorney for health care form grants the agent authority to make all health-care decisions for the individual subject to any limitations which the individual may state in the form. Reference is made to artificial nutrition and hydration and other forms of treatment to keep an individual alive in order to ensure that the individual is aware that those are forms of health care that the agent would have the authority to withdraw or withhold absent specific limitation.

Part 1 (3) of the power of attorney for health care form provides that the agent's authority becomes effective upon a determination that the individual lacks capacity, but as authorized by Section 2(c) a box is provided for the individual to indicate that the authority of the agent takes effect immediately.

Part 1 (4) of the power of attorney for health care form directs the agent to make health-care decisions in accordance with the power of attorney, any instructions given by the individual in Part 2 of the form, and the individual's other wishes to the extent known to the agent. To the extent the individual's wishes in the matter are not known, the agent is to make health-care decisions based on what the agent determines to be in the individual's best interest. In determining the individual's best interest, the agent is to consider the individual's personal values to the extent known to the agent. Section 2(e) imposes this standard, whether or not it is included in the form, but its inclusion in the form will bring it to the attention of the individual granting the power, to the agent, to any guardian or surrogate, and to the individual's health-care providers.

Part 1 (5) of the power of attorney for health care form nominates the agent, if available, able, and willing to act, otherwise the alternate agents in order of priority stated, as guardians of the person for the individual. This provision is included in the form for two reasons. First, if an appointment of a guardian becomes necessary the agent is the one whom the individual would most likely want to serve in that role. Second, the nomination of the agent as guardian will reduce the possibility that someone other than the agent will be appointed as guardian who could use the position to thwart the agent's authority.

Because the variety of treatment decisions to which health-care instructions may relate is virtually unlimited, Part 2 of the form does not attempt to be comprehensive, but is directed at the types of treatment for which an individual is most likely to have special wishes. Part 2(6) of the form, entitled "End-of-Life Decisions", provides two alternative choices for the expression of wishes concerning the provision, withholding, or withdrawal of treatment. Under the first choice, the individual's life is not to be prolonged if the individual has an incurable and irreversible condition that will result in death within a relatively short time, if the individual becomes unconscious and, to a reasonable degree of medical certainty, will not regain consciousness, or if the likely risks and burdens of treatment would outweigh the expected benefits. Under the second choice, the individual's life is to be prolonged within the limits of generally accepted health-care standards. Part 2(7) of the form provides a box for an individual to mark if the individual wishes to receive artificial nutrition and hydration in all circumstances. Part 2(8) of the form provides space for an individual to specify any circumstance when the individual would prefer not to receive pain relief. Because the choices provided in Parts 2(6) to 2(8) do not cover all possible situations, Part 2(9) of the form provides space for the individual to write out his or her own instructions or to supplement the instructions given in the previous subparts of the form. Should the space be insufficient, the individual is free to add additional pages.

The health-care instructions given in Part 2 of the form are binding on the agent, any guardian, any surrogate, and, subject to exceptions specified in Section 7(e)–(f), on the individual's health-care providers. Pursuant to Section 7(d), a health-care provider must also comply with a reasonable interpretation of those instructions made by an authorized agent, guardian, or surrogate.

Part 3 of the form provides the individual an opportunity to express an intention to donate bodily organs and tissues at death. The options provided are derived from a suggested form in the Comment to Section 2 of the Uniform Anatomical Gift Act (1987).

Part 4 of the form provides space for the individual to designate a primary physician should the individual choose to do so. Space is also provided for the designation of an alternate primary physician should the first designated physician not be available, able, or willing to act.

Paragraph (12) of the form conforms with the provisions of Section 12 by providing that a copy of the form has the same effect as the original.

The Act does not require witnessing, but to encourage the practice the form provides space for the signatures of two witnesses.

The form does not require formal acceptance by an agent. Formal acceptance by an agent has been omitted not because it is an undesirable practice but because it would add another stage to executing an advance health-care directive, thereby further reducing the number of individuals who will follow through and create directives. However, practitioners who wish to adapt this form for use by their clients are strongly encouraged to add a formal acceptance. Designated agents have no duty to act until they accept the office either expressly or through their conduct. Consequently, requiring formal acceptance reduces the risk that a designated agent will decline to act when the need arises. Formal acceptance also makes it more likely that the agent will become familiar with the principal's personal values and views on health care. While the form does not require formal acceptance, the explanation to the form does encourage principals to talk to the person they have named as agent to make certain that the designated agent understands their wishes and is willing to take the responsibility.

SECTION 5. DECISIONS BY SURROGATE.

(a) A surrogate may make a health-care decision for a patient who is an adult or emancipated minor if the patient has been determined by the primary physician to lack capacity and no agent or guardian has been appointed or the agent or guardian is not reasonably available.

(b) An adult or emancipated minor may designate any individual to act as surrogate by personally informing the supervising health-care provider. In the absence of a designation, or if the designee is not reasonably available, any member of the following classes of the patient's family who is reasonably available, in descending order of priority, may act as surrogate:

(1) the spouse, unless legally separated;

(2) an adult child;

(3) a parent; or

(4) an adult brother or sister.

(c) If none of the individuals eligible to act as surrogate under subsection (b) is reasonably available, an adult who has exhibited special care and concern for the patient, who is familiar with the patient's personal values, and who is reasonably available may act as surrogate.

(d) A surrogate shall communicate his or her assumption of authority as promptly as practicable to the members of the patient's family specified in subsection (b) who can be readily contacted.

(e) If more than one member of a class assumes authority to act as surrogate, and they do not agree on a health-care decision and the supervising health-care provider is so informed, the supervising health-care provider shall comply with the decision of a majority of the members of that class who have communicated their views to the provider. If the class is evenly divided concerning the health-care decision and the supervising health-care provider is so informed, that class and all individuals having lower priority are disqualified from making the decision.

(f) A surrogate shall make a health-care decision in accordance with the patient's individual instructions, if any, and other wishes to the extent known to the surrogate. Otherwise, the surrogate shall make the decision in accordance with the surrogate's determination of the patient's best interest. In determining the patient's best interest, the surrogate shall consider the patient's personal values to the extent known to the surrogate.

(g) A health-care decision made by a surrogate for a patient is effective without judicial approval.

(h) An individual at any time may disqualify another, including a member of the individual's family, from acting as the individual's surrogate by a signed writing or by personally informing the supervising health-care provider of the disqualification.

(i) Unless related to the patient by blood, marriage, or adoption, a surrogate may not be an owner, operator, or employee of [a residential long-term health-care institution] at which the patient is receiving care.

(j) A supervising health-care provider may require an individual claiming the right to act as surrogate for a patient to provide a written declaration under penalty of perjury stating facts and circumstances reasonably sufficient to establish the claimed authority.

Comment

Subsection (a) authorizes a surrogate to make a health-care decision for a patient who is an adult or emancipated minor if the patient lacks capacity to make health-care decisions and if no agent or guardian has been appointed or the agent or guardian is not reasonably available. Health-care decision making for unemancipated minors is not covered by this section. The subject of consent for treatment of minors is a complex one which in many states is covered by a variety of statutes and is therefore left to other state law.

While a designation of an agent in a written power of attorney for health care is preferred, situations may arise where an individual will not be in a position to execute a power of attorney for health care. In that event, subsection (b) affirms the principle of patient autonomy by allowing an individual to designate a surrogate by personally informing the supervising health-care provider. The supervising health-care provider would then, in accordance with Section 7(b), be obligated to promptly record the designation in the individual's health-care record. An oral designation of a surrogate made by a patient directly to the supervising health-care provider revokes a previous designation of an agent. See Section 3(a).

If an individual does not designate a surrogate or if the designee is not reasonably available, subsection (b) applies a default rule for selecting a family member to act as surrogate. Like all default rules, it is not tailored to every situation, but incorporates the presumed desires of a majority of those who find themselves so situated. The relationships specified in subsection (b) include those of the half-blood and by adoption, in addition to those of the whole blood.

Subsection (c) permits a health-care decision to be made by a more distant relative or unrelated adult with whom the individual enjoys a close relationship but only if all family members specified in subsection (b) decline to act or are otherwise not reasonably available. Consequently, those in non-traditional relationships who want to make certain that health-care decisions are made by their companions should execute powers of attorney for health care designating them as agents or, if that has not been done, should designate them as surrogates.

Subsections (b) and (c) permit any member of a class authorized to serve as surrogate to assume authority to act even though there are other members in the class.

Subsection (d) requires a surrogate who assumes authority to act to immediately so notify the members of the patient's family who in given circumstances would be eligible to act as surrogate. Notice to the specified family members will enable them to follow health-care developments with respect to their now incapacitated relative. It will also alert them to take appropriate action, including the appointment of a guardian or the commencement of judicial proceedings under Section 14, should the need arise.

Subsection (e) addresses the situation where more than one member of the same class has assumed authority to act as surrogate and a disagreement over a health-care decision arises of which the supervising health-care provider is informed. Should that occur, the supervising health-care provider must comply with the decision of a majority of the members of that class who have communicated their views to the provider. If the members of the class who have communicated their views to the provider are evenly divided concerning the health-care decision, however, then the entire class is disqualified from making the decision and no individual having lower priority may act as surrogate. When such a deadlock arises, it may be necessary to seek court determination of the issue as authorized by Section 14.

Subsection (f) imposes on surrogates the same standard for health-care decision making as is prescribed for agents in Section 2(e). The surrogate must follow the patient's individual instructions and other expressed wishes to the extent known to the surrogate. To the extent such instructions or other wishes are unknown, the surrogate must act in the patient's best interest. In determining the patient's best interest, the surrogate is to consider the patient's personal values to the extent known to the surrogate.

Subsection (g) provides that a health-care decision made by a surrogate is effective without judicial approval. A similar provision applies to health-care decisions made by agents (Section 2(f)) or guardians (Section 6(c)).

Subsection (h) permits an individual to disqualify any family member or other individual from acting as the individual's surrogate, including disqualification of a surrogate who was orally designated.

Subsection (i) disqualifies an owner, operator, or employee of a residential long-term health-care institution at which a patient is receiving care from acting as the patient's surrogate unless related to the patient by blood, marriage, or adoption. This disqualification is similar to that for appointed agents. See Section 2(b) and Comment.

Subsection (j) permits a supervising health-care provider to require an individual claiming the right to act as surrogate to provide a written declaration under penalty of perjury stating facts and circumstances reasonably sufficient to establish the claimed relationship. The authority to request a declaration is included to permit the provider to obtain evidence of claimed authority. A supervising health-care provider, however, does not have a duty to investigate the qualifications of an individual claiming authority to act as surrogate, and Section 9(a) protects a health-care provider or institution from liability for complying with the decision of such an individual, absent knowledge that the individual does not in fact have such authority.

SECTION 6. DECISIONS BY GUARDIAN.

(a) A guardian shall comply with the ward's individual instructions and may not revoke the ward's advance health-care directive unless the appointing court expressly so authorizes.

(b) Absent a court order to the contrary, a health-care decision of an agent takes precedence over that of a guardian.

(c) A health-care decision made by a guardian for the ward is effective without judicial approval.

Comment

The Act affirms that health-care decisions should whenever possible be made by a person whom the individual selects to do so. For this reason, subsection (b) provides that a health-care decision of an agent takes precedence over that of a guardian absent a court order to the contrary, and subsection (a) provides that a guardian may not revoke the ward's power of attorney for health care unless the appointing court expressly so authorizes. Without these subsections, a guardian would in many states have authority to revoke the ward's power of attorney for health care even though the court appointing the guardian might not be aware that the principal had made such alternate arrangement.

The Act expresses a strong preference for honoring an individual instruction. Under the Act, an individual instruction must be honored by an agent, by a surrogate, and, subject to exceptions specified in Section 7(e)–(f), by an individual's health-care providers. Subsection (a) extends this principle to guardians by requiring that a guardian effectuate the ward's individual instructions. A guardian may revoke the ward's individual instructions only if the appointing court expressly so authorizes.

Courts have no particular expertise with respect to health-care decision making. Moreover, the delay attendant upon seeking court approval may undermine the effectiveness of the decision ultimately made, particularly but not only when the patient's condition is life-threatening and immediate decisions concerning treatment need to be made. Decisions should whenever possible be made by a patient, or the patient's guardian, agent, or surrogate in consultation with the patient's health-care providers without outside interference. For this reason, subsection (c) provides that a health-care decision made by a guardian for the ward is effective without judicial approval, and the Act includes similar provisions for health-care decisions made by agents (Section 2(f)) or surrogates (Section 5(g)).

SECTION 7. OBLIGATIONS OF HEALTH-CARE PROVIDER.

(a) Before implementing a health-care decision made for a patient, a supervising health-care provider, if possible, shall promptly communicate to the patient the decision made and the identity of the person making the decision.

(b) A supervising health-care provider who knows of the existence of an advance health-care directive, a revocation of an advance health-care directive, or a designation or disqualification of a surrogate, shall promptly record its existence in the patient's health-care record and, if it is in writing, shall request a copy and if one is furnished shall arrange for its maintenance in the health-care record.

(c) A primary physician who makes or is informed of a determination that a patient lacks or has recovered capacity, or that another condition exists which affects an individual instruction or the authority of an agent, guardian, or surrogate, shall promptly record the determination in the patient's health-care record and communicate the determination to the patient, if possible, and to any person then authorized to make health-care decisions for the patient.

(d) Except as provided in subsections (e) and (f), a health-care provider or institution providing care to a patient shall:

(1) comply with an individual instruction of the patient and with a reasonable interpretation of that instruction made by a person then authorized to make health-care decisions for the patient; and

(2) comply with a health-care decision for the patient made by a person then authorized to make health-care decisions for the patient to the same extent as if the decision had been made by the patient while having capacity.

(e) A health-care provider may decline to comply with an individual instruction or health-care decision for reasons of conscience. A health-care institution may decline to comply with an individual instruction or health-care decision if the instruction or decision is contrary to a policy of the institution which is expressly based on reasons of conscience and if the policy was timely communicated to the patient or to a person then authorized to make health-care decisions for the patient.

(f) A health-care provider or institution may decline to comply with an individual instruction or health-care decision that requires medically ineffective health care or health care contrary to generally accepted health-care standards applicable to the health-care provider or institution.

(g) A health-care provider or institution that declines to comply with an individual instruction or health-care decision shall:

(1) promptly so inform the patient, if possible, and any person then authorized to make health-care decisions for the patient;

(2) provide continuing care to the patient until a transfer can be effected; and

(3) unless the patient or person then authorized to make health-care decisions for the patient refuses assistance, immediately make all reasonable efforts to assist in the transfer of the patient to another

health-care provider or institution that is willing to comply with the instruction or decision.

(h) A health-care provider or institution may not require or prohibit the execution or revocation of an advance health-care directive as a condition for providing health care.

Comment

Subsection (a) further reinforces the Act's respect for patient autonomy by requiring a supervising health-care provider, if possible, to promptly communicate to a patient, prior to implementation, a health-care decision made for the patient and the identity of the person making the decision.

The recording requirement in subsection (b) reduces the risk that a health-care provider or institution, or agent, guardian or surrogate, will rely on an outdated individual instruction or the decision of an individual whose authority has been revoked.

Subsection (c) imposes recording and communication requirements relating to determinations that may trigger the authority of an agent, guardian or surrogate to make health-care decisions on an individual's behalf. The determinations covered by these requirements are those specified in Sections 2(c)–(d) and 5(a).

Subsection (d) requires health-care providers and institutions to comply with a patient's individual instruction and with a reasonable interpretation of that instruction made by a person then authorized to make health-care decisions for the patient. A health-care provider or institution must also comply with a health-care decision made by a person then authorized to make health-care decisions for the patient to the same extent as if the decision had been made by the patient while having capacity. These requirements help to protect the patient's rights to autonomy and self-determination and validate and seek to effectuate the substitute decision making authorized by the Act.

Not all instructions or decisions must be honored, however. Subsection (e) authorizes a health-care provider to decline to comply with an individual instruction or health-care decision for reasons of conscience. Subsection (e) also allows a health-care institution to decline to comply with a health-care instruction or decision if the instruction or decision is contrary to a policy of the institution which is expressly based on reasons of conscience and if the policy was timely communicated to the patient or to an individual then authorized to make health-care decisions for the patient.

Subsection (f) further authorizes a health-care provider or institution to decline to comply with an instruction or decision that requires the provision of care which would be medically ineffective or contrary to generally accepted health-care standards applicable to the provider or institution. "Medically ineffective health care", as used in this section, means treatment which would not offer the patient any significant benefit.

Subsection (g) requires a health-care provider or institution that declines to comply with an individual instruction or health-care decision to promptly communicate the refusal to the patient, if possible, and to any person then authorized to make health-care decisions for the patient. The provider or institution also must provide continuing care to the patient until a transfer can be effected. In addition, unless the patient or person then authorized to make health-care decisions for the patient refuses assistance, the health-care provider or institution must immediately make all reasonable efforts to assist in the transfer of the patient to another health-care provider or institution that is willing to comply with the instruction or decision.

Subsection (h), forbidding a health-care provider or institution to condition provision of health care on execution, non-execution, or revocation of an advance health-care directive, tracks the provisions of the federal Patient Self-Determination Act (42 U.S.C. 1395cc(f)(1)(C) (Medicare); 42 U.S.C. § 1396a(w)(1)(C) (Medicaid)).

SECTION 8. HEALTH-CARE INFORMATION. Unless otherwise specified in an advance health-care directive, a person then authorized to make health-care decisions for a patient has the same rights as the patient to request, receive, examine, copy, and consent to the disclosure of medical or any other health-care information.

Comment

An agent, guardian, or surrogate stands in the shoes of the patient when making health-care decisions. To assure fully informed decision making, this section provides that a person who is then authorized to make health-care decisions for a patient has the same right of access to health-care information as does the patient unless otherwise specified in the patient's advance health-care directive.

SECTION 9. IMMUNITIES.

(a) A health-care provider or institution acting in good faith and in accordance with generally accepted health-care standards applicable to the health-care provider or institution is not subject to civil or criminal liability or to discipline for unprofessional conduct for:

(1) complying with a health-care decision of a person apparently having authority to make a health-care decision for a patient, including a decision to withhold or withdraw health care;

(2) declining to comply with a health-care decision of a person based on a belief that the person then lacked authority; or

(3) complying with an advance health-care directive and assuming that the directive was valid when made and has not been revoked or terminated.

(b) An individual acting as agent or surrogate under this [Act] is not subject to civil or criminal liability or to discipline for unprofessional conduct for health-care decisions made in good faith.

Comment

The section grants broad protection from liability for actions taken in good faith. Subsection (a) permits a health-care provider or institution to comply with a health-care decision made by a person appearing to have authority to make health-care decisions for a patient; to decline to comply with a health-care decision made by a person believed to be without authority; and to assume the validity of and to comply with an advance health-care directive. Absent bad faith or actions taken that are not in accord with generally accepted health-care standards, a health-care provider or institution has no duty to investigate a claim of authority or the validity of an advance health-care directive.

Subsection (b) protects agents and surrogates acting in good faith from liability for making a health-care decision for a patient. Also protected from liability are individuals who mistakenly but in good faith believe they have the authority to make a health-care decision for a patient. For example, an individual who has been designated as agent in a power of attorney for health care might assume authority unaware that the power has been revoked. Or a family member might assume authority to act as surrogate unaware that a family member having a higher priority was reasonably available and authorized to act.

SECTION 10. STATUTORY DAMAGES.

(a) A health-care provider or institution that intentionally violates this [Act] is subject to liability to the aggrieved individual for damages of $[500] or actual damages resulting from the violation, whichever is greater, plus reasonable attorney's fees.

(b) A person who intentionally falsifies, forges, conceals, defaces, or obliterates an individual's advance health-care directive or a revocation of an advance health-care directive without the individual's consent, or who coerces or fraudulently induces an individual to give, revoke, or not to give an advance health-care directive, is subject to liability to that individual for damages of $[2,500] or actual damages resulting from the action, whichever is greater, plus reasonable attorney's fees.

Comment

Conduct which intentionally violates the Act and which interferes with an individual's autonomy to make health-care decisions, either personally or through others as provided under the Act, is subject to civil damages rather than criminal penalties out of a recognition that prosecutions are unlikely to occur. The legislature of an enacting state will have to determine the amount of damages which needs to be authorized in order to encourage the level of potential private enforcement actions necessary to effect compliance with the obligations and responsibilities imposed by the Act. The damages provided by this section do not supersede but are in addition to remedies available under other law.

SECTION 11. CAPACITY.

(a) This [Act] does not affect the right of an individual to make health-care decisions while having capacity to do so.

(b) An individual is presumed to have capacity to make a health-care decision, to give or revoke an advance health-care directive, and to designate or disqualify a surrogate.

Comment

This section reinforces the principle of patient autonomy by providing a rebuttable presumption that an individual has capacity for all decisions relating to health care referred to in the Act.

SECTION 12. EFFECT OF COPY.   A copy of a written advance health-care directive, revocation of an advance health-care directive, or designation or disqualification of a surrogate has the same effect as the original.

Comment

The need to rely on an advance health-care directive may arise at times when the original is inaccessible. For example, an individual may be receiving care from several health-care providers or may be receiving care at a location distant from that where the original is kept. To facilitate prompt and informed decision making, this section provides that a copy of a valid written advance health-care directive, revocation of an advance health-care directive, or designation or disqualification of a surrogate has the same effect as the original.

SECTION 13. EFFECT OF [ACT].

(a) This [Act] does not create a presumption concerning the intention of an individual who has not made or who has revoked an advance health-care directive.

(b) Death resulting from the withholding or withdrawal of health care in accordance with this [Act] does not for any purpose constitute a suicide or homicide or legally impair or invalidate a policy of insurance or an annuity providing a death benefit, notwithstanding any term of the policy or annuity to the contrary.

(c) This [Act] does not authorize mercy killing, assisted suicide, euthanasia, or the provision, withholding, or withdrawal of health care, to the extent prohibited by other statutes of this State.

(d) This [Act] does not authorize or require a health-care provider or institution to provide health care contrary to generally accepted health-care standards applicable to the health-care provider or institution.

[(e) This [Act] does not authorize an agent or surrogate to consent to the admission of an individual to a mental health-care institution unless the individual's written advance health-care directive expressly so provides.]

[(f) This [Act] does not affect other statutes of this State governing treatment for mental illness of an individual involuntarily committed to a [mental health-care institution under appropriate statute].]

Comment

Subsection (e) is included to accommodate the legislature of an enacting jurisdiction that wishes to address in this Act rather than by separate statute the authority of an agent or surrogate to consent to the admission of an individual to a mental health-care institution. In recognition of the principle of patient autonomy, however, an individual may authorize an agent or surrogate to consent to an admission to a mental health-care institution but may do so only by express provision in an advance health-care directive. Subsection (e) does not address the authority of a guardian to consent to an admission, leaving that matter to be decided under state guardianship law.

All states surround the involuntary commitment process with procedural safeguards. Moreover, state mental health codes contain detailed provisions relating to the treatment of individuals subject to commitment. Subsection (f) is included in the event that the legislature of an enacting jurisdiction wishes to clarify that a general health-care statute such as this Act is intended to supplement and not supersede these more detailed provisions.

SECTION 14. JUDICIAL RELIEF. On petition of a patient, the patient's agent, guardian, or surrogate, a health-care provider or institution involved with the patient's care, or an individual described in Section 5(b) or (c), the [appropriate] court may enjoin or direct a health-care decision or order other equitable relief. A proceeding under this section is governed by [here insert appropriate reference to the rules of procedure or statutory provisions governing expedited proceedings and proceedings affecting incapacitated persons].

Comment

While the provisions of the Act are in general to be effectuated without litigation, situations will arise where judicial proceedings may be appropriate.

For example, the members of a class of surrogates authorized to act under Section 5 may be evenly divided with respect to the advisability of a particular health-care decision. In that circumstance, authorization to proceed may have to be obtained from a court. Examples of other legitimate issues that may from time to time arise include whether an agent or surrogate has authority to act and whether an agent or surrogate has complied with the standard of care imposed by Sections 2(e) and 5(f).

This section has a limited scope. The court under this section may grant only equitable relief. Other adequate avenues exist for those who wish to pursue money damages. The class of potential petitioners is also limited to those with a direct interest in a patient's health care.

The final portion of this section has been placed in brackets in recognition of the fact that states vary widely in the extent to which they codify procedural matters in a substantive act. The legislature of an enacting jurisdiction is encouraged, however, to cross-reference to its rules on expedited proceedings or rules on proceedings affecting incapacitated persons. The legislature of an enacting jurisdiction which wishes to include a detailed procedural provision in its adoption of the Act may want to consult Guidelines for State Court Decision Making in Life-Sustaining Medical Treatment Cases (2d ed. 1992), published by the National Center for State Courts.

SECTION 15. UNIFORMITY OF APPLICATION AND CONSTRUCTION. This [Act] shall be applied and construed to effectuate its general purpose to make uniform the law with respect to the subject matter of this [Act] among States enacting it.

SECTION 16. SHORT TITLE. This [Act] may be cited as the Uniform Health-Care Decisions Act.

SECTION 17. SEVERABILITY CLAUSE. If any provision of this [Act] or its application to any person or circumstance is held invalid, the invalidity does not affect other provisions or applications of this [Act] which can be given effect without the invalid provision or application, and to this end the provisions of this [Act] are severable.

SECTION 18. EFFECTIVE DATE. This [Act] takes effect on

_____ .

SECTION 19. REPEAL. The following acts and parts of acts are repealed:
  (1)
  (2)
  (3)

APPENDIX D
(i) Values History Form Packet (English)

It is important that your medical treatment be **your choice.**

The purpose of this form is to assist you in thinking about and writing down what is important to you about your health. If you should at some time become unable to make health care decisions, this form may help others make a decision for you in accordance with your values.

The first section of this packet offers suggestions for using the Values History Form. The second section, the form itself, provides an opportunity for you to discuss your values, wishes, and preferences in a number of different areas such as your pers onal relationships, your overall attitude toward life, and your thoughts about illness.

The third section of this packet provides a space for indicating whether you have completed an Advance Directive, e.g., an Advance Directive for Health Care, a Living Will, Durable Power of Attorney for Health Care Decisions or Health Care Proxy, and w here such documents may be found.

You may download this form for free, providing you attribute it to our Health Sciences Ethics Program and the form is not used in a proprietary or for-profit manner.

This form is not copyrighted; you may make as many copies as you wish.
For more information or to obtain a hard copy write to:

Health Sciences Ethics Program
University of New Mexico
Nursing/Pharmacy Bldg., Room 368
Albuquerque, NM 87131
E-mail requests to: pierson@unm.edu
Cost per hard copy: $3.00 (payable to Health Sciences Ethics Program)

I. SUGGESTIONS FOR USING THE VALUES HISTORY FORM

This Values History Form was developed at the Center for Health Law and Ethics, University of New Mexico School of Law. The form **is not a legal document**, although it may be used to supplement an Advance Directive such as a Living Will, a Durable Power of Attorney for Health Care, or a Health Care Proxy, if you have these. Also, the Values History Form **is not copyrighted,** and you are encouraged to make additional copies for friends and relatives to use.

WHY A VALUES HISTORY FORM?

The Values History Form recognizes that medical decisions we make for ourselves are based on those beliefs, preferences and values that matter most to us: How do we feel about our overall health? What personal relationships in our lives are important to us? How do we feel about independence or dependence? About pain, illness, dying and death? What are our goals for the future?

A discussion of these and other values can provide important information for those who might, in the future, have to make medical decisions for us when we are no longer able to do so.

Further, a discussion of the questions asked on the Values History Form can provide a solid basis for families, friends, physicians and other when making such medical decisions. By talking about these issues ahead of time, family disagreements may be m inimized. And when such decisions do need to be made, the burden of responsibility may be lessened because others feel confident of your wishes.

HOW DO I FILL OUT THE VALUES HISTORY FORM?

There are a number of ways in which you might begin to answer these questions. Perhaps you would like to write out some of your own thoughts before you talk with anyone else. Or you might ask family and friends to come together and talk about you—and their—responses to the questions.

Often simply giving copies of the Values History Form to others is enough to get people talking about a subject that, for many of us, is difficult and painful to consider.

The most important thing to remember is that **it is easier to talk about these issues BEFORE a medical crisis occurs.** Feel free to add questions and comments of your own.

WHAT SHOULD I DO WITH MY COMPLETED VALUES HISTORY FORM?

Make sure that all those who might be involved in your health care are aware of your wishes: family, friends, physicians and other health care providers, your pastor, your lawyer. If appropriate, give written copies to these people. But remember, each of us continues to grow and change, and so the Values History Form should be discussed and updated fairly regularly.

Consider attaching a copy of it to your Living Will, Durable Power of Attorney, or Health Care Proxy, if you have one, or filing it with your important medical papers.

WHAT IF I DO NOT HAVE AN ADVANCE DIRECTIVE?

If you would like forms that are legal in your state, contact:

Partnership for Caring, Inc. (formerly Choice in Dying)
1620 Eye Street, NW, Suite 202
Washington, DC 20006
Phones: 202-296-8071; 800-989-9455
Fax: 202-296-8352
www.partnershipforcaring.org

This agency will provide legal information about Living Wills and Durable Powers of Attorney for Health Care, as applicable in your own state.

You might also contact your local Office of Senior Affairs, you State or Area Agency on Aging, agencies providing Legal Services for the Elderly, or your personal attorney.

WHO SHOULD CONSIDER PREPARING A VALUES HISTORY FORM?

Everyone.

While we often focus on older people, it is just as important that younger people discuss these issues and make their wishes known. Often some of the most difficult medical decisions must be made on behalf of younger patients. If they had talked with families and friends, these decisions makers could feel reassured they were following the patient's wishes.

We hope this Values History Form is of help to you, your families and friends. Many people have commented that it is important to reflect, not so much on "How I want to die," but rather on "**How I want to LIVE until I die.**"

II. Values History Form

NAME: ————————————————————————

DATE: —————————————————————————

If someone assisted you in completing this form, please fill in his or her name, address, and relationship to you.

Name: ————————————————————————

Address: ——————————————————————

——————————————————————————————

Relationship: ———————————————————

OVERALL ATTITUDE TOWARD LIFE AND HEALTH

What would you like to say to someone reading this document about your overall attitude toward life?

What goals do you have for the future?

How satisfied are you with what you have achieved in your life?

What, for you, makes life worth living?

What do you fear most? What frightens or upsets you?

What activities do you enjoy (e.g., hobbies, watching TV, etc.?)

How would you describe your current state of health?

If you currently have any health problems or disabilities, how do they affect: You? Your family? Your work? Your ability to function?

If you have health problems or disabilities, how do you feel about them? What would you like others (family, friends, doctors) to know about this?

Do you have difficulties in getting through the day with activities such as: eating? preparing food? sleeping? dressing and bathing? etc.

What would you like to say to someone reading this document about your general health?

PERSONAL RELATIONSHIPS

What role do family and friends play in your life?

How do you expect friends, family and others to support your decisions regarding medical treatment you may need now or in the future?

Have you made any arrangements for family or friends to make medical treatment decisions on your behalf? If so, who has agreed to make decisions for you and in what circumstances?

What general comments would you like to make about the personal relationships in your life?

THOUGHTS ABOUT INDEPENDENCE AND SELF-SUFFICIENCY

How does independence or dependence affect your life?

If you were to experience decreased physical and mental abilities, how would that affect your attitude toward independence and self-sufficiency?

If your current physical or mental health gets worse, how would you feel?

LIVING ENVIRONMENT

Have you lived alone or with others over the last 10 years?

How comfortable have you been in your surroundings? How might illness, disability or age affect this?

What general comments would you like to make about your surroundings.

RELIGIOUS BACKGROUND AND BELIEFS

What is your spiritual/religious background?

How do your beliefs affect your feelings toward serious, chronic or terminal illness?

How does your faith community, church or synagogue support you?
What general comments would you like to make about your beliefs?

RELATIONSHIPS WITH DOCTORS AND OTHER HEALTH CAREGIVERS

How do you relate to your doctors? Please comment on: trust; decision making; time for satisfactory communication; respectful treatment.
How do you feel about other caregivers, including nurses, therapists, chaplains, social workers, etc.?
What else would you like to say about doctors and other caregivers?

THOUGHTS ABOUT ILLNESS, DYING AND DEATH

What general comments would you like to make about illness, dying and death?
What will be important to you when you are dying (e.g., physical comfort, no pain, family members present, etc.)?
Where would you prefer to die?
How do you feel about the use of life-sustaining measures if you were: suffering from an irreversible chronic illness (e.g., Alzheimer's disease)? terminally ill? in a permanent coma?
What general comments would you like to make about medical treatment?

FINANCES

What general comments would you like to make about your finances and the cost of health care?
What are your feelings about having enough money to provide for your care?

FUNERAL PLANS

What general comments would you like to make about your funeral and burial or cremation?
Have you made your funeral arrangements? If so, with whom?

OPTIONAL QUESTIONS

How would you like your obituary (announcement of your death) to read?
Write yourself a brief eulogy (a statement about yourself to be read at your funeral).
What would you like to say to someone reading this Values History Form?

III. LEGAL DOCUMENTS

What legal documents about health care decisions have you signed? (Each state has its own special form—feel free to add yours to this list.)

Advance Directive for Health Care—New Mexico? Yes _____ No _____

Where and with whom can it be found?

Name _____

Address _____

Phone _____

Living Will? Yes _____ No _____

Where and with whom can it be found?

Name _____

Address _____

Phone _____

Durable Power of Attorney for Health Care Decisions?

Yes _____ No _____

Where and with whom can it be found?

Name _____

Address _____

Phone _____

Health Care Proxy? Yes _____ No _____

Where and with whom can it be found?

Name _____

Address _____

Phone _____

(ii) Values History Form Packet (Spanish) (Español)
La Salud Y Sus Valores

Es importante que el tratamiento médico sea **su preferencia.**

El propósito de esta forma es ayudarle a pensar y escribir lo que le es importante acerca de su salud. Si algún día no puede tomar las decisiones en cuanto a su cuidado médico, esta forma ayudará a otros a tomar una decisión por usted según sus deseos y valores.

    La primera parte de esta forma ofrece sugerencias para como usarla. La segunda parte le provee la oportunidad de discutir sus valores, deseos, y preferencias en sus relaciones personales, su actitud sobre la vida, y sus pensamientos sobre la enfermedad. La tercera parte provee un espacio para indicar si usted tiene un Advance Directive for Health Care (Instrucciones y Previa Autorización de Tratamiento Médico), un Living Will (Un Testamento Vivo), un PODER LEGAL DE SALUD DE CUIDADOS MEDICOS y donde puede encontrar estos documentos.

Puede hacer copias de esta forma.
Para más información o para obtener una copia escriba a:
Health Sciences Ethics Program
University of New Mexico
Nursing/Pharmacy Bldg., Room 368
Albuquerque, NM 87131
Teléfono: 505-272-0903
FAX: 505-272-9213

Las solicitudes por correo eléctronico: pierson@unm.edu
Cada copia cuesta $3.00; hacer pago al Health Sciences Ethics Program.
Se puede copiar la forma a http://www.unm.edu/~hsethics

I. SUGERENCIAS PARA USAR ESTA FORMA

Esta forma fue desarrollada por el Center for Health Law and Ethics, University of New Mexico School of Law. Esta forma **no es un documento legal,** pero se puede usar para complementar las Instrucciones y Previa Autorización de Tratamiento Médico (Advance Directive), un Testamento Vivo (Living Will) y un Poder Legal de Salud de Cuidados. Si usted las tiene, favor de hacer copias y dárselas a sus familiares y amigos.

¿POR QUÉ PREGUNTARLE ACERCA DE SUS VALORES?

Se reconoce que las decisiones médicas que tomamos por nuestra cuenta están basadas en las creencias, preferencias y valores que nos son importantes: ¿Qué opinamos acerca de la salud en general? ¿Qué relaciones personales nos importan? ¿Cuáles son nuestras ideas acerca de la independencia o la dependencia? Del dolor, la enfermedad, y la muerte? ¿Cuáles son nuestras metas para el futuro?

Una discusión de estos y otros valores puede proveer información importante para los que hacen las decisiones médicas por nosotros cuando no podamos hacerlas por nosotros mismos.

También, una discusión en las preguntas de esta forma puede proveer una base sólida para las familias, los amigos, los médicos y otros cuando se hacen tales decisiones. De haber hablado de estos asuntos antes de ponerse enfermo, se puede reducir al mínimo las diferencias familiares. Cuando hay que tomar estas decisiones, el cargo de responsabilidad se disminuye cuando otros conocen sus deseos.

¿CÓMO SE LLENA ESTA FORMA?

Hay varias maneras de comenzar a contestar estas preguntas. Tal vez usted quisiera escribir sus pensamientos propios antes de hablar con otra persona. O puede invitar a familiares y amigos a discutir las preguntas y las respuestas. Muchas veces cuando se dan copias de esta forma a otros, ellos quieren hablar de este tema que es difícil y doloroso para muchos.

Es importante recordar que **es mucho más fácil discutir estas cosas ANTES de que ocurra una crisis médica.** Puede añadir sus preguntas y comentarios.

¿QUÉ DEBO HACER CON LA FORMA COMPLETADA?

Es importante que todas las personas que le ayuden con su tratamiento médico sepan de sus deseos: la familia, los amigos, los médicos, el abogado, y el consejero espiritual.

Pero, todos con el tiempo pueden cambiar de idea. Así que es importante repasar la forma de vez en cuando.

Esta forma debe estar junto con sus papeles médicos importantes.

¿Y SI NO TENGO INSTRUCCIONES Y PREVIA AUTORIZACION DE TRATAMIENTO MEDICO?

Si le gustaría a usted tener las formas legales de su estado, puede escribir o llamar:

Partnership for Caring, Inc. (formerly Choice in Dying)
1620 Eye Street, NW, Suite 202
Washington, DC 20006
Phones: 202-296-8071; 800-989-9455
Fax: 202-296-8352
www.partnershipforcaring.org

Esta agencia le puede proveer información legal sobre Los Testamentos Vivos y El Poder Legal de Salud de Cuidados Médicos del estado.

También puede llamar a la Office of Senior Affairs aquí en Albuquerque, a su abogado o varias agencias del estado.

¿QUIEN DEBE PREPARAR ESTA FORMA?

Todo el mundo.

Usualmente pensamos en los viejos, pero también es importante que los jóvenes discutan estos asuntos y digan sus deseos. A menudo los casos más difíciles son de los pacientes jóvenes. Si anteriormente ellos hablaran con su familia y sus amigos, estas decisiones serían menos difíciles porque se sabe de los deseos del paciente.

Mucha gente ha comentado que es más importante pensar en **"Cómo quiero vivir hasta que me muera."** que **"Cómo quiero morir".**

II. LA FORMA DE LOS VALORES

NOMBRE: _____

FECHA: _____
Si alguien le ayudó a cumplir esta forma, favor de llenar su nombre, su dirección, y su relación con usted.

Nombre: _____

Dirección: _____

_____

Relación: _____

LA ACTITUD GENERAL HACIA LA VIDA Y LA SALUD

¿Qué quiere usted decirle a alguien que está leyendo este documento acerca de su actitud general hacia la vida?

¿Cuáles son sus metas para el futuro?

¿Está usted satisfecho con lo que ha cumplido en su vida?

Para usted, ¿por qué vale la vida?

¿De qué tiene usted más miedo? ¿Qué le molesta a usted?

¿Cuáles actividades le gustan? (diversiones, mirar la TV, etc.)

¿Cómo describiría usted el estado presente de su salud?

Si ahora usted tiene problemas de salud o es minusválido, ¿Cómo le afectan a usted? a su familia? su trabajo? su capacidad de funcionar?

¿Qué quiere usted que otros (la familia, los amigos, los médicos) sepan de sus problemas de salud?

¿Tiene usted problemas en comer, preparar la comida, dormir, vestirse y bañarse, etc.?

¿Qué quisiera decirle a alguien que lee este documento de su salud en general?

LAS RELACIONES PERSONALES

¿Qué papel en su vida tienen la familia y los amigos?

¿Cree usted que los amigos, la familia y otros van a apoyar lo que usted decide sobre el tratamiento médico que prefiere ahora o en el futuro?

¿Ya tiene usted planes para que la familia o los amigos tomen decisiones del tratamiento médico por usted? ¿Quién va a seguir las instrucciones que usted ha dejado?

¿Qué comentarios quiere usted hacer acerca de las relaciones íntimas?

SU SENTIDO DE INDEPENDENCIA

¿Qué pasaría si tuviera que depender de la ayuda de otra persona?

Si sus habilidades físicas y mentales disminuyeran, ¿cómo afectaría su actitud acerca de la independencia?

Si su salud física o mental empeorara, ¿Cómo se sentiría?

EL AMBIENTE DE LA VIVIENDA

En los diez años pasados, ¿ha vivido usted solo o con otras personas?

¿Vive cómodo en su medio ambiente? ¿Cómo afectaría este ambiente una enfermedad, la invalidez, o la vejez?

¿Cómo describiría el medio ambiente donde vive?

SU RELIGION Y CREENCIAS

A qué iglesia o religión pertenece?

¿Cómo afectan sus creencias religiosas su concepto de la enfermedad grave, crónica o terminal?

¿En qué manera le apoyan a usted su comunidad de fé, su iglesia or su sinagoga?

¿Qué comentario quiere hacer sobre sus creencias?

RELACIONES CON LOS MEDICOS Y OTROS DEL CAMPO DE SALUD

¿Cómo se lleva con su médico? Favor de comentar en: la confianza que tiene en ellos; cómo toman las decisiones; cómo le tratan a usted, ¿con respecto?

¿Qué piensa usted de las enfermeras, terapistas, pastores, y los trabajadores sociales, etc.?

¿Hay otras cosas que quiere incluir sobre los médicos y otros trabajadores de salud?

LAS IDEAS SOBRE LAS ENFERMEDADES, Y LA MUERTE

¿Hay comentarios generales que le gustaría hacer sobre las enfermedades, y la muerte?

¿Qué le sería importante a usted cuando esté a punto de morir (por ejemplo, la curación, no tener dolor, la presencia de la familia, etc.)?
¿Dónde prefiere usted morir?
¿Cuáles son sus opiniones acerca de los medios de prolongar la vida si usted está sufriendo con una enfermedad crónica e irreversible (por ejemplo, Alzheimer's)? una enfermedad terminal? En un coma permanente?
¿Qué son sus comentarios generales sobre el tratamiento médico?

EL DINERO

Comente sobre su situación económica y el precio del tratamiento médico.
¿Qué opina sobre la necesidad de pagar el tratamiento que uno necesita?

LOS PLANES FUNERALES

¿Qué comentarios le gustaría hacer sobre su funeral y entierro o cremación?
¿Ha hecho usted los planes funerales? ¿Con quién?

PREGUNTAS OPCIONALES

¿Cómo quiere anunciar su muerte?
Favor de escribir un elogio breve para sí mismo (una declaración de sí mismo que se puede leer durante su funeral).
¿Qué quisiera decir a alguien que está leyendo esta Forma de Valores?

Notes

1. Other Values History Forms:

   (a) *Five Wishes*. This document combines an advance health care directive (purportedly valid in thirty-five states and the District of Columbia) with a values history. It is available for purchase through www.agingwithdignity.org/5wishes.html

   (b) *The Medical Directive* was developed by Drs. Linda and Ezekiel Emanuel. A sample may be viewed (and, if desired, purchased) through www.medicaldirective.org

APPENDIX E
Spanish Language Directives

(i) Poder médico

Ley de Directivas Anticipadas (ver § 166. 164, del Código de Salud y Seguridad)
Nombramiento de un agente de atención médica:
Yo, (escriba su nombre) nombro a:
Nombre: __
Dirección: __ Teléfono: __
como mi agente para que tome todas y cada una de las decisiones sobre atención médica por mí, a menos que yo diga lo contrario en este documento. Este poder médico entra en vigor si yo no tengo capacidad para tomar mis propias decisiones sobre la atención médica y mi doctor certifica este hecho por escrito.

La autoridad de mi agente médico para tomar decisiones tendrá las siguientes limitaciones:
Nombramiento de un agente alterno:

(Usted no tiene que nombrar a un agente alterno, pero si quiere puede hacerlo. Un agente alterno puede tomar las mismas decisiones médicas que tomaría el agente designado si el agente designado no puede o no quiere hacer las veces de agente. Si el agente designado es su cónyuge, el nombramiento se revoca automáticamente por ley si su matrimonio se disuelve).

Si la persona designada como mi agente no es capaz o no está dispuesta a tomar decisiones médicas por mí, nombro a las siguientes personas, para que hagan las veces de agente para tomar decisiones de tipo médico conforme yo las autorice por medio de este documento. Lo harán en el siguiente orden:

Primer Agente Alterno
Nombre: __
Dirección: __
Teléfono: __
Segundo Agente Alterno
Nombre: __
Dirección: __
Teléfono: __
El original de este documento se mantendrá en: __
Las siguientes personas o instituciones tienen copias firmadas: __
Nombre: __
Dirección: __
Nombre: __
Dirección: __

Pagina 2
Para *Pagina 1*
Para *Pagina 2 Reverse*
Para regresar al *Indice Directivas Anticipadas*

Poder médico
Ley de Directivas Anticipadas (ver § 166. 164, del Código de Salud y Seguridad)
Duración
Comprendo que este poder existirá indefinidamente a partir de la fecha en que se firma el documento a menos que yo establezca un término más corto o lo revoque. Si no estoy en capacidad de tomar decisiones médicas por mi propia cuenta cuando este poder se venza, la autoridad que le he dado a mi agente seguirá en vigor hasta que yo pueda volver a tomar decisiones por mí mismo.
(Si aplica) Este poder se vencerá en la siguiente fecha: __
Revocación de nombramientos anteriores
Revoco cualquier poder médico anterior.
Acuse de recibo de la Declaración
Me dieron la declaración en la que se explica las consecuencias de este documento. La leí y la entiendo.
(Tiene que escribir la fecha y firmar este poder)
    Firmo mi nombre en este poder médico el (día) de (mes) de (año) en (Ciudad y Estado)

(Firma)

(Nombre en letra de molde)
Declaración del primer testigo

No soy la persona designada como agente por medio de este documento. No soy pariente del poderante ni por sangre ni por matrimonio. No tendré derecho a ninguna parte de la sucesión del poderante después de su fallecimiento. No soy el médico tratante del poderante ni estoy empleado por el médico tratante. No tengo ningún derecho sobre ninguna porción de la sucesión del poderante después de su fallecimiento. Además, si trabajo en el centro de atención médica donde es paciente el poderante, no tengo que ver con el cuidado directo del poderante y no soy funcionario, director, socio, ni empleado de la oficina del centro de atención médica ni de ninguna organización matriz del centro de atención médica.

Firma: __
Nombre en letra de molde: __ Fecha: __
Dirección: __

Firma del segundo testigo
Firma: __
Nombre en letra de molde: __ Fecha: __
Dirección: __
Version 10/25/99
Pagina 2 Reverse
Para *Pagina 1*
Para *Pagina 2*
Para regresar al *Indice Directivas Anticipadas*

Declaración Referente al Poder Médico
Ley de Directivas Anticipadas (ver § 166.163, del Código de Salud
y Seguridad)

**Éste es un documento legal importante.
Antes de firmar este documento debe saber esta
información importante:**

Salvo los límites que usted imponga, este documento le da a la persona que usted nombre como su agente la autoridad de tomar, en su nombre, y cuando usted ya no esté en capacidad de tomarlas por su propia cuenta, todas y cada una de las decisiones referentes a la atención médica conforme con sus deseos y teniendo en cuenta sus creencias morales y religiosas. Puesto que "atención médica" se refiere a cualquier tratamiento, servicio o procedimiento para controlar, diagnosticar o tratar cualquier padecimiento físico o mental, su agente tiene el poder de tomar, en su nombre, decisiones sobre una amplia gama de opciones médicas. Su agente puede dar consentimiento, negar consentimiento o retirar el consentimiento para recibir tratamiento médico y puede decidir si suspender o no dar tratamiento para prolongar la vida. Su agente no puede autorizar su ingreso voluntario a un hospital para recibir servicios de salud mental, ni que le den tratamiento convulsivo, psicocirugía o un aborto. El doctor deberá seguir las instrucciones de su agente o permitir que se le cambie a usted de doctor.

La autoridad de su agente comenzará cuando su doctor certifique que usted no estáen capacidad de tomar decisiones de carácter médico.

Su agente tiene la obligación de seguir sus instrucciones cuando tome decisiones en su nombre. A menos que usted especifique lo contrario, su agente tiene la misma autoridad que usted tendría para tomar decisiones sobre su atención médica.

Antes de firmar este documento, es muy importante que hable sobre éste con el doctor o con cualquier proveedor médico para asegurarse de que entienda la naturaleza y los límites de las decisiones que se tomarán en su nombre. Si no tiene un doctor, debe hablar con alguien más que sepa de estos asuntos y pueda contestar sus preguntas. No necesita la ayuda de un abogado para hacer este documento, pero si hay algo en este documento que usted no entienda, debe pedirle a un abogado que se lo explique.

La persona que usted nombre como su agente debe ser alguien conocido y de su confianza. Debe ser mayor de 18 años, o puede ser menor de 18 años si se le ha retirado la incapacidad de minoría de edad. Si usted nombra al proveedor de atención médica o terapeuta (por ejemplo, su doctor o un empleado del centro de salud, hospital, casa para convalecientes o centro de tratamiento terapéutico, que no sea un pariente) esa persona tiene que escoger entre ser su agente o ser su proveedor de atención médica o terapeuta; conforme con la ley, una misma persona no puede desempeñar las dos funciones a la vez.

Debe informarle a la persona que usted escoja que quiere que ella sea su agente de atención médica. Usted debe hablar sobre este documento con su agente y con su doctor y darle a cada uno de ellos una copia firmada. Usted debe escribir en el documento el nombre de las personas e instituciones a quienes ha dado copias firmadas. Su agente no puede ser enjuiciado por las decisiones sobre atención médica tomadas de buena fe en su nombre.

Aun después de firmar este documento, usted tiene el derecho de tomar decisiones de atención médica mientras esté en capacidad de hacerlo y no se le puede administrar o detener un tratamiento si usted se opone. Tiene derecho de revocar la autoridad otorgada a su agente informándole a su agente o a su proveedor de atención médica o terapeuta, oralmente o por escrito, y firmando un nuevo poder médico. A menos que indique lo contrario, el nombramiento de su cónyuge como su agente se disuelve en el caso de que usted se divorcie.

Este documento no se puede modificar o cambiar. Si quiere hacer algún cambio, tiene que hacer un documento nuevo.

Es aconsejable que nombre a un tercer agente en caso de que su agente no quiera, no pueda o esté incapacitado para actuar como su agente. Cualquier agente alterno que usted nombre tendrá la misma autoridad de tomar decisiones de atención médica en su nombre.

Este poder no tiene validez a menos que se firme en presencia de dos testigos adultos hábiles. Las siguientes personas no pueden actuar como UNO de los testigos:

- la persona que usted ha nombrado como su agente;
- una persona que es su pariente por sangre o matrimonio;
- una persona que, después de su muerte, tenga derecho a cualquier porción de su sucesión de acuerdo con su testamento o con una adición a su testamento firmado por usted o que tenga derecho a ésta por efecto legal;
- el doctor que lo atiende;
- un empleado del doctor que lo atiende;

- un empleado de un centro de atención médica del cual usted es paciente si el empleado le estáprestando servicios directamente a usted o es un funcionario, director, socio o empleado de las oficinas del centro de atención médica o de cualquier organización matriz del centro de atención médica; o
- una persona que, en el momento de firmar este poder, pueda reclamar cualquier porción de su sucesión después de su muerte.

Pagina 1
Para *Pagina 2*
Para *Pagina 2 Reverse*
Para regresar al *Indice Directivas Anticipadas*

Source: State of Texas, Department of Human Services, Office of Long Term Care Policy. www.ltc.dhs.state.tx.us/policy

(ii) Directiva

Directiva a los médicos y a familiares o substitutos
Ley de Directivas Anticipadas (ver § 166.033, del Código de
Salud y Seguridad)

Éste es un documento legal importante conocido como Directiva Anticipada. Su función es ayudar a comunicar sus deseos relacionados con el tratamiento médico para un momento futuro cuando no esté en capacidad de hacer conocer sus deseos debido a una enfermedad o lesión. Estos deseos se basan generalmente en sus valores personales. En particular, querrá considerar qué nivel o dificultades de tratamiento está dispuesto a soportar a cambio del beneficio que obtendría en caso de estar gravemente enfermo.

Se le sugiere que hable sobre sus valores y deseos con su familia y con la persona escogida como su agente, lo mismo que con su doctor. El doctor, otro proveedor médico o una institución médica pueden ofrecerle algunos recursos para ayudarle a completar la directiva anticipada. A continuación se dan unas definiciones breves que le podrán ayudar en sus discusiones y en la planeación. Escriba sus iniciales al lado de las opciones de tratamiento que mejor reflejen sus preferencias personales. Deles una copia de su directiva a su doctor, a su hospital de costumbre, a sus parientes y a su agente. Haga una revisión periódica del documento. Mediante la revisión periódica, puede asegurar que la directiva refleje sus preferencias.

Además de esta directiva anticipada, la ley de Texas estipula otros dos tipos de directivas que pueden ser importantes en caso de una enfermedad grave. Estas son: el Poder médico y la Orden de no revivir fuera del hospital. Debe hablar sobre estos con el doctor, su familia, un representante del hospital o con otros consejeros. También es posible que desee llenar una directiva relacionada con la donación de órganos y tejidos.

Directiva

Yo, reconozco que la mejor atención médica se basa en una relación de confianza y comunicación con mi doctor. Juntos, mi doctor y yo tomaremos las decisiones médicas mientras yo esté en condiciones mentales de hacer conocer mis deseos. Si en algún momento yo no estoy en capacidad de tomar decisiones médicas respecto a mi salud debido a una enfermedad o lesión, ordeno que se respeten las siguientes preferencias respecto al tratamiento:

Si, a juicio de mi doctor, estoy padeciendo de una enfermedad terminal de la que se espera moriré dentro de los seis meses, incluso con tratamientos disponibles para prolongar la vida, suministrado de acuerdo con las normas actuales de atención médica:

―――――Yo pido que no me den o que me retiren todo tratamiento salvo aquellos necesarios para mantenerme cómodo, y que mi doctor me deje morir tan dignamente como sea posible; O

―――――Yo pido que me mantengan con vida en esta situación terminal usando los tratamientos disponibles para prolongar la vida. (**Esta preferencia no se aplica al cuidado de hospicio**).

Si, a juicio de mi doctor, estoy sufriendo de un padecimiento irreversible, que no permitirá que me atienda yo mismo ni que tome decisiones por mí mismo y se espera que moriré si no me suministran tratamientos para prolongar la vida de acuerdo con las normas actuales de atención médica:

―――――Yo pido que no me den o me retiren todo tratamiento salvo aquellos necesarios para mantenerme cómodo, y que mi doctor me deje morir tan dignamente como sea posible; O

―――――Yo pido que me mantengan con vida en esta situación irreversible usando tratamientos disponibles para prolongar la vida. (**Esta preferencia no se aplica al cuidado de hospicio**).

Pagina 1
Para *Pagina 2*
Para *Pagina 3*
Para regresar al *Indice Directivas Anticipadas*

Directiva a los médicos y a familiares o substitutos
Ley de Directivas Anticipadas (ver § 166.033, del Código de Salud y Seguridad)

Peticiones adicionales: (Después de consultarle al doctor, usted querrá escribir algunos tratamientos en el espacio disponible que usted quiera o no quiera que se le den bajo circunstancias específicas, como la nutrición artificial y los líquidos, los antibióticos por vía intravenosa, etc. Asegúrese de anotar si quiere o no quiere el tratamiento en particular).

Después de firmar esta directiva, si mi representante o yo elegimos cuidado de hospicio, entiendo y estoy de acuerdo en que me den solamente aquellos tratamientos para mantenerme cómodo y que no me den los tratamientos disponibles para prolongar la vida.

Si **no** tengo un poder para la atención médica, y no puedo dar a conocer mis deseos, designo a las siguientes personas para que tomen decisiones con mi doctor que sean compatibles con mis valores personales:

1. __

2. __

(Si usted ya ha firmado un poder médico, entonces ya habrá nombrado a un agente y no deberá anotar otros nombres en este documento).

Si las personas nombradas antes no están disponibles, o si no hay un vocero designado, comprendo que se escogerá un vocero para mí, siguiendo las pautas especificadas por la ley de Texas.

Si, a juicio de mi doctor, mi muerte es inminente dentro de minutos u horas, a pesar de que me den todo tratamiento médico disponible suministrado dentro de las pautas de atención actuales, autorizo que no me den o que me retiren todo tratamiento salvo aquellos necesarios para mantenerme cómodo. Comprendo que bajo la ley de Texas esta directiva no tiene efecto si se ha diagnosticado que estoy embarazada. Esta directiva seguirá en efecto hasta que yo la revoque. Nadie más puede hacerlo.

Firmado__ Fecha__

Ciudad, condado y estado de domicilio__

Dos testigos tienen que firmar en los espacios siguientes.

Dos testigos adultos hábiles tienen que firmar a continuación, reconociendo la firma del declarante. El testigo designado **Testigo (1)** no puede ser una de las personas designadas para tomar decisiones relacionadas con el tratamiento para el paciente y no puede estar relacionado con el declarante por sangre o por matrimonio. Este testigo no puede tener derecho a ninguna parte de la sucesión y no puede tener un reclamo en contra de la sucesión del paciente. Este testigo no puede ser el médico que lo atiende ni un empleado del médico que lo atiende. Si el testigo es empleado del centro de salud en el cual se cuida al paciente, este testigo no puede estar directamente involucrado en el suministro de atención al paciente. Este testigo no puede ser funcionario, director, socio o empleado de la oficina del centro de atención médica donde se atiende al paciente o de ninguna organización matriz del centro de atención médica.

Testigo (1)__ Testigo (2)__

Pagina 2

Para *Pagina 1*

Para *Pagina 3*

Para regresar al *Indice Directivas Anticipadas*

Directiva a los médicos y a familiares o substitutos
Ley de Directivas Anticipadas (ver § 166.033, del Código de Salud y Seguridad)

Definiciones:

"Nutrición e hidratación artificial" quiere decir el suministro de nutrientes o líquidos mediante una sonda puesta en una vena, bajo la piel en los tejidos subcutáneos o en el estómago (tracto gastrointestinal).

"Padecimiento irreversible" quiere decir un padecimiento, lesión o enfermedad:

a. que se puede tratar, pero que nunca sana;
b. que deja a la persona incapaz de cuidarse o tomar decisiones por ella misma, y
c. que sin el tratamiento para prolongar la vida, suministrado conforme con las normas actuales de atención médica, podría ser fatal.

Explicación: muchas enfermedades graves como el cáncer, la insuficiencia de cualquier órgano vital (el riñón, el corazón, el hígado o el pulmón) y una enfermedad del cerebro grave, como la demencia de Alzheimer, se pueden considerar irreversibles desde muy temprano. No hay curación, pero el paciente puede mantenerse con vida por periodos prolongados de tiempo si recibe tratamientos para prolongar la vida. Más tarde durante la misma enfermedad, ésta se puede considerar terminal cuando, incluso con tratamiento, se espera que el paciente muera. Usted deberá considerar qué niveles de tratamiento está dispuesto a soportar para lograr un resultado particular. Ésta es una decisión muy personal que usted deberá discutir con el doctor, la familia u otras personas importantes en su vida.

*Tratamiento para prolongar la vida" quiere decir un tratamiento que, a juicio médico, preserva la vida de un paciente y sin el cual el paciente moriría. El término se refiere a medicamentos para preservar la vida y a medios artificiales para mantener la vida como los respiradores mecánicos, el tratamiento de diálisis del riñón, la hidratación y la nutrición artificial. El término no se refiere a la administración de medicamentos para el dolor, la ejecución de un procedimiento quirúrgico necesario para suministrar comodidad ni ningún otro servicio médico ofrecido para aliviar el dolor del paciente.

"Padecimiento terminal" quiere decir una enfermedad incurable causada por lesión, enfermedad o dolencia que a juicio médico produciría la muerte dentro de unos seis meses, incluso con el tratamiento disponible para prolongar la vida suministrado de acuerdo con las normas de atención médica actuales.

Explicación: muchas enfermedades graves se pueden considerar irreversibles desde muy temprano en la evolución de la enfermedad, pero no se considera terminal hasta que la enfermedad ha avanzado bastante. Al pensar en una enfermedad terminal y su tratamiento, deberá considerar los beneficios y las dificultades relacionados con el tratamiento y discutirlos con el doctor, la familia u otras personas importantes en su vida.

Pagina 3
Para *Pagina 1*
Para *Pagina 2*
Para regresar al *Indice Directivas Anticipadas*

Source: State of Texas, Department of Human Services, Office of Long Term Care Policy. www.ltc.dhs.state.tx.us/policy

APPENDIX F
Religious Directives

(i) (Jewish Law Halachic Forms)
The Halachic Living Will
PROXY AND DIRECTIVE WITH RESPECT TO
HEALTH CARE DECISIONS AND POST-MORTEM DECISIONS
FOR USE IN NEW YORK STATE

The "Halachic Living Will" is designed to help ensure that all medical and post-death decisions made by others on your behalf will be made in accordance with Jewish law and custom (*halacha*). This document, the "Proxy and Directive with Respect to Health Care Decisions and Post-Mortem Decisions," is the basic form that provides such protection.

INSTRUCTIONS

(a) Please print your name on the first line of the form.

(b) In section 1, print the name, address, and day and evening telephone numbers of the person you wish to designate as your *agent* to make medical decisions on your behalf if, G-d forbid, you ever become incapable of making them on your own.

You may also insert the name, address, and telephone numbers of an *alternate agent* to make such decisions if your main agent is unable, unwilling, or unavailable to make such decisions.

It is recommended that before appointing anyone to serve as your agent or alternate agent you should ascertain that person's willingness to serve in such capacity. In addition, if you have made arrangements with a burial society (*Chevra Kadisha*) for the handling and disposition of your body after death, you may wish to advise your agents of such arrangements.

Note: *New York law allows virtually any competent adult* (an adult is a person 18 years of age or older, or anyone who has married) *to serve as a health care agent.* Thus, you may appoint as your agent (or alternate agent) your spouse, adult child, parent or other adult relative.

You may also appoint a non-relative to serve as your agent (or alternate agent), unless that individual has already been appointed by 10 other persons to serve as a health care agent; or unless that individual is a non-physician employee of a health care facility in which you are a patient or resident.

(c) In section 3, please print the name, address, and telephone numbers of the Orthodox Rabbi whose guidance you want your agent to follow, should any questions arise as to the requirements of *halacha*.

You should then print the name, address, and telephone numbers of the Orthodox Jewish institution or organization you want your agent to contact for a referral to *another* Orthodox Rabbi *if* the rabbi you have identified is unable, unwilling or unavailable to provide the appropriate consultation and guidance.

You are of course free to insert the name of any Orthodox Rabbi or institution/organization you would like, but before doing so it is advisable to discuss the matter with the rabbi or institution/organization to ascertain their competency and willingness to serve in such capacity.

(d) At the conclusion of the form, print the date, sign your name, and print your address. If you are not physically able to do these things, New York law allows another person to sign and date the form on your behalf, as long as he or she does so *at your direction, in your presence,* and *in the presence of two adult witnesses.*

(e) Two witnesses should sign their names and insert their addresses beneath your signature. These two witnesses must be competent adults. *Neither of them should be the person you have appointed as your health care agent (or alternate agent).* They may, however, be your relatives.

(f) It is recommended that you keep the original of this form among your valuable papers; and that you distribute copies to the health care agent (and alternate agent) you have designated in section 1, to the rabbi and institution/organization you have designated in section 3, as well as to your doctors, your lawyer, and anyone else who is likely to be contacted in times of emergency.

(g) If at any time you wish to revoke this Proxy and Directive, you may do so by executing a new one; or by notifying your agent or health care provider, orally or in writing, of your intent to revoke it.

If you do not revoke the Proxy and Directive, New York law provides that it remains in effect indefinitely. Obviously, if any of the persons whose names you have inserted in the Proxy and Directive dies or becomes otherwise incapable of serving in the role you have assigned, it would be wise to execute a new Proxy and Directive.

(h) It is recommended that you also complete the second component of the Halachic Living Will, the "Emergency Instructions Card," and carry it with you in your waller or billfold.

(i) If, upon consultation with your rabbi, you would like to add to this standardized Proxy and Directive any additional expression of your wishes with respect to medical and/or post-mortem decisions, you may do so by attaching a "rider" to the standardized form. If you choose to do so, or if you have any other questions concerning this form, please consult any attorney.

Halachic Living Will

PROXY AND DIRECTIVE WITH RESPECT TO
HEALTH CARE DECISIONS AND POST-MORTEM DECISIONS

I, —————————————————— , hereby declare as follows:

1. **Appointment of Agent:** In recognition of the fact that there may come a time when I will become unable to make my own health care decisions because of illness, injury or other circumstances, I hereby appoint

Name of Agent: ——————————————————————

Address: ——————————————————————————

——————————————————————————————

Telephone: Day ———————————— Evening ————————————

as my health care agent to make any and all health care decisions for me, consistent with my wishes as set forth in this directive.

If the person named above is unable, unwilling or unavailable to act as my agent, I hereby appoint

Name of Alternate Agent: ————————————————————

Address: ——————————————————————————

——————————————————————————————

Telephone: Day ———————————— Evening ————————————

to serve in such capacity.

This appointment shall take effect in the event I become unable, because of illness, injury or other circumstances, to make my own health care decisions.

2. **Jewish Law to Govern Health Care Decisions:** I am Jewish. It is my desire, and I hereby direct, that all health care decisions made for me be made pursuant to Jewish law and custom as determined in accordance with strict Orthodox interpretation and tradition. By way of example, and without limiting in any way the generality of the foregoing, it is my wish that Jewish law and custom should dictate the course of my health care with respect to such matters as the performance or non-performance of cardio-pulmonary resuscitation if I suffer cardiac or respiratory arrest; the initiation or discontinuance of any particular course of medical treatment or other form of life-support maintenance, including tube-delivered nutrition and hydration; and the method and timing of determination of death.

3. **Ascertaining the Requirements of Jewish Law:** In order to effectuate my wishes, if any question arises as to the requirements of Jewish law and

custom in connection with this declaration, I direct my agent to consult with and follow the guidance of the following Orthodox Rabbi:

Name of Rabbi: _____

Address: _____

_____

Telephone: Day _____ Evening _____

If such rabbi is unable, unwilling or unavailable to provide such consultation and guidance, then I direct my agent to consult with and follow the guidance of an Orthodox Rabbi referred by the following Orthodox Jewish institution or organization:

Name of Institution/Organization: _____

_____

Address: _____

_____

Telephone: Day _____ Evening _____

If such institution or organization is unable, unwilling or unavailable to make such a reference, or if the rabbi referred by such institution or organization is unable, unwilling or unavailable to provide such guidance, then I direct my agent to consult with and follow the guidance of an Orthodox Rabbi whose guidance on issues of Jewish law and custom my agent in good faith believes I would respect and follow.

4. **Direction to Health Care Providers:** Any health care provider shall rely upon and carry out the decisions of my agent, and may assume that such decisions reflect my wishes and were arrived at in accordance with the procedures set forth in this directive, unless such health care provider shall have good cause to believe that my agent has not acted in good faith in accordance with my wishes as expressed in this directive.

If the persons designated in paragraph 1 above as my agent and alternate agent are unable, unwilling or unavailable to serve in such capacity, it is my desire, and I hereby direct, that any health care provider or other person who will be making health care decisions on my behalf follow the procedures outlined in paragraph 3 above if any questions of Jewish law and custom should arise.

Pending contact with the agent and/or rabbi described above, it is my desire, and I hereby direct, that all health care providers undertake all essential emergency and/or life sustaining measures on my behalf.

5. **Post-Mortem Decisions:** It is also my desire, and I hereby direct, that after my death, all decisions concerning the handling and disposition of my body be made pursuant to Jewish law and custom as determined in accordance with strict Orthodox interpretation and tradition. By way of example, and without

limiting in any way the generality of the foregoing, it is my wish that there be conformance with Jewish law and custom with respect to such matters and questions as whether there exist exceptional circumstances that would permit an exception to the general prohibition under Jewish law against the performance of an autopsy or dissection of my body; the permissibility or non-permissibility of the removal and usage of any of my body organs or tissue for transplantation purposes; and the expeditious burial of my body and all preparations lea ding to burial.

Time is of the essence with regard to these questions. I therefore direct that any health care provider in attendance at my death notify the agent and/or rabbi described above immediately upon my death, in addition to any other person whose consent by law must be solicited and obtained prior to the use of any part of my body as an anatomical gift, so that appropriate decisions and arrangements can be made in accordance with my wishes. Pending such notification, it is my desire, and I hereby direct, that no autopsy, dissection or other post-mortem procedure be performed on my body.

6. **Incontrovertible Evidence of My Wishes:** If, for any reason, this document is deemed not legally effective as a health care proxy, or if the persons designated in paragraph 1 above as my agent and alternate agent are unable, unwilling or unavailable to serve in such capacity, I declare to my family, my doctor and anyone else whom it may concern that the wishes I have expressed herein with regard to compliance with Jewish law and custom should be treated as incontrovertible evidence of my intent and desire with respect to all health care measures and post-mortem procedures; and that it is my wish that the procedure outlined in paragraph 3 above should be followed if any questions of Jewish law and custom should arise.

7. **Duration and Revocation:** It is my understanding and intention that unless I revoke this proxy and directive, it will remain in effect indefinitely. My signature on this document shall be deemed to constitute a revocation of any prior health care proxy, directive or other similar document I may have executed prior to today's date.

Date: —————————————————————————

————————————————————— Residing at ———————————————

[Your signature; or, if you
are not physically capable
of signing, the signature   —————————————————————————
of another person signing   [address]
your name on your behalf]

DECLARATION OF WITNESSES

I declare that the person who signed (or asked another to sign) this document is personally known to me and appears to be of sound mind and acting willingly and free from duress. He (or she) signed (or asked another to sign for him or her) this document in my presence (and that person signed in my presence). I am not the person appointed as agent by this document.

_____   Residing at _____
Witness

_____
[address]

_____   Residing at _____
Witness

_____
[address]

Copyright © 1997–1998 by Ira Kasdan. All rights reserved. Used by permission.

(Wallet card)

THE HALACHIC LIVING WILL
EMERGENCY INSTRUCTIONS CARD

The attached "Emergency Instructions" card is designed to be placed in your wallet or handbag. In emergency situations, it will serve to alert medical and other emergency personnel that you have executed a "Halachic Living Will" form that they are to follow if you are incapable of making decisions for yourself.

The Emergency Instructions card should be filled out *only after* you have completed the Halachic Living Will form.

Please complete the artached card in accordance with the following instructions, tear it off along the perforated line, and carry it with you at all times (except on the Sabbath, when Jewish law prohibits carrying in a public domain):

(a) On the front of the card, print your name on the first line, and the date you have completed the Halachic Living Will form on the second line.

(b) On the back of the card, print the names and telephone numbers of the health care agent (and alternate agent) you have designated in section 1 of the Halachic Living Will form, and of the Orthodox Rabbi and the Orthodox Jewish institution/ organization you have designated in section 3 of the Halachic Living Will form.

(c) Keep the card in a conspicuous place in your wallet or billfold.

(d) If there are ever changes in any of the names or telephone numbers listed on the card, please remember to update the information on your card or to fill out a brand new card.

EMERGENCY INSTRUCTIONS

I, ————————, have executed a "Proxy and Directive With Respect to Health Care Decisions and Post-Mortem Decisions," dated ——————. Pursuant to the Proxy and Directive, the persons listed on the reverse of this card are to serve as my agent and alternate agent, respectively, in making health care decisions for me if I become unable to do so on my own. I desire that all such health care decisions, as well as all decisions relating to the handling and disposition of my body after I die, should be made pursuant to Jewish law and custom as determined in accordance with strict Orthodox interpretation and tradition. If there is any question regarding Jewish law and custom, my agent (or any other person making decisions for me) should consult with and follow the guidance of the rabbi identified on the reverse of this card, or as a second choice the rabbi referred by the institution/organization identified on the reverse of this card, or as a third choice an Orthodox Rabbi whose guidance my health care decisionmaker in good faith believes I would respect and follow. Pending contact with the agent and/or rabbi, I desire that health care providers should undertake all essential emergency measures on my behalf; and I desire that no autopsy or other post-mortem procedure be performed on my body.

Name of Agent:————————

Telephone: Day————————

Evening ————————

Name of Alternate Agent:————

Telephone: Day————————

Evening ————————

Name of Rabbi:————————

Telephone: Day————————

Evening ————————

Name of Institution/Organization:

————————————————

Telephone: Day————————

Evening ————————

(ii) Catholic Directives

(a) Health Care Proxy

I, (Name) —————————————— , residing at (Address) ——————
——————————————————— , hereby create a Health Care Proxy and designate the following person to be my health care agent for making any and all health care decisions on my behalf should I ever become incompetent:

—————————————————————————————————————

Name   Address

———————————————————

Telephone

If my agent is ever unable or unwilling to act as my agent, I hereby designate the following person to be my alternative health care agent:

———————————————————

—————————————————————————————————————

Name   Address

———————————————————   —————————————————————————

Telephone   Signature   Date

My health care agent has the authority to make any and all medical decisions on my behalf should I ever be unable to do so for myself. I have discussed my wishes with my agent (and with my alternate agent) who shall base all decisions on my previous instructions. If I have not expressed a wish with respect to some future medical decision, my agent shall act in a manner that he/she deems to be in my best interests in accord with what he/she knows of my beliefs.

My agent has the further authority to request and receive all information regarding my medical condition and, when necessary, to execute any documents necessary for release of such information. My agent may execute any document of consent or refusal to permit treatment in accord with my intentions. My agent may also admit me to a nursing home or other long-term care facility as he/she deems appropriate and to sign on my behalf any waiver or release from liability required by a physician or a hospital.

As a member of the Catholic Church, I believe in a God who is merciful and in Jesus Christ Who is the Savior of the World. As the Giver of Life, God has sent us His only-begotten Son as Redeemer so that in union with Him we might have eternal life. Through His death and Resurrection, Jesus has conquered sin so that death has lost its sting (I Cor. 15:55). I wish to follow the moral teachings of the Catholic Church and to receive all the obligatory care that my faith teaches we have a duty to accept. However, I also know that death need not be resisted by any and every means and that I have the right to refuse medical treatment that is excessively burdensome and would only prolong my death and delay my being taken to God. I also know that I may morally receive medication to relieve pain even if it is foreseen that its use may have the unintended result of shortening my life.

Witness ——————————— Date ————————

Witness ——————————— Date ————————

Note: In many states you must obtain the signature of at least two witnesses. This document is designed to be legally valid in the Commonwealth of Massachusetts. Check with your local Catholic Conference for legal requirements in your state.

When initialed here ——————————— the attached Advance Medical Directive, if completed, shall be considered an extension of this document.

© 1998 The National Catholic Bioethics Center, Boston, MA. Used by permission.

(b) Advance Medical Directive

For the benefit of those who will make decisions on my behalf should I become incompetent, I hereby express my desires about some issues that others may face in providing my care. Most of what I state here is general in nature since I cannot anticipate all the possible circumstances of a future illness. I direct that those caring for me avoid doing anything that is contrary to the moral teaching of the Catholic Church. If I fall terminally ill, I ask that I be told of this so that I might prepare myself for death, and I ask that efforts be made that I be attended by a Catholic priest and receive the Sacraments of Reconciliation and Anointing as well as Viaticum.

Those making decisions on my behalf should be guided by the moral teachings of the Catholic Church contained in, but not limited to, the following documents: *Declaration on Euthanasia*, Congregation for the Doctrine of the Faith, Rome, 1980; *Ethical and Religious Directives for Catholic Health Care Services*, United States Conference of Catholic Bishops, 2001; *Nutrition and Hydration: Moral and Pastoral Reflections*, Committee for Pro-Life Activities, National Conference of Catholic Bishops, March 1995.

I want those making decisions on my behalf to avoid doing anything that intends and directly causes my death by deed or omission. Medical treatments may be forgone or withdrawn if they do not offer a reasonable hope of benefit to me or if they entail excessive burdens, or impose excessive expense on my family or the community. There should be a presumption in favor of providing me with nutrition and hydration, assuming of course they are of benefit to me. In accord with the teachings of my Church, I have no moral objection to the use of medication or procedures necessary for my comfort even if they may indirectly and unintentionally shorten my life.

If, in the medical judgment of my attending physician, death is imminent, even in spite of the means which may be used to conserve my life, and if I have received the Sacraments of the Church, I direct that there be forgone or withdrawn treatment that will only maintain a precarious and burdensome prolongation of my life, unless those responsible for my care judge at that time that there are special and significant reasons why I should continue to receive such care (such as those listed below).

Believing none of the following directives conflicts with the teachings of my Catholic Faith, I hereby add the following special provisions and/or limitations to my future health care: (Examples: I would like my tissue and organs to be used for research or transplants after I am dead. I would like all reasonable steps to be taken to allow me to see my family *or* be reconciled with someone from whom I may have become estranged. If at all possible, I would like to die at home, or at least in a hospice that has the appearance of a home setting.)

_____

_____

_____

_____

_____

_____

_____

Signature _____ Date _____

Witness _____ Date _____

Witness _____ Date _____

Note: This Advance Medical Directive may be completed independently or as an extension of the Health Care Proxy.

APPENDIX G
Mental Health Directives:

(i) Oklahoma
ADVANCE DIRECTIVE FOR MENTAL HEALTH TREATMENT

43A OKl. St. Ann. § 11–106

I. ——————— , being of sound mind and eighteen (18) years of age or older, willfully and voluntarily make known my wishes about mental health treatment, by my instructions to others through my advance directive for mental health treatment, or by my appointment of an attorney-in-fact, or both. I thus do hereby declare:

I. DECLARATION FOR MENTAL HEALTH TREATMENT

If my attending physician or psychologist and another physician or psychologist determine that my ability to receive and evaluate information effectively or communicate decisions is impaired to such an extent that I lack the capacity to refuse or consent to mental health treatment and that mental health treatment is necessary, I direct my attending physician or psychologist and other health care providers, pursuant to the Advance Directives for Mental Health Treatment Act,[1] to provide the mental health treatment I have indicated below by my signature.

I understand that "mental health treatment" means convulsive treatment, treatment with psychoactive medication, and admission to and retention in a health care facility for a period up to twenty-eight (28) days.

I direct the following concerning my mental health care: ——————————

I further state that this document and the information contained in it may be released to any requesting licensed mental health professional.

——————————————	
Declarant's Signature	Date
——————————————	
Witness 1	Date
——————————————	
Witness 2	Date

II. APPOINTMENT OF ATTORNEY-IN-FACT

If my attending physician or psychologist and another physician or psychologist determine that my ability to receive and evaluate information

---

[1] The Oklahoma Advance Directive for Mental Health Treatment, and its enabling legislation, are contained in full on the CD-ROM accompanying this volume.

effectively or communicate decisions is impaired to such an extent that I lack the capacity to refuse or consent to mental health treatment and that mental health treatment is necessary, I direct my attending physician or psychologist and other health care providers, pursuant to the Advance Directives for Mental Health Treatment Act, to follow the instructions of my attorney-in-fact.

I hereby appoint:

NAME _____
ADDRESS _____
TELEPHONE # _____

to act as my attorney-in-fact to make decisions regarding my mental health treatment if I become incapable of giving or withholding informed consent for that treatment.

If the person named above refuses or is unable to act on my behalf, or if I revoke that person's authority to act as my attorney-in-fact, I authorize the following person to act as my attorney-in-fact:

NAME _____
ADDRESS _____
TELEPHONE # _____

My attorney-in-fact is authorized to make decisions which are consistent with the wishes I have expressed in my declaration. If my wishes are not expressed, my attorney-in-fact is to act in what he or she believes to be my best interest.

_____

(Signature of Declarant/Date)

III. CONFLICTING PROVISION

I understand that if I have completed both a declaration and have appointed an attorney-in-fact and if there is a conflict between my attorney-in-fact's decision and my declaration, my declaration shall take precedence unless I indicate otherwise.

_____ (signature)

IV. OTHER PROVISIONS

a. In the absence of my ability to give directions regarding my mental health treatment, it is my intention that this advance directive for mental health treatment shall be honored by my family and physicians or psychologists as the expression of my legal right to consent or to refuse to consent to mental health treatment.

b. This advance directive for mental health treatment shall be in effect until it is revoked.

    c. I understand that I may revoke this advance directive for mental health treatment at any time.

    d. I understand and agree that if I have any prior advance directives for mental health treatment, and if I sign this advance directive for mental health treatment, my prior advance directives for mental health treatment are revoked.

    e. I understand the full importance of this advance directive for mental health treatment and I am emotionally and mentally competent to make this advance directive for mental health treatment.

Signed this ————————— day of ————————— , 20 ———

———————————————————
(Signature)

———————————————————
City, County and State of Residence
This advance directive was signed in my presence.

———————————————————
(Signature of Witness)

———————————————————
(Address)

———————————————————
(Signature of Witness)

———————————————————
(Address)

(ii) Advance Directives for Mental Health Care*
An Analysis of State Statutes

Robert D. Fleischner
Center for Public Representation

State statutes enabling individuals to draft written durable advance directives for health care have approached future decisions about mental health care and treatment in several quite different ways. While some states incorporate mental health care into the generic advance directive law, others exclude some kinds of mental health care from the generic law, and a growing number of states have established distinct processes for mental health directives. The author surveys the state statutes and examines the extent to which the statutes may create barriers to the use of advance directives by people with mental illness.

There is increasing interest among people with mental illness and their clinicians and service providers that advance health care planning may enable individuals to have greater control of their treatment, may provide important information to guide health care providers to make treatment decisions, may reduce the need for formal court adjudications of treatment, and may reduce the costs associated with involuntary care.[1] Likewise, it has been argued that use of written advance directive instruments may have significant therapeutic value and function as an important "safety valve" for difficult treatment and legal issues.[2] However, advance written health care directives are not without significant limitations and are uniquely products of state law.

The potential benefits and problems which attend advance directives for mental health care may best be understood in the context of the right of individuals with mental illness to control their own treatment. This body of

*Copyright © 1998 by the American Psychological Association. Reprinted (or Adapted) with permission.

The preparation of this article was supported by a grant from Center for Mental Health Services, Substance Abuse and Mental Health Services Administration, U.S. Department of Health and Human Services. I thank the Center for Mental Health Services and the Advocacy, Training and Technical Assistance Center of the National Association of Protection and Advocacy Systems for their support of this work. The opinions expressed herein are the author's and do not necessarily express the opinions of the funding agencies.

Correspondence concerning this article should be addressed to Robert D. Fleischner, Center for Public Representation, 22 Green Street, Northampton, Massachusetts 01060. Electronic mail may be sent to rfleischner@gbls.org.

[1]   Paul S. Sherman, *Advance Directives for Involuntary Psychiatric Care, in* Symposium Proceedings, Involuntary Interventions: The Call for a National Legal and Medical Response (1994) 1.

[2]   Bruce J. Winick, *Advance Directive Instruments for Those With Mental Illness,* 51 U. Miami L. Rev. 57, 81–85 (1996) (*Winick I*).

law has been the subject of heated debate, scholarly inquiry, legislation, and litigation. Beginning in the early 1960s, much of the controversy focused on the extent of the government's authority to involuntarily hospitalize—civilly commit—people who are believed to be mentally ill.[3] Since the 1970s, the debate has often concentrated on whether, to what extent, and pursuant to what process the government may medicate individuals with mental illness, despite their unwillingness or inability to consent to such interventions.[4] These issues have often been raised in cases that sought to establish a right to refusetreatment.[5]

---

[3] *See, e.g., Note, Developments in the Law: Civil Commitment of the Mentally Ill,* 87 HARV. L. REV. 1190 (1974); Lessard v. Schmidt, 349 F. 2d. 1078 (E.D. Wisc. 1972), *vacated and remanded,* 414 U.S. 473 (1974), *judgement reinstated,* 413 F. Supp. 1318 (E.D. Wisc. 1976) (procedural rights); O'Connor v. Donaldson, 422 U.S. 563 (1975) (finding of mental illness alone does not justify civil commitment); Addington v. Texas 441 U.S. 418 (1979) (standard of proof).

[4] The body of literature in legal and medical journals regarding the right to refuse treatment is extensive. Some recent articles include Elyn R. Sacks, *Competency to Refuse Psychotropic Medication: Three Alternatives to the Law's Cognitive Standard,* 47 U. MIAMI L. REV. 689 (1993); Bruce J. Winick, *The Right to Refuse Treatment: A Therapeutic Jurisprudence Perspective,* 17 INT'L J. L. & PSYCHIATRY 99 (1994). For a thorough analysis of the right to refuse treatment *see,* MICHAEL L. PERLIN, MENTAL DISABILITY LAW: CIVIL AND CRIMINAL, § 5.00. *See also,* AMERICAN BAR ASSOCIATION, COMMISSION ON THE MENTALLY DISABLED, THE RIGHT TO REFUSE ANTIPSYCHOTIC MEDICATION (1986), a collection of articles by attorneys, psychiatrists, and others expressing a wide range of views about the right to refuse treatment, its implementation, and its impact. The titles alone of two early articles presenting polar views of the right provide some insight into the extent of the debate. *Compare* Paul S. Applebaum and Thomas Gutheil, *Rotting With Their Rights On: Constitutional Theory and Clinical Reality in Drug Refusal by Psychiatric Patients,* 7 BULL. AM. ACAD. PSYCHIATRY & LAW (1979) and Robert Plotkin, *Limiting the Therapeutic Orgy: Mental Patients' Right to Refuse Treatment,* 72 NW. L. REV. 461 (1978).

[5] Among the earliest cases were Rennie v. Klein, 462 F. Supp. 1131 (D.N.J. 1978), *suppl.,* 476 F. Supp. 1294 (D.N.J. 1978) *modified,* 653 F. 2d 836 (3d Cir. 1981), *vacated and remanded,* 458 U.S. 1119 (1982), *on remand,* 720 F. 2d 2661 (3d Cir. 1983) and Rogers v. Okin, 478 F. Supp. 1342 (D. Mass. 1979), *modified* 634 F. 2d 650 (1st Cir. 1980), *vacated and remanded sub nom* Mills v. Rogers, 457 U.S. 291 (1982), *on remand,* 738 F. 2d (1st Cir. 1984). The Supreme Court has considered the extent of the right in several cases including Riggins v. Nevada, 504 U.S. 127 (1992) (forced drugging of a pretrial detainee during trial deprived him of a fair trial) and Washington v. Harper, 494 U.S. 210 (1990) (prisoner has a significant constitutional due process interest in avoiding unwanted administration of antipsychotic medication). For an extensive review of the case law see *Perlin, supra,* n. 4. Although the right to refuse treatment was first articulated in court opinions, several states have codified the right in one form or another. *See, e.g.,* Mass. Gen. Laws. c. 123 § 8B (adopting court-ordered standards for civilly committed inpatients). Most recently, Vermont has amended its involuntary treatment law. Public Act 114 (1998) adding Vt. Stat. Title 18 §§ 7624–7629 and amending §§ 7509 and 7620–7621. The act establishes proceedings for involuntary

Despite nearly 4 decades of reform and retrenchment, civil commitment law remains in flux.[6] The Supreme Court has said that the liberty interest in avoiding involuntary psychiatric hospitalization is a fundamental one.[7] Nevertheless, even without minimizing the increased procedural protections achieved in the early litigation, some states have recently broadened the substantive criteria for commitment and many states have instituted outpatient commitment laws.[8] Important recent research on dangerousness will almost certainly influence ongoing disputes about civil commitment standards.[9]

Debate about the extent of a person's right to make individual medical decisions also continues and has not been limited to mental health care. The issue is just as present in the context of physical health decision making. The Supreme Court and many state courts have recognized or "assumed" a constitutionally protected liberty interest in making health care decisions.[10] In the *Cruzan* case, the Court determined that the state's interest in prolonging life is sufficiently strong to justify a state requirement of clear and convincing evidence to support a person's refusal of life-sustaining treatment or nourishment.[11] The Court thus established a procedural standard requiring that the exercise of this right be clearly expressed, thereby greatly increasing the utility and advisability of written health care directives.

Likewise, the extent of the right of a person with mental illness to refuse treatment remains in question. Although courts have recognized that at least a limited right to refuse exists,[12] the parameters of the right and the

---

medication and purports to supercede agreements reached in a consent decree settling a right to refuse treatment lawsuit. In addition, the act establishes new procedures regarding the effect of durable health care powers of attorney executed by persons who are involuntarily hospitalized. In effect, the law allows a court to override the instructions of an advance directive if the facility can show that, after following the instructions of the directive for 45 days, the incompetent "person has not experienced a significant clinical improvement in his or her mental state." Vt. St. T. 18 § 7626.

[6] *Winick I*, 51 U. Miami L. Rev. *at* 58–59 (1996).

[7] Foucha v. Louisiana, 504 U.S. 71, 80, 86 (1992).

[8] Steven J. Schwartz & Cathy E. Costanzo, *Compelling Treatment in the Community: Distorted Doctrines and Violated Values,* 20 Loyola of L.A. L. Rev. 1329 (1987) (including tables of outpatient commitment statutes).

[9] Henry J. Steadman et al., *Violence by People Discharged From Acute Psychiatric Inpatient Facilities and by Others in the Same Neighborhood,* 55 Arch. Gen. Psychiatry 393 (1998). This important work has already been cited by at least one newspaper editorial calling for reconsideration of civil commitment standards in the wake of the shooting of security guards at the Capitol, allegedly by an individual with mental illness. Editorial, *Rationality About the Mentally Ill,* Boston Globe, City Edition, August 3, 1998, p. A10.

[10] In Cruzan v. Director, Missouri Department of Health, 497 U.S. 261 (1990), the Supreme Court was willing to assume that the Constitution grants a competent person a right to refuse life-sustaining hydration and nutrition. *Id. at* 278–79.

[11] *Cruzan,* 497 U.S. *at* 283.

[12] *See* note 5, *supra.*

protection from the forced treatment that it provides vary from jurisdiction to jurisdiction.

Despite uncertainty about its scope, it seems clear that the right to refuse psychiatric treatment is founded on the same values of autonomy and self-determination as the right to refuse treatment generally.[13] In fact, the *Cruzan* Court cited earlier decisions which involved mental health treatment, including language in *Washington v. Harper*[14] that the Due Process Clause provided that convicted prisoners with mental illness have "a significant liberty interest in avoiding the unwanted administration of antipsychotic medication."[15] Since the basic rights involved in treatment decision making for people with physical illness and those with mental illness appear to be the same, the *Cruzan* decision's emphasis on clearly expressed health care treatment desires has important implications for people who receive or may be referred for psychiatric or other mental health care and treatment. Individuals who, while they are competent, make clear advanced health care decisions, either orally or in writing, should have those decisions respected even if they become incompetent.[16] In fact, every state has enacted some form of advance written health care directive statute which is intended to provide a mechanism for clearly and formally expressing health care choices.[17]

In general terms, a written health care directive is a document that is executed pursuant to certain, usually simple, formalities[18] and that expresses an individual's wishes and desires regarding health care if and when that individual is not capable of making choices or of making those choices known. There are various kinds of advance directives, but most fall within two general categories: instructional or agent driven.

An instructional directive, most often called a "living will," sets out in written form the person's desires for treatment. Living wills are most commonly used in end-of-life situations, and most states that recognize them require that the instructions be followed by health care providers.

Agent-driven directives, often called health care powers of attorney or proxies, may include specific instructions, but also appoint an agent, or attorney-in-fact, to act in the place of the individual when the individual

---

[13] Lester J. Perling, *Health Care Advance Directives: Implications for Florida Mental Health Patients*, 48 U. Miami L. Rev. 193, 198 (1993).

[14] 494 U.S. 210 (1990).

[15] 494 U.S. *at* 221–22 quoted in *Cruzan*, 497 U.S. *at* 278.

[16] *Winick I*, 51 U. Miami L. Rev. *at* 61–65.

[17] Congress has noted the importance of advance directive statutes in the Patient Self-Determination Act, 42 U.S.C. §§ 1395cc(f) & 1396a(w) (1994). The Act encourages the use of advance directives by requiring that any service provider participating in the Medicaid or Medicare programs must inform patients about the state law concerning directives.

[18] Written directives may be followed even when precise formalities are not followed. See *In re Rosa M.*, 597 N.Y.S. 2d 544 (Sup. Ct 1991) (upholding an advance directive by a patient refusing treatment with electroconvulsive therapy).

is not capable of making health care decisions.[19] Usually, the agent-driven directive is not in effect until the individual is determined, ordinarily by his or her treating physician, to be incapable of decision making. When that happens, the agent's authority "springs" into effect and he or she is empowered to act in the stead of the now incapable person. In most states, if the written directive includes instructions to the agent, the agent must follow those instructions. If the directive does not include instructions, the agent may be required to employ a substituted judgment[20] test or to act in what the agent determines to be the individual's best interest. Health care providers are usually required by the statutes to follow the instructions of an agent acting pursuant to an advance health care directive.

The majority of state advance directive statutes expressly or by implication apply to mental health care. Some states, however, have also enacted advance directive statutes that apply specifically and solely to mental health treatment or to some kinds of mental health treatment.

The Table

The table in the Appendix attempts to describe the elements of state advace health care directive statutes that are of particular relevance to people with mental illness.

The table analyzes the statutes of each of the 50 states and the District of Columbia in several areas. Reading from left to right, the informational columns are as follows:

State name: The name of the state appears in this column.
AD St[atute]: This box is checked if the state has some sort of advance directive (AD) law.
Date: The date in this column is the date when the AD statute was first enacted. In states in which existing power-of-attorney statutes were amended to include the right to delegate health care decisions, the date that appears is the

---

[19] For an analysis of the competence of persons with mental illness to consent to treatment see Thomas Grisso & Paul S. Applebaum, *The MacArthur Treatment Competence Study. III: Abilities of Patients to Consent to Psychiatric and Medical Treatments,* 19 L. & HUM. BEHAV. 149 (1995).

[20] In exercising substituted judgment, the decision maker attempts to determine what the incompetent individual would do if he or she was competent. The Massachusetts Supreme Judicial Court, perhaps the leading judicial proponent of the standard in medical decision making for persons who are not capable, explained the doctrine in depth in Superintendent of Belchertown State School v. Saikewicz, 373 Mass. 728, 370 N.E. 2d 417 (1977), and applied it to hospitalized incompetent persons with mental illness in the context of treatment with antipsychotic medications in Rogers v. Commissioner of Department of Mental Health, 390 Mass. 489, 458 N.E. 2d 308 (1983). These cases and their impact on mental health treatment in Massachusetts are analyzed in JOHN H. CROSS, ROBERT D. FLEISCHNER & JINANNE S.J. ELDER, GUARDIANSHIP AND CONSERVATORSHIP IN MASSACHUSETTS, §§ 6.00 and 7.00 (1996).

date the health care authority was added. Some other states have substantially amended their AD statutes. In those cases, the chart reflects the date of the amendment.

Citation and Type of Directive: The information in this column contains the citation to the generic health care advance directive statute or statutes. Following the citation is an indication of the type of statute, often indicated by an abbreviation. The description of the type of statute is derived from the language the legislature chose. Common abbreviations which appear in this column include:

> DPA—durable power of attorney
> DPA/HC—durable power of attorney for health care
> HCAD—health care advance directive
> AD/HC—advance directive for health care
> HCP—health care proxy
> LW—living will

The name may or may not be sigificant.

Agent: If this box is checked, the statute allows for the appointment of an agent or an attorney-in-fact for health care decisions.

Instructio[n]: If this box is checked, the statute allows the principal to include instructions to the agent in the advance directive.

M[ental] H[ealth] Decisions: If this box is checked, the statute allows the generic advance directive to be used for mental health care decisions. In most cases, the statute mentions mental health treatment directly. In others, if there is no mention, but also no exclusion, it is assumed that the directive may be used for mental health purposes.

M[ental] H[ealth] AD Sta[tute]: If this box is checked, the state has some sort of advance directive statute that applies specifically and only to some or all kinds of mental health treatmet.

MH [AD] Cite: If there is an advance directive law statute that applies only to mental health care, its citation will appear in this column. In most cases, the name of the directive and the date the law became effective also appear.

Prescribed form: Virtually every state requires some degree of formality in the execution of an advance directive. This column is intended to state the degree of formality necessary. In particular, it looks at whether there is a mandatory form that must be used for the document to be valid.

Agent's Responsibility & Authority: The information in this column reveals the standard the agent or attorney-in-fact must use in making health care decisions for an incompetent principal.

Notes: The notes that appear in this column detail provisions of the statute that may have some particular relevance to people with mental illness.

Revocation: The information in the final column describes the process and conditions for revocation of the directive. In states in which there is not an explicit requirement that the person be competent to revoke, the assumption is that competency is not a factor.

Analysis

The following general conclusion can be drawn from the review of the state advance directive laws:

- Every state has one or more kinds of instructional advance directive statutes that allow for the appointment of an agent.
- Some states use one kind of advance directive for end-of-life treatment and another for other health care.
- The most common form of advance directive is the durable power of attorney for health care. Most states have either added health care decision making to the authority of an agent-in-fact or have drafted separate laws that track the elements of the standard durable power of attorney law.
- Most states specifically allow non-end-of-life advance directives to be used for mental health treatment, as well as physical health treatment purposes.
- Some states do not mention mental health care in their advance directive laws, but do not exclude it either.
- Several states allow mental health treatment to be addressed in an advance directive, but prevent the agent or attorney-in-fact from making certain mental health treatment decisions—usually convulsive treatment, involuntary commitment, and psychosurgery.
- A very small number of states specifically exclude mental health care from their generic advance directive statutes.
- Most of the states that exclude mental health treatment from the generic advance directive law have other specific laws that address advance planning for mental health care. At least one state has an instructional advance directive for mental health care that does not require the appointment of an agent.
- A few states that allow the generic advance directive to be used for mental health care have also enacted mental health specific advance directive laws, thereby providing an option to the person wishing to plan for future mental health care.
- Just under half the states require that a principal be competent to revoke the advance directive. A few statutes are silent as to whether capacity to revoke is necessary. Most of the other states allow revocation at any time, regardless of capacity.
- Specific mental health advance directives are irrevocable after loss of capacity in nearly every state that has adopted such a device.
- Every state requires that certain elements or language appear in an advance directive for it to be valid. Most states suggest a form in the statute and require at least that the advance directive be substantially similar to the statutory form.
- Every state requires that the agent or attorney-in-fact follow the principal's instruction regarding health care. Usually the statute says that the

instruction may be in the advance directive itself or may be otherwise known to the agent. When the agent does not know or cannot ascertain the principal's wishes, every state that addresses the problem requires that the agent make a decision that he or she determines to be in the principal's best interest. A few states require that when the instructions are unknown, the agent engage in a substituted judgment process to determine what the principal would do if he or she could decide.

* Most of the state laws are silent on the relationship between a health care agent and a guardian, if there is one.

Barriers to Use of Advance Directives by Individuals Wishing to Plan for Future Mental Health Care

In 1994, Paul Sherman, one of the first people to envision the potential benefits of advance directives for people with mental illness, identified barriers to their use in five areas: educational issues; logistical issues, such as the shortage of legal assistance and of people to serve as agents; legal issues; consumer behavioral issues, including the fear of being coerced or manipulated to sign an advance directive; and enforcement issues.[21] An analysis of the statutes and the experience of protection and advocacy system[22] advocates indicate that Dr. Sherman was prescient. The barriers include:

* Advance directives are legal documents that must be executed with some amount of formality. Although preprinted forms are available and it is usually not essential to have an attorney draft the instrument, some individuals may be dissuaded by the formality of the process.[23]
* Advocates report that some individuals do not execute advance directives because they do not have a person available and willing to act as an agent or attorney-in-fact.
* Revocability is an issue for some individuals. Some people may want to write a document that is irrevocable after they have been determined to lack capacity to make decisions. For example, someone who has learned from personal experience that she sometimes stops taking medication, becomes incapable, and then refuses the medication, may want an agent to have the authority to consent for her during her incapacity. She may fear that she will revoke the advance directive or override her agent's directions. If she is in a state that allows revocation

---

[21] *Sherman, supra* n. 2, *at* 8.

[22] Each state has a protection and advocacy program for people with mental illness. The programs are funded by the Center for Mental Health Services pursuant to the Protection and Advocacy for Mentally Ill Individuals Act, 42 U.S.C. § 10801 *et seq.*

[23] The Judge David L. Bazelon Center for Mental Health Law has a model form for a psychiatric advance directive available on its web site (www.bazelon.org). The Bazelon Center believes the form, which can be completed on-line, meets the requirements of every state.

at any time, even when the individual is incompetent, she may feel that writing the advance directive is a useless exercise.

On the other hand, another person may not want to draft a document that is irrevocable. She may feel that she cannot anticipate all future circumstances[24] and may not want ot be bound by even her own words in the circumstances of an uncertain future. This individual might be reluctant to execute an advance directive in a state that does not permit revocation after a determination of incapacity.

Maine and Illinois, which have both a generic advance directive law that allows post-incapacity revocation and a special mental health directive law that does not, may at least offer the individual a choice.

- Some individuals may be concerned about the utility of advance directives when they may be overridden, as in some states by an emergency situation, by a court order for treatment, by a guardian, or for other reasons. In some states the relationship between the advance directive law and the court decisions regarding forced treatment is unclear at best.[25]
- The laws are often confusing. Even the excellent training manuals that some protection and advocacy programs[26] have written for their clients are often necessarily lengthy and may be complicated for some individuals.

Conclusion

Despite their uncertainties, their inherent limitations, and the barriers to their use, advance directives may offer people with mental illness a formidable device to gain more control of their treatment and to promote their autonomy.

---

[24] Some clinicians share this concern, seeing it as an issue in future planning generally. *See,* Paul S. Applebaum, *Advance Directives for Psychiatric Treatment,* 42 HOSP. & COMMUNITY PSYCHIATRY 983 (1991).

[25] For a discussion of the dilemma created by the uncertain relationship of the Massachusetts health care directive law and the substituted judgment process established by the *Rogers* decision, *see,* JOHN H. CROSS ET AL., *supra* n. 21, *at* § 6.08.

[26] Protection and advocacy agencies in several states have published useful manuals describing the use of health care directives in their states. *See, e.g.,* Melissa Daar, Tracy Nelson, and Daniel Pone, *Durable Power of Attorney for Health Care Manual: An Advocacy Tool for Mental Health Consumer Empowerment and Patient Choice* (1994) (available from Protection and Advocacy, Inc., Sacramento, CA) and Equip for Equality, Inc., *The Mental Health Treatment Preference Declaration* (1996) (available from Equip for Equality, Inc., Chicago, IL).

(Appendix follows)

Appendix
Advance Directive Statutes by State

State name	AD	St Date	Citation and Type of Directive	Agent	Instruction	MH Decisions	MH AD Sta	MH Cite	Prescribed form	Agent's Responsibility & Authority	Notes	Revocation
Alabama	✓	1997	Ala. Code 22-8A-1 (AD); Ala Code 26-1-2 (DPA/HC)	✓	✓	✓		NA	DPA: Certain words are required	DPA: Any health care decision principal could make, with exceptions (see notes); AD/HC life sustaining only	DPA agent may not consent to psycho-surgery or involuntary treatment, most abortions, or sterilization	DPA: Yes, at any time, written or oral
Alaska	✓	1988	Alaska Stat. 13.26.332 (DPA)	✓	✓	✓	✓	Alaska Stat. 47.30.950–980 (1996)	DPA and MHAD must be substantially in statutory form	Instruction: best interests if wishes not known	DPA and MHAD agents may serve jointly or separately; DPA agent may not authorize ECT or involuntary treatment	DPA: any time; MHAD is valid for three years
Arkansas	✓	1965	Ark Code Ann. 28-68-201 (DPA) (Short Form); 28-68-301 (DPA) (Long Form)	✓	✓	✓		NA	Certain language required	Not clear from statute; apparently to act in accordance with instructions in the DPA	"Long Form" requires court approval to be in effect. Health care not specifically mentioned in statute. Principal may give agent authority over "principal's person."	Principal may set time limit to directive. Apparently revocation may be any time.

(continued)

Appendix
Advance Directive Statutes by State (continued)

State name	AD St	Date	Citation and Type of Directive	Agent	Instruction	MH Decisions	MH AD Sta	MH Cite	Prescribed form	Agent's Responsibility & Authority	Notes	Revocation
Arizona	✓	1992	Ariz Rev Stat. 36-3221 (LW & HC Directive)	✓	✓	✓	✓	Ariz. Rev. Stat. 36-3281 (1999)	Sample forms included in statute, not mandatory	Authority limited only by express language of power of attorney	MHAD form includes option to make MHAD irrevocable; special provisions re admissions to facilities	Yes, both DPA and MHAD any time, written, oral, or by act demonstrating intent
California	✓	1994	Cal. Probate Code 4600 (DPA/HC)	✓	✓	✓		NA	No, but mandatory elements and language	Act consistent with instructions in AD or as otherwise made known. If wishes unknown, then best interest.	Agent may not authorize treatment over incompetent principal's objection; Agent may not authorize placement in MH facility, ECT, psychosurgery, sterilization, abortion	Yes, when competent; evidentiary presumption of competence
Colorado	✓	1992	Colo. Rev. St. 15-14-503 (Medical DPA)	✓	✓	✓		NA	No	Instructions; best interest if wishes unknown		Yes, no apparent limits.
Connecticut	✓	1990	Conn. Gen. Stat. tit. 1 ch. 7, sec. 1-42 (Short Form Power of Attorney)	✓	✓	✓		NA	Yes, recommended for DPA/HC	Expressed wishes; agent acts as "alter ego" for principal	Health care agent may make decisions re life support; DPA attorney-in-fact may make other decisions	Statute appears to be silent as to conditions for revocation.

State	✓	Year	Citation	✓	✓	✓		Form	Standard	Special Provisions	Revocation
Delaware	✓	1982	16 Del. Code sec. 2501 (Advance Health Care Directive)	✓	✓	✓	NA	Optional form in statute	Instruction, what would want if no instruction, best interest otherwise	"Initiation of emergency treatment shall be presumed to represent a suspension" of AD during treatment	Yes, when competent; guardian may not revoke w/o court authority
District of Columbia	✓	1987	D.C. Code 21-2201 (DPA/HC)	✓	✓	✓	NA	Substantially similar language; sample form	Expressed wishes; best interest if unknown		Yes, when capable; rebuttable presumption of capacity to revoke
Florida	✓	1992	Fla. Stat. Ann. 765.101 (HCAD)	✓	✓	✓	NA	Sample form for health care surrogate, none for AD; must contain elements	According to instruction, what person would want, or, if unknown, best interest	If guardian is appointed for one who has executed AD, judge may or may not honor terms of AD & even may revoke AD.	Yes, any time; no requirement that the person be competent to revoke
Georgia	✓	1990	Ga. Code Ann. 31-36-1 (DPA/HC)	✓	✓	✓	NA	Yes, recommended form	Any decision principal could make, subject to limitations in AD	Principal may authorize agent to admit to mental health facility & nursing home	Yes, at any time; principal may set termination date
Hawaii	✓	1992	Haw. Rev. Stat. 551D-2.5 (DPA/HC)	✓	✓	✓	Haw. Rev. Stat. 327F-1 (1992) ✓	DPA: recommended form; MHAD: required elements	DPA: Expressed wishes; MHAD: No agent	Mental health declaration is an instructional AD; no agent appointed	Yes; MHAD when in remission and competent, oral or written

(continued)

Appendix
Advance Directive Statutes by State (continued)

State name	AD St Date	Agent	Instruction	MH Decisions	MH AD Sta	MH Cite	Prescribed form	Agent's Responsibility & Authority	Notes	Revocation
Idaho Citation and Type of Directive: Idaho Code 39-4505 (DPA/HC)	✓ 1988	✓	✓	✓	✓	I.c. 66-602 (1998)	Suggested form; mandatory elements	Instructions; best interests if wishes unknown	MHAD effective after incompetency determined by court or 2 physicians	Any time, without regard to competence MHAD only while competent MHAD overridden by civil commitment
Illinois Citation and Type of Directive: Ill. Stat. ch. 755 sec. 45/4-1 (DPA/HC)	✓ 1987	✓	✓	✓	✓	Ill. St. c. 755 s 43/1 (Men. Health Treatment Declaration) (1995)	DPA/HC: Suggested form, mandatory elements	DPA/HC: Consistent with instructions & desires of principal	MHTPD applies only to psychotropic meds, ECT, and admission to MH facility for up to 17 days; may be overridden in emergency or by court order; valid for 3 yrs.	PA/HC: Any time; may set term, date; MHTPD: only in writing, w/dr. attesting to capacity & delivery to attending dr.
Indiana Citation and Type of Directive: Ind. Code Ann. 16-36-1-7 (LW) (1993); Ind. Code Ann. 30-5-1 (DPA)	✓ 1991	✓	✓	✓		NA	Yes, substantially in statutory form	Principal's express preference		Yes, in writing; apparently any time
Iowa Citation and Type of Directive: Iowa Code Ann. 144B.1 (DPA/HC)	✓ 1991	✓	✓	✓		NA	Yes, recommended form	Instructions; best interest if wishes unknown		Yes, at any time

		Year			Statute		Statutory form	Standard	Special provisions	Revocation
Kansas	√	1989	√	√	Kan. Stat. Ann. 58-625 (DPA/HC)	NA	Yes, substantially in statutory form	Consistent with expressed desires of principal	Principal may authorize agent to admit to mentalhealth facility or nursing home	Yes, in writing, apparently any time
Kentucky	√	1994	√	√	Ky. Rev. Stat. Ann. 311.621 (Living Will Directive Act)	NA	Yes, substantially in statutory form	"In accordance with desires of grantor as indicated in advance directive."		Yes, if grantor had "decisional capacity"
Louisiana	√	1998	√	√	La. Civ. Code Art. 2989; R.S. 40:1299.50 (1975)	NA	No	Document must expressly state that "the mandate" (i.e., the agent) has authority to make health care decisions	Mandate may be used for mental health decisions, AD may not	Yes, any time; Principal may draft document so as to make it irrevocable.
Maine	√	1989	√	√	Me. Rev. Stat. tit. 18-A, 5-801 (Adv. Health Care Directive)	Rev. Stat. tit. 34-B sec. 11001 (1993) tit. 34-B secs. 3831, 3862 (1999) √	Sample form for both AD & MHAD	AD: instructions; best interest if wishes unknown; No agent w/MHAD	No agent is appointed with a MHAD: 1999 additions re admissions to facilities and law enforcement authority to take person with MHAD into custody in some circumstances	AD: any time; MHAD: only when competent

(continued)

Appendix
Advance Directive Statutes by State (continued)

State name	AD St Date	Citation and Type of Directive	Agent	Instruction	MH Decisions	MH AD Sta	MH Cite	Prescribed form	Agent's Responsibility & Authority	Notes	Revocation
Maryland	✓ 1993	Md. Code Health-Gen. 5-601 (AD)	✓	✓	✓		NA	No particular form required; some oral directives allowed	Instructions; best interest of wishes unknown or unclear	Presumption of competence remains after involuntary commitment, Beeman v. DH&MH, 666 A2d 1314	Yes, apparently any time
Massachusetts	✓ 1993	Mass. G.L. c. 201D (HCP)	✓	✓	✓		NA	No, but mandatory elements	Unlimited, instructions; best interest if wishes are unknown	DPA may apparently also be used for health care decisions; If incompetence of principal with HCP is due to MI or MR, only drs. with relevant experience may decide.	Yes, any time, written or oral and by implication
Michigan	✓ 1990	Mich. Comp. L. 700.496	✓	✓	✓		NA	Some mandatory language	Reasonable effort to follow instructions, then best interest		Yes, any time, even if not capable
Minnesota	✓ 1993	Minn. Stat. 145C.01 (DPA/HC)	✓	✓	✓	✓	Minn. Stat. 253B.03-6d (1991)	DPA/HC: Recommended form; MH Declaration: no	DPA: In accordance with wishes; best interest if unknown; MH Dec: Instructions (intrusive treatment only)	DPA agent may not consent to voluntary mental hospitalization; MH Declaration may be used for intrusive m.h. treatment only	DPA/HC at any time; MH Declaration, only when competent

State	Year		Citation			Form		Standards	Special provisions	Revocation
Mississippi	1990	✓	Miss. Code 41-41-151 (DPA/HC)	✓	✓	Some mandatory wording; substantially in statutory form	NA	Consistent with discussions with principal; best interests if wishes unknown	No treatment may be given over principal's objection; DPA/HC statute does not affect law regarding emergency treatment	Yes, when competent; Presumption of competence to revoke.
Missouri	1990	✓	Mo. Ann. Stat. 404.800 (DPA/HC)	✓	✓	Required language	NA	Instructions; best interest when wishes unknown	Principal may authorize triggering mechanisms other than statutory standard	Yes, any time patient is able to communicate an intent to revoke; principal may set termination date in AD
Montana	1991	✓	Mont. Code 72-5-501 (HCPA)	✓	✓	No prescribed form; durability language probably required	NA	Statute is silent as to agent's responsibilities	Generic DPA may not be used for health care [Mt St. 72-31-201]; In HCPA "health care" defined as treatment for disease, injury, or degenerative condition	Any time under terminally ill directive act [Mt St. 50-9-104(I)]; HCPA law is silent; Conservator may revoke HCPA
Nebraska	1992	✓	Neb. Rev. Stat. 30-3401 (HCPA)	✓	✓	Mandatory elements; suggested form	NA	Wishes; best interest if wishes are unknown	Attempted suicide may not be construed as an indication of principal's wishes regarding health care	Yes, when competent, in any manner in which principal is able to communicate intent

(continued)

Appendix
Advance Directive Statutes by State (continued)

State name	AD	St	Date	Citation and Type of Directive	Agent	Instruction	MH Decisions	MH AD Sta	MH Cite	Prescribed form	Agent's Responsibility & Authority	Notes	Revocation
Nevada	✓		1987	Nev. Rev. Stat. 449.800 (DPA/HC)	✓	✓	✓		NA	Must be substantially in statutory form	In accordance with principal's desires; best interests if wishes unknown	Agent may not consent to commitment to mental hospital, ECT, psychosurgery, sterilization, or abortion	Any time, apparently; principal may set termination date for AD
New Hampshire	✓		1991	N.H. Rev. Stat. 137-J:1 (DPA/HC)	✓	✓	✓		NA	Must be substantially in statutory form	In accordance with agent's knowledge of principal's wishes; best interest if wishes unknown	Treatment may not be given over patient's objection, even when incapable; Agent may not consent to admission to state institution or to sterilization	Any time, written, oral, or by act evidencing specific intent to revoke
New Jersey	✓		1992	N.J. Stat. 26:2H-53 (AD/HC); 46:2B-8 (DPA)	✓	✓	✓		NA	Apparently not	In accordance with wishes; best interest if wishes unknown	DPA may be used for health care; instructional directives w/o appointment of agent are permitted	Yes, while competent; incompetent person may "suspend"
New Mexico	✓		1995	N.M. Stat. 24-7A-1 (DPA/HC)	✓	✓	✓		NA	Optional statutory form	In accordance with individual instructions or other wishes; best interest if wishes unknown		Yes, while competent

State		Year	Citation		Statutory form	Surrogate standard	Additional provisions	Revocation
New York	✓	1990	N.Y. Pub. Health L. 2980 (HCP)	NA	Yes, recommended	Instructions, best interest when wishes not known		Yes, when capable; Principal may set date for AD to expire
North Carolina	✓	1998	N.C. Gen. Stat. 32A-15 (HCPA) (1991)	N.C. Gen. Stat. 122C-71 (1997) ✓	Yes, recommended	MHAD: expressed preference of the principal	MHAD may be combined with HCPA	MHAD-Yes, when capable
North Dakota	✓	1991	N.D. Cent. Code 23-06.5-01 (DPA/HC)	NA	Statutory form provided	In accordance with instructions; best interest if wishes unknown	Agent may not consent to admission to state institution for more than 45 days, to psychosurgery, sterilization, or abortion w/o court order	Any time, apparently; principal may set date for AD to expire
Ohio	✓	1991	Ohio Rev. Code 1337.11 (DPA/HC)	NA	Preprinted forms not prepared by attorney must conform to statute form	Act subject to limitations in AD; if no instruction, then as principal would have acted; if cannot determine, then in best interest		Yes, any time in any manner; principal may set date for AD to expire
Oklahoma	✓	1992	Okla. Stat. tit. 63 sec. 3101.1 (Applies to terminally ill & unconscious only)	Okla. Stat. tit. 43A sec. 11-101 (eff. 1995) ✓	Yes, substantially in statutory form	Instructions; best interest if wishes not known		MHAD: when capable; AD: any time

(continued)

Appendix
Advance Directive Statutes by State (continued)

State name	AD St	Date	Agent	Instruction	MH Decisions	MH AD Sta	MH Cite	Prescribed form	Agent's Responsibility & Authority	Notes	Revocation
Oregon	✓	1989	✓	✓	✓	✓	Or. Rev. Stat. 127.700 (add'd 1993)	AD/HC must be on prescribed form	Both AD/HC and MHAD require attorney-in-fact to follow instruction in AD, or wishes otherwise known. If wishes are unknown, best interest.	AD/HC agent may not consent to MH admit, ECT, psychosurg.; MHAD applies to ECT, psychoactive drugs, admits under 17 days; MHAD invalid post commitment	AD/HC: any time for life-saving treatment provisions, when capable for all other; MHAD: when capable; valid for 3 yrs.
Pennsylvania	✓	1982	✓	✓	✓		NA	None; All powers of attorney presumed to be durable	To act "as principal could...if present."	Principal may grant agent authority to admit to medical, nursing, & residential facilities; Principal may designate the triggering event	Guardian may revoke: Principal may set expiration date: No mention of standards for revocation
Rhode Island	✓	1992	✓	✓	✓		NA	Statutory form provided	Consistent with desires stated in AD or as otherwise known to agent		Yes, any time without regard to competence; principal may set date for AD to expire
South Carolina	✓	1990	✓	✓	✓		NA	Yes, substantially in statutory form	Instructions		Yes, apparently any time

Citation and Type of Directive:
Oregon: Or. Rev. Stat. 127.005 (DPA); 127.505 (AD/HC)
Pennsylvania: Pa. Cons. Stat. tit. 20 sec. 5601 (PA)
Rhode Island: R.I. Gen L. 23-4.10 (DPA/HC)
South Carolina: S.C. Code 62-5-501 (HCPA)

State		Year	Statute				MH Statute		Substantially follow statutory form	Standard	Scope/Limitations	When effective/Revocation
South Dakota	✓	1977	S.D. Codified L. 59-7-2.1 (DPA)	✓	✓	✓	SDLC 27A-16-1 (Declaration for MH Treatment) (1997)	✓	MHAD: Yes, substantially in statutory form	MHAD: Must be consistent w/desires in AD or, if unknown, with best interest; DPA: What the principal would do; best interest if that cannot be determined	MHAD limited to ECT, psychotropic meds & admission up to 30 days; commitment and emergency situation override MHAD	MHAD: yes, when capable; effective upon communication to dr.; MHAD effective for 3 yrs.
Tennessee	✓	1990	Tenn. Code 34-6-201 (DPA/HC)	✓	✓				Yes, substantially in statutory form	To make decisions to same extent principal could if had capacity	Statute "does not affect law governing ... treatment in an emergency."	Yes, when competent, statutory presumption of capacity to revoke
Texas	✓	1989	Tex. Civ. Pract. & Rem. Code 135.001 (DPA/HC)	✓	✓		NA		Yes, substantially in statutory form	Pursuant to instructions	Agent may not consent to mental health admissions, ECT, or psychosurgery	Yes, at any time, oral, written or by implication; principal may set a time for AD to terminate
Utah	✓	1995	Utah Code 75-2-1101 (AD) (Applies only to terminal care)	✓			Utah Stat. 62A-12-501 (Declaration for MH Treatment) (1996)		Must substantially follow statutory form	MHAD: According to instruction; best interest if wishes are unknown	MHAD applies to psychoactive meds, convulsive treatment, admissions to mental hospitals up to 14 days; Not valid after commitment or in emergency	Yes, when capable; revocation valid upon communication to doctor; MHAD in effect for 3 yrs.

(*continued*)

Appendix
Advance Directive Statutes by State (continued)

State name	AD St	Date	Citation and Type of Directive	Agent	Instruction	MH Decisions	MH AD Sta	MH Cite	Prescribed form	Agent's Responsibility & Authority	Notes	Revocation
Vermont	✓	1987	Vt. Stat. tit. 14 s 3451 (DPA/HC)	✓	✓	✓			Substantially in statutory form	Act pursuant to instructions; if unknown, then best interest	Agent may not authorize admission to mental hospital or sterilization; Court may override mental health aspects of AD if after 45 days treatment choice not successful Vt. St. Tit. 18 s 7626	Any time, no requirement of competency
Virginia	✓	1992	Va. Code 54.1-2981 (AD/HC)	✓	✓	✓		NA	Suggested statutory form	Follow desires of principal; if unknown, then best interest	No mention of mental health care in statute; principal may appoint agent to make decisions about health care designated in AD	Any time, no requirement of competency
Washington	✓	1989	Wash. Rev. Code 11.94.010 (3) (DPA/HC)	✓	✓	✓		NA	No, but mandatory elements	To act as attorney-in-fact for principal; DPA may provide instructions	Appointment of guardian trumps DPA/HC (s. 70.02); Agent may not consent to ECT, psychosurgery, restrictions on personal freedom	Yes, apparently any time, no requirement of competency in statute

State		Year	Statute			Substantially in statutory form	Follow instructions		
West Virginia	✓	1990	W. Va. Code 16-30A-1 (Medical Power of Attorney)	✓ ✓	NA	Substantially in statutory form	Follow instructions; if wishes unknown, then best interest		Apparently any time. No mention of competency in statute.
Wisconsin	✓	1989	Wisc. Stat. 155.01 (PA/HC)	✓ ✓	NA	Required language	Instructions; otherwise best interest	Many admit to n. h. for 3 months & comm. res. for 30 day respite; may not consent to admit to MH fac., ICF/MR, ECT	Yes, at any time
Wyoming	✓	1991	Wyo. Stat. 3-5-201 (DPA/HC)	✓ ✓	W.S. 35-22-301 (1999)	Yes, necessary wording Health Dept. to promulgate MH forms	Apparently pursuant to instructions; otherwise best interest	Agent may not consent to commitment, ECT, psychosurgery MH agent's authority appears unrestricted. MHAD may be overriden by court or to prevent permanent physical injury	Yes, when capable MH Directive effective for 2 years

Note. DPA = durable power of attorney; DPA/HC = durable power of attorney for health care; HCAD = health care proxy; LW = living will.

APPENDIX H
Uniform Anatomical Gift Act
(As Enacted by North Dakota)

UNIFORM ANATOMICAL GIFT ACT

CHAPTER 23-06.1
UNIFORM ANATOMICAL GIFT ACT

[Repealed by S.L. 1989, ch. 303, § 5]
Note: For present provisions, see chapter 23-06.2.

CHAPTER 23-06.2
UNIFORM ANATOMICAL GIFT ACT

Section		Section	
23-06.2-01.	Definitions.		anatomical gifts may be
23-06.2-02.	Making, amending, revoking,		made.
	and refusing to make ana-	23-06.2-07.	Delivery of document of gift.
	tomical gifts by individual.	23-06.2-08.	Rights and duties at death.
23-06.2-03.	Making, revoking, and	23-06.2-09.	Coordination of procurement
	objecting to anatomical		and utilization.
	gifts by others.	23-06.2-10.	Sale or purchase prohibited—
23-06.2-04.	Authorization by coroner or		Penalty.
	local public health official.	23-06.2-11.	Examination—Autopsy—
23-06.2-05.	Request for consent to an		Liability.
	anatomical gift—Protocol—	23-06.2-11.1.	Anatomical parts testing—
	Exceptions.		Exception.
23-06.2-06.	Persons who may become	23-06.2-12.	Application.
	donees—Purposes for which		

23-06.2-01. Definitions. As used in this chapter, unless the context or subject matter otherwise requires:

1. "Anatomical gift" means a donation of all or part of a human body to take effect upon or after death.

2. "Decedent" means a deceased individual and includes a stillborn infant or fetus.

3. "Document of gift" means a card, a statement attached to or imprinted upon a motor vehicle operator's license, a will, or any other writing used to make an anatomical gift.

4. "Donor" means an individual who makes an anatomical gift of all or part of the individual's body.

5. "Enucleator" means an individual who has successfully completed a course in eye enucleation conducted by the department of ophthalmology of an accredited college of medicine that has been approved by the state board of medical examiners.

6. "Hospital" means a facility licensed, accredited, or approved as a hospital under the laws of any state and includes a hospital operated by the United States government, a state, or a subdivision thereof, although not required to be licensed under state law.
7. "Part" means an organ, tissue, eye, bone, artery, blood, fluid, and any other portion of a human body.
8. "Physician" or "surgeon" means an individual licensed or authorized to practice medicine and surgery or osteopathy and surgery under the laws of any state.
9. "Procurement organization" means a person licensed, accredited, or approved under the laws of any state for procurement, distribution, or storage of human bodies or parts thereof.
10. "State" means any state, district, commonwealth, territory, insular possession, or other area subject to the legislative authority of the United States of America.
11. "Technician" means an individual who is licensed or certified by the state board of medical examiners to remove or process a part.

Source: S.L. 1989, ch. 303, § 2.

Cross-References.
Disclosure of human immunodeficiency virus test results authorized, see § 23-07.5-05.
Inapplicability of certain sections, see § 23-06-01.2.
Word defined by statute always has same meaning, see § 1-01-09.

Collateral References.
Validity and effect of testamentary direction as to disposition of testator's body, 7 ALR 3d 747.
Enforcement of preference expressed by decedent as to disposition of his body after death, 54 ALR 3d 1037.
Tests for death for organ transplant purposes, 76 AKR 3d 913.

Comparative Legislation.
Jurisdictions which have, like North Dakota, enacted the 1987 Uniform Anatomical Gift act include:
Ark. Stat. Ann. §§ 20-17-601 to 20-17-615.
Cal. Health & Safety Code §§ 7150 to 7156.5

Conn. Gen. Stat. §§ 19a-279a to 19a-280a.
Hawaii Rev. Stat. §§ 327-1 to 327-14.
Idaho Code §§ 39-3401 to 39-3417.
Mont. Code Ann. §§ 72-17-101 to 72-17-312.
Nev. Rev. Stat. §§ 451.500 to 451.585.
R.I. Gen. Laws §§ 23-18.6-1 to 23-18.6-15.
Utah Code Ann. §§ 26-28-1 to 26-28-12.
Vt. Stat. Ann. tit. 18, §§ 5238 to 5247.
Va. Code §§ 32.1-289 to 32.1-297.1.
Wis. Stat. § 157.06.
Jurisdictions which have enacted the 1968 Uniform Anatomical Gift Act include: Alabama, Alaska, Arizona, Colorado, Delaware, District of Columbia, Florida, Georgia, Guam, Illinois, Indiana, Iowa, Kansas, Kentucky, Louisiana, Maine, Maryland, Massachusetts, Michigan, Minnesota, Mississippi, Missouri, Nebraska, New Hampshire, New Jersey, New Mexico, New York, North Carolina, Ohio, Oklahoma, Oregon, Pennsylvania, South Carolina, South Dakota, Tennessee, Texas, Virgin Islands, Washington, West Virginia, and Wyoming.

23-06.2-02. Making, amending, revoking, and refusing to make anatomical gifts by individual.

1. An individual who has attained eighteen years of age may make an anatomical gift for any of the purposes specified in subsection 1 of section 23-06.2-06 or may refuse to make an anatomical gift. An individual may limit an anatomical gift to one or more of the purposes specified in subsection 1 of section 23-06.2-06.
2. An anatomical gift may be made by a document of gift.
   a. A document of gift must be signed by the donor. If the donor cannot sign, the document of gift must state that it has been signed by another individual and by two witnesses, all of whom have signed at the direction and in the presence of the donor and in the presence of each other.
   b. A document of gift may be a statement attached to or imprinted upon a donor's motor vehicle operator's license, subject to subdivision a. Revocation, suspension, expiration, or cancellation of the license does not invalidate the anatomical gift.
   c. Notwithstanding subsection 2 of section 23-06.2-08, a document of gift may designate a particular physician or surgeon to carry out the appropriate procedures. In the absence of a designation or if the designee is not available, the donee or other person authorized to accept the anatomical gift may employ or authorize any physician, surgeon, technician, or enucleator for the purpose.
3. An anatomical gift by will becomes effective upon death of the testator without waiting for probate. If the will is not probated, or if, after death, it is declared invalid for testamentary purposes, the gift is nevertheless valid.
4. The donor may amend or revoke an anatomical gift, not made by will, only by:
   a. A signed statement;
   b. An oral statement made in the presence of two individuals;
   c. Any form of communication during a terminal illness or injury addressed to a physician or surgeon; or
   d. The delivery of a signed statement to a specified donee to whom a document of gift had been delivered.
5. An anatomical gift made by a will may be amended or revoked in the manner provided for amendment or revocation of wills, or as provided in subsection 4.
6. An anatomical gift that is not revoked by the donor is irrevocable and does not require the consent or concurrence of any other person after the death of the donor but is subject to subsection 2 of section 23-06.2-11.
7. A potential donor may refuse to make an anatomical gift by a writing executed in the same manner as an anatomical gift is made or

any other instrument used to identify the individual as refusing to make an anatomical gift. It may be an oral statement or other form of communication during a terminal illness or injury.

8. An anatomical gift of a part by a donor pursuant to subsection 1 is not a refusal to give other parts in the absence of contrary indications by the donor and is not a limitation on a gift or release of other parts pursuant to sections 23-06.2-03 and 23-06.2-04.

9. A revocation or amendment of an anatomical gift by a donor is not a refusal to make another anatomical gift in the absence of contrary indications by the donor. If the donor intends a revocation to be a refusal to make an anatomical gift, the donor must make a refusal pursuant to subsection 7.

23-06.2-03. Making, revoking, and objecting to anatomical gifts by others.

1. Unless an individual at the time of death has refused to make any anatomical gift, then any member of the following classes of persons, in the order of priority stated, may make an anatomical gift of all or any part of the decedent's body for any purpose specified in section 23-06.2-06:
   a. The spouse of the decedent.
   b. An adult son or daughter of the decedent.
   c. Either parent of the decedent.
   d. An adult brother or sister of the decedent.
   e. A grandparent of the decedent.
   f. A guardian of the person of the decedent at the time of death.

2. A gift may not be made by a person specified in subsection 1 if:
   a. A person in a prior class is available at the time of death to make an anatomical gift;
   b. The person has knowledge of contrary indications by the decedent; or
   c. The person has knowledge of an objection by a member of the person's class or a prior class.

3. An anatomical gift by a person under subsection 1 must be made by a document of gift signed by the person, or by the person's telegraphic, recorded telephonic, or other recorded message, or other type of communication from the person that is contemporaneously reduced to writing and signed by the recipient.

4. An anatomical gift by a person under subsection 1 may be revoked by any member of the same or a prior class if, before commencement of procedures for the removal of any part from the body of the decedent, the physician, surgeon, technician, or enucleator taking the part knows of the revocation.

5. A failure to make an anatomical gift under subsection 1 is not an objection to the making of an anatomical gift.

23-06.2-04. Authorization by coroner or local public health official.

1. The coroner may permit the removal and release of any part from a body within the coroner's custody, for transplant or therapeutic purposes, if the following requirements are met:

    a. A request has been received from a person specified in subsection 1 of section 23-06.2-06;

    b. A reasonable effort has been made, taking into account the useful life of the part, to locate and examine the decedent's medical records, and to inform persons specified in subsection 1 of section 23-06.2-03 of the option to make or object to the making of an anatomical gift;

    c. That official does not know of a contrary indication by the decedent or objection by a person having priority to act as specified in subsection 1 of section 23-06.2-03;

    d. The removal will be by a physician, surgeon, or technician; but in the case of eyes, removal may be by an enucleator;

    e. The removal will not interfere with any autopsy or investigation; and

    f. The removal will be in accordance with accepted medical standards and cosmetic restoration will be done if appropriate.

2. If the body is not within the custody of the coroner, the local public health officer may permit the removal and release of any part from a body within the local public health officer's custody for transplant or therapeutic purposes if the enumerated requirements of subsection 1 are met.

3. An official permitting the removal and release of any part shall maintain a permanent record of the name of the decedent, the person making the request, the date and purpose of the request, the part requested, and the person to whom it is released.

23-06.2-05. Request for consent to an anatomical gift—Protocol— Exceptions.

1. When death occurs, or is deemed to be imminent, in a hospital to a patient who has not made an anatomical gift, the hospital administrator or a designated representative, other than a person connected with the determination of death, shall request the person described in subsection 1 of section 23-06.2-03, in the order of priority stated, when persons in prior classes are not available at the time of death, and in the absence of actual notice of contrary indication by the decedent or one in a prior class, to consent to the gift of organs of the decedent's body as an anatomical gift. The hospital shall develop a protocol that includes the training of employees or other persons designated to make the request, the procedure to be followed in making the request, and a form of record identifying the person making the request and the response and relationship to the decedent. The protocol must encourage

reasonable discretion and sensitivity to the family circumstances in all discussions regarding anatomical gifts.

2. If, based upon medical criteria, a request would not yield an anatomical gift that would be suitable for use, there is authorized an exception to the request required by this section.

3. If, based upon the attending physician's special and peculiar knowledge of the decedent or the circumstances surrounding the death of the patient, the attending physician determines that a request will not be made for an anatomical gift, that determination must be noted in the patient's medical record. The determination is an exception to the request required by this section.

4. A reasonable search for a document of gift or other information identifying the bearer as an anatomical gift donor or as an individual who has refused to make an anatomical gift must be made by:
   a. A law enforcement officer, fireman, paramedic, or other emergency rescuer finding an individual whom the searcher believes to be dead or near death; and
   b. A hospital representative upon the admission of an individual at or near the time of death, if there is no other source of that information immediately available.

5. If a document of gift or evidence of refusal to make a gift is located by the search required by subdivision a of subsection 4, a hospital must be notified of the contents and the document must be sent to the hospital with the individual to whom it applies.

6. If, at or near the time of death, a hospital knows that an anatomical gift has been made pursuant to subsection 1 of section 23-06.2-03 or has been authorized pursuant to section 23-06.2-04, or that a patient or an individual identified as in transit to the hospital is a donor, the hospital shall notify the donee if one is specified; if not, the hospital shall notify an appropriate procurement organization. The hospital shall cooperate in the implementation of the anatomical gift.

7. Any person who fails to discharge the duties imposed by this section is not subject to criminal or civil liability but is subject to appropriate administrative sanctions.

23-06.2-06. Persons who may become donees—Purposes for which anatomical gifts may be made.

1. The following persons may become donees of anatomical gifts for the purposes stated:
   a. Any hospital, physician, surgeon, or procurement organization, for transplantation, therapy, medical or dental education, research, or advancement of medical or dental science.
   b. Any accredited medical or dental school, college or university for education, research, advancement of medical or dental science, or therapy.

    c. Any specified individual for transplantation or therapy needed by that individual.

2. An anatomical gift may be made to a specified donee or without specifying a donee. If a donee is not specified or if the donee is not available or rejects the anatomical gift, the anatomical gift may be accepted by any hospital.

3. If the donee has knowledge of contrary indications by the decedent or that a gift by a member of a class is opposed by a member of the same or a prior class under subsection 1 of section 23-06.2-03, the donee may not accept the gift.

23-06.2-07. Delivery of document of gift.

1. Delivery of a document of gift during the donor's lifetime is not necessary to the validity of an anatomical gift.

2. If an anatomical gift is made to a specified donee, the document of gift, or a copy, may be delivered to the donee to expedite the appropriate procedures immediately after death. The document of gift, or a copy, may be deposited in any hospital, procurement organization, or registry office that accepts it for safekeeping or for facilitation of procedures after death. On request of any interested person, upon or after the donor's death, the person in possession shall provide the document of gift or a copy for examination.

23-06.2-08. Rights and duties at death.

1. Rights of a donee created by an anatomical gift are paramount to rights of others except as provided by subsection 2 of section 23-06.2-11. A donee may accept or reject an anatomical gift. If a donee accepts a gift of the entire body, the donee, subject to the terms of the gift, may authorize embalming and the use of the body in funeral services. If the gift is of a part of the body, the donee, upon the death of the donor and before embalming, shall cause the part to be removed without unnecessary mutilation. After removal of the part, custody of the remainder of the body vests in the surviving spouse, next of kin, or other persons under obligation to dispose of the body.

2. The time of death must be determined by a physician or surgeon who attends the donor at death or, if none, the physician or surgeon who certifies the death. Neither the attending physician or surgeon nor the physician or surgeon who determines the time of death may participate in the procedures for removing or transplanting a part, except as provided in subdivision c of subsection 2 of section 23-06.2-02.

3. If there has been an anatomical gift, a technician may remove any donated parts and an enucleator may remove any donated eyes or parts of eyes, after determination of death by a physician or surgeon.

23-06.2-09. Coordination of procurement and utilization. Each hospital, after consultation with other hospitals and procurement organizations in the region, shall establish agreements or affiliations for coordination of procurement and utilization of anatomical gifts.

23-06.2-10. Sale or purchase prohibited—Penalty.

1. A person may not knowingly, for valuable consideration, purchase or sell any part for transplantation or therapy, if removal of the part is intended to occur after the death of the decedent.
2. Valuable consideration does not include reasonable payments for removal, processing, disposal, preservation, quality control, storage, transportation, and implantation of a part.
3. Any person who violates this section is guilty of a class B misdemeanor.

23-06.2-11. Examination—Autopsy—Liability.

1. An anatomical gift authorizes any reasonable examination necessary to assure medical acceptability of the gift for the purposes intended.
2. This chapter is subject to the laws of this state prescribing powers and duties with respect to autopsies.
3. Except as provided in section 23-06.2-10, a hospital, physician, surgeon, coroner, local public health officer, enucleator, technician, or any other person who acts in accordance with this chapter or with the applicable anatomical gift law of another state or a foreign country or attempts in good faith to do so is not liable for that activity in any civil action or criminal proceeding.
4. An individual who makes an anatomical gift and the individual's estate are not liable for any injury or damage that may result from the use of the anatomical gift.

23-06.2-11.1. Anatomical parts testing—Exception. No anatomical parts of human bodies, including whole blood, plasma, blood products, blood derivatives, semen, body tissue, organs, and parts of organs or products derived from parts of organs may be used for injection, transfusion, or transplantation into a human body unless the anatomical parts or the donor have been examined for the presence of antibodies to or antigens of the human immunodeficiency virus and the test is negative for the presence of such antibodies or antigens. The testing requirement of this section does not apply if, in a medical emergency constituting a serious threat to the life of a potential anatomical part recipient, a required anatomical part that has been subjected to the testing required under this section is not available. The state department of health may adopt rules to implement the requirements of this section.

23-06.2-12. Application. This chapter applies to a document of gift or refusal to make a gift signed by the donor before, on, or after July 12, 1989.

APPENDIX I
The Oregon Death With Dignity Act

Or. Rev. Stat. §§ 127.800 to 127.995

(General Provisions)

(Section 1)

Note: The division headings, subdivision headings and leadlines for 127.800 to 127.890, 127.895 and 127.897 were enacted as part of Ballot Measure 16 (1994) and were not provided by Legislative Counsel.

127.800 § 1.01. Definitions. The following words and phrases, whenever used in ORS 127.800 to 127.897, have the following meanings:

(1) "Adult" means an individual who is 18 years of age or older.

(2) "Attending physician" means the physician who has primary responsibility for the care of the patient and treatment of the patient's terminal disease.

(3) "Capable" means that in the opinion of a court or in the opinion of the patient's attending physician or consulting physician, psychiatrist or psychologist, a patient has the ability to make and communicate health care decisions to health care providers, including communication through persons familiar with the patient's manner of communicating if those persons are available.

(4) "Consulting physician" means a physician who is qualified by specialty or experience to make a professional diagnosis and prognosis regarding the patient's disease.

(5) "Counseling" means one or more consultations as necessary between a state licensed psychiatrist or psychologist and a patient for the purpose of determining that the patient is capable and not suffering from a psychiatric or psychological disorder or depression causing impaired judgment.

(6) "Health care provider" means a person licensed, certified or otherwise authorized or permitted by the law of this state to administer health care or dispense medication in the ordinary course of business or practice of a profession, and includes a health care facility.

(7) "Informed decision" means a decision by a qualified patient, to request and obtain a prescription to end his or her life in a humane and dignified manner, that is based on an appreciation of the relevant facts and after being fully informed by the attending physician of:

(a) His or her medical diagnosis;

(b) His or her prognosis;

(c) The potential risks associated with taking the medication to be prescribed;

(d) The probable result of taking the medication to be prescribed; and

(e) The feasible alternatives, including, but not limited to, comfort care, hospice care and pain control.

(8) "Medically confirmed" means the medical opinion of the attending physician has been confirmed by a consulting physician who has examined the patient and the patient's relevant medical records.

(9) "Patient" means a person who is under the care of a physician.

(10) "Physician" means a doctor of medicine or osteopathy licensed to practice medicine by the Board of Medical Examiners for the State of Oregon.

(11) "Qualified patient" means a capable adult who is a resident of Oregon and has satisfied the requirements of ORS 127.800 to 127.897 in order to obtain a prescription for medication to end his or her life in a humane and dignified manner.

(12) "Terminal disease" means an incurable and irreversible disease that has been medically confirmed and will, within reasonable medical judgment, produce death within six months. [1995 c.3 § 1.01; 1999 c.423 § 1]

(Written Request for Medication to End
One's Life in a Humane and
Dignified Manner)

(Section 2)

127.805 § 2.01. Who may initiate a written request for medication

(1) An adult who is capable, is a resident of Oregon, and has been determined by the attending physician and consulting physician to be suffering from a terminal disease, and who has voluntarily expressed his or her wish to die, may make a written request for medication for the purpose of ending his or her life in a humane and dignified manner in accordance with ORS 127.800 to 127.897.

(2) No person shall qualify under the provisions of ORS 127.800 to 127.897 solely because of age or disability. [1995 c.3 § 2.01; 1999 c.423 § 2]

127.810 § 2.02. Form of the written request

(1) A valid request for medication under ORS 127.800 to 127.897 shall be in substantially the form described in ORS 127.897, signed and dated by the patient and witnessed by at least two individuals who, in the presence of

the patient, attest that to the best of their knowledge and belief the patient is capable, acting voluntarily, and is not being coerced to sign the request.

(2) One of the witnesses shall be a person who is not:

(a) A relative of the patient by blood, marriage or adoption;

(b) A person who at the time the request is signed would be entitled to any portion of the estate of the qualified patient upon death under any will or by operation of law; or

(c) An owner, operator or employee of a health care facility where the qualified patient is receiving medical treatment or is a resident.

(3) The patient's attending physician at the time the request is signed shall not be a witness.

(4) If the patient is a patient in a long term care facility at the time the written request is made, one of the witnesses shall be an individual designated by the facility and having the qualifications specified by the Department of Human Services by rule. [1995 c.3 § 2.02]

(Safeguards)

(Section 3)

127.815 § 3.01. Attending physician responsibilities

(1) The attending physician shall:

(a) Make the initial determination of whether a patient has a terminal disease, is capable, and has made the request voluntarily;

(b) Request that the patient demonstrate Oregon residency pursuant to ORS 127.860;

(c) To ensure that the patient is making an informed decision, inform the patient of:

(A) His or her medical diagnosis;

(B) His or her prognosis;

(C) The potential risks associated with taking the medication to be prescribed;

(D) The probable result of taking the medication to be prescribed; and

(E) The feasible alternatives, including, but not limited to, comfort care, hospice care and pain control;

(d) Refer the patient to a consulting physician for medical confirmation of the diagnosis, and for a determination that the patient is capable and acting voluntarily;

(e) Refer the patient for counseling if appropriate pursuant to ORS 127.825;

(f) Recommend that the patient notify next of kin;

(g) Counsel the patient about the importance of having another person present when the patient takes the medication prescribed pursuant to ORS 127.800 to 127.897 and of not taking the medication in a public place;

(h) Inform the patient that he or she has an opportunity to rescind the request at any time and in any manner, and offer the patient an opportunity to rescind at the end of the 15 day waiting period pursuant to ORS 127.840;

(i) Verify, immediately prior to writing the prescription for medication under ORS 127.800 to 127.897, that the patient is making an informed decision;

(j) Fulfill the medical record documentation requirements of ORS 127.855;

(k) Ensure that all appropriate steps are carried out in accordance with ORS 127.800 to 127.897 prior to writing a prescription for medication to enable a qualified patient to end his or her life in a humane and dignified manner; and

(L)(A) Dispense medications directly, including ancillary medications intended to facilitate the desired effect to minimize the patient's discomfort, provided the attending physician is registered as a dispensing physician with the Board of Medical Examiners, has a current Drug Enforcement Administration certificate and complies with any applicable administrative rule; or

(B) With the patient's written consent:

(i) Contact a pharmacist and inform the pharmacist of the prescription; and

(ii) Deliver the written prescription personally or by mail to the pharmacist, who will dispense the medications to either the patient, the attending physician or an expressly identified agent of the patient.

(2) Notwithstanding any other provision of law, the attending physician may sign the patient's death certificate. [1995 c.3 § 3.01; 1999 c.423 § 3]

127.820 § 3.02. Consulting physician confirmation. Before a patient is qualified under ORS 127.800 to 127.897, a consulting physician shall examine the patient and his or her relevant medical records and confirm, in writing, the attending physician's diagnosis that the patient is suffering from a terminal disease, and verify that the patient is capable, is acting voluntarily and has made an informed decision. [1995 c.3 § 3.02]

127.825 § 3.03. Counseling referral. If in the opinion of the attending physician or the consulting physician a patient may be suffering from a psychiatric or psychological disorder or depression causing impaired judgment, either physician shall refer the patient for counseling. No medication to end a patient's life in a humane and dignified manner shall be prescribed until the person performing the counseling determines that the patient is not suffering from a psychiatric or psychological disorder or depression causing impaired judgment. [1995 c.3 § 3.03; 1999 c.423 § 4]

127.830 § 3.04. Informed decision. No person shall receive a prescription for medication to end his or her life in a humane and dignified manner unless he or she has made an informed decision as defined in ORS 127.800 (7). Immediately prior to writing a prescription for medication under ORS 127.800 to 127.897, the attending physician shall verify that the patient is making an informed decision. [1995 c.3 § 3.04]

127.835 § 3.05. Family notification. The attending physician shall recommend that the patient notify the next of kin of his or her request for medication pursuant to ORS 127.800 to 127.897. A patient who declines or is unable to notify next of kin shall not have his or her request denied for that reason. [1995 c.3 § 3.05; 1999 c.423 § 6]

127.840 § 3.06. Written and oral requests. In order to receive a prescription for medication to end his or her life in a humane and dignified manner, a qualified patient shall have made an oral request and a written request, and reiterate the oral request to his or her attending physician no less than fifteen (15) days after making the initial oral request. At the time the qualified patient makes his or her second oral request, the attending physician shall offer the patient an opportunity to rescind the request. [1995 c.3 § 3.06]

127.845 § 3.07. Right to rescind request. A patient may rescind his or her request at any time and in any manner without regard to his or her mental state. No prescription for medication under ORS 127.800 to 127.897 may be written without the attending physician offering the qualified patient an opportunity to rescind the request. [1995 c.3 § 3.07]

127.850 § 3.08. Waiting periods. No less than fifteen (15) days shall elapse between the patient's initial oral request and the writing of a prescription under ORS 127.800 to 127.897. No less than 48 hours shall elapse between the patient's written request and the writing of a prescription under ORS 127.800 to 127.897. [1995 c.3 § 3.08]

127.855 § 3.09. Medical record documentation requirements. The following shall be documented or filed in the patient's medical record:

(1) All oral requests by a patient for medication to end his or her life in a humane and dignified manner;

(2) All written requests by a patient for medication to end his or her life in a humane and dignified manner;

(3) The attending physician's diagnosis and prognosis, determination that the patient is capable, acting voluntarily and has made an informed decision;

(4) The consulting physician's diagnosis and prognosis, and verification that the patient is capable, acting voluntarily and has made an informed decision;

(5) A report of the outcome and determinations made during counseling, if performed;

(6) The attending physician's offer to the patient to rescind his or her request at the time of the patient's second oral request pursuant to ORS 127.840; and

(7) A note by the attending physician indicating that all requirements under ORS 127.800 to 127.897 have been met and indicating the steps taken to carry out the request, including a notation of the medication prescribed. [1995 c.3 § 3.09]

127.860 § 3.10. Residency requirement. Only requests made by Oregon residents under ORS 127.800 to 127.897 shall be granted. Factors demonstrating Oregon residency include but are not limited to:

(1) Possession of an Oregon driver license;

(2) Registration to vote in Oregon;

(3) Evidence that the person owns or leases property in Oregon; or

(4) Filing of an Oregon tax return for the most recent tax year. [1995 c.3 § 3.10; 1999 c.423 § 8]

127.865 § 3.11. Reporting requirements

(1)(a) The Health Division shall annually review a sample of records maintained pursuant to ORS 127.800 to 127.897.

(b) The division shall require any health care provider upon dispensing medication pursuant to ORS 127.800 to 127.897 to file a copy of the dispensing record with the division.

(2) The Health Division shall make rules to facilitate the collection of information regarding compliance with ORS 127.800 to 127.897. Except as otherwise required by law, the information collected shall not be a public record and may not be made available for inspection by the public.

(3) The division shall generate and make available to the public an annual statistical report of information collected under subsection (2) of this section. [1995 c.3 § 3.11; 1999 c.423 § 9]

127.870 § 3.12. Effect on construction of wills, contracts and statutes

(1) No provision in a contract, will or other agreement, whether written or oral, to the extent the provision would affect whether a person may make or rescind a request for medication to end his or her life in a humane and dignified manner, shall be valid.

(2) No obligation owing under any currently existing contract shall be conditioned or affected by the making or rescinding of a request, by a person, for medication to end his or her life in a humane and dignified manner. [1995 c.3 § 3.12]

127.875 § 3.13. Insurance or annuity policies. The sale, procurement, or issuance of any life, health, or accident insurance or annuity policy or the rate charged for any policy shall not be conditioned upon or affected by the making or rescinding of a request, by a person, for medication to end his or her life in a humane and dignified manner. Neither shall a qualified patient's act of ingesting medication to end his or her life in a humane and dignified manner have an effect upon a life, health, or accident insurance or annuity policy. [1995 c.3 § 3.13]

127.880 § 3.14. Construction of Act. Nothing in ORS 127.800 to 127.897 shall be construed to authorize a physician or any other person to end a patient's life by lethal injection, mercy killing or active euthanasia. Actions taken in accordance with ORS 127.800 to 127.897 shall not, for any purpose, constitute suicide, assisted suicide, mercy killing or homicide, under the law. [1995 c.3 § 3.14]

(Immunities and Liabilities)

(Section 4)

127.885 § 4.01. Immunities; basis for prohibiting health care provider from participation; notification; permissible sanctions. Except as provided in ORS 127.890:

(1) No person shall be subject to civil or criminal liability or professional disciplinary action for participating in good faith compliance with ORS 127.800 to 127.897. This includes being present when a qualified patient takes the prescribed medication to end his or her life in a humane and dignified manner.

(2) No professional organization or association, or health care provider, may subject a person to censure, discipline, suspension, loss of license, loss of privileges, loss of membership or other penalty for participating or refusing to participate in good faith compliance with ORS 127.800 to 127.897.

(3) No request by a patient for or provision by an attending physician of medication in good faith compliance with the provisions of ORS 127.800 to 127.897 shall constitute neglect for any purpose of law or provide the sole basis for the appointment of a guardian or conservator.

(4) No health care provider shall be under any duty, whether by contract, by statute or by any other legal requirement to participate in the provision

to a qualified patient of medication to end his or her life in a humane and dignified manner. If a health care provider is unable or unwilling to carry out a patient's request under ORS 127.800 to 127.897, and the patient transfers his or her care to a new health care provider, the prior health care provider shall transfer, upon request, a copy of the patient's relevant medical records to the new health care provider.

(5)(a) Notwithstanding any other provision of law, a health care provider may prohibit another health care provider from participating in ORS 127.800 to 127.897 on the premises of the prohibiting provider if the prohibiting provider has notified the health care provider of the prohibiting provider's policy regarding participating in ORS 127.800 to 127.897. Nothing in this paragraph prevents a health care provider from providing health care services to a patient that do not constitute participation in ORS 127.800 to 127.897.

(b) Notwithstanding the provisions of subsections (1) to (4) of this section, a health care provider may subject another health care provider to the sanctions stated in this paragraph if the sanctioning health care provider has notified the sanctioned provider prior to participation in ORS 127.800 to 127.897 that it prohibits participation in ORS 127.800 to 127.897:

(A) Loss of privileges, loss of membership or other sanction provided pursuant to the medical staff bylaws, policies and procedures of the sanctioning health care provider if the sanctioned provider is a member of the sanctioning provider's medical staff and participates in ORS 127.800 to 127.897 while on the health care facility premises, as defined in ORS 442.015, of the sanctioning health care provider, but not including the private medical office of a physician or other provider;

(B) Termination of lease or other property contract or other nonmonetary remedies provided by lease contract, not including loss or restriction of medical staff privileges or exclusion from a provider panel, if the sanctioned provider participates in ORS 127.800 to 127.897 while on the premises of the sanctioning health care provider or on property that is owned by or under the direct control of the sanctioning health care provider; or

(C) Termination of contract or other nonmonetary remedies provided by contract if the sanctioned provider participates in ORS 127.800 to 127.897 while acting in the course and scope of the sanctioned provider's capacity as an employee or independent contractor of the sanctioning health care provider. Nothing in this subparagraph shall be construed to prevent:

(i) A health care provider from participating in ORS 127.800 to 127.897 while acting outside the course and scope of the provider's capacity as an employee or independent contractor; or

(ii) A patient from contracting with his or her attending physician and consulting physician to act outside the course and scope of the provider's capacity as an employee or independent contractor of the sanctioning health care provider.

(c) A health care provider that imposes sanctions pursuant to paragraph (b) of this subsection must follow all due process and other procedures the sanctioning health care provider may have that are related to the imposition of sanctions on another health care provider.

(d) For purposes of this subsection:

(A) "Notify" means a separate statement in writing to the health care provider specifically informing the health care provider prior to the provider's participation in ORS 127.800 to 127.897 of the sanctioning health care provider's policy about participation in activities covered by ORS 127.800 to 127.897.

(B) "Participate in ORS 127.800 to 127.897" means to perform the duties of an attending physician pursuant to ORS 127.815, the consulting physician function pursuant to ORS 127.820 or the counseling function pursuant to ORS 127.825. "Participate in ORS 127.800 to 127.897" does not include:

(i) Making an initial determination that a patient has a terminal disease and informing the patient of the medical prognosis;

(ii) Providing information about the Oregon Death with Dignity Act to a patient upon the request of the patient;

(iii) Providing a patient, upon the request of the patient, with a referral to another physician; or

(iv) A patient contracting with his or her attending physician and consulting physician to act outside of the course and scope of the provider's capacity as an employee or independent contractor of the sanctioning health care provider.

(6) Suspension or termination of staff membership or privileges under subsection (5) of this section is not reportable under ORS 441.820. Action taken pursuant to ORS 127.810, 127.815, 127.820 or 127.825 shall not be the sole basis for a report of unprofessional or dishonorable conduct under ORS 677.415 (2) or (3).

(7) No provision of ORS 127.800 to 127.897 shall be construed to allow a lower standard of care for patients in the community where the patient is treated or a similar community. [1995 c.3 § 4.01; 1999 c.423 § 10]

Note: As originally enacted by the people, the leadline to section 4.01 read "Immunities." The remainder of the leadline was added by editorial action.

127.890 § 4.02. Liabilities

(1) A person who without authorization of the patient willfully alters or forges a request for medication or conceals or destroys a rescission of that request with the intent or effect of causing the patient's death shall be guilty of a Class A felony.

(2) A person who coerces or exerts undue influence on a patient to request medication for the purpose of ending the patient's life, or to destroy a rescission of such a request, shall be guilty of a Class A felony.

(3) Nothing in ORS 127.800 to 127.897 limits further liability for civil damages resulting from other negligent conduct or intentional misconduct by any person.

(4) The penalties in ORS 127.800 to 127.897 do not preclude criminal penalties applicable under other law for conduct which is inconsistent with the provisions of ORS 127.800 to 127.897. [1995 c.3 § 4.02]

127.892 Claims by governmental entity for costs incurred. Any governmental entity that incurs costs resulting from a person terminating his or her life pursuant to the provisions of ORS 127.800 to 127.897 in a public place shall have a claim against the estate of the person to recover such costs and reasonable attorney fees related to enforcing the claim. [1999 c.423 § 5a]

(Severability)

(Section 5)

127.895 § 5.01. Severability. Any section of ORS 127.800 to 127.897 being held invalid as to any person or circumstance shall not affect the application of any other section of ORS 127.800 to 127.897 which can be given full effect without the invalid section or application. [1995 c.3 § 5.01]

(Form of the Request)

(Section 6)

127.897 § 6.01. Form of the request. A request for a medication as authorized by ORS 127.800 to 127.897 shall be in substantially the following form:

REQUEST FOR MEDICATION TO END MY LIFE
IN A HUMANE AND DIGNIFIED MANNER

I, —————————————, am an adult of sound mind.

I am suffering from ——————————, which my attending physician has determined is a terminal disease and which has been medically confirmed by a consulting physician.

I have been fully informed of my diagnosis, prognosis, the nature of medication to be prescribed and potential associated risks, the expected result, and the feasible alternatives, including comfort care, hospice care and pain control.

I request that my attending physician prescribe medication that will end my life in a humane and dignified manner.

INITIAL ONE:

_____ I have informed my family of my decision and taken their opinions into consideration.

_____ I have decided not to inform my family of my decision.

_____ I have no family to inform of my decision.

I understand that I have the right to rescind this request at any time.

I understand the full import of this request and I expect to die when I take the medication to be prescribed. I further understand that although most deaths occur within three hours, my death may take longer and my physician has counseled me about this possibility.

I make this request voluntarily and without reservation, and I accept full moral responsibility for my actions.

Signed: _____
Dated: _____

DECLARATION OF WITNESSES

We declare that the person signing this request:

(a) Is personally known to us or has provided proof of identity;

(b) Signed this request in our presence;

(c) Appears to be of sound mind and not under duress, fraud or undue influence;

(d) Is not a patient for whom either of us is attending physician.

_____ Witness 1/Date
_____ Witness 2/Date

NOTE: One witness shall not be a relative (by blood, marriage or adoption) of the person signing this request, shall not be entitled to any portion of the person's estate upon death and shall not own, operate or be employed at a health care facility where the person is a patient or resident. If the patient is an inpatient at a health care facility, one of the witnesses shall be an individual designated by the facility.

[1995 c.3 § 6.01; 1999 c.423 § 11]
PENALTIES
127.990 [Formerly part of 97.990; repealed by 1993 c.767 § 29]

127.995 Penalties

(1) It shall be a Class A felony for a person without authorization of the principal to willfully alter, forge, conceal or destroy an instrument, the reinstatement or revocation of an instrument or any other evidence or document reflecting the principal's desires and interests, with the intent and effect of causing a withholding or withdrawal of life-sustaining procedures or of artificially administered nutrition and hydration which hastens the death of the principal.

(2) Except as provided in subsection (1) of this section, it shall be a Class A misdemeanor for a person without authorization of the principal to willfully alter, forge, conceal or destroy an instrument, the reinstatement or revocation of an instrument, or any other evidence or document reflecting the principal's desires and interests with the intent or effect of affecting a health care decision. [Formerly 127.585]

APPENDIX J
Statutory Citations (byState, with Analysis)
(i) Health Care Power of Attorney and Combined Advance Directive Legislation
July 1, 2000

State	Type	Form	Limits on Agent's Powers	Prohibited Agents	Formalities of Execution	Prohibited Witnesses	Authority Over Autopsy, Organ Donation or Remains	Comity Provision
1. ALABAMA Alabama Stat. § 22-8A-2 to –10 (1997). Enacted 1981, substantially revised 1997. Amended 2001. *And* Durable Power of Attorney Act, § 26-1-2, revised 1997.	Combined Advance Directive *[Modeled on UHCDA]**	YES Must be substantially followed	• Mental health facility admission and treatments • Psycho-surgery • Sterilization • Abortion • Pregnancy limitation	• Provider • Facility	• 2 or more witnesses	• Minor • Agent • Proxy • Relative • Heir • Person responsible for care costs	NO	YES
2. ALASKA Alaska Stat. § 13.26.332 to .356 (Supp. 1990). Specifically §§ 13.26.344(l). Health powers enacted 1988.	General DPA	YES Must be substantially followed	• Life-sustaining procedures • Mental health facility admission • Electro-convulsive therapy • Psycho-surgery • Sterilization • Abortion	None specified	• Notarized	N/A	NO	NO
3. ARIZONA Ariz. Rev. Stat. Ann. § 36-3201 to –3262 (1994). Enacted 1992, amended 1994.	Combined Advance Directive	YES Optional	• None specified	None specified	• 1 witness or notarized	• Agent • Provider If only *one* witness, person may not be: • Relative • Heir	Autopsy & Organ Donation	YES

4. ARKANSAS 1999 Ark. Laws Act 1448 (H.B. 1331), enacted 4/15/99. See also Ark. Code Ann. §§ 20-17-201 to –218 (proxy appointment in Living Will Declaration).	Special DPA	NO (But proxy appointment in Living Will Declaration does have optional form)	• Life-sustaining treatment not included, unless the DPA incorporates a proxy authorization from the Living Will Declaration statute, §20-17-202 • Pregnancy limitation on life-sustaining treatment	None specified	• 2 witnesses	None specified	NO	YES, if it is a declaration relating to the use of life-sustaining treatment.
5. CALIFORNIA Cal. Probate Code §§ 4600 to –4948 (West 1999). Enacted 1999.	Combined Advance Directive	YES Optional	• Civil commitment • Electro-convulsive therapy • Psycho-surgery • Sterilization • Abortion	• Provider • Facility • Conservator —unless conditions are met.	• 2 witnesses or notarized • Special institutional requirements	• Agent • Provider • Facility One may not be: • Relative • Heir	YES	YES
6. COLORADO Colo. Rev. Stat. §§ 15-14-503 to –509. Enacted 1992. See also § 15-14-501 (1992)	Special DPA	NO	• None specified	None specified	None specified	N/A	NO	YES
7. CONNECTICUT Conn. Gen. Stat. § 1-43 (1993) and § 19a-570 to –575 (1993). Last amended in 1993.	Combined Advance Directive	YES Optional	• None specified (but authority is described as authority to "convey" principal's wishes, rather than to make decisions for principal.)	• Provider • Administrator or employee of gov't agency financially responsible for care	• 2 witnesses • Special institutional requirements	• Agent	NO	NO

(continued)

Health Care Power of Attorney and Combined Advance Directive Legislation July 1, 2000 (continued)

State	Type	Form	Limits on Agent's Powers	Prohibited Agents	Formalities of Execution	Prohibited Witnesses	Authority Over Autopsy, Organ Donation or Remains	Comity Provision
8. DELAWARE Del. Code Ann. tit. 16, §§ 2501 to 2517 (1996). Enacted 1982, substantially revised 1996.	Combined Advance Directive *[Modeled on UHCDA]**	YES Optional	• Pregnancy limitation	• Provider of residential LTC	• 2 witnesses • Special institutional requirements	• Facility • Relative • Heir • Creditor • Person responsible for care costs	NO	YES
9. DISTRICT OF COLUMBIA D.C. Code Ann. §§ 21-2201 to –2213. Enacted 1989.	Special DPA	YES Optional	• None specified	• Provider • Facility	• 2 witnesses	• Principal • Provider • *One may not be relative or heir*	NO	NO
10. FLORIDA Fla. Stat. Ann. § 765.101 to –.404 (West 2001). Enacted 1990, last amended 2000.	Combined Advance Directive	YES Optional	• Mental health facility admission* • Electro-convulsive therapy* • Psycho-surgery* • Sterilization* • Abortion* • Experimental treatments* • Life-sustaining procedures while pregnant* • Refusal permissible if expressly authorized	• Provider • Facility	• 2 witnesses	• Agent • *One may not be spouse or relative*	Only organ donation	YES

State	Type	Living Will Status	Restrictions	Surrogate Restrictions	Witness/Notary	May Not Be Agent		
11. GEORGIA Ga. Code Ann. §§ 31-36-1 to –13 (1990). Enacted 1990, amended 1999.	Special DPA	YES Optional	• Mental health facility admission • Psycho-surgery • Sterilization • Treatments under Title 37 of Code	• Provider	• 2 witnesses plus attending physician if in hospital or Skilled Nursing Facility	None	YES	NO
12. HAWAII Hawaii Rev. Stat. ɔɔ327E-1 to -16 (West 1999) Enacted 1999, amended 2000. *See also* Hawaii Rev. Stat. ɔ551D, special DPA statute.	Combined Advance Directive *[Modeled on UHCDA]**	YES Optional	• None specified	• Provider	• 2 witnesses *or* notarized	• Provider • Agent *One* may not be • Relative • Heir	NO	YES
13. IDAHO Idaho Code §§ 39-4501 to -4509 (Supp. 1990) Specifically § 39-4505. Enacted 1988. Last amended 2001.	Special DPA	YES Optional	• None specified	• Provider • Facility	• 2 witnesses *or* notarized	• Agent • Provider • Facility *One* may not be relative or heir	NO	NO
14. ILLINOIS 755 ILCS 45/1-1 through 4-12 (1995). Enacted 1987. Last amended 1999.	Special DPA	YES Optional	• None specified	• Provider	None specified	None specified	YES	YES
15. INDIANA Ind. Code Ann. §§ 30-5-1 to 30-5-10 (West 1991), specifically § 30-5-5-17. Enacted 1991. (DPA) See also § 16-36-1-1 to -14 (Health Care Consent Act)	General DPA and health care consent statute	YES Optional, but mandatory language for authority re life-sustaining treatment in DPA	• None specified	None specified	• Notarized (for DPA) • 1 witness (for consent act)	• Agent	YES	YES

(continued)

Health Care Power of Attorney and Combined Advance Directive Legislation July 1, 2000 (continued)

State	Type	Form	Limits on Agent's Powers	Prohibited Agents	Formalities of Execution	Prohibited Witnesses	Authority Over Autopsy, Organ Donation or Remains	Comity Provision
16. IOWA Iowa Code Ann. §§ 144B.1 to .12 (West Supp. 1991). Enacted 1991.	Special DPA	YES Optional	• None specified	• Provider	• 2 witnesses or notarized	• Agent • Provider • Person under 18 *One may not be relative*	NO	YES
17. KANASA Kan. Stat. Ann. §§ 58-625 to –632 (Supp. 1994). Enacted 1989. Last amended 1994.	Special DPA	YES Must be substantially followed	• Cannot revoke previous living will	• Provider • Facility	• 2 witnesses or notarized	• Relative • Heir • Person responsible for care costs	YES	YES
18. KENTUCKY Ky. Rev. Stat. §§ 311.621 to .643 (Supp 1994). Enacted 1994, replacing 1990 Act. Last amended 1998.	Combined Advanced Directive	YES Must be substantially followed	• Nutrition & hydration* • Pregnancy limitation * Refusal permissible if specified conditions are met	• Facility	• 2 witnesses or notarized	• Relative • Provider • Facility • Heir • Person responsible for care costs	NO	NO
19. LOUISIANA La. Rev. Stat. Ann 40:1299.58.1 to .10 (West 1997). Enacted 1990.	Proxy contained in Living Will statute	YES Optional	• Powers implicitly limited to executing a living will declaration on behalf of principal	None specified	None specified* * Only requires that powers affecting real estate be signed before notary and 2 witnesses	• Relative • Heir	NO	YES

State / Citation	Type		Restrictions	Facility	Witnesses	Who May Not Be Agent		
20. MAINE Me. Rev. Stat. Ann. tit. 18A, § 5-801 to § 5-817 (West 1995). Enacted 1995.	Combined Advance Directive *[Modeled on UHCDA]**	YES	• Mental health facility admission, consent permissible if expressly authorized	• LTC Facility	• 2 witnesses	None specified	NO	YES
21. MARYLAND Md. Code Ann. [Health-Gen.] §§ 5-601 to –608. Enacted 1993, last amended 2000.	Combined Advance Directive	YES Optional	• None specified	• Facility	• 2 witnesses • Also recognizes oral directive to a physician with one witness	• Agent • *One* may not be person with No financial interest in person's death	NO	YES
22. MASSACHUSETTS Mass. Gen. Laws Ann. Ch. 201D (West Supp. 1991). Enacted 1990.	Special DPA	NO	• None specified	• Facility	• 2 witnesses	• Agent	NO	YES
23. MICHIGAN Mich. Comp. Laws Ann. 333.5651 to 333.5661 (1997). Enacted 1997.	Special DPA	Only for agent's acceptance	• Pregnancy limitation • Life-sustaining procedures* * Refusal permissible if expressly authorized	None specified	• 2 witnesses Agent must accept in writing	• Agent • Relative • Heir • Provider • Facility • Employee of life/ health insurance provider	NO	NO
Mich. Comp. Laws Ann. § 700.5501 to 5513 (West 1999). Enacted 1998. Amended 1999. Effective 4/1/00.	General DPA	YES	• Pregnancy limitation • Life-sustaining procedures* * Refusal permissible if expressly/authorized	None specified	• 2 witnesses Agent must accept in writing	• Relative • Heir • Physician • Agent • Employee of life or health insurance provider	NO	NO

(continued)

Health Care Power of Attorney and Combined Advance Directive Legislation July 1, 2000 (continued)

State	Type	Form	Limits on Agent's Powers	Prohibited Agents	Formalities of Execution	Prohibited Witnesses	Authority Over Autopsy, Organ Donation or Remains	Comity Provision
24. MINNESOTA Minn. Stat. §§ 145C.01 to .16 (1993). Enacted 1993, substantially revised 1998, as of 8/1/98. See Minn. Stat. § 253B.03 (Subd. 6b) (1993) for mental health advance directive.	Combined Advance Directive	YES Optional	• None specified	• Provider	• 2 witnesses or notarized	• Agent • *One* may not be provider	Organ donation & Disposition of remains	YES
25. MISSISSIPPI Miss. Code Ann. §§ 41-41-201 to −229. (Enacted 1998, replaced 1990 statute)	Combined Advance Directive *[Modeled on UHCDA]**	YES Optional	• Mental health facility admission, consent permissible if expressly authorized	• LTC Facility	• 2 witnesses or notarized	• Agent • Provider • Facility • *One* may not be relative or heir	NO	Only if in compliance with this Act
26. MISSOURI Mo. Ann. Stat. §§ 404.700 to .735 And §§ 800–870 (West 1991). Health powers enacted 1991.	Special DPA (within general DPA statute)	NO	• Nutrition & hydration* * Refusal permissible if expressly authorized	• Physician • Facility	• Must be acknowledged as conveyance of real estate (§ 404.705)	None specified	NO	YES

State & Statute	Type	Living Will	Covered Procedures	Excluded/Qualified	Witnesses	Agent Restrictions		
27. MONTANA Mont. Code Ann. §§ 50-9-101 to -111, and -201 to -206 (1991). Enacted 1985. Proxy added 1991.	Proxy contained in Living Will statute	YES Optional	• Co-extensive with Living Will Declaration • Pregnancy limitation	None specified	• 2 witnesses	None specified	NO	YES
28. NEBRASKA Neb. Rev. Stat. §§ 30-3401 to -3434 (1993). Enacted 1992. Last amended 1993.	Special DPA	YES Optional	• Life-sustaining procedures* • Nutrition & hydration* • Pregnancy * Refusal permissible if expressly authorized	• Provider • Facility • Any agent serving 10 or more principals	• 2 witnesses or notarized	• Agent • Spouse • Relative • Heir • Provider • Insurer *One* may not be administrator or employee of provider	NO	YES
29. NEVADA Nev. Rev. Stat. §§ 449.800 to .860 (Supp. 1989). Enacted 1987. Last amended 1991.	Special DPA	YES Must be substantially followed	• Mental health facility admission • Electro-convulsive therapy • Psycho-surgery • Sterilization • Abortion	• Provider • Facility	• 2 witnesses or notarized	• Agent • Provider • Facility *One* may not be relative or heir	NO	NO
30. NEW HAMPSHIRE N.H. Rev. Stat. Ann. §§ 137-J:1 to -J:16 (1993). Enacted 1991.	Special DPA	Form and disclosure to principal. Must be substantially followed.	• Mental health facility admission • Sterilization • Pregnancy limitation • Nutrition & hydration* * Refusal permissible if expressly authorized	• Provider • Facility	• 2 witnesses • Principal must acknowledge receipt of mandatory notice	• Agent • Spouse • Heir *One* may not be provider or facility	NO	YES

(continued)

Health Care Power of Attorney and Combined Advance Directive Legislation July 1, 2000 (continued)

State	Type	Form	Limits on Agent's Powers	Prohibited Agents	Formalities of Execution	Prohibited Witnesses	Authority Over Autopsy, Organ Donation or Remains	Comity Provision
31. **NEW JERSEY** N.J. Stat. Ann. § 26:2H-53 to –78 (West 1993). Enacted 1991.	Combined Advance Directive	NO	• None specified	• Physician • Facility	• 2 witnesses or notarized	• Agent	NO	YES
32. **NEW MEXICO** N.M. Stat. Ann. §§ 24-7A-1 to –16 (1997). Enacted 1995, amended 1997.	Combined Advance Directive *[Modeled on UHCDA]**	YES Optional	• None specified	• LTC Facility	• 2 witnesses recommended, but not required	None specified	NO	Only if in compliance with this Act
33. **NEW YORK** N.Y. Pub. Health Law §§ 2980 to 2994 (McKinney Supp. 1991). Enacted 1990.	Special DPA	YES Optional	• Nutrition and hydration* * Principal must make his/her wishes "reasonably known"	• Provider • Facility	• 2 witnesses • Special institutional requirements	• Agent	NO	YES
34. **NORTH CAROLINA** N.C. Gen. Stat. §§ 32A-15 to –26 (1993). Enacted 1991. Last amended 1998. See N.C. Gen. Stat. ∋ 122C-71 to –77, enacted in 1997, for mental health advance directive.	Special DPA	YES Optional	• None specified	• Provider	• 2 witnesses *and* notarized	• Relative • Heir • Provider • Facility • Creditor	YES	NO

State / Citation	Type	Status	Special provisions	Provider notification	Witness requirements	Who may be agent	NO	YES
35. NORTH DAKOTA N.D. Cent. Code §§ 23-06.5-01 to –18 (1993). Enacted 1991. Last amended 2001.	Special DPA	YES Optional	• Mental health facility admission >45 days • Psycho-surgery • Abortion • Sterilization	• Provider • Facility	• 2 witnesses or notarized • Agent must accept in writing	• Agent • Provider • Facility • Spouse • Heir • Relative • Creditor	NO	YES
36. OHIO Ohio Rev. Code §§ 1337.11 to .17 (Anderson Supp. 1991). Enacted 1989. Last amended 1991.	Special DPA	Only for mandatory disclosure to principal	• Life-sustaining procedures* • Nutrition & hydration* • Pregnancy limitation * Refusal permissible if specified conditions are met	• Physician • Facility	• 2 witnesses or notarized	• Agent • Relative • Physician • Nursing home administrator	NO	YES
37. OKLAHOMA Okla. Stat. Ann. tit. 63, § 3101.1 to –.16 (West 1993) Enacted 1992. Last amended 1998. See Okla. Sess. Law Serv. Ch. 251 (H.B. 1353) enacted 1995 for mental health advance directive.	Combined Advance Directive	YES Must be substantially followed	• Nutrition & hydration* • Pregnancy limitation * Refusal permissible if expressly authorized	None specified	• 2 witnesses	• Heir	NO	YES
38. OREGON Or. Rev. Stat. §§ 127.505 to .640 (1993). Enacted 1989. Substantially revised 1993. See Or. Rev. Stat. §§ 127.700 to .735 (1993) for mental health advance directive.	Combined Advance Directive	YES Must be followed	• Mental health facility admission • Electro-convulsive therapy • Psycho-surgery • Sterilization • Abortion • Life-sustaining procedures* * Refusal permissible if expressly authorized or if specified conditions are met	• Attending physician • Facility	• 2 witnesses • Agent must accept in writing • Special institutional requirements	• Agent • Attending physician • *One* may not be relative, heir, or facility	NO	YES

(continued)

Health Care Power of Attorney and Combined Advance Directive Legislation
July 1, 2000 (continued)

State	Type	Form	Limits on Agent's Powers	Prohibited Agents	Formalities of Execution	Prohibited Witnesses	Authority Over Autopsy, Organ Donation or Remains	Comity Provision
39. PENNSYLVANIA Pa. Stat. Ann. tit. 20, §§ 5401 to 5416 (1993). Enacted 1992. See also 20 Pa. Cons. Stat. Ann. §§ 5601 to 5607 (Purdon's Supp. 1990). Enacted 1982, amended 1999.	Living Will Statute (Also in General DPA *See Note 2*)	YES Optional	Authorizes agent to act *only* if principal is in a • terminal condition, or • state of permanent unconsciousness • Nutrition & hydration* • Pregnancy limitation * Refusal permissible if expressly authorized	None specified	• 2 witnesses	• Person who signs declaration on declarant's behalf	Organ Donation	NO
40. RHODE ISLAND R.I. Gen. Laws § 23-4.10-1 to –12 (Supp. 1993). Enacted 1986. Last amended 1998.	Special DPA	YES Optional	• None specified	• Provider • Facility	• 2 witnesses • Principal must be Rhode Island resident	• Agent • Provider • Facility • *One* may not be relative or heir	NO	YES
41. SOUTH CAROLINA S.C. Code § 62-5-504. Enacted 1992. See also § 62-5-501 re durable power.	Special DPA	YES Must be substantially followed	• Nutrition & hydration "necessary for comfort care or alleviation of pain"* • Pregnancy limitation * Refusal permissible if expressly authorized	• Provider • Nursing care facility	• 2 witnesses	• Agent • Spouse • Relative • Heir • Attending physician • Creditor • Life insurance beneficiary • Person responsible for care costs • *One* may not be facility	NO	YES

State / Citation							
42. SOUTH DAKOTA S.D. Codified Laws Ann. §§ 34-12C-1 to -8, and §§ 59-7-2.1 to -2.8 (Supp. 1992). Health powers enacted 1990. Last amended 1992.	Special DPA	NO	• Pregnancy limitation • Nutrition & hydration* * Refusal permissible if specified conditions are met	None specified	None specified	None specified	NO YES
43. TENNESSEE Tenn. Code Ann. §§ 34-6-201 to -214 (Supp. 1991). Enacted 1990. Amended 1991.	Special DPA	Only for disclosure to principal (not mandatory)	• Nutrition & hydration* * Refusal permissible if expressly authorized. However, cannot withhold "simple nourishment or fluidsψ"	• Provider • Facility • Conservator* * Unless certain conditions are met	• 2 witnesses and notarized	• Agent • Provider • Facility • *One* may not be relative or heir	YES YES
44. TEXAS Tex. [Health & Safety] Code Ann. §§166.001 to -.166 (West 1993). Enacted 1989. Amended 1999.	Special DPA	YES Must be substantially followed	• Mental health facility admission • Electro-convulsive therapy • Psycho-surgery • Abortion • Comfort care	• Provider • Facility	• Warning disclosure • 2 witnesses	• Agent • Provider • Spouse • Heir • Creditor	NO YES
45. UTAH Utah Code Ann. § 75-2-1101 to -1118 (Supp. 1993). Enacted 1985. Last amended 1993.	Special DPA	YES Must be substantially followed	• Life-sustaining procedures* • Pregnancy limitation * Agent makes health care decisions by executing a medical directive. Decisions may include the withholding of life-sustaining procedures unless principal is pregnant	None specified	• Notarized	None specified	NO YES

(continued)

Health Care Power of Attorney and Combined Advance Directive Legislation
July 1, 2000 (continued)

State	Type	Form	Limits on Agent's Powers	Prohibited Agents	Formalities of Execution	Prohibited Witnesses	Authority Over Autopsy, Organ Donation or Remains	Comity Provision
46. VERMONT Vt. Stat. Ann. tit. 14, § 3451 to 3467 (1989). Enacted 1988.	Special DPA	YES Must be substantially followed	• Mental health facility admission • Sterilization	• Provider • Facility	• Warning disclosure • 2 witnesses • Special institutional requirements	• Agent • Provider • Facility • Relative • Heir • Creditor	NO	YES
47. VIRGINIA Va. Code § 54.1-2981 to –2993 (Supp. 1992). Enacted 1992, last amended 2000.	Combined Advance Directive	YES Optional	• Mental health facility admission • Psycho-surgery • Sterilization • Abortion • Decisions about "visitation" unless expressly authorized	None specified	• 2 witnesses	• Spouse • Relative	NO	YES
48. WASHINGTON Wash. Rev. Code Ann. §§ 11.94.010 to .900 (Supp. 1990). Health powers enacted 1989.	General DPA	NO	• Electro-convulsive therapy • Psycho-surgery • Other psychiatric • Amputation	• Provider • Facility	None specified	N/A	NO	YES
49. WEST VIRGINIA W. VA. Code § 16-30-1 to –24 (Supp. 2000). Enacted 2000.	Combined Advance Directive Law, but maintains separate Living Will and Medical Power of Attorney documents	YES Optional	• None specified	• Provider • Facility	• 2 witnesses *and* notarized	• Agent • Attending physician • Principal's signatory • Relative • Heir • Person responsible for care costs	YES	YES

State / Citation	Type	Disclosure	Restrictions		Execution	Who may not serve		
50. WISCONSIN Wis. Stat. Ann. §§ 155.01 to .80 and 11.243.07(6m) (West 1990). Enacted 1990. Last amended 1998.	Special DPA	YES Optional but disclosure to principal is mandatory	• Mental health facility admission • Electro-convulsive therapy • Mental health research • Drastic mental health treatment • Nutrition & hydration* • Admission to nursing home or residential facility * Refusal permissible only if specified conditions are met	• Provider • Facility	• 2 witnesses	• Agent • Provider • Relative • Heir • Person responsible for care costs	NO	YES
51. WYOMING Wyo. Stat. Ann. §§ 3-5-201 to -214 (Supp. 1991) Enacted 1991. Last amended 1992.	Special DPA	NO	• Mental health facility admission • Electro-convulsive therapy • Psycho-surgery	• Provider • Facility	• 2 witnesses or notarized	• Agent • Provider • Facility • *One may not be relative or heir*	Organ donation and Disposition of remains	YES
UNIFORM HEALTH-CARE DECISIONS ACT	Comprehensive Health Care Decisions Act	YES Optional	• None specified	• LTC Facility	• 2 witnesses recommended, but not required	None	NO	Only if in compliance with this Act

Abbreviations: DPA = Durable Power of Attorney.   UHCDA = Uniform Health Care Decisions Act.
CAUTION: The descriptions and limitations listed in this chart should be viewed as broad characterizations for comparison purposes and not as precise quotations from legislative language.

(ii) Surrogate Consent in the Absence of an Advance Directive
July 1, 2001

State & Citation	General Type of Statute	Priority of Surrogates (in absence of appointed proxy or guardian with health powers)	Limitations on Types of Decisions	Disagreement Process Among Priority Surrogates
1. ALABAMA Ala. Code 1975 § 22-8A-11 and -6 (1997), enacted 1997	Comprehensive Health Care Decisions Act	• Spouse • Adult child • Parent • Sibling • Nearest relative • Attending physician & ethics committee	Patient must be in terminal condition or permanently unconscious	Consensus required
2. ARIZONA Ariz. Rev. Stat. Ann. § 36-3231 (West 1998), enacted 1992	Comprehensive Health Care Decisions Act	• Spouse • Adult child • Parent • Domestic partner • Sibling • Close friend • Attending physician in consult with ethics committee or, if none, 2nd physician	N/A to decisions to withdraw nutrition or hydration	Majority rule

3. ARKANSAS Ark. Code Ann. § 20-17-214 (1997)	Living Will Statute	• Parents of unmarried minor • Spouse • Adult child • Parents • Sibling • Persons in loco parentis • Adult heirs	Patient must be in terminal condition or permanently unconscious N/A if pregnant	Majority rule
4. CALIFORNIA Cal. Probate Code § 4711-4727 (West 1999)	Comprehensive Health Care Decisions Act	An individual *orally* designated as surrogate. No others.	Effective "only during the course of treatment or illness or during the stay in the health care institution when the designation is made." N/A to civil commitment, electro-convulsive therapy, psychosurgery, sterilization, and abortion.	None listed
5. COLORADO Colo. Rev. Stat. Ann. § 15-18.5- 103 (West 1999)	Separate Surrogate Consent Act	The following "interested persons" must decide who among them shall be surrogate decision-maker: • Spouse • Either parent • Adult child • Sibling • Grandchild • Close friend	N/A to withholding or withdrawal of artificial nourishment and hydration unless specified conditions are met	Consensus required

(continued)

Surrogate Consent in the Absence of an Advance Directive
July 1, 2001 (*continued*)

State & Citation	General Type of Statute	Priority of Surrogates (in absence of appointed proxy or guardian with health powers)	Limitations on Types of Decisions	Disagreement Process Among Priority Surrogates
6. CONNECTICUT Conn. Gen. Stat. Ann. § 19a-571 (West 1998)	Comprehensive Health Care Decisions Act	Physician authorized in consultation with next of kin	Limited to the removal or withholding of life support systems, and patient is in terminal condition or permanently unconscious N/A if pregnant	None listed
7. DELAWARE Del. Code Ann. tit. 16, § 2507 (1998)	Comprehensive Health Care Decisions Act	• An individual orally designated as surrogate • Spouse • Adult child • Parent • Sibling • Grandchild • Close friend	Patient must be in terminal condition or permanently unconscious N/A if pregnant	If in health care institution, refer to Aappropriate committee ≅ for a recommendation
8. DISTRICT OF COLUMBIA D.C. Code 1981 § 21-2210 (1998)	Durable Power of Attorney for Health Care Act	• Spouse • Adult child • Parent • Sibling • Religious superior if patient is member of a religiousorder or a diocesan priest • Nearest living relative	N/A to abortion, sterilization, or psycho-surgery, convulsive therapy or behavior modification programs involving aversive stimuli are excluded	None listed

State / Statute	Statute Name	Priority List	Limitations	Resolution
9. FLORIDA Fla. Stat Ann. § 765.401 and .404 (West 2001) Last amended 2000	Comprehensive Health Care Decisions Act	• Spouse • Adult child • Parent • Sibling • Close adult relative • Close friend	N/A to abortion, sterilization, electroshock therapy, psychosurgery, experimental treatment, or voluntary admission to a mental health facility. A decision to withhold or withdraw life-prolonging procedures must be supported by clear and convincing evidence. N/A if pregnant	Majority rule
10. GEORGIA Ga. Code Ann. § 31-9-2 (1998)	Informed Consent Statute	• Spouse • Adult child • Parent • Sibling • Grandparent	Not explicitly applicable to refusals of treatment	None listed
Ga. Code Ann. 31-36A-1 to A-7, enacted 1999	"Temporary Health Care Placement Decision Maker for an Adult Act"	Same as above but priority list continues with: • Adult grandchild • Uncle or Aunt • Adult nephew or niece	Applies only to decisions regarding admission to or discharge from one health care facility or placement, or transfer to another health care facility or placement. Excludes involuntary placement for mental illness.	None listed

(continued)

Surrogate Consent in the Absence of an Advance Directive
July 1, 2001 (*continued*)

State & Citation	General Type of Statute	Priority of Surrogates (in absence of appointed proxy or guardian with health powers)	Limitations on Types of Decisions	Disagreement Process Among Priority Surrogates
11. HAWAII Hawaii Rev. Stat. ₎₎327E-1 to -16 (West 1999) Enacted 1999.	Comprehensive Health Care Decisions Act	An individual orally designated as surrogate If none, the following "interested persons" must decide who among them shall be surrogate decision-maker: • Spouse • Reciprocal beneficiary • Adult child • Parent • Sibling • Grandchild • Close friend	None, except an "interested person" may make a decision to withhold or withdraw nutrition and hydration only if two physicians certify that providing it will merely prolong the act of dying and the patient is highly unlikely to have any neurological response in the future.	Consensus required
12. IDAHO Idaho Code § 39-4303 (Lexis 1998)	Informed Consent Statute	Either: • Parent • Spouse If none, then any relative or . . . any other person representing himself or herself responsible for the health care of such person	None listed	None listed

13. ILLINOIS 755 ILCS 40/25 (Smith-Hurd 1998)	Separate Surrogate Consent Act	• Spouse • Adult child • Either parent • Sibling • Adult grandchild • Close friend • Guardian of the estate	N/A to admission to mental health facility, psychotropic medication or electo-convulsive therapy (see 405 ILCS 5/1-121.5; 5/2-102; 5/3-601.2, amended 1997) If decision concerns forgoing life-sustaining treatment, patient must be in terminal condition, permanently unconscious, or incurable or irreversible condition	Majority rule
14. INDIANA Ind. Code Ann. § 16-36-1-1 to -14 (West 1998)	Health Care Agency and Surrogate Consent Act	Any of the following: • Spouse • Parent • Adult child • Sibling • Religious superior if the individual is a member of a religious order	None listed	None listed

(continued)

Surrogate Consent in the Absence of an Advance Directive
July 1, 2001 (*continued*)

State & Citation	General Type of Statute	Priority of Surrogates (in absence of appointed proxy or guardian with health powers)	Limitations on Types of Decisions	Disagreement Process Among Priority Surrogates
15. IOWA Iowa Code Ann. § 144A.7 (West 1998)	Living Will Statute	• Spouse • Adult child • Parent or both parents, if reasonably available • Adult sibling	Limited to the withholding or withdrawal of life-sustaining procedures, and patient is in terminal condition or comatose N/A if pregnant	Majority rule
16. KENTUCKY Ky. Rev. Stat. § 311.631 (Baldwin 1999)	Living Will Statute	• Spouse • Adult child • Parents • Nearest relative	N/A to withholding or withdrawal artificial nutrition and hydration unless specified conditions are met	Majority rule
17. LOUISIANA La. Rev. Stat. Ann. § 40:1299.58.1 to .10 (West 1999)	Living Will Statute	• Spouse • Adult child • Parents • Sibling • Other relatives	Limited to patient in terminal and irreversible condition and comatose	Consensus required

18. MAINE
Me. Rev. Stat.
Ann. tit. 18-A,
§ 5-801 to
§ 5-817
(West 1999)
	Comprehensive
	Health Care
	Decisions Act
		• Spouse
		• Adult in spouse-like
		  relationship
		• Adult child
		• Parent
		• Sibling
		• Adult grandchild
		• Adult niece or nephew
		• Adult relative familiar with
		  patient's values
		• Close friend
			If decision pertains to
			withdrawal or withholding of
			life-sustaining treatment,
			patient must be in terminal
			condition or persistent
			vegetative state
			N/A to denial of surgery,
			procedures, or other interventions
			that are deemed medically necessary.
				Majority rule,
				although referral
				to dispute resolution
				assistance is
				mentioned as option

19. MARYLAND
Md. Health-Gen.
Code Ann.,
§ 5-605
(Lexis 1998)
	Comprehensive
	Health Care
	Decisions Act
		• Spouse
		• Adult child
		• Parent
		• Sibling
		• Friend or relative
		  who has maintained regular
		  contact with the patient
			N/A to sterilization or treatment
			for mental disorder Applicable to
			life-sustaining procedure only if
			the patient as been certified to be
			in a terminal condition, persistent
			vegetative state, or end-stage
			condition
			Applicable to DNR order only
			under certain conditions
				If in hospital or
				nursing home, refer
				to ethics committee
				If elsewhere,
				consensus required

(continued)

Surrogate Consent in the Absence of an Advance Directive
July 1, 2001 (continued)

State & Citation	General Type of Statute	Priority of Surrogates (in absence of appointed proxy or guardian with health powers)	Limitations on Types of Decisions	Disagreement Process Among Priority Surrogates
21. MISSISSIPPI Miss. Code 1972 Ann. § 41-41-211, ∋41-41-215(9) (1998)	Comprehensive Health Care Decisions Act	• Individual orally designated by patient • Spouse • Adult child • Parent • Sibling • Close friend • Owner, operator, or employee of residential long-term care institution (but see limitations)	If surrogate is owner, operator, or employee of residential long-term care institution, then the authority does not extend to decisions to withhold or discontinue life support, nutrition, hydration, or other treatment, care, or support.	Majority rule.
22. MONTANA Mont. Code Ann. § 50-9-106 (1997)	Living Will Statute	• Spouse • Adult child • Parents • Sibling • Nearest adult relative	Limited to withholding or withdrawal of life-sustaining treatment , and patient is in terminal condition N/A if pregnant	Majority rule
23. NEVADA Nev. Rev. Stat. § 449.626 (1997)	Living Will Statute	• Spouse • Adult child • Parents • Sibling • Nearest adult relative	Limited to withholding or withdrawal of life-sustaining treatment, and patient is in terminal condition N/A if pregnant	Majority rule

State	Statute	Surrogates	Limitations	Dispute resolution
24. NEW MEXICO N.M. Stat. Ann. 1978 ∋ 24-7A-5 (1998)	Comprehensive Health Care Decisions Act	• An individual designated as surrogate • Spouse • Individual in long-term spouse-like relationship • Adult child • Parent • Sibling • Grandparent • Close friend	None listed	Majority rule
25. NEW YORK N.Y. Pub. Health Law § 2965 (McKinney 1999)	Specialized Surrogate Consent Statute (applicable only to **DNR** orders)	• Spouse • Adult child • Parent • Sibling • Close friend	Limited to consent to a DNR order, and patient is in terminal condition, or permanently unconscious, or where resuscitation is futile or extraordinarily burdensome	Refer to dispute mediation system
26. NORTH CAROLINA N.C. Gen. Stat. § 90-322 (Michie 1997)	Living Will Statute	• Spouse • Majority of relatives of the first degree	Limited to the withholding or discontinuance of extraordinary means or artificial nutrition or hydration, and patient is in terminal condition, or persistent vegetative state, and meets other conditions	Majority rule

(*continued*)

Surrogate Consent in the Absence of an Advance Directive
July 1, 2001 (*continued*)

State & Citation	General Type of Statute	Priority of Surrogates (in absence of appointed proxy or guardian with health powers)	Limitations on Types of Decisions	Disagreement Process Among Priority Surrogates
27. NORTH DAKOTA N.D. Cent. Code § 23-12-13 (Michie 1997)	Informed Consent Statute	• Spouse • Adult children • Parents • Siblings • Grandparents • Adult grandchildren • Close adult relative or friend	Not explicitly applicable to refusals of treatment N/A to sterilization, abortion, psychosurgery, and some admissions to a state mental facility	None listed
28. OHIO Ohio Rev. Code Ann. § 2133.08 (Baldwin 1999)	Living Will Statute	• Spouse • Adult child • Parents • Sibling • Nearest adult relative	Limited to consent for withdrawal or withholding of life-sustaining treatment, and patient is in terminal condition or permanently unconscious Nutrition and hydration may be withheld only upon the issuance of an order of the probate court N/A if pregnant	Majority rule
29. OKLAHOMA Okla. Stat. Ann. tit. 63 § 3102A (West 1999)	Specialized provision (applicable only to experimental treatments)	• Spouse • Adult child • Parent • Sibling • Relative	Limited to experimental treatment, test or drug approved by a local institutional revew board.	None listed

30. OREGON Or. Rev. Stat. § 127.635 (1998)	Comprehensive Health Care Decisions Act	• Spouse • Adult designated by others on this list, without objection by anyone on list • Majority of adult children • Either parent • Majority of siblings • Adult relative or adult friend • Attending physician	Limited to withdrawal or withholding of life-sustaining procedures, and patient is in terminal condition, or permanently unconscious, or meets other conditions	Majority rule
31. SOUTH CAROLINA S.C. Code 1976 Ann. § 44-66-30 (1998)	Separate Surrogate Consent Act	• Person given priority to make health-care decisions for the patient by another statute • Spouse • Parent or adult child • Sibling, grandparent, or adult grandchild • Other close relative • Person given authority to make health-care decisions for the patient by another statutory provision	N/A if patient's inability to consent is temporary and delay of treatment will not result in significant detriment to the patient's health	None listed
32. SOUTH DAKOTA S.D. Codified Laws Ann. § 34-12C-1 to -8 (1998)	Separate Surrogate Consent Act	• Spouse • Adult child • Parent • Sibling • Grandparent or adult grandchild • Aunt or uncle or adult niece or nephew	None listed	None listed

(continued)

Surrogate Consent in the Absence of an Advance Directive
July 1, 2001 (*continued*)

State & Citation	General Type of Statute	Priority of Surrogates (in absence of appointed proxy or guardian with health powers)	Limitations on Types of Decisions	Disagreement Process Among Priority Surrogates
33. TEXAS Tex. [Health & Safety] Code Ann. § 166.039 (West 1997)	Advance Directive Act	• Spouse • Reasonably available adult children • Parents • Nearest relative	N/A if pregnant	None listed
Tex. [Health & Safety] Code Ann. ∋166.08to .101, specifically § 166.088(b) (West 1997)	Specialized provision (applicable to **DNR** orders)	(Same as above. Incorporates the terms of § 672.009)	(Same as above)	(Same as above)
34. UTAH Utah Code Ann. 1953 § 75-2-1105, -1105.5, -1107 (Lexis 1998)	Comprehensive Health Care Decisions Act	• Spouse • Parents or surviving parent • Adult child • Nearest reasonably available relative When patient is terminal or in a permanent vegetative state: • Spouse • Parent • Adult children	N/A if pregnant	Majority rule

State	Type of Statute	Surrogate Priority	Limitations	Conflict Resolution
35. VIRGINIA Va. Code 1950 § 54.1-2986 (Michie 1997)	Comprehensive Health Care Decisions Act	• Spouse • Adult child • Parent • Sibling • Other relative in the descending order or blood relationship	N/A to non-therapeutic sterilization, abortion, psychosurgery, or admission to a mental retardation facility or psychiatric hospital	Majority rule
36. WASHINGTON Wash. Rev. Code Ann. § 7.70.065 (West 1998)	Informed Consent Statute	• Spouse • Adult children • Parents • Siblings	Not explicitly applicable to refusals of treatment	Consensus required
37. WEST VIRGINIA W. Va. Code 1966 § 16-30-8 and -9 (2000) Last amended 2000	Comprehensive Health Care Decisions Act	• Spouse • Adult child • Parent • Sibling • Adult grandchild • Close friend • Any other person or entity according to DHHR rules If there are multiple surrogates at the same priority level, the attending physician must choose one who appears best qualified according to statutory criteria. May also choose lower level surrogate if deemed best qualified.	None listed	Conflict among multiple surrogates pre-empted by Physician's authority to select one surrogate. Other permissible surrogates have a 72-hour window to seek court challenge of a decision made by selected surrogate.

(continued)

Surrogate Consent in the Absence of an Advance Directive
July 1, 2001 (*continued*)

State & Citation	General Type of Statute	Priority of Surrogates (in absence of appointed proxy or guardian with health powers)	Limitations on Types of Decisions	Disagreement Process Among Priority Surrogates
38. WYOMING Wyo. Stat. 1997 § 3-5-209 and § 35-22-105(b) (1998)	Durable Power of Attorney Statute and Living Will Statute (Identical provisions)	• All family members who can be contacted through reasonable diligence	Limited to withholding or withdrawal of life-sustaining procedures, and patient is in terminal condition or irreversible coma	Consensus required
UNIFORM HEALTH-CARE DECISIONS ACT	Comprehensive Health Care Decisions Act	• Individual orally designated by patient • Spouse • Adult child • Parent • Sibling • Close friend	None listed	Majority rule

© ABA Commission on Legal Problems of the Elderly, 2001. Used by permission.
The American Bar Association acknowledges The West Group for providing access to on-line legal research.

(iii) Health Care Surrogate Decision-Making Legislation
July 1, 2001

Living Will Statutes	Proxy Statues	Default Surrogate Consent Statutes	EMS-DNR Statutes (Non-hospital DNR Orders)
48 States	51 States	37 States	34 States
Alabama			
† Alaska	Alabama	Alabama	...
Arizona	† Alaska	...	Alaska
Arkansas	Arizona	Arizona	Arizona
California	* Arkansas	Arkansas	Arkansas
Colorado	California	(California—Limited)	California
Connecticut	Colorado	Colorado	Colorado
Delaware	Connecticut	Connecticut	Connecticut
† D.C.	Delaware	Delaware	...
Florida	D.C.	D.C.	...
Georgia	Florida	Florida	Florida
† Hawaii	Georgia	Georgia	Georgia
† Idaho	† Hawaii	Hawaii	Hawaii
† Illinois	† Idaho	Idaho	Idaho
Indiana	† Illinois	Illinois	Illinois
Iowa	Indiana	Indiana	Indiana
Kansas	Iowa	Iowa	...
Kentucky	Kansas	...	Kansas
Louisiana	Kentucky	Kentucky	Kentucky
Maine	Louisiana	Louisiana	...
† Maryland	Maine	Maine	...
...	† Maryland	Maryland	Maryland
...	Massachusetts	...	...
† Minnesota	Michigan	...	Michigan
Mississippi	† Minnesota	...	...
Missouri	Mississippi	Mississippi	...
† Montana	Missouri	...	...
Nebraska	† * Montana	Montana	Montana
Nevada	Nebraska	...	...
New Hamp.	Nevada	Nevada	Nevada
New Jersey	New Hamp.	...	New Hamp.
New Mexico	New Jersey	...	...
...	New Mexico	New Mexico	New Mexico
† North Carolina	New York	(New York—Limited)	New York
North Dakota	North Carolina	North Carolina	North Carolina
Ohio	North Dakota	North Dakota	...
† Oklahoma	Ohio	Ohio	Ohio
† Oregon	† Oklahoma	(Oklahoma—Limited)	Oklahoma
Pennsylvania	† Oregon	Oregon	...
Rhode Island	* Pennsylvania	...	...
South Carolina	Rhode Island	...	Rhode Island
South Dakota	South Carolina	South Carolina	South Carolina
† Tennessee	South Dakota	South Dakota	...
† Texas	† Tennessee	...	Tennessee
† Utah	† Texas	Texas	Texas
Vermont	† Utah	Utah	Utah
Virginia	Vermont	...	...
Washington	Virginia	Virginia	Virginia
West Virginia	Washington	Washington	Washington
Wisconsin	West Virginia	West Virginia	West Virginia
† Wyoming	Wisconsin	...	Wisconsin
	† Wyoming	Wyoming	Wyoming

Code:
Underlined states have a combined advance directive statute merging Health Care Proxies, Living Wills, and (if Surrogate column is underlined) surrogate provisions applicable in the absence of an advance directive.

* Health care proxy is contained only within living will statute. Thus, proxy authority may be limited to terminal illness or PVS.

† State has special mental health advance directive statute.

ABA Commission on Legal Problems of the Elderly, Washington, D.C. (2000).

(iv) Health-Care Decisions Statutes Citations
July 1, 2001

Living Will Statutes

Ala. Code §§ 22-8A-1 to -10 (1997) combined health decisions act, enacted in 1997 (amends earlier statute).

Alaska Stat. §§ 18.12.010 to -.100 (Supp. 1990).

Ariz. Rev. Stat. Ann. §§ 36-3201 to -3262 (1992), combined health decisions act, enacted in 1992 (replaces >86 law).

Ark. Code Ann. §§ 20-17-201 to -218 (Supp. 1989).

Cal. Probate Code §§ 4600 to 4948 (West 1999), combined health decisions act, enacted 1999.

Colo. Rev. Stat. §§ 15-18-101 to -113 (1987 & Supp. 1990).

Conn. Gen Stat. §§ 19a-570 to -575 (1992), as amended by 1993 Conn. Acts 93-407 (H.B. 7244) (Reg. Sess.).

Del. Code Ann. tit. 16, §§ 2501-2517 (substantially revised 1996).

D.C. Code Ann. §§ 6-2421 to 2430 (1989).

Fla. Stat. Ann. §§ 765.101 to .404 (West 1999), combined health decisions act enacted in 1992.

Ga. Code Ann. §§ 31-32-1 to 12 (1985 & Supp. 1989).

Hawaii Rev. Stat. §§ 327E-1 to -16 (West 1999), combined health decisions act, enacted 1999, replacing more limited statute. Idaho Code §§ 39-4501 to -4509 (1985 & Supp. 1989).

Illinois—755 ILCS 35/1 to 35/10 (formerly Ill. Ann. Stat. ch. 110 1/2 para. § 701-710).

Ind. Code Ann. §§ 16-36-4-1 to -21 (West 1994).

Iowa Code Ann. §§ 144A.1 to -11 (West Supp. 1989).

Kan. Stat. Ann. §§ 65-28, 101 to -28, 109 (1985).

Ky. Rev. Stat. §§ 311.621 to .643 (Supp. 1994), combined health decisions act enacted in 1994 (replaces 1990 law).

La. Rev. Stat. Ann. §§ 40:1299.58.1 to -10 (West Supp. 1987).

Me. Rev. Stat. Ann. tit. 18-A, §§ 5-801 to -817 (Supp. 1996), enacted in 1995. combined health decisions act.

Md. Health-Gen. Code Ann. §§ 5-601 to -608 (1993), combined health decisions statute, enacted 1993.

Minn. Stat. §§ 145C.01 to -.16 (Supp. 1998), combined health decisions act enacted 1998, replacing former living will and durable power acts; see also mental health advance directive at § 253B.03, Subd. 6b.

Miss. Code Ann. §§ 41-41-201 to -229 (Supp. 1998), enacted in 1998. combined health decisions act.

Mo. Ann. Stat. §§ 459.010 to -055 (Vernon Supp. 1990).

Mont. Code Ann. §§ 50-9-101 to -111, -201 to -206 (1992).

Neb. Rev. Stat. §§ 20-401 to -416 (1993), enacted 1992.

Nev. Rev. Stat. §§ 449.535 to .690 (1991).
N.H. Rev. Stat. Ann. §§ 137-H:1 to -H:16 (Supp. 1988).
N.J. Stat. Ann. §§ 26:2H-53 to -78 (West 1993), combined advance directive act, enacted 1991.
N.M. Laws Ch. 182 (H.B. 483), combined health decisions act, enacted 1995.
N.C. Gen. Stat. Ann. §§ 90-320 to -322 (1991).
N.D. Cent. Code §§ 23-06.4-01 to -14 (Supp. 1993).
Ohio Rev. Code Ann. §§ 2133.01 to -15 (Anderson Supp. 1991).
Okla. Stat. Ann. tit. 63, §§ 3101.1 to .16 (West 1993), combined advance directive act, enacted 1993; see also mental health advance directive act at Okla. Sess. Law Serv. Ch. 251 (H.B. 1353), enacted 1995.
Or. Rev. Stat. §§ 127.505 to 127.660, and 127.995 (West 1996), combined health decisions act, enacted 1993.
Pa. Stat. Ann. tit. 20, §§ 5401 to 5416 (Purdon 1993), enacted 1992.
R.I. Gen Laws §§ 23-4.11-1 to -14 (1992).
S.C. Code Ann. §§ 44-77-10 to -160 (Law. Co-op Supp. 1988).
S.D. Codified Laws Ann. §§ 34-12D-1 to -17 (1991).
Tenn. Code Ann. §§ 32-11-101 to -110 (Supp. 1988).
Tex. Health & Safety Code Ann. §§ 166.031 to .051 (Vernon Supp. 1990).
Utah Code Ann. §§ 75-2-1101 to 1119 (Supp. 1993).
Vt. Stat. Ann. tit. 18, §§ 5251-5262 and tit. 13, § 1801 (Supp. 1987).
Va. Code §§ 54.1-2981 to -2993 (Supp. 1992), combined health decisions act, enacted 1992.
Wash. Rev. Code Ann. §§ 70.122.010 to -.905 (Supp. 1989).
W. Va. Code §§ 16-30-1 to -10 (1985).
Wisc. Stat. Ann. §§ 154.01 to -.15 (West 1989).
Wyo. Stat. §§ 35-22-101 to -109 (Supp. 1990).

Health Care Power of Attorney Statutes

Ala. Code §§ 22-8A-1 to -10 (1997) combined health decisions act, enacted in 1997 (amends earlier statute that did not contain power of attorney provisions); must be read in combination with Durable Power of Attorney Act, § 26-1-2, revised 1997.
Alaska Stat. §§ 13.26.332 to -.356 (Supp. 1990), particularly § 13.26.344(1), health care agent authority enacted 1988.
Ariz. Rev. Stat. Ann. §§ 36-3201 to -3262 (1992), combined health decisions act, enacted in 1992.
1999 Arkansas Laws Act 1448 (H.B. 1331), enacted 4/15/99. See also proxy authorization in Living Will statute, Ark. Code Ann. §§ 20-17-201 to -218 (Supp. 1989).
Cal. Probate Code §§ 4600 to 4948 (West 1999), combined health decisions act, enacted 1999.

Colo. Rev. Stat., §§ 15-14-501 to -509 (1992), enacted 1992.

Conn. Gen. Stat. § 1-43 (1991) re durable powers of attorney, and Conn. Gen. Stat. §§ 19a-570 to -575 (1992), re health care agents, both amended by 1993 Conn. Acts 93-407 (H.B.7244) (Reg. Sess.).

Del. Code Ann. tit. 16, § 2501-2509 (1983).

D.C. Code Ann., §§ 21-2201 to -2213 (1989), enacted 1989.

Fla. Stat. Ann. §§ 765.101 to .404 (West 1999), combined health decisions act enacted in 1992.

Ga. Code Ann., §§ 31-36-1 to -13 (1990), enacted 1990.

Hawaii Rev. Stat. §§ 327E-1 to -16 (West 1999), combined health decisions act, enacted 1999, replacing more limited statute.

Idaho Code, §§ 39-4501 to -4509, specifically § 39-4505 (Supp. 1990), enacted 1988.

Illinois – 755 ILCS 45/4-1 to 4-12 (formerly Ill. Ann. Stat. Ann. ch. 110 1/2, para. 804-1 to -12, enacted 1987).

Ind. Code Ann. §§ 30-5-1 to 30-5-10 (West 1991), particularly 30-5-5-17 re health care agent authority, enacted in 1991, and see also § 16-36-1-1 to -14 (West 1994) re health care consent.

Iowa Code Ann. §§ 144B.1 to .12 (West Supp. 1991), enacted 1991.

Kan. Stat. Ann. §§ 58-625 to -632 (Supp. 1989), enacted in 1989.

Ky. Rev. Stat. §§ 311.621 to 311.643 (Supp. 1994), enacted in 1994 (replaces a 1990 law).

La. Civ. Code Ann. Art. 2997 (West 1990).

Me. Rev. Stat. Ann. tit. 18A, §§ 5-801 to -817 (Supp. 1996), enacted in 1995, replacing more limited statute.

Md. Health-Gen. Code Ann. §§ 5-601 to -608 (1993), combined health decisions statute enacted 1993.

Mass. Gen. Laws Ann. ch. 201D (West Supp. 1991), enacted 1990.

Mich. Comp. Laws Ann. §§ 333.5651 (West 2001), enacted 1996, and §§ 700.5501 to-.5520 (West 2001), enacted 1998, effective 4/1/00.

Minn. Stat. §§ 145C.01 to -.16 (Supp. 1998), combined health decisions act enacted 1998, replacing former living will and durable power acts; see also mental health advance directive at § 253B.03, Subd. 6b.

Miss. Code Ann. §§ 41-41-201 to -229 (Supp. 1998), enacted in 1998, replacing 1990 act; combined health decisions act.

Mo. Ann. Stat. §§ 404.700 to .735 (West 1991), health care agent authority enacted 1991.

Mont. Code Ann. §§ 50-9-101 to -111, and 50-9-201 to -206 (1992), enacted 1985 with proxy added 1991.

Neb. Rev. Stat. §§ 30-3401 to -3432 (1993), enacted 1992.

Nev. Rev. Stat. §§ 449.800 to .860 (Supp. 1991) enacted 1987.

N.H. Rev. Stat. Ann. §§ 137-J:1 to -J:16 (1993), enacted 1991.

N.J. Stat. Ann. §§ 26:2H-53 to -78 (West 1993), combined advance directive act, enacted 1991.

N.M. Laws Ch. 182 (H.B. 483), combined health decisions act, enacted 1995; see also durable power of attorney for health care act at N.M. Stat. Ann. §§ 45-5-501 and -502 (1989).

N.Y. Pub. Health Law §§ 2980 to 2994 (McKinney Supp. 1991), enacted 1990.

N.C. Gen. Stat. §§ 32A-15 to -26 (1991), enacted 1991.

N.D. Cent. Code §§ 23-06.5-01 to -18 (Supp. 1993), enacted April 18, 1991.

Ohio Rev. Code, §§ 1337.11 to .17 (Anderson Supp. 1991), enacted 1989.

Okla. Stat. Ann. tit. 63, §§ 3101.1 to .16 (West 1993), combined advance directive act, enacted 1992.

Or. Rev. Stat. §§ 127.505 to .660, and 127.995 (West 1996), combined health decisions act created 1993.

20 Pa. Cons. Stat. Ann. §§ 5601-5607 (Purdon's Supp. 1990), enacted in 1982, and see Pa. Stat. Ann. tit. 20, §§ 5401 to 5416 (1993), enacted 1992.

R.I. Gen. Laws §§ 23-4.10-1 to -2 (Supp. 1993), enacted 1986.

S.C. Code §§ 62-5-504, enacted April 8, 1992 (S.B. 541) (See also § 62-5-501 re durable power of attorney).

S.D. Codified Laws Ann. §§ 34-12C-1 to -8, and §§ 59-7-2.1 to -2.8 (Supp. 1992), health care agent authority enacted 1990.

Tenn. Code Ann. §§ 34-6-201 to -214 (Supp. 1991), enacted 1990.

Tex. Health & Safety Code Ann. §§ 166.151 to .166 (West 1993), enacted 1989.

Utah Code Ann. §§ 75-2-1101 to -1119 (Supp. 1993), enacted 1985.

Vt. Stat. Ann. tit. 14, §§ 3451 to 3467 (1989), enacted 1988.

Va. Code §§ 54.1-2981 to -2993 (Supp. 1992), combined health decisions act, enacted 1992, replacing a 1989 act.

Wash. Rev. Code Ann. §§ 11.94.010 to .900 (Supp. 1990) (health care agent authority enacted 1989).

W. Va. Code §§ 16-30A-1 to -20 (Supp. 1990), enacted in 1990.

Wis. Stat. Ann. §§ 155.01 to .80, and 11.243.07(6m) (West 1990), enacted 1990.

Wyo. Stat. §§ 3-5-201 to -214 (Supp. 1993).

Special Mental Health Advance Directives

1996 Alaska Laws Ch. 63 (S.B. 159), enacted 6/17/96, effective 9/15/96, and codified at Alaska Stat. § 47.30.950 to .980 (1996).

1999 Arizona Laws Ch. 83, § 17, effective August 6, 1999, codified at Ariz. Rev. Stat. Ann. §§ 36-3281 to 36-3287.

Idaho, 1998 Idaho Laws Ch. 81 (S.B. 1358), enacted 3/18/98 and effective 7/1/99, codified at Idaho Code §§ 66-601 to 66-613.

Illinois. 755 ILCS 43/1 to 43/115 enacted Dec. 15, 1995, effective June 1, 1996.

Haw. Rev. Stat. ว327F (Michie 1995), enacted 1992.

Md. Laws Ch. 189 (H.B. 127), approved April 20, 2001.

Minn. Stat. Ann. § 253B.03 (West 1995), enacted 1991.

2001 Montana Laws Ch. 533 (H.B. 583), approved May 1, 2001.

N.C. Session Laws 1997-442, effective January 1, 1998, codified at N.C. Gen. Stat. §§ 122C-71 to -77.

Okla. Stat. Ann. tit. 43A §§ 11-101 to 11-113, enacted 1995.

Or. Rev. Stat. §§ 127.700 to 127.735 and 127.995 (West 1996), enacted 1993.

2000 Tenn. Laws Pub. Ch. 947 (H.B. 3004). Eff. June 23, 2000.

Vernon's Texas Code Ann., Civil Practice & Remedies Code § 137.001 to -.011, enacted 1997.

Utah Code Ann. 1953 § 62A-12-501 to -504, enacted 1996.

1999 Wyoming Laws Ch. 167 (H.B. 26), approved 3/3/99.

Surrogate Consent Statutes

Ala. Code §§ 22-8A-1 to -10 (1997), specifically § 22-8A-10, combined health decisions act, enacted in 1997 (amends earlier statute that did not contain surrogate provisions).

Ariz. Rev. Stat. Ann. § 36-3231 (1992), enacted in 1992 as part of combined health decisions act.

Ark. Stat. Ann. § 20-17-214 (1991) and § 20-9-602 (1987), addresses consent generally.

Cal. Probate Code §§ 4711 to 4727 (West 1999), enacted 1999 as part of combined health decisions act; see also Cal. Health & Safety Code § 1418.8 (1996) re: medical interventions affecting nursing facility residents.

Colo. Rev. Stat. §§ 15-18.5-101 to -104 (1992).

Conn. Gen Stat. §§ 19a-570 to -571 (Supp. 1991).

Del. Code Ann. tit. 16, § 2507 (1996).

D.C. Code Ann. § 21-2210 (1989).

Fla. Stat. Ann. §₃765.401 to .404 (West 1999), enacted as part of combined health decisions act.

Ga. Code Ann. § 31-9-2 (1991), addresses consent generally; *see also* Ga. Code Ann. § 31-36A-1 to A-7, enacted 1999, which applies to facility admission, discharge, and transfer decisions.

Hawaii Rev. Stat. §§ 327E-1 to -16 (West 1999), combined health decisions act, enacted 1999, replacing more limited statute.

Idaho Code § 39-4303 (1985), addresses consent generally.

Illinois—755 ILCS 40/1 to 40/55 (1997).

Ind. Code Ann § 16-8-12-4 (1988).

Iowa Code Ann. § 144A.7 (West 1991).

Ky. Rev. Stat. § 311.631 (Supp. 1994), enacted in 1994 as part of combined health decisions act.

La. Rev. Stat. Ann. § 40:1299.53 (1975).

Me. Rev. Stat. Ann. tit. 18a, §§ 5-801 to 5-817 (1996) (see especially § 5-805); and tit. 24, § 2905 (1988), addresses consent generally.

Md. Health-Gen. Code Ann. § 5-605 (1993), enacted 1993 as part of combined health decisions act.

Miss. Code Ann. § 41-41-211 (Supp. 1998), enacted in 1998 and § 41-41-215, enacted 1999; part of combined health decisions act.

Mont. Code Ann. § 50-9-106 (1992).

Nev. Rev. Stat. §§ 449.535 to .690 (1991), specifically § 449.626.

N.M. Laws Ch. 182 (H.B. 483), combined health decisions act, enacted 1995. see also living will act at N.M. Stat. Ann. § 24-7-8.1 (1984).

N.Y. Pub. Health Law § 2965 (McKinney Supp. 1991), restricted to do-not-resuscitate decisions.

N.C. Gen. Stat. § 90-322 (1991).

N.D. Cent. Code §§ 23-12-13 (1991), addresses consent generally.

Ohio Rev. Code Ann. § 2133.08(B) (Anderson Supp. 1992).

Okla. Stat. Ann. Tit. 63, § 3102A, enacted April 16, 1997, effective Nov. 1, 1997, establishes limited surrogate consent, applicable only to experimental treatments, tests or drugs.

Or. Rev. Stat. § 127.635 (1993), part of combined health decisions act created 1993.

S.C. Code Ann. §§ 44-66-10 to -80 (1990).

S.D. Codified Laws §§ 34-12C-3 (1991), addresses consent generally.

Tex. [Health & Safety] Code Ann. §§ 166.035 and 116.039 (Vernon 1989) and Tex. [Health & Safety] Code §§ 313.001 to -007 (Vernon 1993).

Utah Code Ann. § 75-2-1105(2), and § 78-14-5(4) (1991), addresses consent generally.

Va. Code § 54.1-2986 (Supp. 1992).

Wash. Rev. code Ann. § 7.70.065 (West 1991), addresses consent generally.

W. Va. Code §§ 16-30B-1 to -16 (1992), enacted 1992, replacing a more limited provision; revised 1997.

Wyo. Stat. §§ 3-5-201 and -209, and §§ 35-22-101 and -105 (1992).

EMS DNR Statutes

Alaska Stat. §§ 18.12.010 to .100 (Michie 1998).

Ariz. Rev. Stat. Ann. §§ 36-3251 (West 1999).

Ark. Code Ann. §§ 20-13-901 to -911 (1997).

Cal. Probate Code § 4753 (West 1999).

Colo. Rev. Stat. Ann. §§ 15-18.6-101 to -108 (West 1999).

Conn. Gen Stat. §§ 19a-580d (1998).

Fla. Stat. Ann. § 401.45(3)(West 1999), but see §§ 395.1041(3); 400.142(3). 400.4255(3); 400.487(7); 400.6095(8); and 400.621(3) for its application to various health care providers.

Ga. Code Ann. §§ 31-39-1 to -9 (1999).

Hawaii Rev. Stat. § 321-222 and § 321-229.5 (Michie 1998).

Idaho Code Ann. §§ 39-150 to -165 (1998).

210 ILCS 50/3.30(a)(7), implemented by 77 Ill. Admin. Code § 515.380
et seq.

Ind. Code Ann. § 16-36-5-1 to -24 (West 199).

Kan. Stat. Ann. §§ 65-4941 to -4949 (1997).

Ky. Rev. Stat. § 311.623(3) (Banks-Baldwin 1999).

La. Rev. Stat. Ann. §§ 40:1299.58.1 to -.10 (West 1999).

Md. Health-General Code Ann. §§ 5-601, 5-608 and 5-617 (1998).

Mich. Comp. Laws Ann. §§ 333.1051 to .1067 (West 1998).

Mont. Code Ann. §§ 50-10-101 to -106 (1997).

Nev. Rev. Stat. §§ 450B.400 to -.490 (1997).

N.H. Rev. Stat. Ann. § 151-B:18 (1998).

N.M. Sta. Ann. § 24-10B-4(J) (1998).

N.Y. Pub. Health Law §§ 2960-2978 (McKinney 1999).

N.C. Gen. Stat. §§ 32A-15 to -26 and §§ 90-320 to -322 (applicable to DNR
orders according to health an Attorney General Advisory Opinion 1997
WL 858260 (N.C.A.G.) (December 22, 1997).

Ohio Rev. Code §§ 2133.01 to -.26 (Banks-Baldwin 1999).

Okla. Stat. Ann. tit. 63, § 3131.1 to .14 (West 1999).

R.I. Gen Laws § 23-4.11-1 to .14 ((1998):

S.C. Code Ann. §§ 44-78-10 to -65 (Law. Coop. 1998).

Tenn. Code Ann. §§ 68-140-601 to -604, and 68-11-224 (1998).

Texas Health & Safety Code §§ 166.081 to -.101(West 1999).

Utah Code Ann. §§ 75-2-1105.5 (1998).

Va. Code §§ 54.1-2987.1, -2988, -2989, and -2982 (Lexis 1999).

Wash. Rev. Code § 43.70.480 (199 West 1998).

W. VA. Code §§ 16-30C-1 to -16 (1998).

Wis. Stat. §§ 154.19 to -.29 (West 1999).

Wyo. Stat. Ann. §§ 35-22-201 to -208 (Michie 1998).

*Prepared by the ABA Commission on Legal Problems of the Elderly (2000).
Used by permission.*

APPENDIX K
Consumer Education
(How to Make a Community Presentation on Advance Directives)

by Carol Krohm, M.D. and Scott K. Summers

The key to raising consciousness about advance directives is education. As a committed professional, you can do much to spread the word among clients and patients.

Here is a suggested outline for an in-office or community presentation. Use some or all of these ideas; adapt them to suit your own style, expertise, and audience.

    I. Welcome and Introductions.

   II. Basic Premises
      A. Most important legal document you will ever sign?
      B. If you don't decide about your health care, someone else will
      C. Directives are NOT "pull-the-plug" documents
      D. Directives ARE personal contingency plans
      E. This can be an emotional subject—and that's OK!
      F. Directives are not forever! Change them as your needs change
      G. Directives can help head off "living probate" (i.e., guardianship)
      H. Tailor make directives to suit YOUR wishes and needs
       I. Get the advice and help you need: doctors, lawyers, spiritual advisors, social workers, family, friends

 III. Introduction to principal state documents
      A. Durable power of attorney for health care or health care proxy (for most people)
      B. Living will (now a limited use document in most states)
      C. Pros and cons of documents

 IV. "Walk Through" of state directives. (Pass out forms. Break, perhaps, for people who want to leave. Reconvene for those who want to remain and fill out forms. Go paragraph by paragraph and answer audience questions as you go.)
      A. Name/address/phones of principal-patient-maker
      B. Name/address/phones/fax/pager/wireless phone/email of agent/ proxy and successors. ***Designation of agent is the most important decision: she or he may be called upon to make end-of-life choices for you.*** Don't pick an agent who can't handle it.
      C. Concept of power/proxy form as broad and expansive: Adapt and "chip away" to limit it and otherwise suit needs
      D. Inclusion or exclusion of certain medical treatments. Don't be absolute. For example, rather than categorically saying

"no ventilator", condition the statement to, say, permit short-term use in a postoperative situation.

E. For some, disease dictates directives. Those with chronic conditions do well to obtain medical advice and carefully state parameters that square with their underlying illnesses.

F. It's utterly impossible to anticipate all medical scenarios. Give very careful consideration to the "elastic clause" section of the directive, where the patient/principal can indicate a generalized (or fallback) care philosophy in the event of either an unanticipated or a terminal condition.

G. Control implementation: keep it open ended with a springing feature. ("This proxy becomes effective upon the written determinations of two medical physicians that I am no longer capable of making personal decisions.") Or, give the directive to a third party, for delivery to the agent/proxy only upon the indicated date or circumstance.

V. Consider (then execute!) related documents

A. Health
  1. Values history
  2. Living will
  3. Organ donation (i.e., back of driver's license)
  4. Declaration of intention for mental health treatments

B. Financial
  1. Durable power of attorney for PROPERTY
  2. Estate planning: intervivos ("living") trusts, etc.

VI. LEAVE GOOD FOOTPRINTS!

A. Carry a pocket card in a wallet or purse

B. Wear a medallion or bracelet

C. Give copies to others: doctor, agent/proxy, facility, family, friends

D. Leave copies in obvious places at home and work in case of emergency

E. Sign up with a directives registry or online service

VII. SPREAD THE WORD!

OFFICE BROCHURES/CLIENT EDUCATION MATERIALS

Please refer to the authors' website, www.AdvanceHealthCareDirectives.com, for an expansive listing of materials suitable for lay use, including updates on new publications.

- Durable Power of Attorney: Planning for Medical Decision Making. National Academy Elder Law Attorneys, Inc. Ordering information: info@naela.com

- Health and Financial Decisions: Legal Tools for Preserving Personal Autonomy. American Bar Association. Ordering information: 202-331-2297.
- Medical Treatment: Decide in Advance. American Association of Retired Persons. Ordering information: 1-800-424-3410
- Talking with Your Doctor about Advance Directives. Last Acts (through Robert Wood Johnson Foundation). Ordering information: www.lastacts.org
- Advice on Advance Directives: Helping You Prepare for Your Health-care. Last Acts (through Robert Wood Johnson Foundation). Ordering information: www.lastacts.org
- Shape Your Health Care Future with Health Care Advance Directives. AARP, American Bar Association, and American Medical Association. Ordering information: www.abanet.org/ftp/pub/elderly/ad-ftp.wpd.

APPENDIX L
Internet Resources

General Interest

	Description	Address
Last Acts	A national coalition to improve care and caring at the end of life. (Resource center RWJF)	www.lastacts.org
National Public Radio: Exploring death in America	Excellent bibliography, resources, readings	www.npr.org/programs/death
Public Broadcasting Service (PBS)	"Before I Die" (Bill Moyers series)	www.pbs.org/wnet/bid
American Hospice Foundation	Support for professionals and consumers	www.americanhospice.org
ABCD Americans for Better Care of the Dying	Helps organizations and individuals focus on reforms to improve care	www.abcd-caring.org
Hospice Foundation of America	Education for professionals and patients	www.hospicefoundation.org
Growth House, Inc	Comprehensive resources with outstanding links for patients and professionals	www.growthhouse.org
Project on Death in America	Innovations for public and professional education	www.soros.org/death

Professional Resources

American Academy of Hospice and Palliative Medicine	Information for professionals interested in palliative care	www.aahpm.org
Hastings Center	Research institute ethical issues	www.thehastingscenter.org
American Society of Law, Medicine, and Ethics	Interdisciplinary approach	www.aslme.org
Midwest Bioethics Center	Community-based ethics center for professionals and consumers	www.midbio.org
American Bar Association, Commission on Legal Problems of the Elderly	General and state specific information about advance directives	www.abanet.org
Aging with Dignity	Sample directives plus Five Wishes Program (detailed values history)	www.agingwithdignity.org
United States Living Will Registry	National service for registry of advance directives	www.uslivingwillregistry.com
Partnership for Caring	End-of-Life Law Digest; forms for advance directives by state (small fee)	www.partnershipforcaring.org
ASBH	American Society for Bioethics and Humanities	www.asbh.org

Joint commission on Accreditation of Healthcare Organizations (JCAHO)	Performance improvement for organizations	www.jcaho.org
The Park Ridge Center	Study of Health, Faith, and Ethics	www.parkridgecenter.org
The EPEC project	Physician education background and description of program	Epec.net
The EPERC project	Central Repository for educational resources	www.eperc.mcw.edu
McLean Center for Clinical Medical Ethics	University of Chicago	www.uchicago.edu/uchi/ resteach/macleannotice.html
American Medical Association	Medical ethics resources for physicians	www.ama-assn.org
Hospice and Palliative Nurses Association	Education and research for nursing profession	www.hpna.org
Robert Wood Johnson Foundation	Provides grants for education efforts	www.rwjf.org

Organ, Tissue, and Blood Donation

UNOS	General information about tissue and organ donation	www.unos.org
Transplant for Life	Listing of preferences or prohibition by faith	www.transplantforlife.org

| Cord Blood Registry | Education and resources for banking umbilical cord blood | www.cordblood.com |

This listing is but a sample of the many outstanding resources available online. For updates and additional links, please refer to the website maintained by authors Krohm and Summers: www.AdvanceHealthCareDirectives.com

APPENDIX M
Selected Bibliography

Beauchamp, Tom and Childress, James *Principles of Biomedical Ethics*. 4th Edition. New York: Oxford University Press, 1994.

Buchanan, Allen and Brock, Dan *Deciding for Others: The Ethics of Surrogate Decision Making*. New York: Cambridge University Press, 1995.

Byock, Ira *Dying Well: Peace and Possibilities at the End of Life*. New York: Riverhead Books, 1998.

Christakis, N *Death Foretold Prophecy and Prognosis in Medical Care*. University of Chicago Press: Chicago, IL, 1999.

Collin, Francis, et al *Durable Powers of Attorney and Health Care Directives*. Eagan, MN: West Group, 1999.

Cooper Hammon, ML and Taylor, G *Organ and Tissue Donation: A Reference for Clergy*. 4th Edition. SEOPF/UNOS, 2000.

Devettere, Raymond *Practical Decision Making in Health Care Ethics: Cases and Concepts*. Washington, DC: Georgetown University Press, 1995.

Dickson, Donald *Law in the Health and Human Services: A Guide for Social Workers, Psychologists, Psychiatrists, and Related Professionals*. New York: The Free Press, 1995.

End-of-Life Law Digest: A Quarterly Review of Legislative Activity and Case Law. Partnership for Caring, Inc., Washington, DC. (no date)

Joint Commission Topics in Clinical Care Improvement: Advance Directives. Joint Commission on Accreditation of Healthcare Organizations, Oakbrook Terrace, IL, 1999.

Lieberson, Alan *Advance Medical Directives*. Clark, Boardman, Callaghan, Inc., 2000.

Lipson, J, Dibble, S and Minarik, P (editors) *Culture and Nursing Care: A Pocket Guide*. UCSF Nursing Press: San Francisco, CA, 1996.

Lynn, Joanne, Schuster, Janice and Kabcenell, A *Improving Care for the End of Life: A Sourcebook for Health Care Managers and Clinicians*. Oxford University Press, New York: New York, 2000.

Marquis, Damon *Advance Care Planning: A Practical Guide for Physicians*. AMA Press: Chicago, IL, 2001.

The Park Ridge Center for the Study of Health, Faith, and Ethics Religious Traditions and Health Care Decisions: A Quick Reference to Fifteen Religious

Traditions and Their Application in Health Care. The Park Ridge Center, 211 E. Ontario, Suite 800, Chicago, IL 60611-3215, 1995–1999.

Walsh, Arthur, et al. *Mental Capacity: Legal and Medical Aspects of Assessment and Treatment.* Illinois: Clark, Boardman, and Callaghan, 1994.

For additional resources, please refer to the website maintained by authors Krohm and Summers: www.advancehealthcaredirectives.com

APPENDIX N
Sample Wallet Cards

1. LIVING WILL

LIVING WILL NOTIFICATION CARD

I, ——————————————————, have signed a living will. If my condition is critical or life threatening, a copy of it may be obtained from:

Name: ————————————————————

Address: ————————————————————

Phone: ————————————————————

Phone: ————————————————————

Fax/Email: ————————————————————

2. POWER OF ATTORNEY (OR PROXY) FOR HEALTH CARE

POWER OF ATTORNEY FOR HEALTH CARE
NOTIFICATION CARD

I, ——————————————————, have signed a power of attorney or proxy for health care (and/or a declaration for mental health treatment), naming an agent or proxy to make all of my health care decisions for me if I am unable to do so.

My agent is: ————————————————————

Name: ————————————————————

Address:————————————————————

Phone: ————————————————————

Phone: ————————————————————

Fax/Email: ————————————————————

3. ORGAN DONOR CARD   (Note: many jurisdictions also provide for organ donation on the backs of driver's licenses or state-issued identification cards. If organ donation is contemplated, make certain that instructions in both an organ donation card or a driver's license and a health care power of attorney or proxy are consistent.)

(Print on two sides or fold in half:)

ORGAN DONOR CARD

I, —————————————————————————————, hereby make the following anatomical gift, if medically acceptable, to take effect upon my death:

—————— Any organs or parts —————— Entire body

Only the following specific organs or parts:

———————————————————————

Limitations or special wishes, if any:

———————————————————————

Donor signature: ————————————————————————

Date of birth: —————————— Date signed: ——————————

Witness signature: ——————————————————————

Witness signature: ——————————————————————

This is a legal document under the Uniform Anatomical Gift Act or similar laws.

APPENDIX O
Sample Letter from Lawyer to Client Upon Execution of Advance Health Care Directives

Dear Client:

I have been pleased to assist you with the preparation and execution of advance health care directives. You have made a wise set of decisions by putting into place a personal contingency plan in case you someday become unable to make your own medical choices.

As we discussed, it is essential that you now leave good "footprints" about your directives, for they are worthless if others do not know about them. It is for this reason that I am enclosing several photocopies in addition to the (original) (duplicate originals) (conformed copies). Provide copies to your attending or primary care physician and to your (agent) (proxy), as well as any other "need-to-know" personnel such as your spiritual advisor or staff of a hospital or residential facility. Place copies at home and at work where others are likely to find them in the event of an emergency. Also consider placing them with a registry service. On all such copies, attach a notation where the original is located.[1]

As you may see fit, make additional photocopies and give them to family members and friends. With your permission, I am keeping a copy for my files. I do NOT suggest storing the original in a safety deposit box, for it may be difficult to retrieve in case of an emergency. (Instead, keep a photocopy in your box.) Complete your "footprints" by filling out and carrying the attached wallet card.

It is also very important that you now take steps to orally validate your directives with your agent and other key people. I know that this may be distasteful and difficult for both you and your "important others"—but it is an essential step for assuring that your directives are carried out properly. Sit with each individual and go over the document, and pointedly reiterate your wishes. Try to update such conversations at least once a year. Take extra time with your (agent) (proxy) and any nominated successors, for it is they who will be indispensable in carrying out your instructions and wishes.

Know that discussing and orally validating your directives may provide both you and your agent with important measures of assurance and relief. You will achieve a measure of certainty that your intentions are well understood. Similarly, your agent will be able to act on your behalf some day with comfort and self-assurance.

---

[1] Some jurisdictions pointedly provide that photocopies shall be construed to be as valid as an original. Accordingly, adapt this passage to comport with statute.

Also keep in mind that your directives are NOT forever! Over time, your wishes and thinking and needs regarding medical care are likely to change. You may also want or need to change the people who may "stand in your shoes" and make medical decisions for you. If at some future time you wish to make changes, it is best to draw up a new set of directives. In this event, feel free to contact me. Similarly, if you permanently relocate to another state, it is a good idea to re-execute directives using the formalities of your new residence.

You will recall my point that advance health care directives do NOT address your financial concerns. Directives are but a part of a holistic contingency plan for decisional incapacity. In the event you have not done so, I urge that you also take steps to prospectively tend to your financial and property issues through judicious use of (intervivos trusts) (a durable power of attorney for property). A thoughtful plan about your property—in addition to your commendable forward thinking about your health care—will go far to minimize the possibility that you or your money will ever be subjected to "living probate" (that is, a judicially-supervised guardianship or conservatorship, if ever you become decisionally or communicatively incapacitated). As we discussed, a complete plan for your property also includes (wills) (trusts) (gifting programs).

I also wish to commend you for signing the back of your driver's license and becoming a prospective organ donor. As we know, there is a significant shortage of willing donors, and the list of desperately needy patients grows longer each day. It is exceedingly important that you now tell your immediate family that you have committed to organ donation, for they too may need to consent at some future point.

Perhaps you will agree with my observation that advance health care directives now are the most important legal documents any of us will ever sign. I have been pleased and honored to assist you with the exceedingly profound and important decisions you have made.

Very truly yours,

Attorney at Law

APPENDIX P
Sample Instructions to My Agent About My Advance Health Care Directives

To my (agent) (proxy) (surrogate) (representative):

Attached are my (living will) (durable power of attorney for health care) (intention to become an organ donor) (declaration of preferences for mental health treatment). These contain my instructions and desires about my medical care if ever I become decisionally incapacitated or noncommunicative.

It is my wish that you become my "deputy" and make choices on my behalf if ever I'm unable to make my own medical decisions. I have designated you because I believe that you know me well enough to choose as I would likely choose for myself. I also believe that you have the courage—and love—to make exceedingly difficult decisions about me, should the need arise.

Please review these documents now, and from time to time hereafter, for they contain general instructions about the medical care that I wish to have. We also should go over them once a year, so that we keep our understandings up-to-date. If at any time you have questions about my medical preferences, please raise them with me.

We both need to keep in mind that the wishes I've expressed here are necessarily general in nature. Neither you, nor I, nor my doctors, can possibly anticipate every contingency or scenario. I'm counting on you—and your knowledge about me—to work with my doctors, "fill in the blanks" (if need be), and make fitting choices.

I do not wish to impose. If for whatever reason you cannot serve, or choose not to serve, please know that you may resign as my "deputy". I have designated successors to you, just in case.

I am especially grateful that you will "be there" for me some day. Please accept my profound and profuse thanks.

About the Authors

Carol Krohm, M.D. has over twenty years of clinical experience as a family physician. She also has worked in key managerial capacities, including service as a medical director with two health maintenance organizations. Dr. Krohm has taught and lectured extensively in medical school and residency programs and has earned several teaching awards. Krohm holds a medical degree from Rush University, a master of public health (MPH) from the University of Illinois at Chicago, and is board certified in family practice with a certificate of added qualifications in geriatrics.

Scott K. Summers maintains a private law practice in a Chicago suburb. Author of several articles, his writings also include *Guardianship and Conservatorship: A Handbook for Lawyers*, which was published in 1996 by the American Bar Association. A graduate of the Northern Illinois University College of Law, Summers holds a masters from Northwestern University's Kellogg Graduate School of Management. Additionally, he is a Certified Financial Planner.

Dr. Krohm and Mr. Summers trace interest in end-of-life planning to service together in the early 1980s as board members of one of the first hospices to be founded in Illinois. Their subsequent collaborative interest in advance health care directives was demonstrated in an article entitled "Light in the Gray Zones", which appeared in a 1993 issue of EXPERIENCE, a magazine published by the Senior Lawyers Division of the American Bar Association.

In addition to their writings on the subject, Krohm and Summers speak individually and jointly about advance directives, to both institutional and community groups. Their dynamic and highly informative presentations are well received by appreciative audiences.

Index

A

Acceptance of directive, barrier to
  ceding autonomy, § 5.20
  of clergy/spiritual advisor, § 9.26
  cultural/religious beliefs, § 5.18,
    § 6.08
  elastic clause reliance, § 5.19
  for family member, § 6.08
  foreclosure of medical advance,
    § 5.22
  of health care provider, § 8.09
  of medical professional, § 8.09
  opinion/feeling of others, § 5.21
  procrastination/fear, § 5.23
  views on life/death, § 5.17,
    § 6.08
Active duty military personnel,
  § 11.16
Advance health care directive. *See
  also* Advance health care
  directive, future of; Durable
  power of attorney (proxy)
  ambiguous, § 1.08
  conflicting values/philosophy on,
    § 1.05
  cost-effectiveness of, § 12.19
  cost of, § 5.26
  definition of, § 2.01, § 3.03
  disinclination to honor, § 1.06
  electronic, § 12.12
  in emergency situation, § 1.11
  enforcement of, § 1.10
  failure of, § 1.04
  flexibility of, § 1.07, § 5.14
  genesis of, § 7.02
  indicating existence of, § 1.03,
    § 1.09

  lack of permanence of, § 1.07
  as mandatory, § 1.01
  multidisciplinary approach to,
    § 9.02
  poorly drawn, § 1.08
  as provoking controversy, § 1.03
  public reaction to, § 1.02, § 5.01
  re-execution of, § 1.07, § 2.15,
    § 5.12, § 8.24
  revocation of, § 1.07, § 2.01, § 4.19,
    § 5.12, § 8.24, § 11.23
Advance health care directive, future
  of, § 12.01–§ 12.02, § 12.04
  educating professionals, § 12.15
  educating public, § 12.14
  ethical issues, § 12.03
  forum shopping, § 12.18
  implementation, § 12.05–§ 12.12
  shifting attitudes, § 12.16
  utilization, § 12.19
African American, and directive use,
  § 5.06, § 8.15
Agent
  choosing, § 1.05, § 2.12, § 2.17
  decision-making dilemmas for,
    § 6.09
  as guardian, § 2.02
  health care provider as, § 11.14
  honoring of directive by, § 1.03,
    § 1.06
  lack of, § 11.18
  physician as, § 8.08
Allied professionals. *See also*
  Clergy/spiritual advisor
  and ethics, § 3.14
American Bar Association's
  Commission on Legal Problems
  of the Elderly, § 4.03

American Medical Association's
 Code of Medical Ethics, § 3.13,
 § 8.16
Anatomical donation, § 2.07, § 11.03
Ancillary/limited purpose health care
 directive, § 2.01. *See also*
 Durable power of attorney for
 property; Living will; Organ
 donation
 guardian nomination, § 2.09
 for mental health treatment, § 2.05
 oral expressions, § 2.08
Anencephalic infant, § 11.02
Anxiety, § 4.16
Artificial hydration, § 2.04, § 6.09,
 § 7.01
Artificial nutrition, § 2.04, § 6.09,
 § 7.01
Asian, and directive use, § 5.06
Assisted suicide, § 4.17, § 7.02,
 § 10.11
Attorney, and drafting directive,
 § 7.03
 capacity issues, § 7.07
 drafting checklist, § 7.05, § 7.09
 initiating discussion, § 7.04, § 12.15
 moving forward, § 7.06
 tips for, § 7.10
 witness for client interview, § 4.06
Attorney perspective, on directives
 case study, § 7.01
 case study critique, § 7.10
 conflicting philosophy/values,
 § 1.05
Automatic expiration, of directive.
 See Sunset date
Autonomy, patient, § 3.03
 and best interests, § 3.05
 ceding, § 5.20
 effect of beneficence on, § 3.09
 and ethics, § 3.06
 and statutes/case law, § 3.07
 and substituted judgment, § 1.05,
 § 3.04

Autopsy, § 2.11, § 11.04
 family review/consent for, § 6.02

B

Baby Jane Doe regulations, § 11.02
Beneficence, § 10.10
 defined, § 3.09
 difference from nonmaleficence,
 § 3.08, § 3.09
Best interests, § 1.05, § 3.07
 defined, § 3.05
Biomedical ethics committee, § 3.15,
 § 12.09
Biotechnology, § 12.20
Blood donation, § 2.07, § 7.11
Blood product use, religious
 prohibition of, § 1.05
Blood transfusion, religious
 prohibition of, § 1.05
Bone marrow donation, § 2.07, § 7.11,
 § 11.05
Bracelet/medallion/necklace, § 1.11,
 § 2.14, § 8.20
Broad grant of authority, § 2.02, § 2.10

C

Capacity
 American Bar Association on,
 § 4.03
 applicable statute for, § 4.02
 definition of, § 4.02
 lawyer-client interview for, § 4.06
 lay observations of, § 4.07
 legal standards of, § 4.18
 medical assessment for, § 3.16,
 § 4.04–§ 4.05
Capacity on occasion (episodic
 lucidity), § 4.10
Cardiopulmonary resuscitation
 (CPR), § 6.09
Clergy/spiritual advisor. *See also*
 Religious belief; Religious/
 spiritual precept, of end-of-life
 decision

barriers to acceptance, § 9.26
barriers to implementation for,
§ 9.27
case study, § 9.01
case study critique, § 9.29
and end-of-life issues, § 9.03
Client issues. *See also* Client issues,
common misconceptions; Client
issues, literature summary
barriers to acceptance,
§ 5.16–§ 5.23
barriers to implementation for,
§ 5.24–§ 5.33
case study, § 5.01
case study critique, § 5.34
right/wrong client for directive,
§ 5.35
Client issues, common
misconceptions, § 5.08. *See also*
Client issues; Client issues,
literature summary
concerning age/health, § 5.09
directive as arbitrary checklist,
§ 5.14
lack of need for, § 5.15
limitations of directives, § 5.11
loss of right to decide, § 5.13
permanency of directives, § 5.12
"pull the plug" document, § 5.10
Client issues, literature summary,
§ 5.02. *See also* Client issues;
Client issues, common
misconceptions
ethnic trends, § 5.06
increasing interest in directives,
§ 5.07
individuals likely to complete,
§ 5.03
need for discussion about
directives, § 5.05
reasons not to have, § 5.04
Clinical depression, § 4.17
Coma, and determining competence,
§ 4.09

Compassion Sabbath, § 9.03
Competence, § 4.01. *See also*
Capacity
judicial determination of, need for,
§ 4.09
medical *vs.* legal determination of,
§ 4.04
Competence, lay observation
comments/cautions
avoiding snap judgments, § 4.08
being decision-neutral, § 4.11
dementia, § 4.15
depression, § 4.17
episodic lucidity, § 4.10
judging on appearance/habits,
§ 4.12
psychiatric disorders, § 4.16
refusing evaluation, § 4.13
temporary incapacitation, § 4.14
as threshold concept, § 4.09
Conservatorship, § 7.09, § 10.08,
§ 11.12
avoiding, § 2.06, § 10.09, § 12.15
and ethics, § 3.12
and incompetence/incapacity,
§ 4.05
Copies, of directive, § 2.13, § 2.14,
§ 2.15, § 5.33, § 5.35, § 7.06,
§ 8.20
Cord Blood Banking Registry, § 11.05
Cord blood donation, § 2.07, § 7.11,
§ 11.05
Cruzan, Nancy, § 5.09
*Cruzan vs. Director, Missouri
Department of Health*, § 3.07,
§ 7.01, § 7.02, § 9.02, § 11.07
Cryonics, § 11.06

D

Death, western medical view of,
§ 1.05
Death with Dignity Act (Oregon),
§ 4.17, § 7.02, § 8.16, § 10.11,
§ 12.18

Decisionally incapacitated child,
§ 2.09
Decisionally incapacitated patient,
§ 8.14, § 8.24, § 10.10,
§ 11.11
Decisions, validity of, § 6.06
Declaration. *See* Living will
Default/fallback standard. *See* Best
interests
Defective directive, § 11.07
Delirium, § 4.15
Dementia, § 4.15
Depression, § 4.15, § 4.16, § 4.17
Diminished capacity, § 4.09
Disability planning, § 12.15
Disposition of remains, § 2.11,
§ 11.03
Divorce/dissolution/annulment of
marriage, § 11.08
Doctor. *See* Physician
Domestic partner/companion, § 11.09
Domestic partnership termination,
§ 11.08
"Do no harm" premise of medicine,
§ 1.05, § 1.06, § 3.08, § 8.02,
§ 8.04, § 8.09
Do Not Resuscitate (DNR) order,
§ 1.03, § 1.11, § 5.25, § 8.07,
§ 10.05, § 10.08
Duplicate originals, of directive,
§ 2.14, § 5.35, § 7.06
Durable power of attorney for
property, § 2.06
to avoid guardianship, § 10.09
determining capacity for, § 4.04
indicating existence of, § 2.14
and springing powers, § 2.11, § 5.13
updating, § 2.15
Durable power of attorney (proxy).
See also Durable power of
attorney (proxy),
comments/cautions
for adult health care decision,
§ 2.01–§ 2.02

determining capacity, § 4.04
for minor child health care
decision, § 2.01–§ 2.02
narrow/broad grant of authority,
§ 2.02
as not "pull-the-plug" document,
§ 5.10
overlap/conflict with living will,
§ 2.04, § 11.07
Durable power of attorney (proxy),
comments/cautions, § 2.10. *See
also* Durable power of attorney
(proxy)
cause of action if directive not
honored, § 7.09
controlling implementation, § 2.11
indicating existence of, § 2.14
keeping direct control of, § 2.13
selecting agent, § 2.12
updating, § 2.15

E

Education, on directive
for professionals, § 8.11, § 12.15
for public/patient, § 8.13, § 12.14
for staff, § 8.19
Education for Physicians on
End-of-Life Care (EPEC), § 8.11
Elastic clause, § 2.14, § 5.19, § 8.24
Electronic storage, of directive,
§ 2.15, § 12.12
Emancipation of minor, § 11.17
Embryo, § 11.10
Emergency health care exemption,
§ 1.11
Emergency response team, § 1.11
Emergency room staff, § 1.11
End-of-life cost containment,
§ 12.19
End of Life Physician Education
Resource Center (EPERC),
§ 8.11
EPEC. *See* Education for Physicians
on End-of-Life Care

EPERC. *See* End of Life Physician
Education Resource Center
Episodic lucidity, § 4.10
Episodic mental illness, § 2.05
*Estate of Taylor ex rel. Taylor v.
Muncie Medical Investors L.P.,*
§ 5.34
Ethics
of advance health care directives,
§ 3.01, § 3.03
of allied professionals, § 3.14
of beneficence, § 3.09
of best interests, § 3.05
committees for, § 3.15, § 8.07,
§ 8.16, § 8.22, § 10.10, § 12.09
and cost of care, § 3.13
of justice in health care delivery,
§ 3.10
of nonmaleficence, § 3.08
and patient autonomy/privacy,
§ 3.06
of professionals, § 3.11–§ 3.14
of substituted judgment, § 3.04
and withdrawing treatment, § 3.13
and withholding treatment, § 3.13
Ethics consultant, § 12.09
Ethnicity, and end-of-life decision,
§ 5.18
European American, and directive
use, § 5.06, § 8.15
Euthanasia, § 4.17, § 7.02, § 8.16,
§ 12.18, § 12.19
passive, § 10.11
Exemption, for emergency health care
provider, § 1.11
Expiration, of directive, § 2.05,
§ 2.11, § 11.07

F

Failure, of directive, § 1.04
through conflicting philosophy,
§ 1.05
through disinclination to honor,
§ 1.06
through lack of knowledge of
existence of, § 1.09
through lack of permanence, § 1.07
through poorly drawn/ambiguous
instruction, § 1.08
through value judgment, § 1.05
Family member
barriers to acceptance of directive
for, § 6.08
barriers to implementation for,
§ 6.09
case study, § 6.01
case study critique, § 6.10
common misconceptions of, § 6.07
conflict among, § 8.16, § 10.10
as decision-maker, § 6.05
disagreement over treatment by,
§ 1.03
disinclination to honor directive,
§ 1.06
and end-of-life-decision, § 5.18
role of extended, § 6.03
role of immediate, § 6.02
validity of decision by, § 6.06
Federally funded hospital, § 1.01,
§ 5.25
File for Life, § 5.34
Firefighter, § 1.11
"Five Wishes" document, § 11.20
Folstein Mini-Mental State
Examination (MMSE), § 4.05
Foreign nationals, § 11.13, § 12.18
Forms, obtaining, § 5.28
Forum shopping, § 12.18
Fourteenth Amendment, § 3.07,
§ 5.34, § 7.02
Friend, role of, § 6.03
Futile care, § 8.16, § 10.10

G

Garger v. New Jersey, § 7.02
General diversion, in absence of
directive, § 10.02. *See also*
Guardian; Guardianship

General diversion (*cont.*)
Do Not Resuscitate (DNR)
protocol, § 1.03, § 1.11, § 5.25,
§ 8.07, § 10.05, § 10.08
informal practice, § 10.03
surrogacy statutes, § 10.04
"Good footprints" principle, § 1.09,
§ 2.17, § 5.35, § 7.06, § 8.20
Griswold v. Connecticut, § 7.02
Guardian. *See also* Guardianship
judicial appointment of, § 2.09,
§ 3.05, § 8.16, § 8.21, § 10.06
nominating, § 2.09
Guardianship, § 1.05, § 2.12, § 6.03,
§ 7.09, § 11.12. *See also*
Guardian
avoiding, § 2.06, § 10.09, § 12.15
and durable power of attorney,
§ 2.02
and ethics, § 3.12
and incompetence/incapacity,
§ 4.01, § 4.05
limitations to, § 10.08
of minor child, § 2.02, § 2.09,
§ 10.06, § 11.17
proceedings for, § 10.07

H

Health Care Consent Act (Indiana),
§ 5.34
Health care ethics committee,
§ 3.15, § 8.07, § 8.16, § 8.22,
§ 10.10
Health care provider, § 8.03. *See also*
Physician
as agent/proxy, § 11.14
barrier to acceptance of directive
for, § 8.09
case study, § 8.01
case study critique, § 8.25
common misconceptions of, § 8.08
executing directive, § 8.06
fact finding by, § 8.04
improving provider participation,
§ 8.07

issue discussion by, § 8.05, § 8.26
tips for, § 8.26
Health care proxy. *See* Durable power
of attorney (proxy)
HELP. *See* Hospitalized Elderly
Longitudinal Project
Heroic life-sustaining measure
agent interest in, § 1.03
physicians and, § 1.06
Hippocratic Oath, § 1.05, § 3.13
Hispanic, and directive use, § 5.06,
§ 8.15
Home health-care agency, § 1.01,
§ 3.07, § 5.25
Hospice, § 1.01, § 3.07, § 5.25, § 6.08,
§ 12.07, § 12.19. *See also*
Palliative care
Hospilized Elderly Langitudinal
Project (HELP), § 8.07,
§ 8.18

I

Implementation of directive, barrier
to. *See also* Implementation
within medical profession,
barrier to
of clergy/spiritual leader, § 9.27
communication failure, § 5.33
cost, § 5.26
document complexity/readability,
§ 5.29
drafting lag time, § 5.30
execution formalities, § 5.32
family meeting delays, § 5.31,
§ 6.09
lack of prior guidance, § 6.09
meeting with professional advisors,
§ 5.27
obtaining forms, § 5.28
PSDA protocol failure, § 5.25
stale/obsolete directive, § 6.09
surrogate decision-maker
commitment, § 6.09
unfamiliarity with patient health
care delivery system, § 6.09

Implementation within medical profession, barrier to. *See also* Implementation of directive, barrier to
changes in directive, § 8.24
countermanding/overriding patient directive, § 8.22
cultural/ethnic/spiritual, § 8.15
existence of directive, lack of knowledge of, § 8.20
legal issues, § 8.21
patient capacity, § 8.14
patient education opportunity, § 8.13
patient–physician conflict, § 8.16
Patient Self-Determination Act, weakness, § 8.17
professional education, § 8.11
prognosis determination difficulty, § 8.18
staff education, § 8.19
tailoring clinical situation to directive, § 8.23
time, lack of, § 8.12
Incapacity, as effectuating event, § 4.19
Informed consent, § 7.02
Inoperative directive, § 11.07
Institutional ethics committee. *See* Health care ethics committee
Insufficient capacity, § 2.12, § 3.16
International travel, § 11.15, § 12.18
Intervivos trust, § 2.06, § 10.09

J

Joint Commission on Accreditation of Healthcare Organizations (JCAHO), § 12.10
Judicial processes, as last resort, § 8.21, § 10.07
Justice, § 3.10

K

Korean American, and directive use, § 5.06
Kutner, Luis, § 7.02

L

Last will and testament
as different from living will, § 2.04
nominating guardian in, § 2.09
Lawyer. *See* Attorney
Legislation on directive, future of, § 12.09
"Life Prolonging Procedures Declaration" (Indiana), § 5.11
Limited purpose health care directive. *See* Ancillary/limited purpose health care directive
Living probate. *See* Conservatorship; Guardianship
Living trust. *See* Intervivos trust
Living will, § 4.04, § 5.10
as different from last will and testament, § 2.04
overlap/conflict with durable power of attorney, § 2.04, § 11.07
and pregnancy, § 11.21
for very elderly, § 11.18
Long-term care facility. *See* Nursing home

M

Malpractice, § 8.09
Matter of Quinlan, § 9.01
MDS, *See* Minimum Data Set
Medical assessment, for capacity, § 3.16, § 4.04–§ 4.05
Medic Alert, § 5.35
Medical evaluation/report, attorney retention of, § 4.05
Medical examination, for capacity, § 4.05
Medical futility, § 8.16, § 10.10
Medically ineffective treatment, § 8.16
Mental health treatment declaration, § 2.05, § 2.15
Mental retardation, profound, and competence, § 4.09

Mercy killing, § 10.11

Mexican American, and directive use, § 5.06

Middle generation proxy, § 6.06

Military Advance Medical Directive (Louisiana), § 11.16

Military personnel, active duty, § 11.16

Minimum Data Set (MDS), § 12.10

Minor, maturing, and capacity, § 4.09, § 8.14

Minor child

  durable power of attorney for health care for, § 2.01–§ 2.02

  emancipation of, § 11.17

  guardianship for, § 2.02, § 2.09, § 10.06, § 11.17

  life sustaining treatment withdrawal, § 11.17

Missouri Synod, § 9.10

Model Uniform Health-Care Decisions Act, § 2.11, § 2.15, § 4.19

Multidisciplinary approach, to directive, § 9.02, § 9.03

N

Narrow grant of authority, § 2.02

National Marrow Donor Program (NMDP), § 2.07, § 11.05

National Organ Transplant Act, § 2.07

No heroic measures, § 1.03

Nonmaleficence, § 3.08

  difference from beneficence, § 3.08, § 3.09

Notarization, § 5.32

Nurse, § 1.05, § 8.04, § 8.05

Nursing home, § 1.01, § 5.25

  compliance with directives by, § 8.06, § 12.10

  cost-effectiveness of directives in, § 12.19

O

Obtaining forms, § 5.28

Omnibus Reconciliation Act, § 2.07

One minute patient intervention, § 8.26

Oral Expressions, § 2.08

Oral revocation, § 1.07, § 2.02, § 11.23

Organ donation, § 2.11, § 7.11, § 11.19

  from anencephalic infant, § 11.02

  attorney as witness for, § 7.06

  from donated body, § 11.03

  family review/consent for, § 2.07, § 6.02

  myths/misconceptions about, § 2.07

  religious precepts on, § 2.07, § 9.04

Organ transplantation, religious precepts on, § 9.04

Originals, of directive, § 2.13, § 2.14

Out-of-hospital DNR order, § 1.11, § 10.05

Out of state travel/relocation, § 11.20

Ova, § 11.10

P

Palliative care, § 5.10, § 7.02, § 11.13, § 12.07. *See also* Hospice

Paramedic, § 1.11

Partial capacity, § 4.09

Passive euthanasia, § 10.11

Patient abandonment, § 8.22

Patient education, § 8.13, § 12.14

Patient Self Determination Act (PSDA), § 1.02, § 8.05

  failure of protocols of, § 5.25

  heightening awareness of, § 12.11

  mandate to federally funded hospital/nursing home, § 1.01, § 3.07

  and quality improvement, § 12.08

  weaknesses of, § 8.17

Photocopies, of directive. *See* Copies, of directive

Physical destruction, of directive, § 1.07, § 2.02, § 2.15, § 8.24, § 11.23

Physician. *See also* Health care provider; Implementation within medical profession, barrier to
as agent/proxy, § 8.08
barriers to acceptance of directive for, § 8.09
disagreement with directive/agent by, § 1.03
disinclination to honor directive, § 1.06
and ethics, § 3.13
personal beliefs of, § 1.05
relationship with patient, § 8.02
withdrawal from treatment/ substitution of, § 8.16, § 8.22

Pocket card, § 2.14

Power of attorney. *See* Durable power of attorney (proxy)

Pregnancy, § 11.21

Prisoners, § 11.22

Privacy, patient, § 1.05, § 3.03, § 3.04, § 3.05, § 3.07

Professional ethics
for allied professional, § 3.14
for health professionals, § 3.13
for lawyer, § 3.12
rules for, § 3.16

Proxy. *See* Agent; Durable power of attorney (proxy)

Psychiatric disorder, § 4.15, § 4.16, § 4.17

Puerto Rico, lack of statutory provision for directive in, § 1.10, § 3.07

"Pull-the-plug" document, § 2.04, § 5.10, § 5.11

Q

"Qualifying conditions," § 10.04

Quality Improvement Organization (QIO), § 12.10

Quality improvement (QI), § 8.07, § 12.08

Quinlan, Karen Ann, § 5.09, § 9.01, § 9.29, § 10.10

R

Reciprocity, 11.20

Re-execution, of directive, § 1.07, § 2.15, § 5.12, § 8.24

Refusal of treatment
and competence, § 4.09
by prisoner, § 11.22
right to, § 7.02

Registry service, § 2.07, § 5.35, § 8.20

Religious belief. *See also* Religious/spiritual precept, of end-of-life decision
accommodating directive to, § 9.28, § 12.06
as barrier to acceptance of directive, § 5.18, § 6.08
and medical healing, § 1.05, § 5.18

Religious/spiritual precept, of end-of-life decision, § 9.04. *See also* Clergy/spiritual advisor
of American Baptist, § 9.06
of Anglican Church, § 9.24
of Buddhism, § 9.05, § 11.04
of Christian Science, § 9.07
of Church of Bretheren, § 9.15
of Eastern Orthodox, § 9.22
of Evangelical Lutheran, § 9.09
of Hinduism, § 9.13
of Islam, § 9.14
of Jehovah's Witness, § 9.08
of Judaism, § 9.20
of Latter-Day Saints, § 9.23
of Lutheran Church, § 9.10
of Mennonite, § 9.18
of Navajo, § 9.19
of Presbyterian Church (U.S.A.), § 9.17
of Roman Catholic, 9.01, § 9.11
of Seventh-Day Adventist, § 9.25

Religious/spiritual (*cont.*)
  of Unitarian Universalist
    Association, § 9.21
  of United Church of Christ, § 9.12
  of United Methodist Church, § 9.16
Remains, disposition of, § 2.11,
    § 11.03
Revocation
  of directive, § 1.07, § 2.01, § 5.12,
    § 8.24, § 11.23
  of mental health declaration, § 2.05
  required, irrespective of capacity,
    § 4.19
Roe v. Wade, § 7.02, § 9.02

S

Saturation marketing, § 12.10, § 12.13
*Schloendorff v. Society of New York
  Hospitals*, § 7.02
Slow codes. *See* Passive euthanasia
Snap judgments, of competence,
    § 4.08
Social worker, § 1.05, § 3.14, § 8.05
Sperm, § 11.10
Spiritual advisor. *See* Clergy/spiritual
    advisor
Spouse, as proxy, § 6.06
"Springing" power, § 2.11, § 4.19,
    § 5.13
Staff ethicist, § 3.15
Stale directive, § 11.07
"Statement of Preferences for Mental
    Health Treatments," § 4.16
Storing, original/copy of directive,
    § 2.13, § 5.35, § 7.06
Study to Understand Prognosis and
    Preferences for Outcomes and
    Risks of Treatment (SUPPORT),
    § 8.07, § 8.18
Substituted judgment, § 1.05, § 3.07
  definition of, § 3.04
Suicide, assisted, § 4.17, § 7.02,
    § 10.11
Sunset date, § 2.05, § 2.11, § 11.07

SUPPORT. *See* Study to Understand
    Prognosis and Preferences for
    Outcomes and Risks of
    Treatment
Surrogate decision-maker, § 3.04,
    § 3.05, § 3.07
  and beneficence, § 3.09
  dilemmas for, § 6.09
  extended family member as,
    § 6.03
  immediate family member as,
    § 6.02
  lack of, § 11.18
Surrogate statutes, § 10.04
Sustenance, withholding, § 2.04

T

Temporary Incapacity, § 4.14
Ten minute patient intervention,
    § 8.26
Testamentary attestation, § 4.06
Tissue donation, § 2.07, § 9.04,
    § 11.02
Tissue transplantation, § 11.02
Travelers, and directives, § 2.04,
    § 11.15, § 11.20
Treatment, efficacy of, § 6.09
Trust, intervivos, § 2.06, § 10.09

U

Ulysses directive. *See* Mental health
    treatment declaration
Undue influence, § 2.12, § 3.16,
    § 4.10, § 5.32, § 6.03
Uniform Health-Care Decisions Act,
    § 12.10
Union Pacific Railway Co. v. Botsford,
    § 7.02
Updating directive, § 2.15

V

Vacco v. Quill, § 7.02, § 9.02
Values history, § 2.17, § 5.30, § 7.05,
    § 8.24, § 12.06

Values judgment inventory,
§ 1.05
Vial for Life, § 5.34

W

Wallet/purse card, § 2.07, § 2.14,
§ 5.35, § 8.20

Washington v. Glucksberg, § 7.02
Witness, § 5.32
for lawyer–client interview,
§ 4.06
to observe lucid interview,
§ 4.10
to oral expression, § 2.08

Advance Health Care Directives
A Handbook for Professionals

About the CD

This CD-ROM works with any computer capable of running Adobe® Acrobat® Reader 4.0 or later. (Adobe Acrobat Reader 5.05 is recommended; Windows and Macintosh versions are included on this CD-ROM.) Your computer must have a CD-ROM drive capable of reading Windows or Macintosh CD-ROM discs.

To start this CD-ROM, insert the CD-ROM into your computer CD drive and wait 10-20 seconds until a menu screen appears.

If the CD-ROM does not start automatically on your Windows computer, or if you are using a Macintosh or other non-Windows computer, you can open the handbook manually by double-clicking the file "start.pdf." Then click on the link to the document you would like to view.

For more important information about installing Adobe Acrobat and using this CD-ROM, view the file "Readme.txt," located on the CD-ROM.

Produced by the ABA Senior Lawyers Division
Copyright ©2002 American Bar Association. All rights reserved.